Thomas Chatterton and Romantic Culture

Also by Nick Groom

THE MAKING OF PERCY'S RELIQUES

Thomas Chatterton and Romantic Culture

Edited by
Nick Groom

Foreword by Peter Ackroyd

First published in Great Britain 1999 by
MACMILLAN PRESS LTD
Houndmills, Basingstoke, Hampshire RG21 6XS and London
Companies and representatives throughout the world

A catalogue record for this book is available from the British Library.

ISBN 0–333–725867

First published in the United States of America 1999 by
ST. MARTIN'S PRESS, INC.,
Scholarly and Reference Division,
175 Fifth Avenue, New York, N.Y. 10010

ISBN 0–312–22848–1

Library of Congress Cataloging-in-Publication Data
Thomas Chatterton and romantic culture / edited by Nick Groom ;
foreword by Peter Ackroyd.
p. cm.
Includes bibliographical references and index.
ISBN 0–312–22848–1
1. Chatterton, Thomas, 1752–1770—Criticism and interpretation.
2. Literary forgeries and mystifications—History—18th century.
3. Literature and history—England—History—18th century.
4. Medievalism—England—History—18th century. 5. Middle Ages in
literature. 6. Romanticism—England. I. Groom, Nick, 1966– .
PR3344.T46 1999
821'.6—DC21 99–37996
CIP

This book is printed on paper suitable for recycling and made from fully managed and
sustained forest sources.

10 9 8 7 6 5 4 3 2
08 07 06 05 04 03 02 01 00

Printed and bound in Great Britain by Antony Rowe Ltd, Chippenham, Wiltshire

Contents

Part II. The Rowley Controversy and After

Illustrations

1. 'The Last Sleep of Arthur in Avalon' (detail), 1881–98, by Sir Edward Burne-Jones (1833–98), Museo de Arte, Ponce, Puerto Rico, West Indies/Bridgeman Art Library, London/New York. Reproduced by permission.
2. 'Truth Sacrifising to the Muses', Grignion after Ryley, published by Bellamy (1793), BL, C39 f1. Reproduced by permission.
3. John Clare's sketch for a tombstone, photograph © Peter Moyse, ARPS. Reproduced by permission of Northamptonshire Libraries.
4. The 'Goggle-ey'd Portrait'; unknown engraver after unknown artist, published by Baldwin (1797). Reproduced by permission of the National Portrait Gallery.
5. Frontispiece to John Dix's *Life of Chatterton* (1837); Alais after Branwhite, stipple engraving. Reproduced by permission of the National Portrait Gallery.
6. Undated pseudo-portrait; unknown engraver after unknown artist, stipple engraving. Reproduced by permission of the National Portrait Gallery.
7. Larry, after Wallis, from *Punch* (June 1987), 25. Reproduced by permission of Punch Ltd.

Abbreviations

Anecdotes	Nichols, John, *Literary Anecdotes of the Eighteenth Century*, 9 vols (London, 1812–15)
BL	British Library
Bodl.	Bodleian Library
DNB	*Dictionary of National Biography*
GM	*Gentleman's Magazine*
Illustrations	Nichols, John, *Illustrations of the Literary History of the Eighteenth-Century*, 8 vols (London, 1817–58).
Life	Meyerstein, E. H. W., *A Life of Thomas Chatterton* (London, 1930)
Life of Johnson	Boswell, James, *Boswell's Life of Johnson (Together with Boswell's Journal of a Tour to the Hebrides and Johnson's Diary of a Journey into North Wales)*, ed. George Birkbeck Hill, rev. L. F. Powell, 6 vols (Oxford, 1934–50)
Miscellanies	Chatterton, Thomas, *Miscellanies in Prose and Verse*, ed. John Broughton (London, 1778)
NQ	*Notes and Queries*
Poems	Chatterton, Thomas, *Poems, Supposed to have been Written at Bristol, by Thomas Rowley, and Others, in the Fifteenth Century*, ed. Thomas Tyrwhitt (London, 1777)
SJC	*St. James's Chronicle*
Taylor	Taylor, Donald S., *Thomas Chatterton's Art: Experiments in Imagined History* (Princeton, 1978)
TLS	*Times Literary Supplement*
Works	*The Complete Works of Thomas Chatterton*, ed. Donald S. Taylor and Benjamin B. Hoover, 2 vols [continuously paginated] (Oxford, 1971)

Acknowledgements

The editor gratefully acknowledges the kind permission of Bloodaxe Books for the use of the Kamau Brathwaite lines in the epigraph of Williams's chapter, and of Ashley Halpé for lines 17–24, 25–9, and 13–14 of his poem 'The Boyhood of Chitta'. 'Flavor Flav Cold Lampin'' quoted in Morton's chapter from Public Enemy, *It Takes a Nation of Millions to Hold Us Back* (© Def Jam Recordings, 1987). 'The Last Sleep of Arthur in Avalon' (detail), 1881–98 by Sir Edward Burne-Jones (1833–98), Museo de Arte, Ponce, Puerto Rico, West Indies/Bridgeman Art Library, London/New York, is reproduced by permission. 'Truth Sacrifising to the Muses' is reproduced by permission of the British Library. Peter Moyse, ARPS generously provided the photograph of Clare's sketch for a tombstone, from the Northamptonshire Library archive. The three pseudo-portraits of Chatterton are reproduced by permission of the National Portrait Gallery. Larry's cartoon is reproduced by permission of Punch Ltd.

I would like to thank Pelagia Goulimari and Gerard Greenway of *Angelaki*, where this project began, Michael Nath who supported it, Charmian Hearne and Sarah Barrett at Macmillan, and John Goodridge and Jonathan Barry, who very kindly read through the completed typescript. I would also like to extend my heartfelt thanks to all the contributors to this volume, particularly Inga Bryden, for their forbearance. You have been generous, tractable, and above all patient. I trust you are as pleased with the results as I am.

This volume is dedicated to the memory of T.C. (*Elegia*).

Contributors

Peter Ackroyd is a novelist and biographer. His books include *Hawksmoor* (1985), *Chatterton* (1987), *Milton in America* (1996), *Dickens* (1990), *Blake* (1995), and *The Life of Sir Thomas More* (1998).

Paul Baines is a Lecturer in the Department of English Language and Literature, University of Liverpool. His edition of Horace Walpole's *The Mysterious Mother* and other plays of the late eighteenth century, co-edited with Edward Burns, will appear in the Oxford World's Classics series in 1999; his book *The House of Forgery in the Eighteenth Century* was published in 1999.

Inga Bryden is Senior Lecturer in English and Cultural Studies at King Alfred's College, Winchester. She has published articles on eighteenth- and nineteenth-century historicism, and for four years contributed the Victorian culture section to *The Year's Work in English Studies*. A four-volume edited collection of Pre-Raphaelite writing was published by Routledge in 1998. She has co-edited a book on nineteenth-century domestic space and is currently completing a book on the reinvention of the Arthurian legends in Victorian literature and culture.

David Fairer is Professor in Eighteenth-Century Poetry at the University of Leeds. He is the author of *Pope's Imagination* (1984) and *The Poetry of Alexander Pope* (1989), and editor of *Pope: New Contexts* (1990) and *The Correspondence of Thomas Warton* (1995). He has also written widely on eighteenth-century Romanticism, including recent essays on Gray, the Wartons, Burke, Blake, Lamb, Coleridge, and Wordsworth. With Christine Gerrard he has edited *Eighteenth-Century Poetry: An Annotated Anthology* (Blackwell, 1999), and is writing *English Poetry of the Eighteenth Century* for the Longman Literature in English Series.

John Goodridge is a Senior Lecturer in English at Nottingham Trent University. He is the author of *Rural Life in Eighteenth-Century English Poetry* (1995), edits the *John Clare Society Journal*, and has published widely on the eighteenth-century self-taught poets. He is currently working on editions of John Dyer and Robert Bloomfield, and on a monograph on John Clare.

Nick Groom is a Lecturer in English Studies at the University of Exeter. He is the author of *The Making of Percy's Reliques* (1999), general editor for two series on the period 1750–1850 (*Cultural Formations* and *Subcultures and Subversions*, which include his edition of the *Reliques*), and has written essays on subjects ranging from Thomas Chatterton to popular music and contemporary art. He is currently writing a book on forgery, and compiling a history of the Rowley Controversy.

Richard Holmes has won many awards for his biographies, including *Shelley: The Pursuit* (1974), *Coleridge: Early Visions* (1989), and *Dr Johnson & Mr Savage* (1993). He is also the author of *Footsteps: Adventures of a Romantic Biographer* (1985). The second volume of his Coleridge biography, *Darker Reflections*, was published in 1998.

Bridget Keegan is an Assistant Professor of English at Creighton University in Omaha, Nebraska, and Vice-President of the John Clare Society of North America. She has written essays on Clare and Wordsworth, and is currently at work on two books: a monograph entitled *Poets Born and Made: Labor, Lyricism and the Self-Taught Tradition, 1729–1837*, and an annotated anthology, *Literature and Nation: Four Centuries of British and American Nature Writing*.

Georges Lamoine has taught English literature and history at the Université du Mirail since 1970. He has written on eighteenth-century Bath and Bristol, on Swift, Chatterton, and various subjects of the period, including criminal justice and the English constitution. He has edited texts by Fielding and Swift, has contributed to works on poverty and English political thought, and is now researching eighteenth-century newspapers.

Maria Grazia Lolla has recently completed her PhD on eighteenth-century antiquarianism at the University of Cambridge. Her publications include articles on antiquarian aesthetics and on Caribbean literature in English, and she completed this paper as a Senior Fellow at the Center for the Humanities at Wesleyan University. She is currently at work on *Rivers Unknown to Song*, antiquarian explorations of the East and West Indies.

Timothy Morton is an Assistant Professor of English at the University of Colorado, Boulder. His first book, *Shelley and the Revolution in Taste* (1994), has recently been reprinted, and he is the co-editor, with Nigel

Smith, of *Radicalism in British Literary Culture, 1650–1830*, to be published by Cambridge University Press. He is the author of numerous articles on food in literature, ecology, and popular culture, and is currently working on *The Poetics of Spice.*

Claude Rawson is Maynard Mack Professor of English at Yale University, and Chairman of the Yale Boswell Editions. His books include *Henry Fielding and the Augustan Ideal under Stress, Gulliver and the Gentle Reader, Order from Confusion Sprung, Satire and Sentiment: 1660–1830*, and (edited with H. B. Nisbet), *The Cambridge History of Literary Criticism, volume IV: The Eighteenth Century.*

Pat Rogers is DeBartolo Professor of the Liberal Arts at the University of South Florida. Recent books include *The Samuel Johnson Encyclopedia* (1996) and *The Text of Great Britain: Theme and Design in Defoe's Tour* (1997). He is currently completing *Albion's Golden Days: History, Mythology, and Artifice in Pope's* Windsor-Forest, as well as a book on Johnson and the Club.

Michael F. Suarez, SJ, is Associate Professor of English at Fordham University in New York. He has written on many aspects of eighteenth-century literature, theology, and the book trade, and has edited Robert Dodsley's *Collection of Poems by Several Hands* (1996).

Carolyn D. Williams is a Lecturer in the Department of English, University of Reading. She has written *Pope, Homer, and Manliness: Some Aspects of Eighteenth-Century Classical Learning* (1993), and a number of articles on varied aspects of early modern life and literature.

Michael Wood is Professor of English at Princeton University. His books include *Stendhal* (1971), *America in the Movies* (1989), *Gabriel Garcia Márquez: One Hundred Years of Solitude* (1990), and *The Magician's Doubts: Nabokov and the Risks of Fiction* (1995). *Chidren of Silence: On Contemporary Fiction* was published in 1998.

Preface

It is enlightening, and somewhat heartening, to learn that Thomas Chatterton is at last being taken seriously as a poet and dramatist. He was so prodigal of his genius that he attached the names of others such as 'Rowlie' to it; and, in the same manner, he has survived a variety of literary incarnations ranging from Augustan fraudster to Romantic icon and post-modern avatar. His supposed suicide has of course assisted this process, although there are those who believe that it was not self-murder at all. It was, perhaps, an accident that created the 'legend' of the poet to be seen lying on a narrow bed in Henry Wallis's painting.

In reality he is more interesting than many of the stereotypes fixed to his reputation and his work. He pursued that antiquarian passion, for example, which seems inseparable from the native genius – Goethe mocked the English for it in *Faust* – and the moment of his revelation in the muniment room of St Mary Redcliffe in Bristol, whether legendary or not, must stand as one of the most important scenes in English literary history.

Chatterton believed that the past, and the language of the past, might be made to live again. He was, in a very real sense, correct. By writing in the impassioned cadence and ornate vocabulary of the fifteenth century, he was able to move beyond the restricting imaginative climate into which he had been born. He was not a Newtonian, or a Lockean; he was a visionary who understood the world in terms of myths and legends. That is why he was so admired by William Blake, for example, as well as those other eighteenth-century writers and artists who were quite out of sympathy with prevailing poetic and painterly customs. It is a mistake to assume, therefore, that Chatterton was 'discovered' by Wordsworth or by Coleridge. His

1

visionary importance had already been vouchsafed to an earlier generation who were equally distrustful of the materialist culture – and materialist aesthetic – emerging around them.

But if Chatterton remains an example to those who reject the mores of their age, he also possesses a further significance. In renewing the literature of the medieval period, and in a sense actually creating it, he was invoking a tradition which in *The Englishness of Art* Nikolaus Pevsner described as an inalienable aspect of the English sensibility. For many hundreds of years the artists and writers of this country have used a mixture of historical styles as a form of ludic comprehension of the past. Pevsner mentions those Elizabethan tombs which were supposed to look medieval, as well as the architectural plans of Nicholas Hawksmoor which were conceived in Gothic and Baroque styles. The stylistic inventiveness of Walter Pater and Walter Savage Landor, as well as the alliterative line of W. H. Auden, might also be mentioned in this context. It has nothing to do with some 'postmodern' examination of narrative; it is connected, instead, to the enduring consciousness of the nation. We seem to have come a long way from Thomas Chatterton himself, the 'marvellous Boy' who found within himself the living presence of the past, but in fact he can stand as the one great genius of historical restoration and renewal in this country.

Peter Ackroyd

Chapter 1
Introduction
Nick Groom

The most enduring image of Romanticism is that of the poet in a tiny garret, sprawling supine on his bed: young and beautiful, an exquisite corpse. This angelic poet has suffered for his genius – starving and destitute, mad and suicidal, and now dead. The fatal archetype is, of course, Thomas Chatterton. His painting by Henry Wallis is a secular, a literary, *pietà*. The poet crucified by his prodigious genius, his flaming head haloed with shredded manuscripts, his lifeless feet resting against his writing-desk. But no-one is there to cradle him, only fictions ....

Thomas Chatterton, born in 1752 to a recently widowed mother, was a blue-coat boy who trained as an attorney's clerk. He lived and worked and wrote in his native Bristol, before moving to London shortly before his death in 1770; when he died he was only 17. Despite the strictures of education and time, however, in his short life he produced a dazzling body of literature. Chatterton was a voracious reader and a prolific writer: his collected *Works* fill two thick volumes – from reams of poetry (fashionable songs, graveyard Gothic, scathing satire, oriental eclogues) to columns of political journalism. And he produced hundreds of medieval texts: forgeries.

Were they really forgeries? Were they a new form of fiction? Chatterton claimed in about 1768 to have discovered the works of one Thomas Rowley, a fifteenth-century priest, in an old chest in the muniment room over the north porch of St Mary Redcliffe Church, Bristol. (In fact, his father, who had been the writing master of the church, had collected a basket of old parchment scraps from the floor of the muniment room, and the young Chatterton was mesmerized by these paternal relics.) Chatterton's invented Rowley corpus was enormous, and much of it was laboriously fabricated by the teenage boy.

3

He inscribed Rowley's poems and prose in cod-medieval lettering on parchments he decorated with heraldic devices and aged with ochre and soot, and, with an autodidact's acuity, Chatterton laced these beautifully baroque creations together with editorial comments and antiquarian annotations.[1] The works of Thomas Rowley, Priest, appeared to be a major cultural find.

The fictional Thomas Rowley was supposedly employed by the real Bristol merchant and public figure William Canynge as his agent in antique dealing, and as his translator and scribe.[2] Rowley and Canynge were also at the centre of a very active literary circle, and so in addition to fifteenth-century research notes, heraldry, maps, and business memoirs, Rowley's works included poems, poetic translations, plays, and coterie verse by other members of this industrious set (including John Lydgate). The young Chatterton circulated his 'find' among the Bristol literati, and captured the imagination of two local antiquarians: William Barrett, a retired surgeon who was writing a history of Bristol (eventually published, with Rowley material intact, in 1789), and George Catcott, a pewterer and self-publicist. Although Chatterton had plans to publish Rowley, for which he was notoriously rebuffed by Horace Walpole, the publication and ensuing controversy about the authenticity of the works did not properly develop until after his death. In 1777 an edition of Rowley's poems was published, and for the next five years an intemperate debate and pamphlet war raged. The Rowley Controversy proved to be one of the most important cultural debates of the eighteenth century, establishing standards of criticism and scholarship, and also launching the posthumous career of Thomas Chatterton; but, like the row over James Macpherson's Ossianic discoveries in the Highlands of Scotland, the ebb and flow of opinion has yet to be properly mapped.

In the triumphalist wake of the Anti-Rowleyan arguments that ultimately dispatched Thomas Rowley, Chatterton was immediately reinvented as a tragic genius. In this incarnation he inspired Blake, Wordsworth and Coleridge, Keats and Shelley, Byron and De Quincey. His extraordinary life and works were part of the very genesis of Romanticism: Coleridge's first published poem was 'On the Death of Chatterton', Southey and Cottle edited his works in 1803, Wordsworth in 'Resolution and Independence' christened him for ever more as

the marvellous Boy,
The sleepless Soul that perish'd in its pride;

Keats dedicated *Endymion* to his memory, Shelley welcomed his 'frail Form' in *Adonais*, and the Pre-Raphaelite poet and painter Dante Gabriel Rossetti was utterly infatuated by him: 'He was as great as any English poet whatever, and might absolutely, had he lived, have proved the only man in England's theatre of imagination who could have bandied parts with Shakespeare.'[3] The extraordinary Thomas Chatterton occupies therefore a unique position in Romantic culture: a precocious talent, a literary forger, an apparent suicide: a Romantic icon of massive and enduring influence. He is a seminal figure in English literature.

And yet, some two centuries after his death, at the Eighth International Congress on the Enlightenment held in Chatterton's home town of Bristol in 1991, only two out of over 500 speakers mentioned Thomas Chatterton.[4] The city itself discloses only the scantiest memorial in St Mary Redcliffe, the church where Chatterton perched and prowled during his childhood and where he supposedly discovered in an ancient chest the works of Rowley. Bristol booksellers have no books by or about Chatterton; some even claim never to have heard of him.

This is nothing unusual. There is almost no critical work on this prodigy – a handful of books and a few essays devoted to his stupendous achievement and profound influence. For the critic, Chatterton is too mercurial, too confusing: perpetually challenging the genres of writing, mixing national histories, national fictions, and national myths in a great post-Enlightenment reinvention of the past. And he has been condemned as a forger: a writer who belongs in anecdotal histories rather than in serious critical studies. Chatterton's iconicity has eclipsed his very work as a writer.

Consequently, Chatterton has inspired a good deal more creative work than he has generated scholarship, and most of the scholarship has concentrated on his biography or on sources for the forgeries.[5] Part of the reason for this has been the eccentric longevity of the Rowley myth: not until Walter Skeat's etymological 'Essay on the Rowley Poems' in his edition of Chatterton's *Poetical Works* (1872) was the controversy really laid to rest, the waters having been considerably muddied in the nineteenth century by John Dix's semi-fraudulent biography, and there are still oddballs who entertain doubts today.[6] Still, only six significant books have been devoted to Chatterton in this century: a resilient biography, a magisterial edition, two bibliographies, and just two critical works. E. H. W. Meyerstein's great *Life*

(1930) and Donald Taylor and Benjamin Hoover's monumental *Complete Works* (1971: appearing almost a century after Skeat's edition) have made available a wealth of material which scholars and critics have, as yet, failed to capitalize upon.[7] Taylor has written a monograph, *Thomas Chatterton's Art* (1978), which is a critical reading of Chatterton's achievement, re-enacting the compositional techniques of Chatterton, his problems with structure and poetic idiom, and his revolutionary solutions. In direct contrast, Louise Kaplan's *The Family Romance of the Impostor-Poet Thomas Chatterton* (1988) picks up A. Alvarez's psychoanalysis of Chatterton (in *The Savage God*, 1971) and considers him as a psychological case of 'imposturous narcissism': the consequence of his traumatic, fatherless infancy. Together with these works are a clutch of significant articles: Ernest Clarke's recovery of several important manuscripts and documents; L. F. Powell's bibliographic account of Thomas Tyrwhitt's editorship of the *Rowley Poems*; and Richard Holmes's brilliant critical biography.[8] It is, however, disappointing to find that critics have not been quick to assimilate new interpretations – such as the accidental death of Chatterton. The myth of suicide, like the crime of forgery, is too powerful, too enticing.

Yet the tide is turning, and reassessments of Chatterton are gaining ground.[9] This has been enabled in part by a reconsideration of the status of literary forgery. Foremost is Ian Haywood's *The Making of History* (1986), which argues that Chatterton developed an historical aesthetics and constructed an entirely self-sufficient world that found its fullest expression in the historical novels of the nineteenth century. Marilyn Butler has examined Chatterton in terms of divergent British nationalisms, whereas Susan Stewart develops Kaplan's psychoanalytic reading to argue that the 'imposture' arises from Chatterton's interdisciplinarity and genre-hopping.[10] In other recent works, such as Andrew Motion's 1997 biography of Keats, it is encouraging to see outlined Chatterton's formative role on the impressionable young poet.[11]

The current collection of new essays – evidently the first ever devoted to Chatterton – grew out of a special issue of the journal *Angelaki*, 'Narratives of Forgery' (1993/4). 'Narratives of Forgery' suggested imaginative new directions for Chatterton studies, with contributors discussing the Bristol context, Chatterton's periodical publications, the 1770s criminal forgery trials, the ideological influence of Chatterton, and the implications of literary forgery.[12] But although the current collection was inspired by *Angelaki*, only one essay recognizably derives from the journal: instead there are 14 original essays and two think-pieces on the life, works, and influence of Thomas Chatterton – a testament to the energy of contributors and the scope of the field. It should be stressed that there is no methodological orthodoxy in this collection, rather a series of interventions are made in such debates as the formation of the eighteenth-century canon and literary antiquarianism, the archaeology of early Romanticism, and, of course, forgery; yet it is revealing how often problems of context and originality, elegy and memory are addressed and re-addressed in the following pieces. Most of all, however, the essays demonstrate with a rare clarity the major significance of Chatterton. Chatterton is fundamentally reassessed and situated in new critical contexts, and so the book develops theoretical positions as well as introducing significant new historical evidence to the *oeuvre*.

The first part considers the life and work of Chatterton, the second traces the Rowley Controversy and Chatterton's influence. First, two surveys: Claude Rawson establishes Chatterton's work within a bracing canon of eighteenth-century literature, neatly inverting the problem of forgery by arguing that it arises from an unorthodox use of Pope and other satirical writers; the dazzling form of Chatterton's verse then receives a much-needed reappraisal in Georges Lamoine's new critical analysis of originality. Examining the orientalist *African Eclogues* alongside Rowley, Carolyn Williams develops a postcolonial reading that explores Chatterton's anxieties about cultural alienation, whether Bristolian marginalization or his own lack of a classical education, while national dilemmas of empirical as opposed to legendary history are discussed by Inga Bryden, who reads the signs of heraldry in the Rowley works to discover startling similarities between the respective canonizations of Chatterton and King Arthur. The Round Table becomes the dining-table for Timothy Morton, who interprets two food-fight poems in terms of signification and consumption, dramatizing Chatterton's riotous entry into political life, and the first part concludes with Michael Suarez's new findings on the professional writer's meat and drink: the culmination of research into Chatterton's deft handling of the press, exploding the myth that he was a penniless writer.

Chatterton's reputation is explored in the second part, initially by examining the unfolding drama of the Rowley Controversy. Pat Rogers's survey of the Literary Club's response to the burgeoning debate and their ideological deployment of coterie scholarship sets the context for Maria Grazia Lolla's treatment of the controversy as the pretext for a sustained rebellion against Enlightenment systems of knowledge in which the question of authenticity became irrelevant. Paul Baines then focuses on Johnson's remarkable and indulgent sympathy for Chatterton (he made as fruitless a trip to Rowleyan Bristol as he had to Ossianic Scotland), in contrast to Chatterton's boiling filial antipathy, while my own contribution focuses on another protagonist, Thomas Percy, suggesting that Rowley's supporters embarked almost immediately on a disastrous collision course with the *Reliques*, the touchstone of authenticity, that would eventually annihilate both the Rowleyans and Percy's own literary career. But Chatterton thrived far beyond the Rowley affair. Bridget Keegan shows the compelling fascination he held for the milkwoman and peasant poets Yearsley and Clare, who saw in Chatterton both a model and a voice for reclaiming the lost poetic traditions of autodidact culture, and David Fairer analyses the profound implications of the life and works of Chatterton for the lifelong artistry of Coleridge, read through the extraordinary evolving poetic canonization that followed the Rowley controversy. Further cases will, one hopes, be made on the model of these exempla. Finally, Richard Holmes traces the Chatterton myth through a series of pseudo-portraits; just as the phrase 'the marvellous Boy' echoes through this volume, so a figure of Chatterton haunts literature, a myth literally built on madness. We end on a paradox of authenticity and inauthenticity – but the last twist is left for Michael Wood, who weaves further silky paradoxes from the threads of these essays. In conclusion, John Goodridge's magisterial bibliography 'Rowley's Ghost' speaks most loquaciously of Chatterton's deep cultural influence: from a scrap of eighteenth-century ephemera – a biography printed on a souvenir handkerchief – to a pop song recorded by Serge Gainsbourg.

As Peter Ackroyd suggests, Chatterton begins in the past, and although each beginning, renewal, and reinvention attempts to deliver him from history, it is this nostalgic and elegiac figment of Chatterton as past/passed that captivates poets, painters, and pop stars. But it is worth asking: what would Chatterton have become if he had not died – whether an adolescent suicide or the victim of a lethal cocktail of drugs? Samuel Johnson was one of Chatterton's earliest pseudo-biographers: he suggested to Hannah More that she should have married Chatterton, 'that posterity might have seen a propagation of poets' (!), and Ackroyd has hinted at another ingenious counterfactual biography in his novel, *Chatterton*; others could be written.[13] In Brooke Street, where he died, Chatterton spent days and nights writing with an almost maniacal intensity, eating little and sleeping less, taking laudanum, perhaps dosing himself with arsenic; he was burning himself out like the searing glare of a magnesium flare. Had he survived the night of the 24 August 1770, he might simply have died the following week in equally depressing and mysterious circumstances. But it is more daring to imagine Chatterton in old age. He would have lived through the most remarkable literary times, and moulded them as they touched him. Chatterton would have been 70 years old on 20 November 1822. He might have just lost his friend P. B. Shelley, who died in August of that year (he had already outlived Keats, who died 18 months earlier in February 1821) – if indeed these young men would have kept company with a writer 20 years older than Coleridge. He could have read the 'Essays of Elia' in the *London Magazine*, or *Confessions of an English Opium Eater*, or *The Fortunes of Nigel*, all published in 1822. But while this life-span reminds us that the debuts of both *Tristram Shandy* and *Frankenstein* could be enjoyed in his single lifetime, Chatterton would not have been a 'marvellous Boy' in the eyes of any of his later acolytes: he would have been in his manly mid-40s when *Lyrical Ballads* was published, perhaps having already dabbled in radical politics, mixing with Godwin and Wollstonecraft and of course William Blake. (Blake, born in 1757, died in his 70th year in 1827 and offers a suggestive trajectory; he too echoes through this collection.) Would Chatterton have remained a poet? He was eager to write political propaganda for Wilkes (with whom he really did communicate), but was willing, it appears from his promiscuous output, to have tried his pen at anything and to write for any side. He certainly had great literary expectations, and was handling himself very adeptly in London. Perhaps he would have recognized the profit and fame to be won from writing Gothic novels; the heady mix of history and legend would have appealed. If so, his Rowley works might have been put aside as frisky juvenilia, not unlike the miniature magazine histories of Angria and Gondal produced by the Brontës. But Chatterton also suggested he might join the navy as a surgeon's mate (as Smollett had done 30 years previously), tossed on strange and distant seas when the Rowley Controversy broke ....

We can never know. No matter: all the following essays demonstrate that the material we do have is extraordinarily rich and compellingly intricate, supple and responsive to an astonishing and diverse range of critical interrogations, and will perhaps ultimately prove Peter Ackroyd's bold challenge to read Chatterton as the prototypical English poet. And if the old chests in the dusty muniment room of St

Mary Redcliffe have been long since emptied, fantastic riches clearly remain to be discovered elsewhere.

Notes

1. I use 'baroque' in the sense of Jorge Luis Borges, who defines it as 'the name of one of the forms of the syllogism' (*A Universal History of Infamy*, Preface to the 1954 edn (Harmondsworth, 1975), 11).
2. From Taylor's dating of *Rowley*, the result of recording the frequency of words derived from the glossaries and dictionaries Chatterton had access to at different times, it appears that from the beginning Chatterton aimed to create a single definable author (*Works*, ii. 1176–228): see Groom, Nick, 'Thomas Rowlie Preeste', in *The Early Romantics: Pope to Wordsworth*, ed. Thomas Woodman (London, 1998).
3. Caine, T. Hall, *Recollections of Dante Gabriel Rossetti* (Boston, 1869), 184.
4. Baines, Paul, 'Literary Forgery and the Ideology of Detection', and Suarez, Michael F., SJ, 'Trafficking in the Muse: The Sale and Distribution of Dodsley's *Collection of Poems* 1748–1782'. Both have contributed to the present volume.
5. See John Goodridge's 'Rowley's Ghost', below.
6. *The Poetical Works of Thomas Chatterton*, ed. Walter W. Skeat (London, 1872), ii. vii–xlvi; Dix, John, *The Life of Thomas Chatterton including his Unpublished Poems and Correspondence* (London, 1837). For Dix's duplicity and forgery, see the Chatterton entry by Penny Boumelha in Margaret M. Smith (ed.), *Index of English Literary Manuscripts* (London, 1986), iii. 1, 195–200.
7. The manuscript of Meyerstein's *Life* is in Bristol Reference Library, 24567. In the same year as Taylor's incomparable edition, Grevel Lindop also edited *Thomas Chatterton: Selected Poems* for Carcanet (Manchester, 1972). The two bibliographies are Warren, Murray, *A Descriptive and Annotated Bibliography of Thomas Chatterton* (New York, 1977), and Rowles, Jean C., 'Thomas Chatterton 1752–1770: An Annotated Bibliography', Library Association thesis, 1981.
8. Clarke, Ernest, 'New Lights on Chatterton', *Transactions of the Bibliographical Society* 13 (1916), 219–51; Powell, L. F., 'Thomas Tyrwhitt and the Rowley Poems', *Review of English Studies* 7 (1931), 314–26; Holmes, Richard, 'Thomas Chatterton: The Case Re-opened', *Cornhill Magazine*, 178 (1970), 200–51. Holmes's thesis, that Chatterton's death was not an adolescent suicide but a dreadful accident, is suggested by Donald S. Taylor, 'Chatterton's Suicide', *Philological Quarterly* 31 (1952), 63–9, and anticipated by Neil Bell, *Cover His Face: A Novel of the Life and Times of Thomas Chatterton, the Marvellous Boy of Bristol* (London, 1943). It is also, of course, the inspiration for Peter Ackroyd's *Chatterton: A Novel* (London, 1987) – and the most plausible reading of the evidence.
9. For example, Marjorie Levinson, *The Romantic Fragment Poem: A Critique of a Form* (Chapel Hill, NC, 1986), 34–9.
10. Butler, Marilyn, 'The Country Movement', in *Romanticism in National Context*, ed. Roy Porter and Mikuláš Teich (Cambridge, 1988), 41–51; and

'Against Tradition: The Case for a Particularized Historical Method', in *Historical Studies and Literary Criticism*, ed. Jerome J. McGann (Madison, 1985), 25–47, esp. 37–41; Stewart, Susan, *Crimes of Writing* (Oxford, 1991), 148–53.

11. Interestingly, Jerome McGann disagrees with what one might call the 'Keatsianization' of Chatterton, and instead sees him as the precursor of Poe and Wilde ('Infatuated Worlds', *London Review of Books*, 22 September 1994, 7).

12. Baines, Paul, 'The Macaroni Parson and the Marvellous Boy: Literature and Forgery in the Eighteenth Century'; Barry, Jonathan, 'The History and Antiquities of Bristol: Chatterton in Bristol'; Goodridge, John, 'Identity, Authenticity, and Class: John Clare and the Mask of Chatterton'; Groom, Nick, 'Forgery or Plagiarism? Unravelling Chatterton's Rowley'; McGowen, Randall, 'Forgery Discovered, or The Perils of Circulation in Eighteenth-Century England'; Suarez, Michael F., SJ, 'What Thomas Knew: Chatterton and the Business of Getting into Print'.

13. *Johnsonian Miscellanies*, ed. G. B. Hill (London, 1897), ii. 197. For a theory of counterfactuals, see *Virtual History: Alternatives and Counterfactuals*, ed. Niall Ferguson (London, 1997), 1–90.

I
Life and Works

Chapter 2

Unparodying and Forgery: The Augustan Chatterton

Claude Rawson

Thomas Chatterton (1752–70) is famous for inventing the fifteenth-century poet Thomas Rowley, writing the latter's poems, passing them off as authentic articles, and doing all this before he died at 17. He fooled some of the people most of the time, but judges competent in the history of English language and prosody refused to be taken in, not always as quickly as one might have expected. The enterprise was a perverse variant of the 'medievalism' which produced Percy's *Reliques* (1765), as well as part of the curious mid-century flowering of pre-Romantic 'forgery' whose other famous example was Macpherson's Ossian. Samuel Johnson, who rejected both, said 'For Ossian there is a national pride, ... for Chatterton there is nothing but the resolution to say again what has once been said', though Chatterton's Bristolian *campanilismo* can be seen as a scaled-down version of Ossianic nationalism, and Chatterton wrote some Ossianic imitations of his own.

Chatterton also wrote poems in modern English from the age of 11, and by the time of his death at 17 had produced an *oeuvre* that fills nearly 700 pages of the big Oxford edition (1971). The modern poems, some of them highly accomplished, were in a variety of recognized eighteenth-century styles, not in the least Romantic. But it was Chatterton's 'medieval' creations which captured the imagination, and their exposure as fraudulent fostered the scenario of a tender Romantic genius stifled by the hard-faced men of an eighteenth-century cultural rearguard. Chatterton's writings, including his famous sonnet to Horace Walpole, first published in Dix's *Life* (1837), contributed to the later evolution of this mythology, though their own more limited point was concerned with poverty oppressed by the arrogance of power:

> Had I the Gifts of Wealth and Lux'ry shar'd
> Not poor and Mean – Walpole! thou hadst not dared
> Thus to insult, But I shall live and Stand
> By Rowley's side – when Thou art dead and damned.

When Chatterton died at 17 of arsenical poisoning in his London attic, he became the prototype of that favourite Romantic figure, the poet slain by the critics, whose culminating exemplar was Keats, 'snuff'd out', in Byron's jeering phrase, 'by an article'. Shelley placed Chatterton, 'pale, his solemn agony ... not / Yet faded from him', first in the celestial welcoming party for the martyred Keats in *Adonais*. Henry Wallis's painting of the dead Chatterton (1856), for which George Meredith sat (or rather lay), perpetuates the tragic scene at the Tate to this day.

Long before this the paradox had established itself that it was Chatterton's 'Rowleyan' supporters who argued that he couldn't possibly have had the talent to write those medieval masterpieces, so that recognition of his genius actually depended on the exposure of the forgery. When Chatterton himself spoke out for wounded poets against reviewers, he did so not in accents of Romantic defiance or self-pity, but in an Augustanizing idiom crudely derived from Pope and Churchill ('Let busy Kenrick vent his little Spleen/And spit his Venom in a Magazine'), like the Byron of *English Bards*.

None of this impeded the myth of a Chatterton martyred by Augustan persecutors, promoted by nearly all Romantic poets except Byron. It is seldom noticed that even Wordsworth's 'marvellous Boy' (the phrase itself an unwitting reprise of the ambivalent or contemptuous sarcasms about 'that marvellous young man', 'that marvellous creature', by Chatterton's arch-enemy Horace Walpole), the most memorable evocation of Chatterton as exemplar of the tragic fate of poets, is hardly a simple case:

> I thought of Chatterton, the marvellous Boy,
> The sleepless Soul that perished in his pride;...
> We Poets in our youth begin in gladness;
> But thereof come in the end despondency and madness.

Wordsworth's 'Resolution and Independence', in which these lines appear, is known to have close links with Chatterton's late poem, the 'Excelente Balade of Charitie'. Its stanza (rhyme royal with a final alexandrine, as in Milton's *Nativity Ode*) was formally the same, and like Chatterton's poem it is a fable describing an encounter with a destitute old man. Its official moral contains more than a hint that the mythology of 'mighty Poets in their misery dead', including Wordsworth's own investment in it in some of the poem's most memorable passages, is mere self-indulgence when compared with the misfortunes of the old leech gatherer.

The explicit tendency is thus more conventional than the lines on Chatterton might lead us to expect, and the point of real interest is that it is actually closer to Chatterton's poem by that fact. The 'Excelente Balade', perhaps the last of the Rowley poems, is a Good Samaritan parable about a pauper who gets no charity from a rich abbot but is given a groat of silver and an under-cloak by a humbler priest. It's not obviously a statement about neglected genius, but may have been written close to the time of Chatterton's death and is commonly read, as his editor Donald S. Taylor says, 'as a pre-suicide statement'. Taylor believes it to be somewhat earlier, and Chatterton's 'suicide' is a part of the legend which has itself been questioned.

A persistent counter-scenario, promoted by several scholars and lately reactivated in Peter Ackroyd's novel Chatterton, has Chatterton dying of an accidental overdose of anti-venereal medication, at a period when his post-Rowleyan literary career was undergoing a successful launch (exceptional for a boy of 17), and when, to judge by his letters, he seems to have been in a mood quite remote from despondency and madness. However Wordsworth read the 'Balade', he is hardly likely to have designed 'Resolution and Independence' as a putdown of Chatterton. He said in a letter that the poem describes how the leech gatherer rescued him 'from my dejection and despair almost as an interposition of Providence', and Chatterton's biographer Meyerstein, with his usual preening positiveness, says the 'burden' of the two poems 'is the same'. But in Wordsworth the broken old man is the rescuer and not the rescuee, and an inability on Wordsworth's part to register this difference would have been an extraordinary illustration of the self-absorption actually targeted in the poem itself.

The most immediately arresting thing about Chatterton's work is in fact his power and fluency in modern English and in 'Augustan' literary modes. His first two poems, written in 1764, when he was 11, are in flat hard Hudibrastics with a take-it-or-leave-it sarcasm which is aggressively and extraordinarily adult. They are derivative, in part, from Swift and from Gay's Fables, but their brassy force has a timbre of its own. In 'Apostate Will', about a Vicar of Bray character,

> He'd oft profess an hallow'd flame,
> And every where preach'd Wesley's name;
> He was a preacher and what not,
> As long as money could be got;
> He'd oft profess with holy fire,
> The labourer's worthy of his hire,

the amalgam of sanctimonious cant and slangy harshness invites comparison with the invective of Swift's later poems or with Fielding's angrier fictions.

The other poem, 'unfinished' in a Swiftian way (*'Caetera desunt'*), is 'Sly Dick':

> Sharp was the Frost, the Wind was high
> And sparkling Stars bedeckt the Sky
> Sly Dick in arts of cunning skill'd,
> Whose Rapine all his pockets fill'd,
> Had laid him down to take his rest
> And soothe with sleep his anxious breast.
> 'Twas thus a dark infernal sprite
> A native of the blackest Night,
> Portending mischief to devise
> Upon Sly Dick he cast his Eyes,
> Then strait descends th'infernal sprite,
> And in his Chamber does alight:
> In visions he before him stands ...

The dark infernal sprite, less a Gothick figure than a sharply efficient, mock-portentous property from the satiric 'visions' of eighteenth-century satire (a general influence of Gay's *Fables* on Chatterton is well recognized), proposes to Sly Dick a piece of thievery which Meyerstein believes to be a schoolboy exploit by a fellow pupil at Colston school. If so, it belongs with that schoolboy world which many writers, from the Fielding of *Jonathan Wild* to Auden and Isherwood, have identified with the gangster virtues of adult criminality as well as of epic heroes.

Meyerstein, a fervent devotee of the Rowley poems, speaks of 'that conversational style which he always managed with a glib gusto', but even if that's all it was, it's not in the mode with which he is normally identified: among 'conversational' styles, it is that of Butler or Swift rather than Coleridge or Keats. Chatterton went on to write many more poems in modern English, sometimes in Popeian couplets which, like Byron, he managed less successfully than the low-key metres he learned from Swift and Gay.

This Augustanism extends to his 'medieval' imitations. The first of these, the 'Bristowe Tragedie' (1768), is more remarkable for the garrulity and repetitiousness of its narrative (which it shares with many of the 'authentic' ballads of the kind it mimics, so that it testifies more to his skills as a *pasticheur* than to formal indiscipline or Romantic 'freedom') than for other conversational properties, but its opening stanza

> The feather'd songster Chaunticleer
> Han wounde his bugle horne,
> And told the earlie villager
> The commynge of the morne

announces itself as self-consciously different from some classicizing alternatives of Renaissance or Augustan tradition, as Chatterton's own note cheekily indicates: 'In my humble Opinion the foregoing Verses are far more elegant and poetical than all the Parade of Aurora's whipping away the Night, unbarring the Gates of the East &&.' But this note, ostensibly expressing Chatterton's liberation from the 'imprisoning canons' of eighteenth-century poetry, actually evokes the parody of poetic dawns in Swift's 'Description of the Morning' and in the prose of Fielding, as well as being a satirical footnote in a widely practised Augustan mode.

It's a mode whose legacy is more far-reaching than is sometimes realized, especially in the literature of romantic irony and the self-conscious modernism which derives from that, and it has left its mark in other Rowley poems too. The boastful rant about Aurora may be compared with a non-satiric note in the same poem: 'I defy Homer, Virgil, or any of their Bardships to produce so great a Hero as Syr Chas. Bawdyn ...', which, though intended straight, also has perceptible resemblances with the species of mock-note of which Pope's *Dunciad* offers many examples. The elaborate authenticating footnotes to some of Chatterton's other Rowley works, especially those purporting to correct errors or expose textual shenanigans in his invented authors, have an air of poker-faced mystification similarly reminiscent of Pope's Dunciadic commentary, of which they may be thought to be an underisive counterpart: 'I think this Line is borrow'd from a much better one of Rowley's ... The Reason why I think Iscam guilty of the Plagiary is that the Songe to Ella ... was wrote when Rowley was in London ...'.

'Ella' is also the eponymous hero of the play *Ælla,* which Chatterton and some Chattertonians regard as a dramatic masterpiece. It's based, anachronistically for a fifteenth-century work, on *Othello,* and has been shown, in structure and sensibility, to resemble Restoration and eighteenth-century adaptations of Shakespeare. The manner, as the admiring Taylor says, is that of the heroic play: 'complexities of action, character, and situation are conflated, reduced, or eliminated; individualizing character detail is dropped; symmetries and echoing in plot, character relationships, and scene structure are underlined or emphatically introduced'. But like the notes to the poems, which sometimes read like a scholarly commentary composed by Squire Western, this work of Shakespearean derivation has absorbed the spirit of Augustan parody along with the more primary forms. It is, as Taylor says, 'operatic … even grandiose', but the yokel ranting ('Thou are [*sic*] a warrioure, Hurra, thatte I kenne, / And myckle famed for thie handie dede') is less like the grandiloquence of Dryden or Lee than the kind of thing which parodies of the heroic play, from the *Rehearsal* to Fielding's *Tragedy of Tragedies,* perceived in the originals.

Chatterton might be said to be unparodying these parodies, in an unwitting upward reformulation of a kind to which eighteenth-century writing, especially addicted to parodic forms, had a predisposition not always adequately recognized. Better writers did it with greater control and clairvoyance, as when Pope's *Dunciad* breaks through the parody-barrier into its own stratosphere of primary heroic grandeur, whose epic stature, though disfigured, remains oddly undiminished; or when Sterne's *Tristram Shandy,* a more or less exact contemporary of Chatterton's, ostentatiously outfaced the parody of self-cherishing modernism in Swift's *Tale of a Tub* and created a generic self-mockery which wilfully escalates the Romantic egomania Swift was exposing in the first place.

Chatterton's activity is less self-aware. And his idea, at the end of a Hudibrastic satire of 1769, of switching to 'a Shandeyan Stile', amounts to asking 'your favor and your Smile', unpicking parody in the direction of sentimental geniality rather than of incremental convolutions of ironic self-regard. The enterprise of authenticating the Rowleyan forgery entailed a parallel simplification, a non-derisive version of Augustan hoaxes of the Bickerstaff kind as well as of better-known and more transparent ironic impersonations. It is also comparable in its way to the epistolary novel's 'editorial' *donnée,* which can be seen as an unparodying of the mock-editorial routines of the *Tale* or *Dunciad* (novels-in-letters were fictive 'editions'); or to the editorial special effect of a post-Shandean novel like Mackenzie's *Man of Feeling*, where the device of an incomplete or mutilated manuscript is offered as something patently other than mockery of the habits of editors of ancient texts, and where even Shandean self-parody is peeled away, leaving a residue of fond unmirthful pathos.

It is here if anywhere that the shadowy presence of a 'pre-Romantic' Chatterton is to be detected. And it's another of the contradictions of the Romantic myth that if Chatterton is to be considered a poet of talent (as the logic of undeceived admirers of the Rowley poems demanded), the talent not only showed itself in work outside the domain of the inspired medievalizing pasticheur whom Romantic poets admired as a precursor in the break with eighteenth-century forms, but may be seen as that of a pervasively Augustanized sensibility in the Rowley poems themselves. In this he resembles Smart, whose reputation as a visionary poet has often obstructed a proper perception of Augustan loyalism, strongly embodied in many lyric, georgic or satirical poems, but also actively proclaimed in unlikely places, including the declaration in *Jubilate Agno*, 'For I bless the Lord Jesus for the memory of GAY, POPE and SWIFT'. That the *Jubilate* has moments of eruptive comedy, part of the poem's strange power whether they were offered as comic or not, strengthens the resemblance, though Smart's 'Let Nebai rejoice with the Wild Cucumber … Let Jaalah rejoice with Moly wild garlick' has a disconcerting *exalté* humour more energetic and vivid than Chatterton's often unfocused or ambivalent jests.

We are not always sure, in Chatterton, when a potential for mirth derives mainly from the gaucheness of the writing, and when it's the product of an awareness of the jokey potential of the whole enterprise of large-scale linguistic and imaginative counterfeiting. Chatterton was certainly capable of mildly libertine jokerie, as in

> There was a Broder of Orderys Blacke
> In mynster of Brystowe Cittie
> Hee layd a Damoisell onne her Backe
> So guess yee the Taile of mie Dittie,

whose street-ballad urbanity and thrust might, for all its Rowleyan fancy dress, have passed Rochester's test for the 'mannerly obscene', a style evidently envisaged by Rochester as more 'mannerly' than Rochester's own. Chatterton fancied himself as a bit of a lad, though his bawdy, such as it is, displays the coy attenuation of Restoration raffishness which began over half a century earlier and was to culminate in the anodyne naughtiness of Tom Moore's *Poetical Works of Thomas Little* (1801), which had the power to shock Coleridge and Byron. In this stanza from a minstrel duet in *Ælla*, a dialogue perhaps derived from Dryden's version of the 27th *Idyll* of Theocritus,

> I've hearde erste mie grandame saie,
> Yonge damoyselles schulde ne bee,
> In the swotie moonthe of Maie,
> Wythe yonge menne bie the grene wode tree,

we are on the way to the winking sub-Shandean libertinage of *Under Milk Wood*. It's preferable to the callow sexual bravado Chatterton displayed in his own name, and perhaps one of the virtues of the Rowleyan idiom is that it may have protected him from some unprocessed expressions of adolescent silliness.

Much attention, notably in the heavily annotated *Poems* (1782), and in anti-Rowleyan writings by Malone and Warton, is given to parallels with Dryden, Rowe, Pope, and others (as well as some earlier writers, chiefly Shakespeare). These are often weak in specific resemblance, and tend not so much to establish a close textual similarity or to indicate plagiarism (i.e. from 'later' writers than Rowley) as to identify the pervasiveness of linguistic usages and poetic conventions unavailable at the presumed time of writing.

The 'Battle of Hastynges', a stanzaic epic, is laced with reminders of Pope's Homer, in later Romantic eyes an especially culpable repository of bad poetic habits. The reminders include extended similes, and also some gory special effects, frequently concerned, for example, with eyes extinguished by death or gouged out by weapons. Such items were not invented by Pope, but Chatterton was hardly likely to get them direct from Homer. The line 'Before his Optics daunced a shade of nyghte', for example, has a Popeian ring, and the word 'optics', as Thomas Warton pointed out, was post-Rowleyan (it is used by Pope, but not in his Homer). But none of the parallels adduced in 1782 is verbally very close, the closest being from Pope's *Iliad*, v. 575, 'His eyeballs darken with the shades of death'. In another example,

> And from their Sockets started out his Eyes,
> And from his Mouth came out his blameless Tonge,

all the parallels cited have eyes falling out, but the detail is commonplace and specific resemblances are not close.

These special effects were routines of Homeric cruelty which Pope was usually disposed to 'soften'. Chatterton went to Pope mainly as an epic model, but perhaps not because he shared any Popeian agenda for sanitizing ancient barbarities: it is he who added the Hitchcockian macabre humour of the extruded tongue. The adjective 'blameless' (Warton says the usage is Popeian, though Pope doesn't actually use it with 'tongue') is a heaving piece of sentimental overkill, and also borders on comedy. This isn't likely to be by design, but it would be rash to discount an active element of schoolboy glee, a callow exuberance in violent narrative which offers another illustration of Auden's insight into the link between what Chatterton's antagonist Walpole called (in another connection) the 'mimic republic' of schoolboys, and the gangster virtues of epic and saga. Grotesque scenes of mutilation come up with a cascading frequency, a relentless flat-footed automatism, suggestive of an adolescent gusto not wholly unamused at its own power or innocent of playing to a gallery of absent schoolmates:

> Into his Bowels then his Launce he thrust:
>   And drew therout a steemie drierie lode,
> Quod he these Offals are for ever curst;
>   Shall serve the Coughs and Rooks and Daws for Food.
>   Then on the Pleine the steamie Lode he throwde,
>   Smokinge with life and dyde with crymson bloude.

Smoking and steaming gore and viscera (blood 'smokde in Puddels on the dustie Pleine', 'The Normans Bowels steemde upon the Feeld') are almost a Chatterton trademark, though they partly derive from Pope. In at least one place,

>   The Greie Goose pinyon that thereon was set,
>   Eftsoones with smokynge Crimson bloude was wet,

which seems to derive from 'Chevy Chace', cited in *Poems* (1778),

>   The grey goose-wing that was thereon
>   In his harts bloode was wett,

we can witness Chatterton actually superimposing the 'smokynge' on a 'medieval' analogue or source.

A character in Ackroyd's novel exclaims that 'half the poetry of the eighteenth century is probably written by him'. The literal point is that Chatterton, at one stage in the fiction, is supposed to have faked his death in 1770 in a deal with a bookseller in which he would devote his time, now that his medieval cover was blown, to forging poems by his eighteenth-century predecessors and contemporaries, including Thomson, Collins, Gray, Goldsmith and Churchill. It's a way of acknowledging Chatterton's extraordinary versatility in eighteenth-century styles, not only those evoked within the antique Rowleyan mode, styles which included those of non-satiric writers as well as of Swift and Gay (and Pope, often mediated through Churchill: though Chatterton's Popeian satires – the 'Consuliad', the 'Whore of Babylon' – like Byron's, are crude by comparison with his work in lighter, less grandiloquent modes). Chatterton is made to say in Ackroyd's book, 'I was a very Proteus to those who read my Works'. The description also includes the boasted 'Skill in the Art of Personation' which made him relate, 'in their own Voices', the adventures of a man 'pursewed by Bailiffs ..., a malefactor chain'd in Newgate,... a young ripe Girl about to be pluck'd'. This makes him sound, perhaps pointedly, like a Defoe narrator.

Parody and impersonation or 'forgery' are connected. They're not the same thing, as Defoe discovered to his cost when his 'final solution' pamphlet, the *Shortest-Way with the Dissenters*, was taken straight. A lesson which eighteenth-century writers, including Swift, Pope and Fielding, confronted with varying combinations of anxiety, discomfiture, or unexpected satisfaction, was that works of sustained parodic irony – an idiom which had only recently become a widely practised mode of literary discourse – ran risks of being understood literally. When that happened, the satisfaction on offer was that of the hoax, a success, usually unlooked for, in impersonation rather than in the intended parodic mode. The corresponding cost was that if most readers missed the irony, the satirical point would be lost, which may be one reason why Swift's extermination tract, *A Modest Proposal*, unlike Defoe's, was couched in terms so outlandish that only an exceptionally obtuse minority might have been disposed to take it straight.

Parody is an act of interpretation rather than impersonation, and, usually through its disposition or need to signal derision, breaches impersonation by that fact. But the readiness with which the one collapses into the other brings home the fact that parody involves an exercise in imaginative sympathy which has at some point to be stopped in its tracks. Chatterton's exercises in what I have called unparodying may be part of an instinctive resistance to this process, a kind of affirmation of the impersonating process, the impulse to imaginative sympathy, which is both contained and denied in the parodic act. That such unparodying was a strong if underrecognized feature of eighteenth-century writing suggests that a degree of self-division on these issues was cultural. A period remarkable and perhaps unique in the centrality it accorded to parodic expression, in which some of the most important works of the best writers (*A Tale of a Tub*, *Gulliver's Travels*, the *Dunciad*, *Jonathan Wild*, and in their way even *Joseph Andrews* and *Tom Jones*) were wholly or mainly parodic in structure and idiom, was drawing to a close, while an unprecedented valorization of unmediated impersonating empathy, whose application to poetry was later to be crystallized in the Keatsian notion of the 'chameleon' poet, had begun to establish itself in the Richardsonian novel.

To the generation of Swift and Pope, and more ambiguously to Richardson's contemporary Fielding, the idea of the 'chameleon' would have evoked the unreliably and reprehensibly changeable behaviour of the hypocrite, just as Proteus, the god of disguises, often disreputable in older texts, was more likely to suggest the routines of the confidence man than the powers of the artist (a long time was to elapse before those two figures could be equated, as in Mann's *Confessions of Felix Krull*). Augustan protocol, towards which Chatterton had little of the disloyalty imputed to him, shrank from full impersonation, for reasons which included gentlemanly inhibitions against self-surrender, and a residue of Platonic objections against play-acting (*hypocrite*, we are often reminded, was the Greek word for actor). The lofty disdain felt for Defoe and Richardson well into Chatterton's lifetime was an expression of class-contempt in which their character as literary impersonators of disconcerting power played an acknowledged or half-acknowledged part: 'the Fellow that was *pilloryed*, I have forgot his Name', said Swift of the Defoe of the *Shortest-Way* (naming him in a footnote in a later printing, without removing the bit about forgetting the name). The signposted derisions of parody in effect provided, even in the most serious works, the defence against the impersonating potential which was inherent in the mode of parody itself. Perhaps the decisive merging of the two antagonistic trends occurs in *Tristram Shandy* (1759–67), whose publication fell wholly within Chatterton's short life and stretched over half of it.

It's within this unstable two-way traffic between parody and impersonation that it is appropriate to view the Rowley forgeries. They are an extension of the eighteenth-century styles Chatterton practised before he invented Rowley and continued after that fiction was abandoned. In this they perhaps differ from Ossian or even Walpole's *Castle of Otranto*, being more ambivalent or uncertain in circumventing parodic survivals even as they share the new predilection for stylistic fancy dress. Walpole said it was the success of Ossian rather than his own hostility that was 'the ruin of Chatterton'. Chatterton himself wrote Ossianic imitations, where impersonation is sometimes more overtly compromised by parody than in the Rowley poems, though with what may have been a similar uncertainty of purpose.

The fancy dress was important too. The invention of Rowley and his milieu may or may not have been conceived as a simple 'forgery', but it soon acquired a density and imaginative commitment in the evocation of period and place analogous to those called for by the more ambitious historical novels, and especially by those extended fictional creations whose 'historical' context exists semi-independently of an individual work and is typically shared by several. It has been compared with Hardy's Wessex or Faulkner's South, for example, though these imaginative worlds did not in the same way require the factual 'authentication' Chatterton felt called upon to supply. He was after all claiming a specific historical existence, not just a fictional likeness, for both his 'ancient' texts and their *dramatis personae*. Nevertheless, like Hardy or Faulkner, he created a Bristol based on real local knowledge as well as on a considerable exercise of invention, into which the lives and doings of his authors and the events of their narratives could be seen to fit.

To that end – on a scale which resembles the historical, topographical, linguistic and grammatical support-system compiled to sustain Tolkien's fictions, more than anything in Hardy or Faulkner – he generated in a short period a large number of pseudo-historical documents, deeds, wills, accounts, heraldic notes, catalogues of antiquities, topographical and architectural drawings and notes, accounts of Bristol, its castle and its churches, with a special emphasis on his own district of Redcliffe and its church of St Mary, genealogies, historical and biographical writings concerning the city of Bristol and its mayor Canynge, Rowley's patron, letters by both men, and so on. An enterprise on this scale is likely in its nature to transcend mere 'authentication', especially when it supports and is supported by a corpus of poems and plays rooted in the material and often celebrative of it.

Chatterton's local pride acts at least as strongly as the excitations of

Tolkien's fantasy in investing his fabrications with a mythologizing radiance. The prose 'Discorse on Brystowe', historical notes assembled by Rowley for Canynge, includes within itself the poem 'Stay curyous Traveller and pass not bye', about St Mary Redcliffe:

> this Maystrie of a human hand
> The Pride of Bristowe and the Westerne Lande,

It is perhaps the most eloquent expression of mythologizing *campanilismo* in the whole of Chatterton, his local Bristolian version of Ossianic 'nationalism', with a touch of Yeatsian elation in its conferment of a heroic glow on the place and its great man:

> Well maiest thou be astound but view it well
> Go not from hence before thou see thy fill
> And learn the Builder's Vertues and his name
> Of this tall Spyre in everye Countye telle
> And with thy Tale the lazing Rychmen shame
> Showe howe the Glorious Canynge did excelle
> How hee good Man a Friend for Kynges became.

Mythologizing isn't left to the poetry, and is in fact evident in the flattest of the 'documentary' texts. Even the early series of heraldic notes, 'Extracts from Craishes Herauldry', far from being confined to mere pseudo-authenticating objectives, makes sure to invent exalted ancestries for Chatterton's friends and family. The latter gets an especially ancient Norman lineage (from 'Johannes Sieur de Chateau tonne'), also a not unYeatsian touch. Such things were sometimes enlivened by *diablerie*, as when, in an extended free-standing document, Chatterton concocted a distinguished ancestry of De Berghams for a Bristol pewterer called Henry Burgum, and later derided his snobbish cravings that way: another example of the volatility of Chattertonian impersonation, and its openness to satirical subversion.

The verses in which Burgum is derided are prefixed to Chatterton's 'Will'. This document, which is superscribed 'wrote bet 11 and 2 oClock Saturday in the utmost Distress of Mind', and is sometimes taken as a prelude to Chatterton's 'suicide', is in fact a satirical exercise, bequeathing 'all my Vigor and Fire of Youth to Mr. George Catcott being sensible he is in most want of it' and 'to Mr. Burgum all my Prosody and Grammar likewise one Moiety of my Modesty, the other moiety to any young Lady who can prove without blushing that she wants that valuable Commodity'. It belongs to a well-established type of mock-will, of which the 'Last Will and Testament' by Auden and MacNeice in *Letters from Iceland*, and an adolescent imitation of the latter by Larkin and Noel Hughes (written at about the same age as Chatterton's), are modern examples. Such a mock-will had recently appeared in the *Town and Country Magazine* (in an issue, as Meyerstein points out, to which Chatterton himself contributed), by Samuel Derrick, the poet whom Johnson refused to measure against Smart on the grounds that one couldn't settle the 'precedency between a louse and a flea'.

The invention of the Rowleyan language is a central part of the authentication project. It differs from Spenser's because of the importance of the authentication factor, but shared Spenser's impulse to evoke a glamourized older English time, was aware of Spenser as a model, and displayed similarly rudimentary linguistic expertise. Nevertheless, Chatterton took some trouble over his invented language. It consists of about 1800 words, virtually all of which can be traced to probable sources (Bailey's *Universal Etymological English Dictionary*, supplemented by other dictionaries, including two Anglo-Saxon dictionaries, and a few authors, principally Chaucer, Spenser, Shakespeare, Camden, Percy). There are a number of Gallicisms, despite Keats's idea that Chatterton purified English of such things, though Chatterton may not have known they were French, and himself insisted on the Englishness of his medieval 'authors'. The rest of his vocabulary, as Taylor says, was based on a notion, evidently not restricted to him, that 'fifteenth-century spelling, syntax, and word forms' were essentially 'lawless', so that he could make free with the spellings and inflections of eighteenth-century English.

The archaizing follows a few crude principles. Make as many words end in 'e' or (as Tyrwhitt noted) begin with 'a' as possible, change 'i' to 'y' at will, duplicate or otherwise add consonants freely: 'Whatteverre schalle be Englysch wee wylle slea … Eftsoones we will retourne, and wanquished bee no moere', says Hurra the Dane in *Ælla*, where both foreigner and Bristolian sometimes sound like demented 'medieval' prefigurations of *Guys and Dolls* ('Unmanned, uneyned, exclooded aie the lyghte', 'I have a mynde wynged wythe the levyn ploome'), as though old Dan Runyounne himself had been included in the Rowleyan-roll call. Dramatic reversals of purpose, and the pathos of heroic carnage, come over thus:

Seconde Dane

Yette I wylle synglie dare the bloddie fraie.
Botte ne; I'lle flie, and morther yn retrete ...

Thyrde Dane

Enthoghteynge forr to scape the brondeynge foe ...
Farr offe I spied a syghte of myckle woe ...

The 'Mynstrelles Songe' in *Ælla*, 'O! synge untoe mie roundelaie', elaborately and sometimes delicately derivative (from Shakespeare, Percy's *Reliques*, and elsewhere), and possessed of some unusual accesses of metrical finesse, is seen off by the heroine with the words:

Thys syngeyng haveth whatte coulde make ytte please;
Butte mie uncourtlie shappe benymmes me of all ease.

One looks to Chatterton's schoolboy humour for a Larkinesque eruption on the lines of 'And he yaf hym a sodynge gode kyk in the balles, causing him grete dole and lamentacions', alas in vain.

Nevertheless, it has at its best a claim to be taken as an artificial language, serviceable to the creation of its poetic world. Even as an exercise in learned authentication, it wasn't bad for its time, and studious efforts had to be activated to detect the fraud. An extraordinary amount of scholarship was devoted to Chatterton soon after his death, including, as Malone said, 'a magnificent and accurate edition of his works', which even Shakespeare lacked. The forgery debate called for linguistic analysis of Chatterton's English, enormously in excess of the hard work Chatterton himself put into the business. Learned men like George Steevens and Thomas Tyrwhitt were stopped in their tracks, not initially certain of themselves as they embarked on heavy labours of refutation.

There is no doubt that the plan was to make money and reputation for Chatterton from the publication of ancient texts and the supply of information to William Barrett, the barber-surgeon historian of Bristol, who was largely taken in, and for the antiquarian and art-historical researches of Horace Walpole, who, after a brief hesitation, was not. But it is evident that the whole enterprise became charged with imaginative as well as imaginary elements in a way that suggests that the borders between forgery and fiction are not always clearly distinct, as Chatterton himself self-consciously noted, when, with insecure logic, he threw back at Walpole the example of his own *Castle of Otranto* in the angry poem he wrote (but did not send) in response to Walpole's rejection of his forgeries:

> Walpole! I thought not I should ever see
> So mean a Heart as thine has proved to be;
> Thou, who in Luxury nurs'd behold'st with Scorn
> The Boy, who Friendless, Penniless, Forlorn,
> Asks thy high Favour, – thou mayst call me Cheat –
> Say, didst thou ne'er indulge in such Deceit?
> Who wrote Otranto?

You might say that in Chatterton's own case the distinction between faking and fiction was not only unclear but artificial: he was quite clearly doing both. Hence everyone on all sides of the authenticity question regarded the genuineness of the material as marginal to a recognition of his abilities. Johnson, an early non-believer, said 'it is wonderful how the whelp has written such things', and Walpole himself reported, 'he was a colossal genius and might have soared I know not whither.' In a sense, the forgery proved the genius of the fiction, since if the material had been genuine Chatterton's achievement would merely have been that of a lucky antiquarian find. For some of Chatterton's Romantic admirers indeed, the genius of the fiction made the fake true by fiat. Blake said: 'I believe both Macpherson & Chatterton, that what they say is Ancient Is so ... I own myself an admirer of Ossian equally with any other poet Rowley and Chatterton also.' A character in Ackroyd's novel says that he's the 'greatest forger ... the greatest plagiarist in history', to be told by the hero that he's 'the greatest poet in history'. Chatterton himself is imagined as saying 'the truest Plagiarism is the truest Poetry', and George Meredith, who modelled as Chatterton for Wallis's famous portrait, as asking the painter whether 'the greatest realism is also the greatest fakery'.

The example of Ossian and his forger Macpherson, also an object of devotion long after the exposure of the fraud (which took place shortly before the Chatterton affair; the two cases are variously related), suggests the existence of cultural factors which may help to place Romantic conceptions of Chatterton's genius in a more sober perspective. Johnson's comments, and even Walpole's, suggest remarkable accomplishment for a youth in Chatterton's circumstances, perhaps in the spirit of Johnson's famous quip about women preachers: one was surprised to see it done at all. For both authors, as for the great Romantic admirers, the spuriousness of the documents hardly blocked recognition of talent, but it did not suggest the supreme imaginative gifts perceived by Coleridge or Keats. That perception was aided by a post-Rowleyan mythology, of the tragic destitute youth struck down by a harsh and unfeeling establishment, which is itself one of Chatterton's imaginative achievements, most crisply expressed in the lines to Walpole. But for the fact that these were not published until 1837 in Dix's *Life*, one might say that the poem partly wrote the script of Chatterton's future reputation.

Note

This article was first published in *The Times Literary Supplement* 4753 (6 May 1994), 3–4.

Chapter 3

The Originality of Chatterton's Art

Georges Lamoine

> Horrid Idea! If on Rolls of Fame,
> The Twentyeth Cent'ry only find thy Name
> Unnotic'd this in Prose or tagging flower ...
> 'Happiness'[1]
> *In Memoriam* Bertrand M. Davis, M.A., of Bristol

Section xxvi of Thomas Warton's *The History of English Poetry* opens with the statement: 'But a want of genius will no longer be imputed to this period of our poetical history, if the poems lately discovered at Bristol ... are genuine' – he was then writing of the late fifteenth century.[2] A few years after the young forger's death, this viewpoint illustrates the attitude of Chatterton's contemporaries to his poetry: if such poems were genuine, they were admirable; if only forged, they were at best an amusing performance. Those Chatterton had duped would not recognize the talents of one clever enough to have deceived them. When the Rowley controversy was at its peak, George Hardinge wrote:

> Whatever be the opinion of their authenticity, and whether the disquisitions on this matter tend to the advancement of real science ..., the world is undoubtedly in possession of some most admirable and finished poems of any age or of any country.[3]

Thus was the question humorously settled: whatever the origins of these poems, what mattered was their quality. Unfortunately, it was only posthumously that Chatterton began to be recognized as a poet: the specific qualities of his writings were not explored by his immediate contemporaries. If we can readily accept that his fake prose texts about Burgum did not immediately arouse much critical interest, his pseudo-archaic poetry needs reappraisal, and an enquiry into the originality of his works is necessary.

The attitude of a man like Walpole, advising Chatterton to return to his original occupation, probably betrayed the prejudice of a great man and learned antiquarian towards a youth scantily educated at Colston's Hospital, with no Latin and less Greek.[4] What nobody was willing to take into account was the discrepancy between the intellectual background provided by Colston's school and Chatterton's family on the one hand and his achievements on the other. Meyerstein does note that a few other boys were also of 'a poetical turn', which tends to prove that poetic genius is not confined to brilliantly educated minds.[5] Considering that most poets and artists begin by trying their hand at imitating their elders, the fact that Chatterton imitated Pope and a few lesser-known writers is not a major fault. The ability to imitate to such an extent might indeed be commendable rather than blameworthy.[6] But poetry, or more simply prose-writing, was considered as the province of educated, leisured gentlemen, and not of indentured apprentices.

In order to explain why the Rowley poetry represents his principal claim to fame, Chatterton's attitude to the past must be briefly examined. Other critics have made a detailed study of his use of history, but what is at issue here is the originality of his method. Chatterton believed in the necessity of historical proof, which he fabricated as he needed it. Since he was dealing with a period prior to the printing press, although he does mention its invention, like Percy he had to produce manuscripts: only they could be acceptable evidence of the reality of the world which he was painting.[7] Thus could he solve the problems that had bedevilled Macpherson, producing texts supporting the fiction of Ossian, and Walpole, who supported his own creation with the fiction of an edition printed 'in the black letter in 1529'. Walpole was as much a 'cheat' as Chatterton; he realized that history was to be explained or made visible through material evidence. Chatterton's own antiquarian attitude is best demonstrated by the fact that Rowley is first employed by Canynge to 'get together auncient drawynges, if of any Account ; at any Price'.[8] Whether or not Chatterton had heard of, or read, John Leland, appointed by Henry VIII 'to make a search after England's antiquities', Rowley became Canynge's antiquary just as Leland had become 'the King's antiquary' *c.* 1538.[9] That is, as Chatterton collected fake documents on the history of Bristol that could be of interest to Barrett or Burgum, so

Rowley collected what he could of the past of the city. Thus was the whole world authenticated by the fabrication of manuscripts. This is further confirmed by the first of the 'three Rowley Letters', with the family coat of arms; but the antiquarian leaning is obvious in this series.[10] Not only was Chatterton interested in the period which he tried to reconstruct, but he was also capable of appreciating what the period could offer: the famous note to 'Bristowe Tragedie', showing 'a specimen of the Poetry of those Days, being greatly superior to what we have been taught to believe', anticipated the later rehabilitation of the 'gothic' Middle Ages and of the period's various forms of art, including literature.[11]

Donald S. Taylor's edition of Chatterton's complete works is of great assistance in demonstrating some aspects of the poet's originality. If 'by September 1768'[12] the boy had already composed 'Bristowe Tragedie', 'Tournament', and 'Battle of Hastings I' among his major texts, in October and November of the same year he had written 1234 lines of Rowley poetry, plus 196 lines of modern verse: 'Battle of Hastings II', 'The Merrie Tricks', 'Discourse of Brystowe', and 'The Parlyamente of Sprytes'. Then, in the period up to the early days of July 1770, he wrote another 2600 Rowley lines. The mere number might seem unimportant, until we bear in mind that he wrote in pseudo-medieval English, thereby compounding the difficulties of quaintness and poetic structure. After Meyerstein, Taylor has shown from whom Chatterton borrowed, both in the *Works* and in his study *Thomas Chatterton's Art*. From Chaucer, whom he quoted, to Junius, whom he imitated and copied, Chatterton chose his models among the contemporary canon: Shakespeare, Pope, Churchill, Macpherson, and also Emmanuel Collins, a local 'rhymester'. The diversity of his texts partly results from his choice of sources. Satire is directed at individuals and particular forms of hypocrisy as early as 1764 and as late as 1770, in short poems and long political pieces. The various Rowley prose texts represent the whims or needs of the young forger, and will be dealt with later. The prose pieces imitating Ossian or Junius correspond to the prevailing fashion and to the political journalism and issues of the time. Dramatic poetry, like Shelley's *Prometheus Unbound*, cannot be performed, but does exist in the form of *Ælla*. 'The Eclogues', and 'An Excelente Balade of Charitie' are examples of Chatterton's power of adaptation to genres and models. Few authors can boast of having given the world so much, in such a comparatively short time, and at so early an age. Without calling the boy a universal poetic genius, it must be admitted that he was able to strike many different chords of the lyre; the name of Mozart comes to mind, at only a few years' distance. The satires of the last months are an interesting exercise in juvenile indignation, a good example of poetry that might be used as secondary sources by historians.

Apart from – and until – Taylor's work, Chatterton's verse was little studied as poetry *per se*. The spelling is probably responsible for this. Parts of the Rowley texts need to be read aloud to be thoroughly enjoyed; rhyme-reading is not made easy by archaic spelling, vowel shifts, apparent extra syllables not to be pronounced, and a few archaic words or forms. Because of these peculiar aspects, the rhythm is also more difficult to scan naturally. The opinions of Wordsworth and Keats are too important to allow anybody simply to dismiss the whole as a piece of fabricated text without interest. When Chatterton produced the first Rowley poems in 1768, the taste of the time was antiquarian; the publication of *Otranto* and Percy's *Reliques* are two main ingredients of the boy's literary background. The books made their authors famous, and dealt with a reconstruction of part of the Middle Ages; why should not Chatterton try to gain the same fame? We can safely say that he was at least the equal of the Bishop of Dromore. If Percy collected texts and improved on them, Chatterton created his characters, or made them live from a very few elements of historical reality. This is one of the aspects of his originality.[13] In this period of intense antiquarian production, he may have collected names and ideas from his professional activity, but he transformed all this into a world of his own. He transposed the local setting into the past by recreating a world with a wealth of historical and geographical detail. Chatterton tried to compose a sort of saga, 'ab Bristoliense urbe condita' down to the time of Rowley. The whole was supported by texts not directly relevant to the Rowley saga; but such pieces as 'The Account of the De Berghams' are part of the world of fifteenth-century Bristol, not forgetting the drawings, or the description of the 'Bridge Narrative'. Whether he was dealing with early invasions in *Ælla* or later ones with the battle of Hastings, he drew Bristolians into the past of Bristol, in the process enlarging the scene from a local to a nationwide setting. In these and further texts, Chatterton wrote on Bristol and Bristolians, or people, places, and events (more or less loosely) connected with Bristol. Even 'Englysh Metamorphosis. Bie T. Rowleie', imitated from *The Faerie Queene*, is located in Bristol and the Avon Gorge with the Rock of St Vincent. No other poet seems to have written so much about his native place or town in all sorts of texts with drawings, fake coats of arms, modern satires, and so on. Another paradoxical aspect of Chatterton's work is that the Rowley texts sing the praises of old Bristol, whereas the modern prose or verse despises the city, criticizing it in very strong, if conventional, terms. Bristol is almost the only subject-matter, if we except the poems to Miss Hoyland or Miss Cotton, and the verse satire of the last London period on Bute and so forth. But even here he mixed up Bristol and London in one common attack on 'the powers that be'.

The Rowley poetry is characterized by a variety of rhythms and rhyme patterns where difficulty rather than ease is cultivated. 'A Bristowe Tragedie' is the first of the series, with four-line stanzas in which only lines 2 and 4 rhyme, creating an unexpected effect. Repetitions draw attention to some aspect of the tragic opposition: Canynge's stanzas 4, 18, 23 framing his last appeal for mercy. Stanzas 56 and 57 are the sentenced man's adieu answered by 'sweet Florence': thus stand opposed duty and loyalty, unforgivingness, love. 'There was a Broder of Orderys Whyte' follows an *aabccb* rhyme scheme. More complex is the 'Tournament', with four-beat lines rhyming *aabbbacc*. The 'Song of St Werburgh' abounds in successions of trochees and iambuses, plus either anapests or cretics. The short 'Song to Ælla' mixes three-foot lines with heroic couplets, 'Battle of Hastings II', like Part I, is made up of 10-line stanzas rhyming *ababbcbcdd*, the last line being an hexameter mixing trochees/iambuses, cretics/anapests. Each section of 'The Merrie Tricks of Laymyngetowne' has a different rhyming pattern for each stanza ('Discoorse 1st', 'Discourse the Second', 'Discoorse 3rd'). The 'Stay curyous Traveller' enclosed in 'A Discourse on Bristowe' is an interesting use of the 8-line stanza, the last line being an hexameter again. 'The Parlyament of Sprytes' is original in the variation of line and foot numbers, and the use of the iambic, trochaic, anapestic, dactylic, amphibrachic forms. Chatterton's masterpiece is, in my opinion, *Ælla, a Tragical Enterlude*. The 'Letter to ...' introduces the *ottava rima*. The first speeches in 10-line stanzas are contrasted with the 'Mynstrelles Songe' recalling the simple form of the ballad. The next 'Mynstrelles Songe', with its quatrain followed by a refrain, and the use of the 7-foot prosodic substitution, is justly famous.[14] 'An Excelente Balade of Charitie' is the last great poem, with rime royal in a 7-line stanza, the last of which is an alexandrine. Such variety in all the genres so happily explored is the mark of a (young) original poet.

Chatterton was also capable of thinking about the poetry of his time. His 'Bristowe Tragedye' already shows that he felt the need to seek inspiration in sources other than classical mythology. His somewhat naive comment on his own verse, 'far more elegant and *poetical* than all the Parade', is true to the etymological meaning of the term.[15] 'Letter to the Dygne Master Canynge' contains what I take to be his *Ars Poetica*:

> shapelie poesie hath loste yttes powers,
> And pynant hystorie ys onlie grace.[16]

History and antiquarianism were all that interested men like Burgum or Walpole, and Chatterton's Rowley poetry was not appreciated. Therefore the poet claimed the right to pick flowers, and to mount the winged horse of personal inspiration: he would 'sometimes soare 'bove trouthe of hystorie', regretting the time of 'verse of dayes of yore, Fine thoughts and couplettes fetyvelie', although he himself made extensive use of history.[17] Like all poets, the boy asserted his right to follow inspiration, and to go beyond facts and reality. Poetry should also tell the truth.[18] Poetry should be the expression of one's imagination, even if historical facts or characters may be the foundation of poetry not contained within the limits of bare reality.

Chatterton wrote what he imagined or wished the truth of fifteenth-century Bristol to have been. Another original aspect of his creative work is the paradoxical attitude of a poet divided between the two worlds. His very first poem lashes out at an apostate, and his attacks on Dr Newton show him apparently no friend of the Church. But in Canynge's world, everything is different: piety and religion are shown and sung (nearly) everywhere, at least in descriptive pieces. Chatterton's attitudes are completely opposed in the worlds between which he plied in his poetry. The poet follows the semantic evolution of the word 'gothic' in his attitude to the past.[19] It is rather the people's faith that is shown, either the fact of individuals like Sir Bawdyn on the scaffold, or of the crowd, piously participating in public life. The several orders alluded to are not seen as enemies of the people, with the exception of the rich man in the 'Excelente Balade of Charitie'; Canynge is generous in his alms, churches abound in Bristol, and St Mary is evidently important.[20] The evocation of the several orders of friars in the 'Bristowe Tragedie' proves that in Rowley's world, the universal Catholic Church was part of social life. Sir Charles and Canynge are true Christians. St Werburgh, turned into a male character for the time, has 'cast asyde his earles estate' to become a religious man.[21] He too can walk on the waters; his staff, like that of Moses, helps him work miracles. St Cuthbert is often prayed to, his shrine is one of the holy places often mentioned, and the saint himself appears to Ethelgar.[22] St Mary Redcliffe is the object of special fervour, since it was built by Canynge. The religious atmosphere of Rowley's world, himself being a priest, is one of the questions raised by the creation: why did the poet so evidently contrast the world he lived in and his construction? One possible answer is that in Rowley's time there was only one Church, unsullied by apostates, mountebanks, or sects; another possibility is that before the Reformation the Church would have been more concerned with the poor; charity was apparently more common in Canynge's days, as Chatterton believed. The Abbot of St Godwyn is not a true Christian, and this ungodly man of God suggests Walter Scott's Prior Aymer de Jorvaulx. But Celmonde notes: 'The seynctes att distaunce stonde ynn tyme of nede', which is closer to Chatterton's attitude in Bristol towards faith and the Church.[23] This parallels his criticism of several divines of his time in his modern verse satires. His defence of freedom of thought, in 'IX Proclamation of Canynge & Rowley', is an interesting position: it goes further than the right to speak, since Rowley and Canynge admit that violence and death will never suppress thought, with the proviso that in matters concerning the Trinity, no man in the wrong may be allowed to preach. Still the man thought to be in the wrong will be allowed to confute his opponents' arguments.

Apart from his attitude to religion, Chatterton believed in the myth of 'the good old times'. Most antiquaries thought that the reign of Queen Elizabeth had been the golden age of England, best depicted in William Camden's *Britannia*. Canynge's time belongs to the preceding century. This is another original aspect of Chatterton's creation, even if the temporal boundaries of his world are elastic: Bristolians took part in the battle of Hastings, Ælla defended his territory much earlier; Bristolians began trading with Ireland in 1231, and with the Isles in 1073.[24] Chatterton could not suppress the basic reality of his 'Bristowe Tragedye', which shows the kingdom divided for and against the 'tyrant'. But he was yearning for some social peace, of which his origins made him feel the urgent need: he was excluded from part of what the world had to offer. So his Rowley world was thought wonderful because it was the product of wishful thinking. It was a world, then, in which evil necessarily existed, as did cruelty and lack of charity, but where the qualities of such men as Rowley, Canynge, and chiefly Bishop John Carpenter could redeem the blackness of others. The passage following the introduction to the 'Parlyament of Sprytes' depicts the man of God.[25] It is difficult to say whether Chatterton intended Carpenter to be a better image of Dr Newton, the Bishop of 1768. But in Carpenter's diocese, the Church is not at war with part of the population on religious grounds, nor with theatre-lovers. 'The Parlyament of Sprytes' is a play acted by the Carmelite Friars on the occasion of the dedication of the church of St Mary Redcliffe, thus contrasting with the attitude of Bishop Newton when Parliament was petitioned to obtain a patent to erect a theatre-house in Bristol.[26] Chatterton reminds his readers that medieval performances before the nobility were given by clerks. Now in his own world, indentured apprentices like himself were forbidden to go to plays. The Rowley world is also torn by political quarrels, as was George III's kingdom: the 'Four Letters on Warwycke' evoke the impossibility of remaining neutral in the crisis between Henry and Edward. But Canynge manages to be saved by the Bishop when he disobeys his sovereign about marriage. Moreover, he is a charitable man who founds and endows a college and a chapel. A Rowley letter mentions one Sister Isabel who impatiently awaits the arrival of John Iscam. But except for Bertha in *Ælla*, almost no other female character appears in this world. Is it because Canynge refused to remarry? Although death is sometimes gruesome, as in the 'Bristowe Tragedie', in the several texts dealing with justice in Rowley's world (the 'IX Deeds' for instance) penance and fine are the sentences inflicted, far from the brutal 'Bloody Code' of the eighteenth century. And in Bristol the poet could often see people hanged or whipped at the cart's tail, not to mention the frequent Tyburn sessions in London.[27] Therefore life as created, or imagined, by Chatterton seems less harsh than that of his own time, but his characters are mainly 'merchants and princes of the earth': the transformation of the shepherd boy into the prince charming is obvious and understandable.

Rowley's world is evidently not that of a fairy-tale; but at times one thinks of medieval romances where the *merveilleux chrétien* plays so considerable a role. In this sense, the Rowley fabric is more tragic than anything else: apart from the use of the word 'tragedy' in a title, *Ælla* is borrowed from *Othello*, other pieces from *Macbeth* and elsewhere. If the tragic flaw is an element of old Bristol, characters are elevated, or correspond to the higher walks of life: in the eighteenth century the mayor and the bishop were probably the most influential men in the city, both wielding enormous power, spiritual and worldly.

The supernatural and the Gothic are worked together to build up the material reality of this world, which Chatterton took care to illustrate with drawings. If the Gothic is abundantly alluded to in 'A Discorse on Brystowe', the poet did not expatiate on the beauty of it; he simply quoted elements of the old city still to be seen. This is one more proof of his assimilating the two worlds. He felt the influence of the beautiful Gothic church of St Mary. We should remember the many coats of arms he drew or imagined that were not reproduced in Taylor's second volume.[28] They too are part of the Gothic world, at least as much as Walpole's *Castle of Otranto*. Chatterton was doing with his pen what his contemporaries did with stone when they built sham ruins or even complete Gothic abbeys like Strawberry Hill, 'a little Gothic castle'. But whereas Walpole created a new kind of prose narrative round a single medieval castle, Chatterton built the complete world of a city with its gates and towers, churches and colleges, its dignitaries and/or imagined characters recalled from the oblivion of history into which they had sunk: his own city lived from the Roman times to the reign of Edward IV. What is Gothic here is the outward form: drawings, coats of arms, the visible antiquated form of his poetry or prose. His creation was passed off as genuine documents, remnants of Saxon texts and other relics. He was no more guilty of forgery than the Squire of Strawberry Hill, or the character from the comedy *The Clandestine Marriage* (1766), who explains that it cost him '£150 to put [his] ruins in thorough repair'.

Another original aspect of the Rowleyan world is the presence of freemasons in 'IX Deeds'. The 'Deed of the Foundation of an Additional College' mentions 20 Brethren being the scholars to be educated, 'the Brethren being Free Masons to observe the rule of Canyng's red Lodge'. The Red Lodge was an old building, but in 'Lyfe of W: Canynge' the subject is taken up again in some detail. 'To Rowley. 1432' clearly mentions a masonic lodge, made up of gentlemen and aldermen, which probably reflected the state of the matter in 1768–9, and the 'lost mysteries'. On the next page Canynge goes on, with a 'most full Lodge', and 'laying the fyrste Stone of the buyldeynge'. Obviously Chatterton made use of what was common knowledge, for the local newspapers regularly reported masonic activities in *The Bristol Oracle* or *Felix Farley's Bristol Journal*: to parade the streets, or attend concerts and theatrical performances in their regalia.[29] Few authors and still fewer poets mention freemasons, and this is yet another example of how Chatterton turned to his own use the present he knew, and incorporated it into the past.

Two questions are raised by the creation of the Rowleyan world: why did Chatterton disguise his texts under a pseudo-archaic form, and why did he so clearly oppose the 'old' and the 'new' worlds? His poetry, as proposed above, is at least as oral as visual. Therefore the visible basis of it remains genuine eighteenth-century English, except where he could squeeze in a few archaic words borrowed here and there. In this instance, it was the case of the cowl making the monk. But the cowl was what drew attention to his writings: who would have noticed a few lines in plain and honest English on the opening of a new bridge and Mr Burgum's eccentricity? It would have merited at most a small column in *Farley's Journal*. Is it sufficient to say that Chatterton used this subterfuge to make money, or to become famous locally? It may have been little more than a game to start with, but it is not enough to explain that he played the demiurge. In fact the two questions come to this: Rowley's world is the fifteenth-century foil to the world of George III's time. I would easily adopt Jonathan Barry's formula, 'In short, the past is a resource for criticism of the present in Chatterton', if only it is agreed that the satires of the last months show an evident extension and generalization of the situation.[30] Chatterton satirized the Bristol local elites, but after May 1770 he soon discovered that there were also London elites to criticize, and that if the metropolis was after all merely larger in size, the foibles of men were the same everywhere. The models proposed by Churchill, Junius, and others in the newspapers of the time suggested 'The Constabiliad' and its second version 'The Consuliad', 'The Whore of Babylon', 'Resignation', 'Kew Gardens', and 'The Exhibition', paralleled by the 'Decimus Letters'. That he wrote for money in London or just before leaving Bristol is evident; the letters sent home are quite clear on the point.

Poverty, and the consciousness of not being a member of the local intelligentsia for want of money, education, and consideration, were motives for the creation of the Rowley world, in which the poet could assimilate himself with the all-powerful Canynge, the counsellor of kings, friend of the princes of the Church and of half a dozen heroes. The usual attitude of rebellion in young men against the established powers is but an aggravating factor, since apprentices were barred from so many things by their indentures. We can then suppose that every one of the Rowleyan characters is a projection of Chatterton, in the way of boys' games in which a child identifies himself with one of his heroes. The creation of this world may have been a sort of self-justification of the dream, to give to 'airy nothing / A local habitation and a name', which developed with time and with the discovery that others (like William Barrett) might be interested in it. It is not 'airy nothing', but the attempt made by a young dreaming poet to compensate through his creative writing for all the negative sides of his own real life. The elements given by Taylor in his analysis of 'the imaginative matrix' can be accepted without discussion; the three stages of the Rowley world – to imagine a language, create a physical city, and fabricate documents to authenticate the whole – are convincing.[31] I may again accept Taylor's view that in late 1768 Chatterton left Rowley as an historical figure to make him an artist, a poet. But I am struck by the fact that, from what has been handed down to us of his work, the boy's literary career began with a personal satire, and that the last important texts were satires in verse or prose: was he at heart a satirist, even if he did not always use this form?

The Rowley world would then have been a compensation for all the aspects of life, personal or general, with which Chatterton was dissatisfied. Fifteenth-century Bristol would be a complete creation in the cosmological meaning of the term, where everything was for the best in the best of worlds, with due allowance for human faults, such as war, treachery, cruelty, and lack of brotherly love. But this could only be a makeshift, considering the reality of Bristol in the 1760s. Imagining and creating the world of Rowley, Canynge, Iscam, and others was satisfactory as long as the boy remained content with replacing ugly reality and daily disappointments by beautiful poetry. Not only was art a self-sufficient satisfaction for the young man because it was his creation, and something difficult for others to understand; but he too could compete with famous men (Walpole, Percy, and others), and some could be attracted by his world. Positive portraits of his characters were as many foils for those met in the flesh. Some of the elements put forward by Meyerstein explain the shift from the fifteenth to the eighteenth century: the boy's urge to write, his conviction that he would make neither a fortune nor a name for himself in Bristol as an attorney's apprentice, the attitude of the Catcott brothers, and so on. After the poem written, but never sent, to Walpole, he wrote plain English. 'Clifton' gives an interesting insight into the author's frame of mind: if in this case he was contemplating the landscape of the Avon Gorge, it inspired him to sing of Britain's heroes; he did so in modern English, but when at other times 'on that spot [his] glowing fancy dwells', it led him to write in the pseudo-Middle English of Bristolian heroes.

> O'er the historick page my fancy runs,
> Of Britain's fortunes, of her valiant sons.

(ll. 47–8)

The rest of the passage (down to line 58) shows Chatterton's interest in history and why he came to use it, in spite of what he wrote elsewhere. The vista of the city also reminds him of the town's wealth, 'by commerce richly blest', and creates an opposition between the present and the past. As in a sort of crescendo, the poet insists on men's vices and defects, 'Amphitryon' being the first such instance with 'Air 7th'.[32] Satire becomes stronger with 'Hobbinol & Thyrsis' but lines 65–70 lead one to think that Chatterton is confessing to becoming a hack writer. 'Journal the 6th' is again satirical, attacking those that love money, a theme repeated very soon after in 'Intrest'. There he bluntly displays his new vein:

> Then if the rage of Satire seize my brain,
> May none but brother Poets meet the Strain ....

Although 'Conversation' is supposed to treat of a simple theme, it 'Descends below My Satyres soaring sting'. 'Happiness' goes on attacking categories or individuals. The 'Epistle to Catcott' he himself calls an 'innocent Effort of Poetical Vengeance', but 'The Whore of Babylon' and the long 'Resignation' are not innocent poems, neither are 'Kew Gardens' or 'The Exhibition'.[33] The prose texts signed 'Decimus' or 'Probus' are very strong pieces of political criticism, even if they were lost in the mass of material published by the Opposition papers, in tune with the political writings of the time. It seems that Chatterton's systematic attack is on man's vice, and mainly concentrated on what he observed more clearly when in Bristol. His repeated criticism of those 'sparynge of Almes Deedes' and 'greedie of Gaine' reminds us of the Bristolians among whom 'the very parsons talk of nothing but trade and how to turn a penny', maybe thereby opposing the charity of Canynge and Colston and the present lack of charity among his fellow-citizens.[34]

Chatterton behaved as did the moralists: Pope, Swift, Gay, Arbuthnot, and other Tory writers of the Augustan age. He rejected the worship of the golden calf, suggesting that men should be more friendly, less proud. 'Epistle to the Revd. Mr. Catcott' takes the Reverend to task, and shows throughout the 268 lines of the poem, that Catcott is too narrow-minded, too sure of his own truths. The opening lines give the flavour of the piece:

> What strange Infatuations rule Mankind,
> How narrow are our Prospects how confin'd

> With universal Vanity possesst
> We fondly think our own Ideas best
> Our tottring Arguments are ever strong.[35]

This is not the denunciation of man's pride under all possible forms in the pulpits of Swift's time, and of 'the glory, jest, and riddle of the world'. We may suppose Chatterton was speaking of and for himself when writing of the 'jeering Ridicule of Youth', a few lines further on. The lines directly aimed at Catcott are applicable to all: 'Confute with Candor ... Infallibility is not for Men ...'. Rowley's world is after all as far away from eighteenth-century Bristol as the worlds of Gulliver from George II's Britain, from the point of view of the reality of the beings that people it. The greedy men imagined as reciting 'The Gouler's Requiem' are as imaginary, and as full of faults, as the horses that Gulliver dreamed of imitating are full of qualities. Therefore his imagined world, the creation of a lofty mind disdaining the vile gold earned through slavery and trade, can also be a utopian country founded on a very firm material basis, but remote in the past: instead of sailing on unknown seas and finding unexplored lands, Chatterton's reader travels back through time, from the landing of Danes, Saxons, and others to the Wars of the Roses. Erewhon is generally situated in the present but nowhere, whereas the world of Canynge is evidently present and visible, under a somewhat altered and enlarged form, but not available in the present. 'There was once upon a time a City where mighty Canynge lived ...' introduces a new way to write utopia. Nothing is more suitable to social criticism and satire than utopian fiction, whether in verse or in prose. Did Chatterton wish to lash mankind *in toto*, or did he pick on figures whom he particularly disliked? The second option would be more likely, since he attacks categories such as merchants, aldermen, or clergymen; sometimes he calls upon characters by name, moving from general to particular satire. Is he even speaking for himself when he exclaims in *Ælla*, through Celmonde's speech:

> Honnoure, whatt bee ytte? tys a shadowes shade,
> A thing of wychencref, an idle dreme;[36]

since he was perhaps not able to apply the maxim to his own case?

Some elements of the later texts can be seen as biographical indications, or perhaps fragments of self-revelation intended to explain why he was writing. But if his tenets do not seem to have been very consistent, Chatterton says very little on his motivation.[37] His few letters give no reasons for his writing. We must be content to show in what respect Chatterton's work was original and give our own explanations, without knowing why from his own pen. The several invocations of 'Happiness' end on a disenchanted note of egotism; in 'The Defence', Chatterton complains that he is 'The Butt of every Critic's little wit'. 'Kew Gardens' gave him more scope for self-justification:

> Here in the malice of my stars confind,
> I call the Muses to divert my Mind.[38]

This is not inconsistent with what has been said so far concerning the Rowleyan world: the reasons for its creation, the use of history mixed with reality, the opposition between past and present and all that it could represent in the poet's mind, the return to the present when material or psychological circumstances led him to give up the Rowleyan myth. Nor does it contradict the special quality of the Rowley poetry. Recognition of Chatterton's originality as a writer is certainly not limited to the enumeration of his reasons for writing and to agreement on the excellence of his verse. There must be something special about his work that should be felt and experienced, which will always defy analysis.

> The Composition of my Soul is made
> Too great for Servile avaricious Trade
> When raving in the Lunacy of Ink
> I catch the Pen and publish what I think.

> ('The Whore of Babylon', 535–8)

Many new readers will enter the world of his 'Lunacy of Ink', and discover in their turn reasons for finding Chatterton an original artist.

Notes

1. *Works*, 405.
2. Warton, Thomas, *The History of English Poetry* (London, 1870; reprint of 1778–81), xxvi. 408.
3. Hardinge, George, *Rowley and Chatterton in the Shades: or, Nugæ Antiquæ et Novæ* (London, 1782), ed. Joan Pittock (Los Angeles, 1979; Augustan Society Reprint 193), Preface, iii.

4. *The Yale Edition of the Correspondence of Horace Walpole*, ed. W. S. Lewis *et al.* (New Haven, 1937–83), xvi. 113: 'I am obliged to you, Sir, and will go a little beyond it, by ... never using my pen again but in the law'. See *Life*, 27.
5. *Life*, 30. This seems to have been true, not only of Chatterton's generation, but also of a later group of young Bristolians round Robert Southey. See Lamoine, Georges, *La Vie littéraire de Bath et de Bristol, 1750–1800* (Paris, 1978), Bibliography, ii. 898–900, for a few local names and titles.
6. See Plato's opinion on the subject: *Sophist*, 234 c; *Timæus*, 19 d & ff.; *Rep.* 10 600 e.
7. 'Rowley's Printing-Press', *Works*, 60.
8. Ibid., 51.
9. He could find relevant information in Thomas Hearne's *De Britannicis Collectanea* (London, 1712), and in early eighteenth-century editions of Camden's *Britannia*.
10. *Works*, 35–42.
11. Ibid. 6.
12. Ibid. 6–59.
13. Originality is to be understood in our modern sense, not in that explained for instance by Edward Young in 1759, in *Conjectures on Original Composition in a Letter to the Author of Sir Charles Grandison*, in *English Critical Essays*, ed. E. D. Jones (London, 1924, repr. 1975), 270–311.
14. *Works*, 210–12.
15. Ibid. 6, 17.
16. Ibid. 176, 51–2.
17. Ibid. 88, 89–90.
18. 'Battle of Hastings II', l. 2 (ibid. 68).
19. See Lévy, Maurice, *Le Roman 'gothique' anglais*, 2nd edn (Paris, 1995), ch. 1 for the history of this evolution.
20. 'Churches in Bristol', *Works*, 247ff.
21. Ibid. 21, 57–9.
22. Ibid. 255.
23. Ibid. 218.
24. Ibid. 139.
25. Ibid. 107–8.
26. It is no coincidence that Colston's school, which Chatterton had attended, was built on the site of a Carmelite convent.
27. See, for example, Lamoine, Georges (ed.), *Bristol Gaol Delivery Fiats, 1741–1799* (Bristol Record Society, 1989), xl. 26ff, for the years 1768 and 1769.
28. *Works*, 784–7.
29. See Lamoine (1978), i. iii, 26ff.
30. Barry, Jonathan, 'The History and Antiquities of the City of Bristol, Chatterton in Bristol', *Angelaki* 1.2 (1993/4), 72.
31. Taylor, 45ff.
32. *Works*, 358.
33. Ibid., 419.
34. *Life*, 15.The same idea applies to the 'Unfaithful Cocknies', *Works*, 90, l. 32.

35. *Works*, 412.
36. Ibid., 195.
37. His profession of faith seems to be at variance with 'The Defence', ll. 67–70, 'To Miss Lydia C—n' in st. 6, 'The Articles of Belief of Me Thomas Chatterton' (426), 'The Unfortunate Fathers', 'The Whore of Babylon', ll. 561–62, 'Will' (504), down to 'Impromptu on the Immortality of the Soul (682–3), etc. I have changed my mind since I wrote 'La Pensée religieuse et le suicide de Chatterton', *Études Anglaises* 22.4 (1972), 369–79, and now think that he did not commit suicide but died from ill-dosed medication.
38. *Works*, 526.

Chapter 4

'On Tiber's Banks': Chatterton and Post-Colonialism

Carolyn D. Williams

> Rome burns
> & our slavery begins
> > Kamau Brathwaite, 'The Sahell of Donatello', ll. 1–2[1]

In her introduction to *Rowley and Chatterton in the Shades* (1782) by George Hardinge (1743–1816), Joan Pittock finds it ironical that the Rowley controversy culminated during a political crisis, 'while monarchy and ministry were beset by the secession of the American colonies and corruption in the affairs of the East Indian company'.[2] Hardinge himself considers it a momentary distraction, diverting attention 'from the *Res Romanae perituraque regna*, to the kingdom of the Muses, and the disputed claims to different estates on Parnassus'.[3] Nevertheless, Chatterton's poetry resonates with political significances, unwittingly highlighted by Hardinge's identification of British and Roman empires, and introduction of English literature into the realms of classical myth.

Chatterton's work betrays a deeply ambiguous attitude to British literary and political aspirations, generated by consciousness of talent hampered by educational and social disadvantages. His ignorance of Greek and Latin sharpened his perception of classical cultural hegemony as an alienating force in British culture. Chatterton's sense of exclusion, not only from his partially-obliterated native heritage but from the alien cultures that superseded it, encouraged him to cast a critical eye on contemporary British dealings with less developed nations. Yet marginality does not guarantee objectivity. Chatterton never completely broke free from established critical and political assumptions: the values he saw as alien were, nevertheless, so thoroughly assimilated that he often seemed oblivious of their presence, acting under their influence even while seeking to defy them. It seems appropriate to consider how far an understanding of Chatterton's work could be developed by readings often defined as 'post-colonial', and whether Chatterton is perhaps best understood, not as a cantankerous exception, but as a rather uncomfortable case of the 'synthetic compromise that characterizes the complex eighteenth-century British identity'.[4]

'Post-colonial' tendencies in authors commonly placed at the core of the canon have already been discussed in Richard Helgerson's *Forms of Nationhood* (1992). Helgerson notes a common 'anxiety and uncertainty' in Edmund Spenser (1552–99), Philip Sidney (1554–86), and other young poets of the generation which included William Shakespeare (1564–1616).[5] He found twentieth-century parallels in the situation and mood of his West African pupils.[6] This chapter contends that the sense of alienation expressed in the 1590s survived at least until the end of the eighteenth century; Chatterton's career both illustrates the prolonged continuation of the tensions generated in the Renaissance, and reflects some of the developments that eventually resolved them.

'My native Cittye'

In their standard repository of critical overviews, *The Empire Writes Back* (1989), Bill Ashcroft, Gareth Griffiths, and Helen Tiffin use the term 'post-colonial' to 'cover all the culture affected by the imperial process from the moment of colonization to the present day', because 'there is a continuity of preoccupations throughout the historical process initiated by European imperial aggression'. According to these definitions, 'the literatures of African countries, Australia, Bangladesh, Canada, Caribbean countries, India, Malaysia, Malta, New Zealand, Pakistan, Singapore, South Pacific Island countries, and Sri Lanka are all post-colonial literatures. The literature of the USA should also be placed in this category'.[7] They do not mention the colonization of Europeans by other Europeans, or events that took place before the voyages of Vasco da Gama (?1469–1524). Nevertheless, they offer no reason why the geographical and historical limits of their otherwise broad perspective should not be extended to include the effects of Roman imperial aggression on western Europe. They discuss British cultural hegemony in terms which suggest striking connections between the two, maintaining that, 'through RS-English (Received Standard English), which asserts the English of south-east England as a universal norm, the weight of antiquity continues to dominate cultural production in the post-colonial world'.[8] 'Antiquity' rings with an echoing chime. Normally applied to classical civilization, it initially seems more appropriate to the Roman empire than the British. But English literature can still be defined as a vehicle of 'antiquity' to the extent that it reflects and transmits traditions of Græco-Roman influence.

When considering Renaissance and early modern responses to classical culture, it seems justifiable to ask who was colonizing whom. According to Edward Said, 'Texts by dead people were read, appreciated and appropriated by people who imagined an ideal commonwealth'.[9] His reference to appropriation reveals the colonizing ethos of the Renaissance humanists who exploited classical learning for their own ends. This seems a trivial point: if nobody suffered or lost anything, differentiation between colonists and colonized hardly mattered. Unfortunately, many people, including Chatterton, did endure pain and loss. At the very least, the high status accorded to classical learning encouraged that symptom of post-colonialism which Said defines as consciousness of foreign lands as 'distant repositories of the Word'.[10] Two closely related problems were linguistic alienation and 'cultural denigration, the conscious and unconscious oppression of the indigenous personality and culture by a supposedly superior racial or cultural model'.[11]

Chatterton's works display a characteristically post-colonial combination of 'cultural dependence and antagonism together'.[12] Cultural confusion is exacerbated by the fact that these ambiguous reactions are directed towards three different centres: Bristol, London, and Rome. Conflict is ever-present; whichever city is favoured, there is always a strong sense that it has been chosen in opposition to at least one of the others. His attitude to Bristol is typically ambivalent. His chronicles of its history reveal a firm determination to prove that his birthplace is not just a provincial backwater but a great city that could stand comparison even with the capital. In Chatterton's 'Discorse on Brystowe', the early medieval historian Turgot is painstakingly made to record 'The fyrst noticynge of this my native Cittye yclepen Brightstowe'.[13] But why should Chatterton have taken that trouble if he had not suspected that Bristol's status needed defence? The eagerness with which he seized the first available opportunity to get to London, not to mention the scabrous satire of individual Bristolians in 'The Exhibition', tells a different story. His conflicts were partially resolved by emphasizing the romantic and heroic elements of Bristol's past, while condemning its present state as sordid and trivial. Nevertheless, Chatterton's readers must come to terms with the fact that, when he wanted a native city worthy of his talents, he felt a pressing need to invent one.

Chatterton's problems were the result of complex processes, beginning in the Middle Ages, which set the majority of the population of the British Isles at a linguistic disadvantage. Michael Hechter's *Internal Colonialism* (1975) has made available a model for the construction of early modern English literature as a post-colonial phenomenon. Hechter's main concern was the colonization of outlying parts of Britain by the English. He depicts the early modern period as an age of increasing anglicization, forced upon the reluctant peasants and seized eagerly by the gentry of the Celtic fringe: 'since the dissolution of the monasteries formal educational institutions had ceased to exist in Wales. Consequently, the gentry began to send their sons off to English schools. Jesus College at Oxford was established in 1571, largely for Welsh students'.[14] But the fathers' hopes extended beyond the acquisition of English language and culture: the languages principally taught at university, and employed in the learned professions, were Latin and Greek. Anglophone parents of English schoolboys and undergraduates cherished similar aspirations. Even the colonizing culture was either unwilling or unable to function in its mother tongue.

The impact of a supposedly 'superior' culture on an 'inferior' community creates or deepens class divisions. Those natives who aspire to high status within the new order assimilate themselves to the invaders, while losing their sense of fellow-feeling with less adaptable compatriots.[15] In Chatterton's England, snobbery often accompanied respect for classical culture and contempt for Britain's Teutonic heritage. James Harris (1709–80), the well-connected author of *Hermes: Or, A Philosophical Inquiry Concerning Language* (1751), wishes that 'those amongst us, who either write or read, with a view to employ their liberal leisure (for as to such, as do either from views more sordid, we leave them, like Slaves, to their destined drudgery) 'twere to be wished, I say, that the liberal (if they have a relish for letters) would inspect the finished Models of *Grecian Literature*'.[16] By 'sordid', Harris means 'commercial'. (Dr Johnson, ever a consummate professional, regarded him as a 'coxcomb'.)[17] To Harris, the Greeks were supermen: on contemplating classical Greece, he feels that 'one can hardly help considering THAT GOLDEN PERIOD, as a Providential Event in honour of human Nature, to shew to what perfection the

Species might ascend'.[18] Their language was appropriately sublime, *'from its Propriety and Universality, made for all that is great, and all that is beautiful, in every Subject, and under every form of writing'*.[19] Latin, though less perfect, is still a splendid language. English, by contrast, is a 'motley and compounded' affair, an accumulation of borrowed terms from 'many and different Sources', including Greek, Italian, French, Flemish, and Low Dutch. This 'may be the cause, why it is so deficient in *Regularity* and *Analogy'*.[20] Harris's attitude appears to be a typical case of 'intellectual colonization'. In such circumstances, imaginative, religious and aesthetic rifts tend to open, as the lower orders adhere to traditional beliefs, ritual, and narratives which were formerly the heritage of the whole nation, but which the upper classes, educated in new ways, now regard with disdain.

'Familiar to us from our childhood'

Painful conflicts can arise when privileged families employ members of the lower orders to look after their children. Conscientious early modern gentlemen wished their sons to acquire correct religious principles, and to find models of good conduct and literary perfection in classical history and poetry. These could be acquired, it was hoped, from the attentions of educated men: clergy, tutors and schoolmasters. Before this training could begin, however, the boys spent several years in the care of female relatives, whose own education had often been neglected, and of servants of both sexes, who were believed to contaminate impressionable young minds by exposing them to the beliefs of a debased and discredited culture. Nurses, in particular, were singled out as sources of superstition.[21] Literary tastes acquired in these early years must either be ignored, or condemned as positively harmful: the ballads and fairy-tales little boys first heard as infants, then read for themselves in broadsides and chapbooks, were perceived as the offspring of a debased, native, 'Gothic' tradition. Such tastes were not encouraged in the early stages of a boy's classical education.[22]

   Similar cases can be found in twentieth-century Sri Lanka, where the lower classes have become custodians of native culture. In 'The Boyhood of Chittha', Ashley Halpé depicts a burgeoning imagination nurtured by stories belonging to the homeland, told by 'a servant/vatic with childish fancy' (ll. 13–14).[23] They are a colourful, exciting mixture of the heroic, the awe-inspiring, and the terrifying:

> Gemunu, tearing out brilliant ear-rings
> for the starved monk, reeked copious blood
> on golden shoulder-blades; his famous elephant
> was huge as a double-decker, wise as father,
>
> and Yasodhara blushed in every breeze,
> so fine her noble skin. Behind the trees
> behind the garden wall toothed demons lurked:
> the servant, not surprisingly, was sacked.

(17–24)

Formal education was a second-hand importation from Britain:

> And so to Robin Hood, Drake-filled Devon,
> Prince Arthur, and Lancelot of the Lake
> (Abridged and Simplified). At seven
> he versified – after a fashion –
> Horatius, Columbus, the evening star.

(25–9)

The examples selected by Halpé as subjects of childhood versification are nicely calculated to reveal the invading culture's motley antecedents: the evening star represents the subjective strains of a specifically English Romantic lyricism; Columbus is the most famous of all Renaissance European explorers and colonizers; Horatius was presented as a model for generations of empire-building British schoolboys in *Lays of Ancient Rome* (1842) – a work which Thomas Babington Macaulay (1800–59) began during his own empire-building stay at Ootacamund.[24] According to D. C. R. A. Goonetilleke, Chittha's 'bitterness towards both the circumstances into which he was born and his own divided personality is evident'.[25]

An early modern British boy undergoing a liberal education in his native land incurred similar distress. Forced to read, write and speak in languages other than his native tongue, he faced grim prospects if he failed to master his subject: years of alternating boredom and terror, physical anguish and public humiliation, with (if he were a sensitive lad) a broken spirit into the bargain. To appreciate this, we have only to read the plea by Richard Steele (1672–1729) in *The Spectator* 157 (1711) that boys should not be birched for incorrect Latin prosody.[26] Success might be equally, but more subtly, problematic. For many, their daily grind at the learned languages was no more than a means to an end. Edward Said describes a similar state of affairs today in one of the Gulf states, where young people studied English in order to get jobs with banks or airlines, which 'all but terminally consigned English to the level of a technological language'.[27] Keen pupils, on the other hand, internalized classical standards so thoroughly that they adopted individual Greeks or Romans as heroes, taking them as role models in adult life.[28] A typical example is Conyers Middleton (1683–1750). In the preface to his *History of the Life of M. Tullius Cicero* (1741) he defends his work from the prejudice of readers who have chosen different heroes:

> The scheme of it is laid in a place and age, which are yet familiar to us from our childhood: we learn the names of all the chief actors at school, and chuse out several favorites according to our tempers or fancies; and when we are least able to judge of the merit of them, form distinct characters of each, which we frequently retain through life. Thus Marius, Sylla, Cæsar, Pompey, Cato, Cicero, Brutus, Antony, have all their several advocates, zealous for their fame, and ready even to quarrel for the superiority of their virtues.[29]

This is cultural alienation with a vengeance.

Still, a lad of parts who acquired a classical education in eighteenth-century England need suffer little conscious discomfort: this form of cultural alienation had, itself, become part of the national culture. Greater troubles might beset a bright boy who did not get a classical education. In his *Life of Thomas Chatterton*, E. H. W. Meyerstein points out that Chatterton was sent to the 'wrong school'. The right school would have been the Grammar School, where 'Latin was taught, and there were two thirty pounds a year fellowships at St John's College, Oxford, for "qualified boys," besides five exhibitions; the pupils there declaimed in Vergilian hexameters and English verse'. Instead, he was sent to Colston's Hospital, where 'nothing was *taught* but writing and accounts'.[30] For Chatterton, a classical education would have been a desirable form of alienation. He responded to this double displacement with resentful confusion.

He tried to diminish the importance of a liberal education by reducing it to a matter of language rather than substance. His 'Epistle to Mastre Canynge on *Ælla*' portrays an aristocratic, pretentious dunce:

Syr Johne, a knyghte, who hath a barne of lore,
Kenns Latyn at fyrst syghte from Frenche or Greke,
Pyghtethe hys knowlachynge ten yeres or more,
To rynge upon the Latynne worde to speke.
Whoever spekethe Englysch ys despysed,
The Englysch hym to please moste fyrste be latynized.

(13–18)

In this context of satiric protest, Chatterton's attempts to write in medieval English and his fabrication of English medieval documents – some of them harking back to an even more authentically English Anglo-Saxon past – can be viewed as a form of post-colonial resistance. His activities appear to be a form of that 'nativism' whereby, according to Said, those who resist colonialism have gained inner strength by returning 'to a pre-imperial period to locate a "pure" native culture'.[31] Chatterton's frequent revisions of local history and geography are also typical: Said believes that 'One of the first tasks of the culture of resistance was to reclaim, rename, and inhabit the land', a process accompanied by 'an almost magically inspired, quasi-alchemical redevelopment of the native language'.[32] The Rowleyan writings fit neatly within this paradigm.

'Thys nyghte I'll putte stronge poysonn ynn the beere'

A post-colonial reading has the merit of accounting for the imaginative limitations which led Chatterton to vindicate the value of native English literature by producing allegedly medieval works that conformed to neoclassical critical standards. Ashcroft, Griffiths, and Tiffin describe similar activity (without the element of conscious forgery) in their account of post-colonial demands for 'an entirely new or wholly recovered pre-colonial "reality"'.[33] Unfortunately, after contact with colonizers, 'It is not possible to return to or to rediscover an absolute pre-colonial cultural purity'.[34] Inevitably, Chatterton looked to the classical tradition for authentication of his efforts: 'The Battle of Hastynges' and *Ælla* are not simply offered as equivalents to classical epic and tragedy, but as examples of those forms. He probably remained unaware of the self-defeating nature of his enterprise.

It has often been noted that Chatterton's poems on the Battle of Hastings are full of quotations from Dryden, Rowe, and Pope's Homer. According to Nick Groom, 'there was a consistent dynamic of plagiarism working beneath the veneer of forgery, fundamentally denying Rowley's own pretensions to originality'.[35] Given the imitative ways of poets, however, especially poets composing secondary and tertiary epics, Chatterton may have felt that it was only by copying others that he could give his Rowleyan writings a truly authentic appearance. In 'The Battle of Hastynges I', Chatterton conscientiously fulfils an agenda set by the notes and criticism he encountered, as well as the poetry. 'The Essay on Homer's Battels' between Books IV and V of Pope's Homer's *Iliad* (1715–20) suggests many characteristics of Chatterton's poem. The reader's attention is directed to 'that Diversity in the Deaths of his Warriors, which he has supply'd by the vastest Fertility of Invention. These he distinguishes by several ways: Sometimes by the Characters of the Men, their Age, Office, Profession, Nation, Family, &c'.[36] Chatterton duly supplies a variety of interesting biographical details for his warriors. Then there is 'the Difference of the Wounds that are given in the Iliad: They are by no means like the Wounds described by most other Poets, which are commonly made in the self-same obvious Places'.[37] Chatterton accepts the challenge with gusto: Howel ap Jevah 'strook de Tracie thilk a crewel Wound, / His Harte and Lever came out on the Launce' (ll. 193–4); Earl Egwarde 'hyt Walleris onn the dexter cheek: /Peerc'd to hys Brayne, and cut hys Tongue ynn two' (ll. 562–3). Chatterton also satisfies the demand for 'Comparisons', which relieve 'the perpetual Horror of Combates'.[38] The simile with which he embellishes the death of Auffroie de Guel is particularly instructive, because it displays not only the requisite diversion to some other area of activity, but also that stern disapproval of unmanliness which it was epic's prime function to instil into its audience:

> This Auffroie was a Manne of mickle Pride,
> Whose featliest Bewtie ladden in his Face:
> His chaunce in War he ne before han tryde,
> But livd in Love and Rozatines Embrace -
> And like a useless Weed among the Haie,
> Among the sleian Warriors Guel laie –

> (205–10)

De Guel is here portrayed as soft and effeminate, his vigour sapped by excessive sexual indulgences. His courage is also suspect: there is something he enjoys better than fighting, and he is a bowman (l. 197) rather than a specialist in hand-to-hand combat. In all these respects he bears a strong resemblance to the Trojan seducer, Paris, often condemned as an effeminate coward.[39] Where epic is concerned, it is often very hard to distinguish between plagiarism and the responsible maintenance of didactic tradition.

In *Ælla*, Chatterton does defy the conventions of polite literature, but neoclassical attitudes are so deeply ingrained in English readers that the result does not win the approbation it apparently deserves. The point at issue is the poetical use of beer. Jasper Griffin observes that English poetry is unable to accommodate subjects which ancient Greeks and Romans despised: 'I remark in passing that it is because the ancients did not drink beer (the marks of utter savagery included the drinking of beer, the wearing of trousers, and the sporting of a moustache without a beard) that English poetry is so full of allusions to wine, so empty of references to beer. The stuff itself is incapable of elevation, and the word is as resistant to poetic use as "mother-in-law"'.[40] At first, Griffin claims that the failure of beer to make itself at home in serious English poetry is a historical accident: the reader is free to conclude that, if beer had been the favourite drink of the Graeco-Roman world, existing poetic requests for the true, the blushful Hippocrene would have been replaced by appeals for a pint of porter, without any diminution of beauty or sublimity. Griffin's second sentence, however, abandons cultural relativism for a more essentialist approach: he claims that there is, after all, something intrinsically unpoetic about beer. This disjunction is a nice example of post-colonialist conflict between emotional internalization of the colonizers' values and intellectual resistance.

Chatterton's use of beer in *Ælla*, and the reaction it provokes, proves how thoroughly the attitude which Griffin both describes and exemplifies has been assimilated in our culture. The villain, Celmonde, consumed with an obsessive passion for Birtha, Ælla's bride, resolves to combine suicide with double murder:

> And cann I lyve to see herr wythe anere!
> Ytt cannotte, muste notte, naie, ytt shalle not bee.
> Thys nyghte I'll putte strong poysonn ynn the beere,
> And hymm, herr, and myself, attenes wyll slea.

> (133–6)

There is no logical reason why beer should not feature in a play set in

Saxon Bristol, where it would have been the most easily available alcoholic beverage. Yet the native, working-class connotations of beer lower the tone in a manner which is not conducive to the suspense and solemnity appropriate to eighteenth-century tragedy. Even today, it is hard to take this passage seriously. When Chatterton tries to use Rowley as a way of escape from neoclassical constraints, he can find no viable route. But the fault probably lies in us, his readers.

'A national pride'

Chatterton makes his most direct attack on imperialism in his three *African Eclogues*. Although not among his 'Rowleyan' compositions, they help to clarify their political context. Written in London, they are the work of a poet operating at a third remove, attacking one cultural centre after another. They adopt the viewpoint (as Chatterton sees it) of native Africans, who regard Europeans as alien invaders. In 'Heccar and Gaira', two African warriors discuss the aftermath of a battle with European slavers. The brave Africans have won, but the enemy have captured Gaira's wife and family:

> The palid shadows of the Azure Waves
> Had made my Cawna and my children slaves.

(77–8)

Gaira expresses no disapproval of slavery in general; his indignation is fired by conjugal love and awareness of his high status. He is horrified to see that 'Cawna mingled with a worthless train / In common slav'ry drags the hated Chain' (ll. 85–6). Nevertheless, when a poem like this emerges from the pen of a poet born in a major slaving port, currently living in the capital of an empire heavily dependent on the slave trade, it is fair to assume a certain amount of authorial discontent. In 'Narva and Mored', Chatterton presents an idyllic, self-sufficient African community, where Europeans are regarded with pitying contempt:

> the pale children of the feeble sun,
> In search of gold, thro' every climate run:
> From burning heat, to freezing torments go,
> And live in all vicissitudes of woe.

(55–8)

So far, the situation has been comparatively simple: Britons treat
Africans as Romans and Normans used to treat Britons. In 'The Death
of Nicou', Chatterton adds another twist: this eclogue is set 'ON Tiber's
banks' (l. 1), a phrase repeated at the beginning of lines 15, 21, and 37.
How does the river upon which Rome was built come to be flowing
through Africa? In his *Observations upon the Poems of Thomas Rowley*
(1781), Jacob Bryant, wishing to prove Chatterton incapable of
writing the Rowley poems, argues that ignorance of classical culture
combined with incompetent map-reading led him to confuse the
Tiber with the Tigris.[41] Now that Chatterton's authorship of the
Rowley poems is established, it is fair to assume that he knew what he
was doing. His provocatively frequent repetitions of the river's name,
and the conspicuously barbaric exoticism of his descriptions, attract
attention to his choice:

> On Tiber's banks, where scarlet jasmines bloom,
> And purple aloes shed a rich perfume:
> Where, when the sun is melting in his heat,
> The reeking tygers find a cool retreat.

> (15–18)

In 1939, an article by Wylie Sypher showed that Chatterton was using
geological theories from Alexander Catcott's *Treatise on the Deluge*
(1768): the underlying conception of all three Eclogues is that 'waters
from the surface of the earth plunge into subterranean areas – caves or
seas – and that these waters regurgitate violently'.[42] This explains how
a Roman river can flow through other continents; Chatterton need
not be regarded as an ignorant blunderer. His choice of the Tiber may
be a deliberate attempt to bring the imperial story full circle by associating eighteenth-century Africa with ancient Rome. Where, now,
does cultural authenticity lie? In the first two Eclogues, it is possible
to see similarities between Africans and Britons of various periods.
Their present resembles remote events in the history of Chatterton's
own society. Their future history will consist of recapitulating
Europe's past. 'The Death of Nicou' suggests more promising parallels:
are the Africans destined to conquer their conquerors, thus becoming
the equals of the Romans?

Time is one of the most controversial topics in post-colonial criticism. Homi Bhabha argues that it 'bears witness to those countries
and communities – in the North and the South, urban and rural –

constituted, if I may coin a phrase, "otherwise than modernity"'.[43]
Contact with 'modernity' transforms them into hybrid borderlands,
requiring them to perform spectacular temporal acrobatics: 'to be part
of a revisionary time, a return to the present to redescribe our cultural
contemporaneity; to reinscribe our human, historic commonality; to
touch the future on its hither side'.[44] Some observers see the matter
differently. Laura Brown, in *Ends of Empire* (1993), advocates 'The
notion of a relatively autonomous native position, of a site of resistance that is not produced and controlled by the ideological
apparatuses of colonialist power', believing that 'although sites of
resistance may be produced within a dominant ideology, they are not
produced by it, and they do not serve it'.[45] This approach is cogently
recommended in *Time and the Other* (1983), Johannes Fabian's
critique of anthropology. He argues that it is a serious falsification of
evidence to claim that an encounter with a different culture is equivalent to an examination of one's own past: 'The Other's empirical
presence turns into his theoretical absence, a conjuring trick which is
worked with the help of an array of devices that have the common
intent and function to keep the Other outside the Time of anthropology'.[46] We must understand that 'What are opposed, in conflict,
in fact, locked in antagonistic struggle, are not the same societies at
different stages of development, but different societies facing each
other at the same Time'.[47]

Chatterton occupies the middle ground. His use of historical and
geographical parallels suggests a tendency to see the African present
in terms of a more or less remote European past. But the poet in him
envisages something radically different, to whom Europeans appear as
inhuman monsters – an opinion justified by European behaviour. But
time is still an important factor in the equation. According to Susan
Stewart, the Rowleyan forgeries 'share with Chatterton himself an
imaginary and altered relation to time'.[48] So do the *African Eclogues*.
In the late twentieth century, we can see the likely future for the
enslaved Cawna in terms of a known and hideous historical past. The
cultural deadlock of slavery is portrayed by Toni Morrison in *Beloved*
(1987), where the spirit of a dead Negro girl recreates the horrific
middle passage as a nightmarish temporal stasis: 'All of it is now it is
always now   there will never be a time when I am not crouching
and watching others who are crouching too   I am always crouching   the man on my face is dead   his face is not mine   his
mouth smells sweet but his eyes are locked.'[49]

The most salient aspect of Chatterton's own relationship with time was hideously simple: he was a promising young poet for whom time ran out. It is necessary to remember his tragically brief life-span in order to set his achievement in perspective. By 1782, the status of English language and literature was improving. The question of definition, however, was still open to debate. A century later, in his 'Essay on the Rowley Poems' (1891), Walter Skeat was to berate Chatterton's contemporaries for their ignorance of Anglo-Saxon. He was particularly incensed by Horace Walpole (1717–97), who 'knew less about the older forms of *his own language* than could have been (and was) picked up by a schoolboy, in the course of a single half-holiday'.[50] But would Horace Walpole have recognized Anglo-Saxon as his own language? That perception was destined to flourish in the Victorian age, with its greater confidence in the value of all things English, bolstered by the knowledge that the British empire far exceeded the Roman.

Chatterton's patriotism was not always recognized by his contemporaries. In the same year that Hardinge discounted Chatterton's political relevance, Dr Johnson made a similar misjudgment. On 27 February 1782, he wrote to Edmond Malone, 'In Ossian there is a national pride, which may be forgiven, though it cannot be applauded. In Chatterton there is nothing but the resolution to say again what has once been said'.[51] It is easy to see why the Romantics turned this rebellious stripling, outcast from the educational establishment and champion of an undervalued cultural heritage, into a laureate of resistance. But if Chatterton had lived as long as Johnson, he would have lasted well into the nineteenth century, and the new and increasing pride in British achievements – a pride which Chatterton had helped to foster – would have made it easy for the Victorians to look back on him as a Grand Old Man.

Notes

1. Brathwaite, Kamau, *Middle Passages* (Newcastle upon Tyne, 1992), 56. With the kind permission of Bloodaxe Books, Ltd.
2. Hardinge, George, *Rowley and Chatterton in the Shades: or, Nugæ Antiquæ et Novæ* (London, 1782), ed. Joan Pittock (Los Angeles, 1979; Augustan Reprint 193), introduction, iii.
3. Ibid. iv.
4. Weinbrot, Howard D., *Britannia's Issue: The Rise of British Literature from Dryden to Ossian* (Cambridge, 1993), 74.
5. Helgerson, Richard, *Forms of Nationhood: The Elizabethan Writing of England* (Chicago & London, 1992), 1.
6. Ibid. 17.
7. Ashcroft, Bill, Griffiths, Gareth, & Tiffin, Helen, *The Empire Writes Back:*

Theory and Practice in Post-Colonial Literatures (London & New York, 1989), 2.

8. Ibid. 10.
9. Said, Edward W., *Culture and Imperialism* (London, 1993), 235.
10. Ibid. 270.
11. Ashcroft *et al.*, 9.
12. Said, *Culture and Imperialism*, 266.
13. *Works*, 93.
14. Hechter, Michael, *Internal Colonialism: The Celtic Fringe in British National Development, 1536–1966* (London, 1975), 111.
15. See Collingwood, R. G., and Myers, J. N. L., *Roman Britain and the English Settlements*, 2nd edn (Oxford, 1937), 225.
16. H[arris], J[ames], *Hermes: Or, a Philosophical Inquiry concerning Language and Universal Grammar* (London, 1751), ed. R. C. Alston (Menston, UK, 1968), 424.
17. *Life of Johnson*, v. 377.
18. Harris, 417.
19. Ibid. 423–4.
20. Ibid. 408
21. See, for example, John Dryden's reference to 'Nurses Legends', in 'The Cock and the Fox' (1700), l. 335, in *Poems*, ed. J. Kinsley (Oxford, 1958), iv. 1613.
22. But see Dr Johnson's protest in *Life of Johnson*, iv. 8, n. 6.
23. Halpé, Ashley, 'The Boyhood of Chittha', in *Silent Arbiters Have Camped in My Skull* (Dehiwala, 1976), 2–3. With the kind permission of the author.
24. Clive, John, *Thomas Babington Macaulay: The Shaping of the Historian* (London, 1973), 295.
25. Goonetilleke, D. C. R. A., 'Sri Lankan Poetry in English: Getting Beyond the Colonial Heritage', in *From Commonwealth to Post-Colonial*, ed. Anna Rutherford (Sydney, 1992), 336.
26. Addison, Joseph, *The Spectator*, ed. D. F. Bond (Oxford, 1965), i. 117.
27. Said, Edward W., 'Figures, Configurations, Transfigurations', in Rutherford (ed.) (1992), 5.
28. See Johnson, J. W., *The Formation of English Neo-Classical Thought* (Princeton, 1967), 101.
29. Middleton, Conyers, *The History of the Life of M. Tullius Cicero* (London, 1755), i. xvi [italics reversed].
30. *Life*, 26–7.
31. Said, *Culture and Imperialism*, 332.
32. Ibid. 273.
33. Ashcroft *et al.*, *The Empire Writes Back*, 194.
34. Ibid. 194–5.
35. Groom, Nick, 'Forgery or Plagiarism? Unravelling Chatterton's Rowley', *Angelaki* 1.2 (1993/4), 49.
36. *The Twickenham Edition of the Poems of Alexander Pope*, ed. John Butt *et al.* (London, 1939–69), vii (1967), 252.
37. Ibid. 253.
38. Ibid. 254.
39. See Williams, Carolyn D., *Pope, Homer, and Manliness: Some Aspects of*

Eighteenth-Century Classical Learning (London & New York, 1993), 96–9.

40. Griffin, Jasper, *The Mirror of Myth: Classical Themes and Variations* (London, 1986), 58. For more on foodstuffs in Chatterton, see Timothy Morton, below.

41. See Bryant, Jacob, *Observations upon the Poems of Thomas Rowley: in which the Authenticity of those Poems is Ascertained* (London, 1781), 477.

42. See Sypher, Wylie, 'Chatterton's *African Eclogues* and the Deluge', *PMLA* 55 (1939), 251. See also Michael Suarez, below.

43. Bhabha, Homi K., *The Location of Culture* (London & New York, 1994), 6.

44. Ibid. 7.

45. Brown, Laura, *Ends of Empire: Women and Ideology in Early Eighteenth-Century English Literature* (Ithaca & London, 1993), 63.

46. Fabian, Johannes, *Time and the Other: How Anthropology Makes Its Object* (New York, 1983), xi.

47. Ibid. 155.

48. Stewart, Susan, 'Anxiety and Authenticity: Fragments of an Eighteenth-Century Day-dream', *Critical Studies* 1 (1989), 90.

49. Morrison, Toni, *Beloved* (London, 1988), 210.

50. *The Poetical Works of Thomas Chatterton*, ed. Walter W. Skeat and Edward Bell, 2 vols. (London, 1891), ii. xxix.

51. *Life of Johnson*, iv. 141.

Chapter 5

The Mythical Image: Chatterton, King Arthur, and Heraldry

Inga Bryden

In a letter to Dr Milles, Dean of Exeter, James Thistlethwaite speculated on Thomas Chatterton's employment prospects: 'One day he might be found busily employed in the study of Heraldry and English Antiquities, both of which are numbered amongst the most favorite of his pursuits'.[1]

This essay is concerned with teasing out the connections between Chatterton's interest in heraldry and his references to that perennial English Antiquity, King Arthur. In poetry, prose, and letters Chatterton makes use of the legends of Arthur, or the 'Matter of Britain', in ways which have particular cultural resonances in the context of eighteenth-century attitudes to Arthur. His preoccupation with heraldry is revealed not only in his pseudo-medieval writing, but also in the form of illustration. My exploration of the relationship in Chatterton's work between, particularly, the coat of arms as symbol and the icon of Arthur will focus on the construction of mythical identities: regional and national identities, and Chatterton's identity as a poet. The process of construction itself is one which relies on the past, or on the idea of a past.

The legendary Arthur was a protean figure, appearing in medieval texts as a historical person, as one of the Christian members of the Nine Worthies, and as an exemplar of chivalry.[2] Indeed, the contradictory nature of his status has always been exploited for a variety of ideological purposes. Throughout the eighteenth century the English view of the historical Arthur owed most to Geoffrey of Monmouth's *Historia Regum Britanniae*, albeit in a scholarly context which increasingly questioned Arthur's historical credentials. The *Historia* was one of the earliest appropriations of Arthurian material for the purposes of constructing a mythical, national identity. It was translated into

English in 1718 by Aaron Thompson, and three more editions were published in the eighteenth century. Thompson, in a preface on the *Historia*'s authority, championed the tradition of chronicling Britain's legendary kings.[3] Moreover, Arthur's historical reputation as a Christian worthy remained intact throughout the eighteenth century. Nathaniel Crouch's *History of the Nine Worthies* went through at least five editions between 1687 and 1759.[4] And Thomas Malory had emphasized this aspect of Arthur's identity in his preface to the 1485 edition of *Le Morte d'Arthur*.

The figure of Arthur crystallized debates about the status of history, inviting the question of how the past could be both mythical and real. This question was central to the construction of a new British national identity which could partly be achieved through the writing of literary epics. Eighteenth-century writers inherited a tradition of failed attempts at producing Arthurian epics. Consequently they were sensitive to the difficulties of rewriting the Arthurian legends: Arthurian material had been dismissed as lightweight fantasy and had proved problematic as political propaganda. With the *Faerie Queene* (1596) Edmund Spenser had retold Arthur's story as mythical allegory while glorifying the monarch via Arthur the perfect knight and courtier. John Milton had considered writing an Arthurian epic, although he omitted Arthur from his 'historical' notes, thus rejecting a legend associated with Tudor absolutism.[5] In negotiating the complex interrelations of the legendary past and a literary epic which would honour the nation, John Dryden had recast his dramatic opera *King Arthur, or, The British Worthy* (1691) after James II's deposition.[6] Alexander Pope had contemplated writing an epic based on Brutus's founding of Britain and the poetaster Richard Blackmore had produced the poems *Prince Arthur* (1695) and *King Arthur* (1697) which paralleled Arthur with William III.

In the eighteenth century Arthur rather 'fell out of literary fashion'.[7] Nonetheless, in the context of new scholarly work on the Anglo-Saxon period, there existed a strong cultural sense that native history should be memorialized in poetry. In his *Essay on the Writings and Genius of Pope* (1756), Joseph Warton defined history in specifically nationalistic terms. 'Historical' fiction was deemed preferable to literature characterized by improbability, and Arthurianism was central to this literary debate. The Arthurian 'mythologists' were criticized, for example, by David Hume in *The History of England* (1763). Hume argued that history was largely fictional, although poets could still be said to distort history.

Two years later the publication of Thomas Percy's *Reliques of Ancient English Poetry* (1765), which included six Arthurian ballads, relegitimized the Arthurian legends as historical relics.[8] Increasingly, scholars and antiquarians were intrigued by the materiality of Britain's legendary past. Thomas Warton, in *Observations on the Faerie Queene of Spenser* (1754), adopted an historicist approach to describing the impact of *Le Morte d'Arthur* on Spenser and created a renewed interest in Malory's text.[9] Warton was eager to trace the origin of fictional or romantic histories and in his own Arthurian poems he was interested in the 'physical vestiges of medieval times'.[10] 'Britannia's Issue' mentioned in Thomas Gray's poem 'The Bard' (1757) – 'No more our long-lost Arthur we bewail / All hail, ye genuine Kings, Britannia's Issue, hail!' – signified both the dynastic line of monarchs and a literary tradition constructed from the mythical past.[11] Indeed the reinvention of Arthur came about partly through the study of medieval romance. The antiquarians Thomas Percy, Thomas Warton, Joseph Ritson, and George Ellis were familiar with the manuscripts of English metrical romances such as 'Arthour and Merlin', 'Sir Tristrem', 'Awntyrs of Arthure', 'The Alliterative Morte Arthure', and 'Le Morte Arthur'.[12]

So it was that during Chatterton's lifetime (1752–70) the figure of Arthur haunted the boundaries of history and fiction, problematizing the notion of place (both geographical and historical) and the relationship between the mythical past and literature. Writing in the late 1760s, and recreating the past in a double sense (as fiction and as fiction later accredited to someone else's hand), Chatterton exposed the dilemma in representing the dynamics between historical, romantic, and mythical traditions.

The overlapping traditions surrounding Arthur in the eighteenth century, which included the pseudo-historical, the topographical, and the burlesque, are clearly evident in Chatterton's writing.[13] The cultural desire to reinvent Arthurian legend in nationalistic terms had been parodied notably in Henry Fielding's dramatic burlesque *Tom Thumb, A Tragedy* (1730). Arthur as a curiosity, and the apparent marginal cultural status of the Arthurian legends, were arguably represented by the neo-Gothic Merlin's Cave. This satirized hermitage, commissioned by Queen Caroline, housed not only the 'Thresher Poet' Stephen Duck, but also wax models of historical and Arthurian figures.[14] In popular tradition Arthur was very much part of ballad culture. William Nicolson, for example, noted that 'King Arthur's story in English' was 'often sold by the Ballad-singers, with the like

Authentic Records of *Guy of Warwick* and *Bevis of Southampton*.[15] Nonetheless, Arthurian romances were often associated with child-hood nostalgia, another reason why Arthur was not accorded central literary status in the eighteenth century.

Chatterton's awareness of the Arthurian stories in popular culture, together with his reading, would probably have given him a sense of a legendary king whose lineage was uncertain and yet whose relics were part of the fabric of Britain. It is worth noting a parallel here – that Chatterton's own past was 'uncertain' in the sense that he was a posthumous son of his father. He had access to accounts of the nation's past which particularly dealt with questions surrounding Arthur's dynastic identity (his birth) and his memorialization (the supposed relics found at Glastonbury). Richard Baker's *A Chronicle of the Kings of England* (1674) mentions how during Richard I's reign Arthur's bones were found at Glastonbury in a sepulchre which bore a leaden cross inscribed 'Here lyeth the Noble K. of Britain, Arthur' and that during Henry II's reign the bones of Arthur and Guynevour were reputedly located in the 'Vale of Avolan, under an hollow Oak, fifteen foot under ground'.[16] The memorial inscription was in itself evidence of Arthur's historicity, according to William Borlase in *Antiquities, Historical and Monumental, of the County of Cornwall* (1754).[17] Similarly, Thomas Fuller's *Church-History of Britain* (1655), which Chatterton also consulted, names Arthur as one of the Nine Worthies and gives the 'corps, coffin, and Epitaph' at Glastonbury as the only certainty of Arthur's existence.[18] These authors also disputed Arthur's dynastic status – was he the son of Gorlois or of Uter?[19] Yet they simultaneously represented Arthur as interested in social hierar-chy – Arthur instituted the Order of the Knights of the Round Table so that 'to the end there might be no question about Precedence'.[20]

Among the texts read by Chatterton which discussed the Arthurian legend, William Camden's *Britannia* (1586) was crucial.[21] Edmund Gibson's 1695 and 1722 revised editions of *Britannia* were used by Chatterton and were a particularly significant source for the creation of the Rowleyan world.[22] Accounting in *Britannia* for the last remains of Britain as a Romanist civilization, Camden cited Arthur's memorial inscription and dealt with the significance of the legend in the context of the nation's geographical, linguistic, and heraldic identities.[23]

A renewed interest in heraldic and genealogical discourses (which were medieval in origin) came with the Reformation. In the eight-eenth century the antiquarian record was perceived as both visual and verbal, and heraldic signification had a particular relevance amidst social fluidity. As a 'shorthand' for history, heraldry seemed to preserve the ideology of the gentry. It was also simply another form of memorial. In *Ancient Funerall Monuments*, which Chatterton read, John Weever mentions tombs and their inscriptions as a means of discerning rank.[24] Continuing the linking of hierarchy with memorials, a section on heralds covers etymology, manner of creation, office, antiquity, catalogue, and succession. Heralds themselves were once heroes.[25] More importantly, Weever issues a plea to the reader, given the present destruction of memorials, to keep a written record of inscriptions. Weever himself intends to compile a list of inscriptions on the monuments of the nation's dead – a project he compares to William Camden's *Britannia*. Camden had referred to the 'silent names' of armories in particular in *Remaines of a Greater Worke concerning Britaine* (1586).

It is probable that Chatterton took up heraldry some time after being apprenticed to John Lambert, gentleman attorney, in July 1767.[26] Clearly, in the years immediately following, Chatterton is positioning himself within debates surrounding heraldic signification.[27] In a letter to Ralph Bigland, the Somerset herald who was writing a book of heraldry, Chatterton gives notes on curious 'coats' (of arms) in and around Bristol.[28] Later commentators noted Rowley's 'zeal for the honour of heraldry' evidenced for example in 'Rowley's Heraldic Account of Bristol Artists and Writers' (1768–9) and indeed, heraldic references and imagery are integral elements in Chatterton's pseudo-medieval poetic world.[29]

In 'The Tournament: An Interlude' (1769) the figure of the herald exercises his 'modern office as an arbiter of heraldic usage'.[30] Chatterton positions himself as an 'arbiter of heraldic usage' in works such as 'Account of the Family of the De Berghams' and 'Extracts from Craishes Herauldry'.

'Account of the Family of the De Berghams from the Norman Conquest to this Time' (1768–9) is one of Chatterton's more elaborate heraldic and genealogical creations, written for Henry Burgum, a Bristol pewterer and George Catcott's partner.[31] Joseph Cottle, in the 1803 collection of Chatterton's works he edited with Robert Southey, offers a commentary on the 'Account' which summarizes the ways in which Chatterton's pedigrees are fabrications.[32] No 'Burgum' can be found on record as being entitled to a coat of arms, claims Cottle. Moreover, the coats of arms referred to are the reverse of those which the families would have borne. The emblazonment given to the Chatterton family in the De Bergham manuscript is different from that which Chatterton assigns himself in his 'Will', and although Chatterton elaborates his genealogy by using well-known heraldic terms, such as 'March' and 'Garter', these have no particular reference as authorities.[33]

So the use of heraldry as a means of memorializing a (fictitious) dynasty legitimates Chatterton's project as historical. On another level, Chatterton is employing heraldry only as a sign-system with arbitrary referents, thereby subverting the notion of heraldry as the province of aristocratic lineage.

'Extracts from Craishes Herauldry', an early Rowleyan work dated pre-October 1768, is the most thorough imagining of a Chatterton dynasty based on heraldry.[34] Other heraldic pieces deal with the 'Chattertons' of the eleventh and twelfth centuries, whilst the 'Will' lists a thirteenth-century Chatterton and a fifteenth-century Chatterton, although there is virtually no consensus between the different accounts.[35] In 'Extracts' Chatterton uses imaginary names combined with names from his daily life in Bristol. In addition he makes extensive use of Camden's *Britannia* and its catalogue of noble families. By doing this Chatterton dignifies himself, his associates, and Bristol, in effect giving the present a history.[36] In describing the Chatterton arms

> Name – Chatterton – Or a Lyon Rampant Azure Gules
> within a Border engrailed Ermine – Guillams Heraldry.[37]

Chatterton inscribes himself within a 'shorthand' for history, setting up the co-ordinates of a family. Yet taking into account other specific descriptions (verbal and illustrative) of Chatterton arms,[38] the signifier 'Chatterton' is clearly prone to slippage, even when Chatterton's autograph accompanies a sketch of his coat of arms.[39] Usually in heraldic practice the same family had the same arms, but with established differences, whereas Chatterton's have different shields.

Moreover Chatterton fictitiously dignifies his family, a question of invention addressed by Joseph Cottle in 'Observations on Chatterton's Arms'.[40] Cottle acknowledges that working-class people cannot easily trace their descent back more than one hundred years. Bearing this in mind Chatterton can be seen to artistically engineer a kind of social sabotage. The unsung Miltons of this world have just as much right to be memorialized as any aristocratic heroes.[41] Cottle also sees Chatterton's reasons for inventing pedigree as lying in flattery; a 'radical tendency of mind' to test others' credulity, '(the grand key to his character!)', and Barrett's eagerness to establish Bristol's antiquity.[42]

Indeed there are interesting connections between Chatterton's drawings of arms and his illustrations of notable buildings and monuments which comprise the city of Bristol in 'A Discorse on Brystowe' (1768). Many of the sketches in 'A Discorse on Brystowe' are distinctly heraldic in terms of their stylized crennelations and patterned divisions – the two-dimensionality of the heraldic shield.[43] Symbolically they memorialize Bristol in a work which discusses the very naming of the city 'Brugstowe'. For Chatterton the city itself is a monument, in the sense in which Weever had defined a monument as any 'thing erected, made, or written'.[44] And the fabric of the city is heraldic. Elsewhere Chatterton praises both the building techniques of the past and heraldry, which was expressed in building.[45] Heraldry and heraldic design were part of the fabric of Bristol's architectural landmarks. St Mary Redcliffe, notably, contains impressive coats of arms on tombs and monuments and each of the 1200 bosses on its roof vaulting is unique (although it possessed virtually no stained glass in the eighteenth century). In effect, 'A Discorse on Brystowe', a response to Camden's statement on Bristol's history and owing a great deal to Camden, is, as Taylor has pointed out, 'a *Britannia* for Bristol'.[46]

Frequently Chatterton associated heraldry with the collecting and interpreting of other 'relics' such as coins. In a letter to his relation Mr Stephens he comments on his collection of antiques and expresses his keenness to look at any Roman, Saxon, or English coins. He goes on to trace the Stephens family and adds 'When you quarter your Arms, in the Mullet say Or a Fess Vert by the name of Chatterton'.[47] In 'Saxon Atchievements' (sent to the printer of the *Town and Country Magazine*) Chatterton gives an 'explanation' of Saxon heraldic bearings, a coin, and an amulet.[48]

There is a direct link here between heraldry, coinage, and references to Arthur in Chatterton's Rowleyan prose fragments. 'Yellowe Rolle: Of the Auntiaunte Forme of Monies' (1768) is intended to show Bristol as an historically important city, and significantly, it gives Arthur's reign as the time when a King first coined quantities of metals for use.[49] Arthur made a piece of silver to adorn those winning honour in battle: 'neyther anie Kynge tylle Arthurres tyme coyned Quantytye of Metalle for anie Use nor dyd Arthurre make Moneie butte a Peece of Silverre toe bee worne rounde of thoese whoe had wonne Honour in Battles'.[50] 'Explayneals of the Annexed Yellowe Rolle [Purple Rolle]' tells how Arthur's 'coynage' was supposedly discovered at Redcliff

Hill. And other Arthurian relics are associated with Bristol: 'Rowley's Collection for Canynge: The Gate of Sayncte Marye' mentions a stone located at Redcliff Hill which possibly belonged to a man fighting for Arthur in the Bath wars. In Arthurian legend Arthur fought the Saxons at Badon Hill in 520.[51]

Furthermore, the contingency of Arthur's reign and developments in the heraldic system may not have gone unnoticed by Chatterton. John Guillim's *A Display of Heraldrie*, one of the heraldic texts used by Chatterton, was specifically conceived as a new methodology for interpreting rank and order in heraldry. In forming this partly histor-ical methodology, Guillim names the reign of King Arthur as when a distinction between metals and colours in heraldry began.[52]

However, as Chatterton was busily invoking Arthur as a dignified personage in the context of his own search for an identity rooted in history, he was simultaneously using the figure of the legendary king as a means of critiquing that very process. In 'Extracts from Craishes Herauldry' under the 'Name – Cross' (1140) entry, which follows the Chatterton entry, declaring descent (in this case Tudor descent) from Arthur 'ap Uther Pendragon' by taking up arms is regarded as folly by the next generation.[53] Taylor adds that the 'Cross' section does seem to be a 'spoof on those who invent distinguished ancestors'.[54] The notion of noble descent from Arthur is also satirized by Chatterton in 'The Constabiliad' (1769), an allegorical satire on the Grafton admin-istration which was reworked as 'The Consuliad' (1770):

> Thrimso undoubtedly of Arthurs race
> You see the mighty Monarch in his Face ...
> And toast the great Pendragon of the Hill
> Mab Uther, Owen, a long train of Kings
> From Whom the royal Blood of Thrimso springs.[55]

With 'The Constabiliad', and in the context of the literary and cultural rejection of Arthur discussed earlier, Chatterton is appropriating Arthur to highlight the futility of contemporary politics. There is definitely a sense in which, in Chatterton's handling, Arthur symbol-ically articulates an anxiety about both kinship and kingship.

In many ways King Alfred, rather than Arthur, commanded wide-spread admiration in eighteenth-century Britain, viewed as the patriot king and guardian of Saxon liberty.[56] As Chatterton commented in a letter to Horace Walpole, 'we are indebted to Alfred and other Saxon Kings for the wisest of our Laws and in part for the British constitution'.[57] Elsewhere Chatterton continued to associate royalty with political turmoil. The title 'Decimus: To the Princess of Gotham' (1770) alludes to Churchill's 'Gotham', a satire on England and the royal family in which current political affairs are likened to the start of Charles I's troubles.[58]

Paralleling Chatterton's observations on the fate of absolute monarchs was John Hamilton Mortimer's visual representation of, significantly, the discovery of 'Arthur' via interpretation of the memorial inscription at Glastonbury. Supposedly the only eighteenth-century painting to refer to Arthur, Mortimer's *The Discovery of Prince Arthur's Tomb by the Inscription on the Leaden Cross* can be read as a moral on the fallibility of kings.[59] The subject was taken from John Speed's *The Historie of Great Britaine* (1611) which included an account and illustration of the discovery of the leaden cross. John Sunderland sees Mortimer's depiction as 'an assertion of the mortality of monarchs and a rejection of the divinity and implied immortality with which kings were sometimes invested'.[60] The figure of Arthur, with its legendary associations of immortality (the 'once and future king'), allowed Chatterton to insert himself into the tradition of speculating on the business of manufacturing history and on the political claims of actual monarchs.

After Chatterton's untimely death the theme of Arthur's passing still exercised a fascination for writers eager to explain the workings of history and fiction. Thomas Warton's 'The Grave of King Arthur' (1777) focuses on Arthur's supposed grave to reveal a dichotomy between the historico-chronicle tradition (which gives Christian Glastonbury as the grave's location) and fictitious romance (which has Arthur pass to a pagan otherworld). Texts such as John Whitaker's *History of Manchester* (1771–5) did support the notion of a historical Arthur although the more general lack of interest in Arthur was evident following the Rowley Controversy. Horace Walpole, writing to a friend, compared the disgracing of Rowley to Arthur's marginalization: 'As to Rowley, when Dr. Glynn is gone, he will be as much abandoned as King Arthur'.[61]

Yet eighteenth-century antiquarianism did a great deal to set in motion a major Arthurian Revival in nineteenth-century Britain, so that by the 1840s the Arthurian legends were relatively familiar matter.[62] Arthurian material appeared in Thomas Warton's *History of English Poetry* (1774–81) and in Joseph Ritson's *Ancient Engleish Metrical Romanceës* (1802). Walter Scott's edition of *Sir Tristrem* (1804), reprinted five times until 1848, was influential in textual dissemination of the legends.

A key figure in the revival of Arthur was Robert Southey, whose two-volume edition of Thomas Malory's *Le Morte d'Arthur, The Byrth, Lyf and Actes of Kyng Arthur* (1817), precipitated the publication of other Arthurian editions in England.[63] Southey's text was printed from Caxton's 1485 edition and included a new introduction and scholarly notes. Part of Southey's project in historicizing and revalorizing Arthur was to explain Arthur's arms. Quoting from John Bossewell's *Workes of Armorie* (1572), Southey portrayed Arthur as

> ... mighty conqueror and worthy ... 3 dragons, an other of 3 crownes, and assumpted or tooke to his armes ... a Crosse silver in a field vert; and on the first quarter thereof was figured an Image of oure Ladye with her sonne in her armes. And bearinge that signe he did many marveiles in Armes, as in his bookes of Actes and valiant conquestes are remembred.[64]

Here, heraldry, or the bearing of a sign, is seen as inseparable from heroic action, as for Chatterton heraldry had been a crucial point of entry into the past. Southey had also been concerned with constructing another hero in the form of Chatterton, particularly in editing *The Works of Thomas Chatterton* with Joseph Cottle (1803): more so than other writers and antiquarians he figures the proximity of the critical reconstruction of Chatterton to the nineteenth-century rehabilitation of Arthur. After all, as Southey and his fellow editor Cottle had commented

> Heroes, patriots, and statesmen, are not only entitled to the love and veneration of their contemporaries during their lives, but their virtues and services ought to be transmitted to the latest posterity.[65]

The editors go further in envisaging the textual homage to Chatterton as a means of 'rescuing' an orphan figure. A note to 'Apostate Will' (1764) tells how Chatterton 'knew no tutor, no friend, no parent – at least no parent who could correct or assist him'.[66] In constructing an identity for Chatterton Southey acknowledges that the project is also another form of *Britannia* for Bristol, just as Chatterton's tracing of imagined, individual heraldic identities was inseparable from the making of a history for Bristol and the creation of a regional identity. Southey comments in the preface that the editors 'have felt peculiar pleasure, as natives of the same city, in performing this act of justice to his fame and to the interests of his family'.

Chatterton's textual, imaginative creation of both his and a nation's 'family' was legitimated by the symbolic use of heraldic terms and devices and by references to Arthurian artefacts and a pseudo-historical, mythical King Arthur. In the context of an eighteenth-century market for heraldry it is arguable that Chatterton's 'heraldic' systems were to a degree elevated to the status of art.[67] In Chatterton's writing, as in heraldry, both visual and verbal languages interconnect and involve a fixing of what is transitory; principally, history. In the end these interconnections, together with those between Chatterton's references to heraldry and to Arthur, point up what Sheila Emerson explains as 'the ambiguity of interaction in which connections are everywhere, and every ending is arbitrary'.[68] Emerson is referring to the nineteenth-century writer and artist John Ruskin's texts, but the comment might equally apply to Chatterton's writing. Where Chatterton attempts to invent and fabricate his heritage, Ruskin is just as concerned with retrospectively rearranging the past and, significantly, with the publicity of reinventing his genesis. And as for Chatterton, for Ruskin both verbal and visual arts are material 'methods' of expression.[69]

Where both Chatterton and Arthur were concerned, their ambivalent status and mysterious 'endings' particularly fascinated eighteenth- and nineteenth-century writers, historians, and critics. However, whereas the subject of Arthur was largely ignored by the Romantic poets, Chatterton was excluded from the Romantic critical canon.[70] It is worth noting here that heraldry was used by writers of the Romantic period apart from Chatterton, references to it ranging from the sublime to the ridiculous. For Thomas De Quincey the heraldic city, set out in emblems and jewel-like colours, was a metaphor for dreamwork.[71] Contrastingly, Charles Lamb constructed elaborate coats of arms for his guinea-pigs and had a Camelot of battlemented hutches made for them.[72]

Yet, resurrected in nineteenth-century art, the icons of Arthur and Chatterton perpetuate myths. It is tempting to assert that the figure of the dead Chatterton in Henry Wallis's famous *The Death of Chatterton* (1856) has more than arbitrary connections with the recumbent Arthur of, most notably, Edward Burne-Jones's 'The Last Sleep of Arthur in Avalon' (1881–98) (Fig. 1).[73] Nineteenth-century commentators debated the whereabouts of Arthur's 'final' resting-place, whilst acknowledging the myth of his eternal 'return' in times of national need. In this context Wallis's painting can be read as an illustration of both the life and death of Chatterton. In a lecture delivered probably in 1857, John Cobley draws attention to the painting as a system of signs which correspond to the history of the boy poet. This, then, is the image of death as genealogy; the painting as *memento mori*, but also as a heraldic code for history. Cobley lists the 'emblems':

> That stump bedstead and miserable pallett: those gorgeous vestments of azure and crimson: those torn letters and memoranda: that gloomy old chest: that expired candle ... that vision of the domes and spires flashing in the light of the morning, of some Capital City; and, more than all, that form, placid and beautiful, sleeping in death.[74]

Chatterton is 'sleeping in death' like 'King' Arthur, but in terms of his pedigree, Cobley provides us with a further reading: the poet's 'heritage was amongst the real kingships – the intellectualities of the earth'.[75] That may be so, yet such a reading ignores Chatterton's insistence, evidenced in the use of heraldry in his writing, on constructing his own social origins. In his 'Will' (1770), and recalling Camden's description of the legend on Arthur's supposed tomb, Chatterton gives elaborate instructions for the building of his own monument, inscribed with heraldic terms.[76]

Notes

1. *The Works of Thomas Chatterton*, ed. Robert Southey and Joseph Cottle (London, 1803), iii. 471.
2. Dean, C., *Arthur of England: English Attitudes to King Arthur in the Middle Ages and Renaissance* (Toronto, 1987), 163.
3. Thompson comments that the *Historia* is still 'most frequently quoted by our most Learned Historians and Antiquaries'.
4. For the purposes of this discussion it is worth noting that James II's deposition and the Glorious Revolution was preceded by widespread debate about the nature of kingship and political authority.
5. See Merriman, James, *The Flower of Kings: A Study of the Arthurian Legend in England Between 1485 and 1835* (Lawrence, Kan., 1973), 56–7, for a summary of the critical explanations for Milton's abandonment of Arthur. See also Ian Haywood, *The Making of History* (London, 1986).
6. The opera was staged with Henry Purcell. In the original version Arthur competes with the Saxon Oswald for possession of Britain and has a vision of future political and racial harmony.
7. Lagorio, Valerie and Mildred Leake Day (eds.), *King Arthur Through the Ages* (New York, 1990), ii. 149.
8. Percy's letters to William Shenstone and Thomas Warton discuss the Arthurian significance of the *Reliques*.

9. After William Stansby's corrupt 1634 version of Caxton's 1485 text, no new editions of Malory appeared until 1816. Robert Southey's *The Byrth, Lyf, and Actes of Kyng Arthur* (1817), with scholarly introduction and notes, inspired republication of a range of medieval Arthurian material.

10. Merriman, 102. Warton's Arthurian poems include 'On King Arthur's Round Table at Winchester' and 'The Grave of King Arthur' (1777).

11. Weinbrot, Howard, *Britannia's Issue: The Rise of British Literature from Dryden to Ossian* (Cambridge, 1993), 14.

12. Johnston, Arthur, *Enchanted Ground: The Study of Medieval Romance in the Eighteenth Century* (London, 1964), appendix ii, 223–33.

13. See Simpson, Roger, *Camelot Regained: The Arthurian Revival and Tennyson, 1800–1849* (Cambridge, 1990) for discussion of these traditions in late eighteenth-century periodicals and literary magazines.

14. See Colton, Judith, 'Merlin's Cave and Queen Caroline: Garden Art as Political Propaganda', *Eighteenth-Century Studies* 10 (1976–7), 1–20. I am grateful to Chris Brooks for drawing my attention to this article.

15. Nicolson, William, *The English Historical Library* (London, 1714), 38.

16. Baker, Richard, *A Chronicle of the Kings of England*, 2nd edn (London, 1679), 59.

17. Borlase, William, *Antiquities, Historical and Monumental, of the County of Cornwall*, 2nd edn (London, 1769), 14.

18. Fuller, Thomas, *Church-History of Britain* (London, 1655), 39. Sections v and vi of Chatterton's 'Nine Deeds and Proclamations' are concerned with the endowment of a Bristol chapel to Our Lady of Glastonbury in 1198. The 1750s witnessed the resurrection of Glastonbury as a healing spa.

19. Borlase, 408.

20. Baker, 4.

21. Meyerstein, 67, notes that the attorney's office where Chatterton worked after his apprenticeship in July 1767 contained an old edition of *Britannia*.

22. *Works*, xliv.

23. *Britannia* was translated into English by Philemon Holland in 1610. Editions followed in 1695, 1722, 1753, 1772, and 1789.

24. Weever, John, *Ancient Funerall Monuments*, ed. W. Tooke (London, 1767).

25. Ibid. 431.

26. *Works*, 920. Meyerstein (70) notes that Lambert's business moved to new premises at an unconfirmed date. Chatterton was given instruction in painting coats of arms by Thomas Palmer, apprentice to a jeweller who occupied the same premises. See also Ingram, John H., *The True Chatterton* (London, 1910), 107–9.

27. See for example 'Saxon Tinctures', sent to the printer of the *TCM* (4 Feb. 1769), 171.

28. *Works*, 170.

29. See Cottle's account of Rowley's MSS, iii. 517.

30. *Works*, 969.

31. With the subtitle 'Collected from Original Records, Turnament Rolls, and the Herald's of March and Garter's Records' (*Works*, 316–38).

32. Southey and Cottle, ii. 455–62.

33. *Works*, 503.

34. Ibid. 44–51.

35. Ibid. 837.
36. Ibid. 835.
37. Ibid. 48. In his heraldic items Chatterton makes use of John Guillim's *A Display of Heraldrie*, 6th edn, published together with a tract of precedency (London, 1724). An abridgement of Guillim by S. Kent, *The Banner Display'd*, was published in two volumes in 1726–8.
38. See Bristol Public Library, MSS B21040, 22, which contains illustrations of eight heraldic shields and dates under the name Chatterton (also the frontispiece of *Works*). See also 'Items Not Printed: Heraldic Items' in *Works*, ii. 784–6.
39. See Bristol Public Library, MSS B5375 (front page). 'The above is the autograph of Chatterton given to G. C. [George Catcott] as a receipt for Ten guineas. The subjoined is also by him – the date of each is probably about – 1770.'
40. Southey and Cottle, ii. 507–19.
41. Goodridge, John, 'Some Predecessors of Clare: "Honest Duck"', *John Clare Society Journal*, 8 (July 1989), 5–10 discusses the idea of the 'peasant poet', which became current in the early eighteenth century. The connected issues of the self-educated poet, class, and memorialization are addressed in poems ranging from Thomas Gray's 'Elegy Written in a Country Churchyard' to Tony Harrison's 'V' and 'On Not Being Milton'. See Bridget Keegan's essay below.
42. Southey and Cottle, ii. 518.
43. *Works*, plates 1 and 2(a).
44. Weever, ch. i.
45. See Bristol Public Library, MSS B5304, 57–62.
46. *Works*, 866.
47. Ibid. 338–9.
48. Ibid. 275–6.
49. Ibid. 851. Taylor points out that coins were favourites with eighteenth-century antiquarians and earlier historians such as Camden.
50. Ibid. 64.
51. Ibid. 117, 881.
52. Guillim (1724 edn), 6.
53. *Works*, 49.
54. Ibid. 838.
55. Ibid. 395, ll. 19–20, 28–30.
56. Alfred was celebrated with monuments such as the sham ruin King Alfred's Hall in Cirencester Park and associated with Thomson's ode 'Rule Britannia' (Weinbrot, 499).
57. *Works*, 273.
58. Ibid. 507.
59. Later visual representations of Arthur's passing and memorialization include George Cattermole's *Henry II Discovering the Relics of King Arthur in Glastonbury Abbey* (1826) and W. B. Scott's *King Arthur Carried to the Land of Enchantment* (1847).
60. See Sunderland, John, 'Mortimer, Pine and some Political Aspects of English History Painting', *Burlington Magazine*, cxvi. 855 (June 1974), 321. I am grateful to Christine Poulson for drawing my attention to this article.

61. *The Yale Edition of Horace Walpole's Correspondence*, ed. W. S. Lewis *et al.* (New Haven, 1937–83), xvi. 228.
62. A revival whose roots also lay in Romanticism, Medievalism, and the Gothic Revival.
63. Brewer, Elisabeth, and Beverly Taylor (eds.), *The Return of King Arthur: British and American Arthurian Literature since 1800* (Cambridge, 1983), appendix i.
64. *The Byrth, Lyf and Actes of Kyng Arthur*, ed. Robert Southey (London, 1817), ii. 488–9, fo. 22.
65. Southey and Cottle, iii. 103.
66. Ibid. 7.
67. As opposed, in the case of illuminated manuscripts, to being regarded as relics of a barbarian age. A. N. L. Munby, *Connoisseurs and Medieval Miniatures 1750–1850* (Oxford, 1972) discusses the increasing appreciation of the medieval miniature as a work of art.
68. Emerson, Sheila, *Ruskin: The Genesis of Invention* (Cambridge, 1993), 27–8.
69. Ruskin, John, *Modern Painters*, iii (London, 1856), 5, 31.
70. William Wordsworth (in *The Prelude*, 1805; 1850) and Samuel Taylor Coleridge (in *Table Talk*, 1833) both rejected Arthur as a suitable subject for 'adult', national poetry. Walter Scott did make more direct use of Arthurian material in, for example, 'The Bridal of Triermain' (1809). As part of medievalism, Arthurianism exercised an imaginative influence on Romantic writers. Interestingly, the heraldic references in John Keats's 'The Eve of St Agnes' (1819) were probably influenced by Chatterton (*Life*, 73).
71. De Quincey, Thomas, *Confessions of an English Opium Eater* (1822; Harmondsworth, 1971), 106-7. Elsewhere in *Confessions* De Quincey expresses concern that his social status will not accord with the 'rigorous constructions of the herald' (85).
72. See Girouard, Mark, *The Return to Camelot: Chivalry and the English Gentleman* (New Haven & London, 1981).
73. See plates in Wood, Christopher, *The Pre-Raphaelites* (London, 1981), 68, 127 (detail).
74. Cobley, John, *The Death of Chatterton: Suggestions from the Celebrated Painting by Wallis: A Lecture* (Manchester, 1857?), 4.
75. Ibid. 26.
76. *Works*, 503–4.

Chapter 6

In Your Face

Timothy Morton

> Excuse me sir, some of the food is going in your mouth.
> (Unidentified extra talking to Burt Lancaster, *Vera Cruz*, 1953)

Introduction

'The Constabiliad' (1769) and a revision entitled 'The Consuliad' (1770) are superb narratives of forgery. They enact Chatterton's entry into political life, the move from Rowley to Chatterton the satirist, from Bristol to London, from Aldermen to the Grafton ministry, which he invokes coyly by using coded proper names without specific referents like 'Twitcher', 'Madoc', 'Thrimso', 'Bumbulkins', 'D–s–n'. Both works are, however, much more than psychologically titillating stories about how an impostor enters the symbolic order. Moreover, they do not merely present 'a tediously brutal picture'.[1] They describe how consumption plays with figuration in a highly politicized way. Their status as food fights, and the representations of food and eating, or non-eating, which they employ, are both poetically and politically significant.

Rather than reading the second poem as an improvement of the first, this essay will read both together. It begins by considering the qualities of the poems as political satires, forgeries of archaic verse and representations of food. The second section discusses the ways in which they depict violence towards animals and characterize their protagonists as regressive, uncivilized groups. The final section comments on the specific items of food mentioned in the poems, and draws some general conclusions.

Politics, simulation, and materiality

In contrast with the writing that presents the language of forgery and simulation as rather etherial and disembodied, this essay shows how the representation of food, the gross body, and the use of visceral, aversive 'kinetic' rhetoric, as Joyce called it, plays into forgery and dissimulation, through narratives of violence. The concept of narratives of violence is supposed to suggest not only the content of the poems, but also their form as disruptive, grotesque, and parodic. It also suggests something about the extremity of forgery itself.

'The Consuliad', accepted in the *Freeholder's Magazine*, was Chatterton's 'first major appearance in London print'.[2] 'The Consuliad' is 'a lengthy Patriot burlesque', unlike the non-political 'Constabiliad'; Patriotism was 'pro-Wilkes, anti-Burke, antiministerial'. Taylor considers this politicization to be serious: 'The changes made ... are so slight as to incline one to take the piece as opportunism rather than settled political conviction. The poem is followed, however, from mid-February through mid-May, by a concentration on Patriot satire done with apparent fervour'.[3] It has been consistently undervalued because it has been considered 'anti-Rowleyan'. Taylor argues, however, that 'The verse satires have more dash, more structural cogency, and, when thoughtfully read, more power than they have been allowed'.[4] Chatterton's food fights are described by Taylor as 'Mock Contention', one of his four types of satire, the others being 'Satiric Epistles', 'Burlesque Libretti', and 'Topical Satires'.[5] Emphasizing their physical quirks, Chatterton satirizes the vestrymen in 'The Constabiliad' as 'middle-class yahoos' who seem rather ridiculous in relation to London.[6]

Chatterton forges a narrative voice that is both rationally distant, removed as far as possible from the protagonists, and frantically 'in your face'. The poems thus seem both crude and sophisticated. Food's diverse attributes as biological necessity, cultural symbol, and commodity suggest the many-headed quality of the commodity fetish, both a materially dense object and a symbolic item of exchange and alienability or abstract representation. As Appadurai has noted, objects may enter and leave commodity phases. By the time it reaches the plate, food is rapidly ceasing to be a commodity, but the act of throwing it around might delay or even arrest this process. Material culture may be divided into two types of commodity according to the familiar medieval typology of *meuble* and *immeuble*.[7] Goods that are *meuble* (mobile) would include food. Food flying around a vestry is a parody of the *meuble* category, and thus a parody of social mobility and the fluidity of goods, contrasted with the motivation for the food fight, a diametrically opposed rigid concept of ancestral lineage and entitlement.

We do not read about the food being produced, only consumed, appropriated, and destroyed. But the food-missiles are little museums of anthropology. They carry within their farcical repetition of epic traces of lineages and territories which may be absorbed into other cultural strata. Just as a satire about vestrymen is reterritorialized onto a satire about councillors, polite urban culture bears within itself traces of other times and other territories. Simultaneously, differences in the figuration of food between 'The Constabiliad' and 'The Consuliad' map social and political differences between two classes of civil maintenance. Food riots, associated with incipient famine, were a popular form of protest in the eighteenth century, and several had taken place as recently as 1757 and 1766.[8] E. P. Thompson notes that 'In Ashby-de-la-Zouche in 1766, when a farmer put up his butter by 2d. a pound, "an old woman clapped one hand around the nape of his neck and with the other smeared his face with butter"'.[9] The poems exude a politically charged atmosphere of threat.

Chatterton's mock epics exploit differences between abusing the property and propriety of others: the social duties which the vestrymen and councillors are supposed to be performing, and the novel uses to which property is put in acts of consumption – the use of food as a weapon. Food riots were a form of British working-class protest in the late eighteenth century, when the price of grain could soar prohibitively high and meat was unavailable on a regular basis.[10] Riots followed Wilkes's election to Parliament; he had been chosen by the shopmen of London as sheriff and alderman, and 'checked abuses in [the] ... meat-market'.[11] Chatterton's protagonists ought not to be behaving in similar ways: they are on the executive and disciplinary sides of the law. The poems mockingly raise food-as-weapon to the level of epic contestation. Food becomes a blow-up fantasy of abused power.

Chatterton's self-presentation as 'teetotaller and ascetic', is in contrast with his poetic representation of coarse behaviour.[12] He dined abstemiously on offal sausages and oysters. Meyerstein notes his refusal of meat at school and his frequent diet of bread and water.[13] Posthumous reports by Croft (1780) and Blake (in *An Island in the Moon*, 1784) depicted an etiolated starveling.[14] In this light 'The Constabiliad' and 'The Consuliad' are rather playful and yet rather menacing. There are broader cultural contexts, however, in which the poems may be read as Bakhtinian carnival. Late eighteenth-century urbanization and the division of labour in food production and preparation locked diners into their dining rooms where it was harder to notice the kitchen and the slaughterhouse. The poems invert this world of rationalization and repression.

Near the end of Peter Ackroyd's disturbing tale, *Chatterton* (1987), Charles Wychwood, a poet who is too honest for the forgery business but who nevertheless becomes embroiled in a dangerous narrative of contemporary Chatterton forgery, visits a third-rate Indian restaurant in London for a celebratory meal (alas, too soon; he dies afterwards): 'The Mutton Tantras are very nice ... Some people prefer the Bhagavad-Gita, but it's very hot'.[15] Wychwood, who neurotically munches books, is well placed to discuss bizarre relationships between consumption, materiality, and simulation. Naming some spurious Indian dishes after real Hindu texts, Charles wishes not simply to show how brilliant his falsifying imagination might be, but how real and substantial his discourse is: 'Have you never heard about poetry being the food of love ...?' he continues, twisting Orsino's line about music into a further statement about the consumption of the text.[16] (*Tantra* and *text* share a Sanskrit derivation.)

What is the similarity between a Mutton Tantra, 'The Constabiliad', and 'The Consuliad'? They are *simulacra*, to use Deleuze's and Baudrillard's word for a 'copy' whose relationship to an 'original' is of no importance: 'A simulation is different from a fiction or a lie in that it not only presents an absence as a presence, the imaginary as the real, it also undermines any contrast to the real'; it is a reality with 'no referent, no ground, no source'.[17] Baudrillard describes a shift in capitalism from political economy to the rule of 'code': 'the signified and the referent are now abolished to the sole profit of a play of signifiers, of a generalized formalization in which the code no longer refers back to any subjective or objective "reality", but to its own logic'.[18]

Baudrillard's mapping of the history of European relationships with the object and the status of truth into three eras of deduction, production, and seduction is too teleological and idealist.[19] Chatterton's forgery of highly seductive simulacra negotiates with both materiality and politics *avant la lettre*. Baudrillard's over-schematic history equates different periods with different modes of representation and criteria for ascertaining truth. Chatterton should exist somewhere between the feudal milieu of deduction and the industrial era of production. Chatterton stages the real without ground or referent in three different ways: through archaism; by using fictional characters with a palpable but indeterminate social or political referent; and through food as simulated weaponry. Chatterton's forgeries are not just fictions or lies.

It is not sufficient, however, to delight in these poems as airy fabrics. The serious relationship between historiography and fiction in the eighteenth century is evident in the works of Macpherson and Chatterton.[20] In a post-humanist environment no longer content with the reality-effect of *auctoritas*, philosophers of history emphasized three elements: the empiricism of the historical real; the need to authenticate history with footnotes, close reading of sources and so forth; and a sense of determinate cultural history. Chatterton's satires present all three in an obscene, perverse form. The 'in-your-face' gristle and slop simulates the 'reality-effect' of empiricism; the knowingly pro-Patriot jibes of 'The Consuliad' are an authentication of Chatterton's entry into the *monde* of public discourse and social commentary; and the food-fight form is a comic cultural history of bad manners. The indeterminacy of names in 'The Consuliad' may have appealed to the 'voraciousness' of Patriot paranoia.[21] The evidence of parallels between food riots and the substance of Chatterton's poems also shows that they are not merely simulations.

Moreover, the substantiality of food is related to the figurative properties of food in both poems. In Hjelmslevian terms, the substance of both content and expression is food and eating. At the same time, the form of content is a meal, and the form of expression is an epic. A bizarre do-se-do between content and expression takes place. Chatterton's mock-epic style refigures Milton's representation of Satan's journey into hell ('The Constabiliad', 159); but food may become a parodic object in itself. Forged aesthetic objects only *appear* to be innocuous. Fake food is still material, greasy, sticky, for all its fakery. The representation of fake food in a novel or a poem is a *mise-en-abîme* which, instead of whisking us up to the empyrean or down into the deconstructive abyss, trickles down our shirts.

The trickles and flows of the commodity-form congregate on the plate before it is hurled at an unwitting diner. An 'Indian meal' in London is a simulation of an absent original, with its own tropes of presentation and spicing. An 'Indian meal' on Long Island is quite different. Indeed, the 'originality' of a particular locus or style of consumption, in this instance, post-Raj orientalism, is predicated on its simulation elsewhere. Food lives through allegory. 'The Constabiliad' and 'The Consuliad' are fictions of deterritorialization:

epics ending up in the wrong place (Bristolian constabular and council dinners), food ending up not in one's mouth but on one's face. Tropology and representation permeate the spicy, sticky materiality; conversely, representation itself is spicy and sticky.

In a twist, the *surface* of things emerges as the *objet petit a* or the *Ding an Sich*.[22] Acts of consumption do not dissolve social reality into sublime air, but materialize and embody it. Appearance, *species*, spice, is also capital, and Chatterton's food fights are ways of capitalizing on the commencement of a career in political poetry. Ackroyd describes how, posing as the dead Chatterton, the novelist Meredith comments to the painter Wallis on the furniture purchased for the picture that now hangs in the Tate: 'I suppose it makes everything more real? When you buy something, when it is your own, does it acquire a deeper reality?'[23] Chatterton's food fights contest heroic identity, and the poems as attempts at satire stage Chatterton's identity.

Food is a well-chosen form for this play between simulation and reality, because of its liminal status as both matter and sign. Food is never just unmediated 'life', nor is it purely conceptual. In the structural anthropology of Lévi-Strauss, cooked food in tribal mythology assumed the role of a sign of culture, that 'second nature' interposed between humans and the natural world. However, the idea of food also blurs those clear boundaries between 'nature' and 'culture' which Lévi-Strauss kept in play. A structural approach would be too neat for the kinds of splattering figure which fill 'The Constabiliad' and 'The Consuliad'. It could not account for the nesting and layering of figures. Before it is represented in literary language, food is already its very own epic. A dish in an Indian restaurant is a narrative about local and national traditions, flows of lineage and ownership, orientalism and colonialism. Chatterton's poems are rich layerings of simulation, metaphor, metonymy, mimesis. The comedy of the mock-epic genre, its juxtaposition of mundane and lofty elements, is also what is somewhat serious about consuming a meal, an everyday activity of profound social significance.

Epic, butchery, and civilization

In epic fashion, let us start *in medias res*: 'Here broken Tarts with bloody Wounds appear' (*C1*, 108; henceforth *C1* will be used to denote 'The Constabiliad', *C2* to denote 'The Consuliad'; where the poems agree, *C1*'s spelling will be used). The tarts are both bleeding jam and, in the conceit of the epic, displaying the blood they have spilt in an expressive play on tarts/hearts. From the late Middle Ages to the seventeenth century, banquets were adorned with 'subtleties', sugar models which often displayed elaborate heraldic or symbolic messages.[24] Famous subtleties included hinds that bled fruit sauce when pierced.[25] The survey of the *disjecta membra* of the battle deploys the 'here ... here' trope characteristic of topographical poetry, a tradition that included works like Pope's *Windsor-Forest*. *Windsor-Forest* celebrated the aggressive consumption of nature under Queen Anne, both as capital and as a resource for sport. Chatterton's poems parody the scene of consumption as a scene of battle, and the scene of battle as a meal. Furthermore, the mock-epic implications of the following lines are distinctly Popeian:

> Sauces encountered Sauces Bottles smashed
> Butter with Butter swims Knives with Knives clash
> Each Honord Garment shines with martial Oil
> And all the Fields a massy Hill of Spoil.
>
> (*C1*, 183–6)

Chatterton recalls the mock heroics of the clashing coaches in *The Rape of the Lock*.

Epics and meals are both narratives of violence. Epics are simulated battles between opposing social interests or 'destinies'. Chatterton's food fights resemble the vegetarian tradition of describing meals as violent narratives. This tradition is often found in texts which also contain arguments about anti-slavery, anti-blood sports, or prison reform. The protagonists are not eating, however; they are throwing and slapping. Mock-epics appear more violent than they are. Yet, this very appearance is represented ironically as itself a kind of violence. The conceit of Chatterton's poems turns Achilles' and Hector's, Aeneas' and Turnus' weapons into soft and deliquescing foodstuffs. But this lightening-through-mockery is also what is so weighty: the mock-consumption of violence *is* the consumption of violence. This sublime hysteria characterizes the commodity-form, and civic institutions like councils or constabularies, extensions of the powers that control the flow of property. In simulating an epic, the contestants hit each other with bleeding pieces of the real. As in *The Rape of the Lock*, the objects often seem more apparent than the human protagonists: 'Sauces encountered Sauces Bottles smashed / Butter with Butter swims Knives with Knives clash' (*C1*, 183–4). Our laughter at these poems is somewhat hysterical. Hysteria may have wider implications, as it is manifested for example in Chatterton's love poetry. Chatterton is notorious for the extremity with which he mythologizes.

The poems converge in passages that employ the aversive rhetoric familiar to eighteenth- and early nineteenth-century apologists for animal rights and vegetarian diet. The 'mangled Pigeon' (*C1*, 36, *C2*, 50), the roaring butchers and screaming ladies, connoting a bull-baiting (*C1*, 83, *C2*, 157), and the carving knife stained by mangling 'Pris'ners' or 'captive carcases', in other words, penned animals (*C1*, 119–20, *C2*, 163–4), would all be familiar to writers like Soame Jenyns, John Oswald, Joseph Ritson, Percy Shelley, and Thomas Young.[26] The vegetarian lines from Shelley's radical poem *Queen Mab* (1813) read: 'No longer now / He slays the lamb that looks him in the face, / And horribly devours his mangled flesh' (viii. 211). 'Captive carcases' implies that the animals are already butchered before being sent to the butcher: confined and marked for the slaughterhouse, they are already as good as dead. Mock-epic consumption overcodes the animal bodies as human bodies in *C1*'s final exhortation: 'Let evry sweating Champion strip the Slain' (204). *C1* adds the description of Bumbulkins falling: 'so falls the Arrow-wounded Goose / When from the murdring Poultrers Pen broke loose' (93).

Meat is most certainly murder in this register, employing the rhetoric of butchery or *macellogia*, denoting the actions of the butcher and the carver in killing and cutting up the body of the dead animal, revealing the process of the production of meat. The passages about the bull-baiting were echoed in the period by complaints mounted by humanitarian members of the upper class against working-class sports. The implied mixing of class discourses is notable in *C2*, which plays upon the degeneracy of the rich councillors' behaviour. In *C1*, the vestrymen's actions betray their class.

Elaine Scarry has shown how in discourses of social or spiritual disfiguration, the sign regresses to the state of being a weapon, demonstrating the '*referential instability*' of the primary sign of the weapon'.[27] This occurs in the degeneration of iconic meat, first into a weapon, and then into a document of *macellogia*. Norbert Elias has described the special position granted to meat in medieval eating manners. The whole animal was displayed at table and carved by a prominent guest or member of the household. In the eighteenth century, the meat would have been more likely to be hidden, removed from the table and/or present only as a 'joint', not the whole but a part of the animal. The loin of veal (*C1*, 47, *C2*, 59) is rather large, and it is excessively consumed: the narrator compares the consumption of three a day with the aldermen and priests of old. Elias indicates that such excesses were commonly associated with the medieval secular 'upper class', and here this association appears both regressive and corrupt. The priest is the kind of Friar Tuck typical of medieval anti-clerical satire.[28] The archaism of the behaviour is grotesquely comic: contemporaries would have perceived it as regressive. There is no need for anachronistic psychological theories to explain this; indeed, that is our own version of a theory of manners. Though it is often assumed that *C2* is a revision of *C1*, the poems are particularly amusing in the light of what they say about manners as a diptych. The councillors' behaviour apes the crudity of the aldermen.

Both poems can be read in Elias's terms as satirizing a regression, in both content and expression, to forms of feudal table behaviour and figuration, from a more 'advanced' state of civility. The sight of the gander hurled through the air after the passage about the murdering poulterer is particularly disturbing (*C1*, 99ff.). It has been suggested that 'Chatterton seems to have had a sort of fascinated disgust at heavy feeding', a reason for his representation of 'Canynge's alder-men-diners'.[29] Meyerstein has noticed a significant similarity between the representation of bloody sacrifice in Chatterton's 'Elegy, written at Stanton Drew' (27 October 1769) and the vegetarian-style rhetoric in these poems.[30]

The narrator's position is typical of the extreme aversion of certain eighteenth-century people to the sight of meat, the 'more or less rationally disguised feelings of disgust' which led some to vegetarian-ism.[31] Erasmus had advised, 'Discenda a primis statim annis secandi ratio' in *De civilitate morum puerilium* (1530): 'The rules of carving should be taught immediately from the earliest age.' But in Chatterton's time certain people were less likely to value carving.[32] The description of the carving knife as 'The lineal Representative of Kings' (*C1*, 117) is satirically charged. Within fifty years, Charles Lamb's 'A Dissertation upon Roast Pig' (1822) expressed a delight in the sight of the cooking of the whole animal which may normally have been regarded as lower-class or coarse.[33]

Elias tries to read morals back into manners in a slyly Freudian way – one's reasons for not eating meat are just disguised aversion. Rationality and disgust aid each other, and in certain cases the ration-al distance of the subject enables disgust. This is to invoke a much larger argument about the state of the division of labour, urbanization and other advancing capitalist phenomena, and the premium placed upon reason in the Enlightenment. However, it is worth noting that it is precisely the achieved phobic distance of the narrator from his satirized subjects in *C1* and *C2* which enables him to be so 'in your face' with the carnivalesque, grotesque, and vegetarian rhetoric. It is the 'fascinated disavowal' which Stallybrass and White discuss as characterizing the eighteenth-century middle-class poetics and politics of containment.[34]

The protagonists are not simply acting like butchers. The councillors and vestrymen are obviously being bad-mannered. The sight of melted butter dripping around the mouth was rude then and now: 'His op'ning Mouth the melted Butter fills / And dropping from his Nose and Chin distills' (*C1*, 37, *C2*, 51–2). In the Middle Ages, new codes prevented nobly-born Europeans from slobbering over their food, touching it with the fingers, or throwing it around. The behaviour of the lower classes and children did not begin to be proscribed to such an extent until the early modern period. The narrator combines mock epic with satire at the level of expression, and medieval display with modern affect at the level of content. But there may be another more immediate context for the fight. Bonnell Thornton (1724–68) was a member of the Nonsense Club whose literary core included William Cowper, and which was associated with the defence of Wilkes. His *Ode on Saint Cæcilia's Day* (1749) was performed in 1763 at Ranelagh Gardens, and employed:

> The ubiquitous instruments of the British vulgar: the hurdy-gurdy, Jew's harp, salt-box, and marrow-bone and cleaver. These instruments were to be found in the hands of hundreds of street musicians in London, as well as doing yeoman's duty (in the case of the cleavers) in the butchers' shambles of Clare Market.[35]

The carnivalesque mood which the *Ode* exemplifies is also occupied by Chatterton's two mock epics. There is a class register here. Rough instruments can be found in the hands of the rude mechanicals in Shakespeare's *A Midsummer Night's Dream*. There is also an urban register. E. P. Thompson has noted how French *charivari* resembled the 'rough music' performances that 'often occurred in conjunction with popular protests against deviant or exploitative social behaviour'. A review of the *Ode* in the *St. James's Chronicle* (1763) enjoyed 'the marrow bones and cleavers of Wilkes' as 'instruments of English liberty'.[36] The table conversations in both poems get out of hand precisely when the question of feudal or Romance-style lineage begins

to be contested: the actors forget their present-day occupations. The
translation of affect from the inside (safe and regulated) to the outside
(unsafe and unregulated) is figured in the pleas of Flaccus:

> 'Friends let this Clang of hostile fury cease
> Ill it becomes the Officers of Peace
> Shall Turkeys for internal Battle drest
> Like Bullets outward perforate the breast
> Shall jav'lin Bottles, Blood etherial spill
> Shall luscious Turtle without Surfeit kill.'

(*C1*, 147–52)

The poetics of food

What sorts of food are represented in the poems? 'Turtle' could mean
turtle doves. The reference in *C2* to the shield of Bristol as a turtle *shell*
suggests the much more luxurious reptile dish. *C2* substitutes 'pleni-
pos' (people vested with full authority) for 'Officers' and 'olio's' for
'Turkeys'. This makes the patterning of social degradation more
complex. There is a greater mock-heroic fall involved from plenipo to
rabble-rouser, but an olio is hardly more socially elevated than a
turkey. The dish, of Portuguese origin, consisted of 'pieces of meat and
fowl, bacon, pumpkins, cabbage, turnips, and other ingredients stewed
or boiled together and highly spiced'.[37] It came to imply a kind of
hotchpotch. Johnson's dictionary traced 'satire' to the Greek *'satura'*,
or medley, a 'dish containing various kinds of fruit'.[38] Brydone had
commented in *A Tour through Sicily and Malta* (1733) on the dominat-
ing presence of olio at tables which the English would consider rustic.
Highly-spiced food had gone out of fashion by the beginning of the
century. The language of social status travels upward, but the language
of food status remains the same or travels downward, and becomes
exoticized (Mediterranean) in form. Antiquarianism was partially
responsible for the emergence of orientalism, with its association of
hot spice with hot tales.

Some foods appear in both poems: the custard pudding, the red
wheat manchet, the Gallic roll (a self-important French roll), the
pigeon, Pactolian gravy, the loin of veal, the pot full of flaming hot
oil, pepper, the bottle of meat juice. However, *C1* has a 'Pear Pie' while
C2 substitutes a 'court-pie', which is also divided at the end in a
reconciliatory ceremony. *C1* employs 'ambrosia', while *C2* employs

'Manilla sauces'. The councillors pick at 'ortolans, and chicken slain, / To form the whimsies of an a-la-reine' (*C2*, 11–12); the vestrymen mangle 'with resistless Teeth the chine / Of pullet slain at sacred Friendship's shrine' (*C1*, 5–6). The vestrymen drink 'almighty Beer' but the councillors go continental with 'Prussian beer' (*C1*, 7, *C2*, 15). These apparently small touches achieve a greater sense of social elevation and fine cuisine in *C2*. *C2* is more sophisticated in its message about the councillors: 'refined, but not that refined'.

The vestrymen throughout are represented as guzzling gluttons: their conflict is resolved in 'Come Guzzle and be Friends again, He said / The Vestry God returned and discord fled' (207–8). *C2* concludes:

> 'See this court-pie with twenty thousand drest;
> 'Divide it, and be friends again,' he said.
> The council god return'd; and discord fled.

> (249–52)

In contrast, the vestrymen divide the 'Spoil' of battle (186), and Chatterton plays on the archaic and modern connotations of the word: the slain, and wasted food. The 'court-pie' is either the coarse woollen material worn as a cloak, tabard or coat in the fourteenth and fifteenth centuries, or a dish whose name refers to it: hence the 'drest', the 'twenty thousand' perhaps referring to pudding decorations.[39] 'Hundreds and thousands', comfits used as cake decorations, arrived in English around 1830 – could this be an early reference?[40] 'Ambrosia' technically speaking was a beverage spiced with cloves or cinnamon alluding to the food and anointing oil of the gods.[41] In *C1* it jokingly refers to the greasy gravy dripping from the gander which Currara whirls around his head. The 'Manilla sauces' may be a more recent, fashionable kind of condiment, as Manila was only named the capital of the Philippines in 1697.[42] The south-east Asian connotation may suggest something rather spicy. The 'Pactolian Gravy' (*C1*, 22, *C2*, 32) refers to the golden sands of Pactolus in India, a mock-epic food epithet.[43]

Using food imagery, *C2* comments on commerce. Curraras (not Currara as in *C1*) has been hit on the ear with the French roll, and falls to the ground (93–4). A description of him runs from the anti-Semitic reference to his 'Jewish soul' (93, repeated 127) to the following:

> Curraras, vers'd in every little art,
> To play the minister's or felon's part:

Grown hoary in the villanies [*sic*] of state,
A title made him infamously great.
A slave to venal slaves; a tool to tools:
The representative of knaves and fools.
But see! commercial Bristol's genius sit,
Her shield a turtle shell, her lance a spit.
See, whilst her nodding aldermen are spread,
In all the branching honours of the head;
Curraras, ever faithful to the cause,
With beef and ven'son their attention draws:
They drink, they eat, then sign the mean address;
Say, could their humble gratitude do less!

(95–109)

As well as framing Curraras, this is a general remark about gluttonous politics. The image of commercial Bristol, ekphrastic like Virgil's depiction of Aeneas' shield, parodies Britannia with her culinary equipment. Depictions of meals often served an ekphrastic function in Classical literature. This is emphasized in Chatterton's ekphrastic figure of commerce as a gourmand.[44] Unlike the more archaic *C1*, *C2* incorporates a modern image of the executive lunch. Simultaneously Chatterton exploits medieval modes of signification, denigrating Jews as treacherous and hypocritical, and associating them with flows of money.

In both poems, food ends up on the face rather than in the mouth. The slapstick register interrupts the monolithic presence of the gaze and the face, efficiently disrupting the pristine unity of face and soul.[45] The best example of this is the 'burning Pepper' which 'sparkles' in the eyes of Sallust or Balluntun (*C1*, 102, *C2*, 134). In Galenic terms, pepper is a hot, dry spice which can burn any soft-tissued organ with which it comes in contact, not just the mouth. *To be blinded with flavour* is an extraordinary synaesthetic disability. The poetic power of this image has been commented on recently by the rapper, Flavor Flav: 'Now I got a murder rap cause I bust ya cap wit Flavor – pure Flavor' as he declares in 'Flavor Flav Cold Lampin''. Slapstick also provides a way of figuring the materiality of haphazard, everyday life. The facial custard-pie is an obvious example of the carnivalesque. The British comedians Mel Smith and Griff Rhys Jones once played two yuppies having a power lunch dressed as babies, doing everything with their food except eating it. The comic content of such a scene is 'typicality' – how typical for yuppies to act like babies. Its expressive juxtapositions, however, are highly unusual.

Conclusion

There are many different kinds of food register in Chatterton's food fights:

Content	Expression
Butchery (quasi-vegetarian)	Exoticism (olios, Manilla sauce)
Coarse manners (social degradation and regression)	Mock epic (Pactolian gravy)
Social elevation (minimal and ironic; Manilla sauce vs. ambrosia; Gallic roll for French roll)	Slapstick
Social degradation/ironic similitude Commerce (commercial Bristol)	Violence

These registers create complex and amusing patterns of identification and differentiation within and between *C1* and *C2*. When read together, the poems comment on each other through gustatory language.

C1 'antiques' the substances and forms composing its content (food, meals, food-fights). Its substance and form of expression (mock-epic slapstick, archaic spellings and lack of modern punctuation) also sustains the forgery of antiquity. The common image of antiquarian 'mumbling' or gnawing over relics could be found in Pope's *Dunciad* (1743), in the brief description of Wormius 'On parchment scraps y-fed' (iii. 184); compare the pot 'Where bubbled scrips and contracts flaming hot' (*C2*, 168).[46] *C2* is more complex. At the level of expressive content it is a simulation of *C1* while doubling up as an urbane satire. Its expressive form is more modern; for example, punctuation is added. The councillors are seen emulating the crude behaviour of the boorish law-enforcers; hegemony apes coercion. *C2* is thus all the more disgustingly visceral in the social and temporal degradation of the councillors back to the land of Arthur or down to the level of the vestrymen. The details which recontextualize the food missiles only serve to satirize the councillors' behaviour further. The poems also implicate racial myths about Gothic identity as an authentically

'British' form. The cult of Gothic liberty is associated with medieval food, while the manners of the French are associated with the fancy pretensions of its cuisine, denigrated in the popular press for nearly a century: the Norman yolk. The verbal register of conquest appears in: 'Now Storming castles of the newest taste, / And granting articles to forts of paste' (*C2*, 13). The 'garter' which is covered with the stage-blood of meat in 'A double river of congealing blood, / O'erflows his garter with a purple flood' (*C2*, 155) suggests a post-Conquest style of heraldic display. What ultimately renders this register comic is its archaism in relation to English history. Capitalism is what really renders absurd the mock-heroic squabble of the characters Thrimso and Bumbulkins about the former's lineage.

Chatterton exploits two aspects of satire, urbane wit and the intrusion of the gross body on the masked, urbane world. 'The Constabiliad' and 'The Consuliad' narrate a breakdown in modern professionalization, while the author seeks to professionalize his satirical persona. In addition, both poems employ quasi-vegetarian rhetoric, based on discourses of sympathy, faciality, and kinetic, aversive figures of disgust. Manners (social degradation) and morals (aversion to cruelty) remove the narrator from the disgusting, mock-cruel slop in which he mixes himself at the level of expression.[47] Chatterton writes satire out of mock epic replete with presiding gods and Classical and Miltonic allusions, but eschews pristine urbanity. He ends up in your face.

Notes

1. *Life*, 301.
2. Taylor, Donald S., *Thomas Chatterton's Art: Experiments in Imagined History* (Princeton, 1978), 208.
3. Ibid. 175.
4. Ibid. 177.
5. Ibid. 186.
6. Ibid. 203.
7. See Thomas, Nicholas, *Entangled Objects: Exchange, Material Culture, and Colonialism in the Pacific* (Cambridge, Mass., 1991), 14–15, 24.
8. Thompson, E. P., *Customs in Common: Studies in Traditional Popular Culture* (New York, 1991), 297.
9. Ibid. 323.
10. See Erdman, David, *Blake; Prophet against Empire: A Poet's Interpretation of the History of His Own Times* (Princeton, 1954; repr. 1977; reissued 1991), 8.
11. Ibid. 13.

12. Kaplan, L. J., *The Family Romance of the Impostor-Poet Thomas Chatterton* (New York, 1988), 133.
13. *Life*, 32.
14. Ibid. 438–9.
15. Ackroyd, Peter, *Chatterton: A Novel* (London, 1987), 145.
16. Ibid. 145.
17. Baudrillard, Jean, *Selected Writings*, ed. Mark Poster (Stanford, 1988), 6, 7 (introduction). See Deleuze, Gilles, *Différence et répétition* (Paris, 1968), 92.
18. Baudrillard, Jean, *The Mirror of Production*, tr. Mark Poster (St Louis, 1975), 127.
19. Ibid. 120, 125, 128–9.
20. Haywood, Ian, *The Making of History* (London, 1986), 15–45.
21. Taylor, 209.
22. Žižek, Slavoj, *The Sublime Object of Ideology* (London & New York, 1989), 153–99. Žižek may be satisfied by this Hegelian custard-pie, which was thrown by Chatterton, an unlikely master of dialectic.
23. Ackroyd, 155.
24. Mintz, Sidney W., *Sweetness and Power: The Place of Sugar in Modern History* (New York, 1985), 89.
25. Ibid. 93.
26. See Morton, Timothy, *Shelley and the Revolution in Taste: The Body and the Natural World* (Cambridge, 1994), ch. 1, for an overview and a description of *macellogia*.
27. Scarry, Elaine, *The Body in Pain: The Making and Unmaking of the World* (Oxford & New York, 1985), 243; see also 38–45, 239–40.
28. Elias, Norbert, *The History of Manners: The Civilizing Process*, tr. E. Jephcott, vol. i (New York, 1978), 118.
29. Taylor, 202.
30. *Life*, 91–2.
31. Taylor, 120.
32. Ibid. 119.
33. Lamb, Charles, 'A Dissertation upon Roast Pig', *London Magazine* (Sept. 1822).
34. Stallybrass, Peter and Allon White, *The Politics and Poetics of Transgression* (Ithaca, 1986), 108.
35. Bertelsen, Lance, *The Nonsense Club: Literature and Popular Culture, 1749–1764* (Oxford, 1986), 16.
36. Ibid. 157, 160.
37. *OED*, 'olio', sb.1.
38. *OED*, 'satire', sb.i.1.
39. *OED*, 'courtepy', sb.obs.
40. My thanks to John Simpson for pointing this out.
41. *OED*, 'ambrosia', sb.4., 3.
42. *OED*, 'Manilla', 1.
43. *OED*, 'pactolian', a.1.
44. For further classification of *ekphrasis*, see Mitchell, W. J. T., *Picture Theory: Essays on Verbal and Visual Representation* (Chicago, 1994), 151–81.
45. See Magli, P., 'The Face and the Soul,' in *Fragments for a History of the Human Body*, ed. M. Feher, R. Nadaff, and N. Tazi (New York, 1989), ii. 86–127.

46. *Dunciad Variorum (The Twickenham Edition of the Poems of Alexander Pope),* v, ed. James R. Sutherland (London, 1963), 171.

47. Similar arguments have been presented about other modern texts in Stallybrass and White.

Chapter 7

'This Necessary Knowledge': Thomas Chatterton and the Ways of the London Book Trade

Michael F. Suarez, SJ

Thomas Chatterton was no Emily Dickinson. Like most writers, he did not merely want to write; he wanted to publish. Publication brought financial gain and reputation. Bred in Bristol, arguably the English provincial city with the most advanced commercial print-culture, Chatterton learned early about the business of getting into print.[1] He was 15 when his first composition, a forgery, appeared in a local journal. He began corresponding with London booksellers shortly after his 16th birthday, and saw his first works printed in a London periodical just two months later. By the time the cocksure Chatterton came to the capital in late April 1770 to win fame and fortune with his pen, he had published 31 titles in seven different journals, five of which were London publications. He was 17 years old.

In both Bristol and London, Chatterton's strategies and practices for publishing his work were far removed from the archetypal image of the hapless and naive Romantic poet he was later imagined to be. Rather, Chatterton approached the problem of seeing his writings into print with remarkable inventiveness and acumen. He studied the ways of the book trade and worked hard to establish the contacts he knew would be necessary for his success. This essay examines Chatterton's relationship with the four London booksellers he visited immediately upon arriving in the capital; it analyses evidence from his correspondence both to establish his habits as a networker and to explore the publishing prospects that resulted from his professional connections, and it considers three booksellers from whom he would most likely have sought patronage because of their close links to his own native city. Determining the nature and extent of Chatterton's knowledge of the book trade enables us to understand his career as a professional

96

writer and to comprehend his relationship with the London literary marketplace where he sought to make his name.

Four London booksellers

While still resident in Bristol, Chatterton conducted a correspondence with four London publishers, all of whom he claimed to have visited almost immediately upon arriving in London: 'called upon Mr. Edmunds, Mr. Fell, Mr. Hamilton, and Mr. Dodsley. Great encouragement from them; all approved of my design ...'.[2] Evidence both from surviving letters and from Chatterton's pre-London publication record suggests that he had good reason to expect at least mild approbation from these booksellers. Who were they and why were they important to Chatterton's 'design' of becoming a professional writer in London?

William Edmunds, in Shoe Lane, edited the *Middlesex Journal*, a thrice-weekly Patriot organ that published seven of Chatterton's eight extant Decimus letters, beginning with 'To the Duke of G—n' on 24 February 1770. Edmunds had printed 'Decimus. To the Princess of Gotham' on April 17th, just eight days before Chatterton's arrival in London. By the end of May, Edmunds's periodical had published the five remaining political missives modelled on the satires of Junius. In addition to the Decimus letters, Chatterton sent Edmunds his long Churchillian satire, 'Kew Gardens', in several parts. Having already seen his first Decimus letter appear some three weeks earlier in the *Middlesex Journal*, Chatterton now tried to capitalize on his success by selling the publisher a loosely constructed and highly digressive work of nearly 1100 lines cobbled together from four earlier couplet satires.[3] Not surprisingly, Chatterton signed his poem 'Decimus'.

Although Edmunds continued to be interested in Chatterton's work, he elected not to publish the poem. We may surmise that Edmunds's rejection of 'Kew Gardens' must not have been too severe, however, since on 26 April, presumably Chatterton's first full day in the capital, his political poem 'The Hag' appeared in the *Middlesex Journal*. As the piece is dated 'Bristol, April 10', it seems likely that Chatterton would have left for London knowing that Edmunds's publication had accepted two of his satires in prose and one in verse.

Despite its change in editorship in mid-May 1770, Chatterton's connection with the *Middlesex Journal* appears to have been solid. It is, however, curious that, after his initial flurry of publication – 11 works in slightly more than six weeks between mid-April and late May –

Chatterton did not publish in the *Middlesex Journal* again until 16 August, just eight days before his death. A notice in the *Journal* for 11 August 1770 indicates that Chatterton had submitted a sheaf of satires, only one of which was sufficiently timely.[4] Nevertheless, Chatterton's submission, the tone of the *Journal*'s notice, and the publication of 'Menenius' five days later, all suggest that, had Chatterton lived, the *Middlesex Journal* would have continued to be an important venue for his political satires in prose and verse. Given the available evidence, Chatterton's failure to publish there in June, July, and the first half of August remains a mystery.[5]

The second literary contact Chatterton called upon soon after his arrival in London was Isaac Fell, a bookseller in Paternoster Row who sold *The New Bath Guide* (along with Dodsley and many Bristol booksellers), and who had published Thomas Mortimer's *A New History of England, from the earliest accounts of Britain, to ... 1763* (3 vols., 1764–6). Most importantly, Fell edited the *Freeholder's Magazine*, a Patriot monthly that published two of Chatterton's early political poems: 'The Consuliad' in January 1770 and 'Resignation. A Poem' in April and May of the same year.

Within two weeks of his arrival in London, Chatterton wrote to his mother and other friends in Bristol with great excitement about his prospects as a writer for the Patriot group:

> I get four guineas a month by one magazine…. Mr. Wilkes knew me by my writings since I first corresponded with the booksellers here. I shall visit him next week … he affirmed that what Mr. Fell had of mine could not be the writings of a youth: and expressed a desire to know the author. By means of another bookseller I shall be introduced to Townshend and Sawbridge.

> *For Mr. T. Cary.*

> I have set you a task… . Tell all your acquaintance for the future to read the Freeholder's Magazine.

> Mr. Mat: Mease

> Begging Mr. Meases Pardon…. I hope he will remember me and tell all his Acquaintance to read the Freeholders Magazine for the future.

Tell – [a list of 13 names]
to read the Freeholders Magazine.[6]

Even for the normally enthusiastic Chatterton, this is too much. What
is going on here?

It seems that Fell, a zealously anti-Ministry bookseller and editor
who in 1769 also contributed to the production of the pro-Patriot
Middlesex Journal, recognized Chatterton's potential usefulness as a
political satirist and decided to take the young writer under his wing.
Although Chatterton may be exaggerating for effect, it appears that
Fell had accepted a number of his works, shown some of his poems to
Wilkes, promised to introduce him to the Opposition chief, and
offered him a generous maintenance allowance. In the same letter,
Chatterton, typically overstepping the mark, tells several friends that
they should send him material and he will most certainly see to its
publication. Does it not seem possible, then, that Fell – on the basis of
the poems he had accepted for the *Freeholder's*, the Decimus letters
appearing in the *Middlesex*, and the additional works he had received
since Chatterton's arrival in London – had decided to make the quick-
witted satirist a junior member of the *Freeholder's* staff? At the very
least, Chatterton's repeated insistence that his Bristol friends read the
Magazine must indicate that a major work of his was soon to appear
there.[7]

Yet, after the publication of the two poems noted above, *none* of
Chatterton's poems ever appeared in the *Freeholder's Magazine*. How,
then, are we to understand Chatterton's letter? Within a week of that
most optimistic epistle, Isaac Fell was arrested for his anti-Ministry
publications. Chatterton's latest 'patron' was obliged to resign his
editorship of the *Freeholder's*, and it seems that Chatterton's great
prospects vanished with Fell's incarceration. Although he continued
to publish in the *Middlesex*, Chatterton's work never appeared in the
Freeholder's again.

Chatterton's third publishing connection in London was with
Archibald Hamilton, Jr of St John's Gate, bookseller and editor of the
Town and Country Magazine. By the time Chatterton first met with
Hamilton in April 1770, he had already published 22 pieces in the
Town and Country. Chatterton's timing in developing a relationship
with the monthly could scarcely have been better. Hamilton's fledg-
ling magazine, an *omnium gatherum* subtitled *Universal Repository of
Knowledge, Instruction, and Entertainment*, needed a steady flow of

diverse contributions to fill its pages; the aspiring author's first works to appear in a London periodical were printed in the second issue.

Although Chatterton remained on good terms with Hamilton while in London, he became less dependent upon the *Town and Country* after his arrival in the capital. While he was still in Bristol, Chatterton published 31 works, of which 22 – or just over 70 per cent – were in the *Town and Country*. When in London, however, Chatterton placed just seven of his 24 publications – or slightly under 30 per cent – in Hamilton's magazine. I take this as a healthy sign of Chatterton's desire to build a reputation as a writer, rather than merely make a living from his pen. Although Chatterton's rate of publication in the magazine declined only slightly – 1.75 works per month in Bristol versus 1.47 in London – the pattern of his periodical publications became more diverse.

Presumably, Chatterton could have fed and clothed himself well enough by writing primarily for the *Town and Country*, though that is not what he had come to London to do. While neither Archibald Hamilton, Jr nor his father, who became editor of the *Middlesex Journal*, appears to have paid Chatterton especially well, the fact that he did not rely on the *Town and Country* as an almost certain source of income suggests that Chatterton's fiscal situation was sufficiently stable to allow him to focus on his more serious antiquarian and political writings. Contrary to popular belief, Chatterton was earning quite a decent living through the sale of his writings at the time of his death in August 1770.[8] Although he clearly had given greater priority to other projects, Chatterton's intention to continue publishing in the *Town and Country* on a regular basis may be inferred from the appearance of his Ossianic poem 'Gortmund' in the September 1770 issue of the magazine.

James Dodsley was the ascendant author's fourth and most prestigious bookselling contact in London. He was also the most problematic for Chatterton. The younger brother of Robert Dodsley (d. 1764), James owned and operated one of London's wealthiest and most respected publishing concerns at Tully's Head in Pall Mall. In addition to publishing the *Annual Register*, an established serial where Chatterton would surely have liked to place his work, Dodsley was, on several accounts, the bookseller most ideally suited to see Chatterton's Rowley poems into print.

The first surviving letter from Chatterton's pen was sent to Dodsley on 21 December 1768, informing the bookseller that, 'I can procure

Copys of several ancient Poems; and an Interlude, perhaps the oldest dramatic Piece extant; wrote by one Rowley, a Priest in Bristol ...'.[9] Less than two months later, Chatterton again wrote to Dodsley, though this time his epistle is pathetically ingenuous:

> Having intelligence that the Tragedy of Ælle [*sic*], was in being, after a long and laborious Search, I was so happy as to attain a Sight of it.... I have endeavoured to obtain a Copy ... but the Present Possessor absolutely denies, to give me one, unless I give him a Guinea for a Consideration. As I am unable to procure such a sum ... I have made bold to apply to you.... was I able, I would print it on my own Risque. It is a perfect Tragedy, the Plot, clear, the Language, spirited, and the Songs interspersd in it ... Elegantly Simple.... the Motive that actuates me to do this, is, to convince the World that the Monks ... were not such Blockheads....
>
> P.S. My reason for concealing my Name, was, lest my Master (who is now out of Town) should see my Letters and think I neglected his Business....[10]

For all his apparent self-assurance and prodigious gifts, Chatterton sometimes could not avoid acting like the 16-year-old adolescent that he was. Whatever prospects Chatterton may have had with the bookseller, they almost certainly vanished upon Dodsley's receipt of this hopelessly artless and ill-conceived letter.

Why was Dodsley apparently the only London bookseller Chatterton approached from Bristol about publishing any of his substantial Rowley forgeries? Most obviously, Chatterton set his sights on Dodsley because Percy's *Reliques of Ancient English Poetry* – a work essential to the Rowley forgeries – was issued from Tully's Head in 1765. Yet Chatterton's knowledge of the Dodsleys' publications went far beyond Percy's *Reliques* and included Robert Dodsley's *Collection of Poems* (1758), *Select Collection of Old Plays* (1744 [1746]), and *The Oeconomy of Human Life* (1750).[11] Because of his antiquarian researches, Chatterton would have encountered the Dodsleys as publishers at almost every turn. In addition to the three-volume *Reliques*, a work that went into its second edition in 1767, Percy's *Five Pieces of Runic Poetry* (1763) and Evan Evans's *Some Specimens of the Poetry of the Ancient Welsh Bards* (1764) almost certainly came into Chatterton's purview. Among other important antiquarian texts from Tully's Head were *England Illustrated, or, A Compendium of the Natural*

History, Geography, Topography, and Antiquities Ecclesiastical and Civil, of England and Wales (1764), Alexander Thomson's *Letters on the British Museum* (1767), and Horace Walpole's *Historic Doubts on the Life and Reign of King Richard the Third* (1768). This last work would have been of particular interest to Chatterton, not only because of Walpole's status as an antiquary, but also because Rowley was supposed to have lived in the reigns of Henry IV and Edward IV, the kings who immediately preceded Richard III. As a forger, Chatterton would have also noticed that Robert Dodsley published *Hardyknute: A Fragment. Being the First Canto of an Epick Poem* (1740), a well-known forgery of ancient Scottish verse that was first printed in 1719.

On the evidence of a whole host of publications, then, Chatterton would have been well aware of the Dodsleys' reputation for popularizing antiquarian poetry and works of related interest. He most probably knew, too, that Robert Dodsley had himself been a footman in livery who rose from modest beginnings through the publication of a volume of his own poems, and he almost certainly would have found reason for hope in the reputation of Tully's Head for assisting similarly disadvantaged poets. James Dodsley's obvious importance to the aspiring author may be measured by the fact that, of the four booksellers Chatterton visited on first coming to London, only Dodsley had not published a single work of Chatterton's. Ironically, he would not appear in a Tully's Head publication until after his death, when some of his pieces were reprinted in the *Annual Register*.

Chatterton on the make

Five weeks after his arrival in London, Chatterton wrote to his sister from 'Tom's Coffee-house':

> There is such a noise of business and politicks, in the room, that my inaccuracy in writing here, is highly excusable. My present profession obliges me to frequent places of the best resort.... I employ my money now in ... getting onto good company; this last article always brings me in interest. But I have engaged to live with a gentleman ... who is going to advance pretty deeply into the bookselling branches.... My employment will be writing a voluminous history of London, to appear in numbers the beginning of next winter ... this will not, like writing political essays, oblige me to go to the Coffee-house....
>
> [He has met the Lord Mayor on the occasion of his] remon-

strating and addressing the King.... But the devil of the matter is, there's no money to be got of this side the question. Interest is of the other side. But he is a poor author, who cannot write on both sides. I believe I may be introduced ... to a ruling power in the court party. I might have a recommendation to ... an East India Director....

Essay writing has this advantage, you are sure of constant pay; and when you have wrote a piece, which makes the author enquired after, you may bring the booksellers to your own terms. Essays on the patriotic side, fetch no more than what the copy is sold for....[12]

Even allowing for Chatterton's egotism and his desire to impress 'the folks back home', this letter tells us that Chatterton was sedulously networking, that he was constantly on the make for connections and for possible publishing outlets. He writes from Tom's in Cornhill – which Bryant Lillywhite describes as 'an extremely busy, important, and well-patronized commercial coffee-house' – a place he frequents because of the 'interest' or profitable contacts he makes there.[13] Intriguingly, Johnson's *Dictionary* defines 'interest' not only as 'advantage' and 'regard to private profit', but also as a 'share; part in any thing'.

Chatterton's biographer E. H. W. Meyerstein wrongly dismisses Chatterton's news that he is engaged to work on a history of London: 'The history of England has turned into this. J. Noorthouck, who published *A New History of London* (1773), denied having seen Chatterton.'[14] Meyerstein's incredulity is understandable but misguided: Noorthouck's *New History of London* was supposed to have been printed in monthly numbers, but was published more than two years after Chatterton said his work was to appear.[15] In fact, there is a history of London that exactly conforms to Chatterton's description: a unique copy of a publisher's advertisement, now in the Public Record Office, reveals that the 'voluminous history of London, to appear in numbers the beginning of next winter' is no chimera:

On Saturday, February 23rd, 1771, will be published, price six-pence, Number I. To be continued weekly, or may be had complete, in two volumes folio,... *The History and Survey of London, Westminster, Southwark, and their Environs....* By William Maitland, ... Improved with a great variety of authentic Pieces,... and continued down to 1771, by the Rev. John Entick....[16]

The History of London from Its Foundation by the Romans to the Present Time (1772), by the antiquary and topographer William Maitland (1693?–1757), was first published in 1739. It grew to two folio volumes in 1756, reached a third edition in 1760, and in 1769 was printed 'by subscription, in weekly numbers'.[17] The market for the old work now being saturated, but still wishing to capitalize upon a best-selling title, the booksellers commissioned the schoolmaster and miscellaneous author John Entick (1703?–73) to produce a revised and substantially expanded edition of Maitland's *History*. Entick, a man of only moderate learning who styled himself 'Rev.' and 'M.A.', though there is no evidence that he was ever ordained nor that any university ever awarded him a degree, routinely worked as a bookseller's fac-totum, especially for Charles and Edward Dilly.

The *DNB* describes Entick's edition of Maitland's *History* as 'consid-erably enlarged', yet we also know that while he was editing the *History* he was also producing his *New Latin and English Dictionary* (1771), and was writing *The Present State of the British Empire* (1774), a work published in four octavo volumes in the year after his death. At the time of Chatterton's appearance in London, John Entick was a 67-year-old schoolmaster of limited abilities who was occupied with several substantial booksellers' projects. Maitland's *History* was a proven best-seller, but required significant improvements in order to continue turning a profit.[18] Chatterton was surprisingly knowledge-able, enthusiastic, ambitious, energetic, and – being young – able to be hired for modest wages.

Though we can never be certain, it seems altogether reasonable to surmise that the project Chatterton mentioned to his sister entailed being a researcher and ghost writer for the ageing and overburdened Entick. Chatterton told his sister that his 'employment' would take him to 'Oxford, Cambridge, Lincoln, Coventry, and every Collegiate Church near', yet he also described the history as 'voluminous' and ready for publication in seven or eight months ('the beginning of next winter').[19] It makes sense, then, that Chatterton had been commis-sioned by the booksellers (or was at least was negotiating with them) to check, revise, augment, and bring up to date Maitland's *History*. The prospectus for Entick's edition was issued months after Chatterton's letter, though his description closely matches the work described there, a work that began to appear six months after his death. Was Chatterton's knowledge of this nascent publishing project merely hearsay that he had picked up in coffee-houses, or was it, as his letter indicates, the result of his future 'employment'?

More generally, the particulars of Chatterton's letter – his frequenting Tom's and other 'places of the best resort', his encounter with the Lord Mayor, his anticipating an introduction to a member of the Court party after having established important connections with the Patriots, his seeking a link with an East India director, his intended arrangement with 'a gentleman ... who is going to advance pretty deeply into the bookselling branches', and his talk of bargaining with the booksellers – all suggest at the very least that the young author well understood that his rise in the world of letters depended upon securing political and publishing patronage.[20] Everything we know of Chatterton's personal history suggests that we may read in this letter a fair indication of his almost relentless quest for the contacts and patronage that would lead to his success. We see this behaviour in his Bristol correspondence with Dodsley, Walpole, and the editors of the *Town and Country*, *Freeholder's*, and *Middlesex*; we see this behaviour in his first days after arriving in London.

In one of his earliest letters home, Chatterton boasted that he had lost no time in networking with the booksellers:

I am quite familiar at the Chapter Coffee-house, and know all the geniuses there. A character is now unnecessary; an author carries his character in his pen.... The poverty of authors is a common observation, but not always a true one. No author can be poor who understands the arts of booksellers – Without this necessary knowledge, the greatest genius may starve; and, with it, the greatest dunce live in splendor. This knowledge I have pretty well dipped into.[21]

The rising author's new-found refuge was on Paul's Alley and Paternoster Row in the precincts of St Paul's Churchyard. Being in the heart of London's most dense concentration of booksellers' shops, the Chapter Coffee-house, more than any other public place, was the frequent resort of many members of the London book trade.[22] Though he had been in London for only 12 days, the Bristol lad had conned his lessons well – the money he spent at the Chapter was an investment to further his education into the world of London publishing; his presence among the bookmen could lead to a useful contact, perhaps a commission to work on a history of London, or, ideally, the publication of one or more books filled with his antiquarian writings and Rowley poems.

Chatterton's purchase on the London publishing world is evident in his satirical poem 'The Art of Puffing by a Bookseller's Journeyman', a work he wrote in July 1770, after having been in London for some three months. Since the persona of the poem purports to be an insider in the book trade revealing to the public how books are fraudulently promoted for sale, much of the poem's success depends upon Chatterton's ability to exploit his knowledge of the trade in an off-hand and cynical fashion. In the course of 38 lines, Chatterton refers to no fewer than seven London booksellers, two periodicals, two successful recent books, two legal cases involving government censorship of the press, the latest literary trends, the booksellers' practices of selling patent medicines and sensationalist criminal biographies, the motives behind political and literary essays, book illustration, binding, and type sizes – all with a *sprezzatura* that makes it clear that in the world of bookselling, as in so much else, Chatterton was a quick study.[23]

With typical single-mindedness, Chatterton wanted to use whatever he could to make the connections necessary to realize his dream of being a successful (i.e. financially independent and renowned) author. In his letter to his sister, he even explained that he was learning to dress for success: 'I employ my money now in fitting myself fashionably; and getting into good company'.[24] If it is impossible, from this distant vantage, to know which booksellers Chatterton would have visited at their shops or attempted to impress at the Chapter or Tom's, we may very reasonably assume that the networking lad fresh from home would have sought to exploit whatever connections he could summon from Bristol.

The Bristol–London connection

What Chatterton wanted, above all else, was to publish his Rowley poems and other antiquarian forgeries as a book with a major London bookseller. Evidence from his notebooks and correspondence indicates that Chatterton had for some time been editing his writings and seeking out proper connections for publishing one or more books.[25] But James Dodsley had failed him; his exchanges with Horace Walpole had led to nothing. The periodical publishers he associated with were publishing neither antiquarian nor literary books. Soon after Chatterton had arrived in London, it must have been clear that the connections he had made through his correspondence from Bristol with Messrs. Edmunds, Fell, Hamilton, and Dodsley, no matter how useful in some cases for enabling him to sustain a living by periodical contributions, would be of no help to him in obtaining the great breakthrough he most desired. Ever the overreacher and convinced of his own genius, Chatterton wanted to publish his masterpiece. Patience was not one of the young man's virtues. He needed to establish some contacts.

Although we cannot be certain whom he may have solicited at the Chapter, Tom's, or various bookshops, it seems obvious that Chatterton, a tireless opportunist almost constantly in search of a new 'patron', would have attempted to exploit his Bristol connection. His associations with Bristol booksellers, his correspondence with members of the London book trade, and the patronage he received from Alexander Catcott would quite naturally have led him to three important bookselling contacts in London. Because Chatterton's resourcefulness and cockiness were exceeded only by his ambition, it is difficult to imagine the aspiring author not trying to capitalize upon these London links to his native Bristol. The three London booksellers with the most obvious Bristol links were all publishers whose lists were highly suitable for Chatterton's purposes; any of the three might have agreed to publish the Rowley poems.

Perhaps the most prominent London bookseller with strong Bristol connections was Thomas Longman (1730–97) [hereafter, Thomas II], nephew of Thomas Longman (1699–1755) [Thomas I]. The Longman ancestors had been prosperous Bristol citizens, making their fortune in the soap manufacturing business and being related by marriage to two mayors of Bristol.[26] In 1719, while still serving his apprenticeship, Thomas the elder came into his majority and inherited his father's property, including a family estate at Winford, near Bristol. Thomas's half-brother Ezekiel (1684–1738), an immensely wealthy linen merchant, served as a Bristol councillor and sheriff. Thomas II was apprenticed in 1745 and, having been freed from his indenture in 1752, immediately became the business partner of his uncle.

In the 1760s, Longman's list included many of the most notable authors of the Restoration and eighteenth century: John Milton, Sir John Vanbrugh, William Wycherley, Thomas Otway, John Gay, Alexander Pope, Jonathan Swift, Colley Cibber, Daniel Defoe, Henry Fielding, Voltaire, and Samuel Johnson – writers whose fame would certainly have attracted Chatterton's notice. In addition, several of Longman's publications would have appealed to Chatterton's antiquarian interests, perhaps most especially *The Extinct Peerage of England: Containing a Succinct Account of all the Peers whose Titles are Expired: ... from the Conquest to the Year 1769* (1769). Would

Chatterton have failed to notice that Longman published Stephen Duck's *Poems on Several Occasions* (1753, 1764),[27] or that Longman and Dodsley were on the imprint of the anonymous *Poems on Several Occasions* (1769)? This last publication may have been particularly encouraging to the aspiring writer, since it carried the auspicious note in the 'Advertisement' that most of the poems in the volume were written when the author, one Thomas Moss (1738–1808), was about 20 years of age.

It seems that the Longman family maintained its Bristol connections throughout its London years; in November 1764 John Palmer, the son of a Bristol bookseller of the same name, was apprenticed to Thomas II.[28] The apprentice's father had been a member of the Bristol book trade since 1748 and remained in business until 1777. Throughout Chatterton's youth and adolescence Palmer the elder was one of the more productive publishers in Bristol. Although we have no record of their meeting, it seems most unlikely that the aggressive and enterprising Chatterton would not have attempted to make contact with Longman, either through John Palmer the elder in Bristol, or simply on his own.

An even closer Bristol–London bookselling association was available to Chatterton in the Cadell family. In 1739 Thomas Cadell, whose father was a Bristol linen-draper, began business as a bookseller in Wine Street, Bristol.[29] He remained in business until 1775.[30] His nephew, Thomas Cadell II (1742–1802), sometimes confusingly known as Cadell the elder, was born in Wine Street in 1742 and bound to the great London bookseller Andrew Millar in 1758. When Cadell completed his apprenticeship in 1765, Millar took him on as his business partner, almost certainly with a view to his retirement two years later. Such was Millar's prominence that many of Cadell's 1767 and 1768 imprints read 'T. Cadell, successor to A. Millar'.

In 1767 when Millar retired, Thomas Cadell II, whose uncle was working in Bristol as the leading bookseller of that city, owned one of the most distinguished publication lists in the capital. In the years 1767–69, Cadell published *Joseph Andrews, Tom Jones, Peregrine Pickle*, Sterne's *Sermons, The Seasons*, Young's *Night-thoughts*, William Robertson's *History of Scotland*, Elizabeth Montagu's *Essay on the Writings and Genius of Shakespear*, and a revised edition of Hume's *History of England*. Cadell was also the publisher of Sir William Fordyce's *A Review of the Venereal Disease, and its Remedies* (1767), which Chatterton may have used in treating his own infection.[31]

Cadell and Dodsley were also on the imprint of two works that must have been of special interest to the young antiquary: *Proposals for Printing a Dictionary, Anglo-Saxon and English. A Work Never Before Attempted* (1767; the *Dictionarium Saxonico et Gothico-Latinum* was published in 1772), and James Kennedy's *A Description of the Antiquities and Curiosities in Wilton-House* (1769). Given that Cadell II had an uncle who was one of the most important and active members of the Bristol book trade, was himself a Bristol native just ten years Chatterton's senior, and was publishing works whose reputation and subject matter would have quite naturally attracted the notice of the young author, it seems almost impossible to believe that Chatterton would not have tried to make use of this publishing connection.

Another association that Chatterton may have attempted to exploit was the London bookseller Benjamin White, who was the sole London seller for the second edition of Alexander Catcott's *Treatise on the Deluge* (1768). As much as Chatterton wished to establish his independence from his Bristol mentor and patron, he might well have attempted to capitalize upon his long-standing relationship with Catcott by approaching White. In a letter of 14 May 1770 to Sarah Chatterton, Thomas made a special request of his mother: 'My box shall be attended to; I hope my books are in it – if not, send them; and particularly Catcott's Hutchinsonian jargon on the Deluge, and the larger M. S. Glossary ...'.[32] This is typical Chatterton: he denigrates Catcott's work even as he is obviously quite anxious to have it with him in London. Although it is easy to see that Chatterton would need his own 'M. S. Glossary' for his own writing, why would he have asked his mother to send Catcott's volume when it had no discernible connection with any of his own work?

Could it be that Chatterton wanted to have his own copy of Catcott's *Treatise* with him in London, not because of its contents, but rather because he could present to White his mentor's inscription as evidence of Catcott's patronage and high regard? Although White's publication list throughout the 1760s consisted mostly of biblical commentaries and paraphrases, sermons, and controversial theology, he also published two titles relating to Horace Walpole, whom Chatterton sought out as an ally and, when rebuffed, saw as an enemy: *An Answer to Mr. Horace Walpole's Late Work, Entitled, Historic Doubts on the Reign and Life of King Richard the Third; or An Attempt to Confute Him from His Own Arguments* (1768) and *A Letter to the Honourable Mr. Horace Walpole, Concerning the Dispute between Mr.*

Hume and Mr. Rousseau (1767).[33] In addition, White was one of several publishers of *The History and Antiquities of the County of Essex* (vol. i, 1766; vol. ii, 1768), and *The History and Antiquities of the Most Ancient Town and Borough of Colchester* (1768). White's links to antiquarian studies and his connection with Catcott would have made him an obvious choice for Chatterton's publishing proposals.

Of course, Chatterton could not have attempted to capitalize upon these relationships if he were not aware of them. He would presumably have learned about Benjamin White directly from Catcott, or, at the very least, from the title-page of Catcott's book. The Cadell connection between uncle and nephew would have been apparent from reading newspaper advertisements, if he had not already been informed about the 'Bristol-boy made good' by the proprietors of the Bristol bookshops he habitually frequented – the establishments of Messrs. Long, Shiercliff, Green, and Goodall.[34] Similarly, the Longman association, though in some ways the least obvious of the three, could have come to Chatterton's attention through John Palmer's apprenticeship. If Palmer were 14 when he was bound as an apprentice in 1764, then he would have been just two years older than Chatterton.[35] It is easy to imagine Palmer the elder's boasting to anyone who would listen about his son's great future as a London bookseller. Yet, because Chatterton appears to have moved in a very limited circle in Bristol, due in no small measure to his age, class, and education, it is perhaps safest to assume that Chatterton's publishing contacts in London – with Edmunds, Fell, Hamilton, and Dodsley, and possibly with Longman, Cadell, and White – were largely the result of his surprisingly far-reaching knowledge of the book trade.

Chatterton's familiarity with 'the arts of booksellers' was remarkably extensive before he left Bristol, and became even more comprehensive during the four months he lived in London. Applying the 'necessary knowledge' so vital to his success, Chatterton assiduously cultivated the patrons and booksellers who could help him to realize his ambitions. Had he lived, he might easily have become a successful 'miscellaneous writer' with a secure financial future. His intelligence, energy, and antiquarian interests would, in time, have won him commissions from booksellers, as the intriguing prospect of his employment in Entick's edition of Maitland's *History* suggests. It seems, however, that Chatterton's education, inventiveness, and temperament would not have suited him well to remain in such an occupation for very long.

Instead, we may infer from his publications in the *Freeholder's Magazine* and *Middlesex Journal*, and from the trajectory of his brief career, that Chatterton's ambition, fluency, imitative gifts, sheer pluck, and readiness to sell his services to the highest bidder made him a promising candidate for patronage as a party political writer. Had he lived, he might well have become the successor to the masterful satirist Charles Churchill (1732–64), whose work the young author had already begun to imitate. If Chatterton's only aim had been to make a decent living from his pen, then he might have already counted himself a modest success and been reasonably sanguine about his future prospects. Chatterton wanted something more than employment as an editorial factotum or political satirist, however. His principal ambition was to publish Rowley, and for this he needed to find a bookseller willing to take a significant capital risk. Publishing an author's book was a different kind of investment in his talent from printing his work in a periodical. Chatterton's knowledge of the book trade must have told him so.

Notes

1. On Bristol, see Barry, Jonathan, 'The Press and the Politics of Culture in Bristol 1660–1775', in Jeremy Black and Jeremy Gregory (eds), *Culture, Politics and Society in Britain, 1660–1800* (Manchester, 1991), 49–81; see also Barry's D.Phil. thesis, 'The Cultural Life of Bristol, 1640–1775' (Oxford University, 1985).
2. To Sarah Chatterton, 26 Apr. 1770 (*Works*, 511).
3. Ibid. 1069–70.
4. Ibid. 776.
5. Chatterton's concern about saturating a single market is not a plausible explanation for the hiatus in his relationship with the *Middlesex Journal*; from February 1769 to January 1770 he placed 21 pieces in the *Town and Country Magazine*. For a calendar and analysis of the works Chatterton published in his own lifetime, see Appendix I.
6. To Sarah Chatterton *et al.*, 6 May 1770 (*Works*, 560–3).
7. While it is impossible to know for certain what Chatterton had in mind, the appearance of part of 'The Resignation' does not seem to be a sufficient explanation for the tenor of his letter; *pace Life*, 362.
8. Taylor, Donald S., 'Chatterton's Suicide', *PQ* 31 (1952), 63–9, 'one can see [from Chatterton's memorandum book] that [he] was doing well by himself during the four months in London. The documented sum alone refutes any notion that Chatterton's payments from the periodicals were small enough to drive him to suicide' (69).
9. *Works*, 157.
10. Ibid. 171–2.

11. Ibid., 339; *Life*, 192n; and Chatterton's copy of the 1765 Dublin edition in the Bristol Public Library.

12. To Mary Chatterton, 30 May 1770 (*Works*, 587–9).

13. Lillywhite, Bryant, *London Coffee Houses* (London, 1963), 583; 'it is highly probable that Tom's, Birchin Lane [which Taylor proposes as Chatterton's location] ceased to exist after the fire in 1748' (581).

14. *Life*, 371n.

15. See *Proposals for Printing in one large Volume, quarto, (to be published in monthly Numbers) A New History of London.... By John Noorthouck* [London, 1772]. The only known surviving copy of this proposal is in the Cambridge University Library: 7850.c.54/1. None of the copies of Noorthouck's *New History* I have examined reveals evidence of publication in numbers; the work was published in quarto in April 1773.

16. PRO: CO.5/38 [20] [London, 1771].

17. *Proposals for Printing by Subscription, in weekly Numbers.... The History and Survey of London ...* [London, 1769]. The only known surviving copy of this proposal is in the Bodleian Library: Gough Lond 265(6a). In 1756, Maitland's *History* was issued both under the 1739 title and as *The History and Survey of London, Westminster, Southwark, and their Environs*; the 1769 edition is therefore called 'The Third Edition', though it is actually the fourth. The imprint of the 1772 edition reads, 'London: Printed for J. Wilkie; T. Lowndes; G. Kearsley; and S. Bladon, 1772'.

18. The title-page of the 1772 edition claimed that Maitland's work had been 'Improved with a great Variety of *Authentick Pieces* ... Wherein all the Defects in the former Edition of this Work, and in other Authors ... are supplied, their Errors corrected, and the History brought down ... to the present Time.'

19. *Works*, 587.

20. On the need for patronage in this period, see Griffin, Dustin, *Literary Patronage in England, 1650–1800* (Cambridge, 1997).

21. To Sarah Chatterton *et al.*, 6 May 1770 (*Works*, 560–1).

22. See West, William, *Tavern Anecdotes ... and Reminiscences, connected with Taverns, Coffee Houses, Clubs, &c.* (London, 1825), 119–20; Wheatley, Henry B., *London Past and Present: Its History, Associations, and Traditions* (London, 1891) i. 350; and Lillywhite, 151–3.

23. *Works*, 650–1. A further example of Chatterton's extensive knowledge of the book trade may be found in his Astrea Brokage letter (ibid. 431).

24. Ibid. 587.

25. See Haywood, Ian, 'Chatterton's Plans for the Publication of the Forgery', *RES* 36 (1985), 58–68, reprinted in Haywood's *The Making of History* (London, 1986), 175–84.

26. Information on the Longman family is taken from Philip Wallis, *At the Sign of the Ship: Notes on the House of Longman, 1724–1974* (printed for private circulation, Harlow, 1974), 7–16; the *DNB*; and Turner, Michael L. and D. F. McKenzie, *The London Booktrades* (a privately circulated computer database).

27. John Rivington and L. Hawes also appear on both imprints for the third (1753) and fourth (1764) editions of Duck's *Poems on Several Occasions*.

28. For further evidence supporting the possibility of the Longman family's

continued contact with Bristol, see Wallis, 14–16.

29. Plomer, H. R., *A Dictionary of the Printers and Booksellers ... 1726 to 1775* (Oxford, 1932), 41.

30. Information on the Cadell family is taken from *The Publishing Firm of Cadell & Davies: Select Correspondence and Accounts, 1793–1836*, ed. and intro. Theodore Besterman (Oxford, 1938), viii; the *DNB*; and Turner and McKenzie.

31. On the theory that Chatterton did not commit suicide, but mistakenly poisoned himself while treating his disease, see Holmes, Richard, 'Thomas Chatterton: The Case Re-opened', *Cornhill Magazine* 178 (1970), 243–9.

32. To Sarah Chatterton, 14 May 1770 (*Works*, 571). For Catcott's *Deluge*, see Carolyn Williams, above.

33. Chatterton first wrote to Walpole on 25 March 1769; by the end of July their falling-out was complete; see *Life*, 250–84.

34. Ibid. 46–8.

35. Because Palmer's father, John, was a member of the trade, John Palmer was eligible to be freed from his indenture at 21 (rather than 24), and thus might well have begun his seven-year apprenticeship at the age of 14.

Appendix I: Works by Chatterton Published in His Own Lifetime[1]

1. 'Bridge Narrative', *Felix Farley's Bristol Journal* 1 Oct. 1768 [56, 843].
2. 'On Mr. Broderip's Excellent Performance on the Organ', *Bristol Journal* 28 Jan. 1769 [168, 919].
3. 'On Mr. Alcock of Bristol, an Excellent Miniature Painter', *TCM* 1 (Feb. 1769) 104 [169, 919].
4. 'Saxon Tinctures', *TCM* 1 (Feb. 1769) 100 [171, 921].
5. 'The Court Mantle', *TCM* 1 (Mar. 1769) 136 [252, 949].
6. 'Ethelgar. A Saxon Poem', *TCM* 1 (Mar. 1769) 144 [253, 949].
7. 'Elegy I', *TCM* 1 (Apr. 1769) 217 [270, 961].
8. 'Kenrick', *TCM* 1 (Apr. 1769) 174 [274, 964].
9. 'Saxon Atchievements', *TCM* 1 (May 1769) 244 [275, 964].
10. 'Cerdick', *TCM* 1 (May 1769) 233 [276, 965].
11. 'Elinoure and Juga', *TCM* 1 (May 1769) 273 [291, 970].
12. 'To Mr. Holland', *TCM* 1 (July 1769) 385 [339, 985].
13. 'Godred Crovan', *TCM* 1 (Aug. 1769) 425 [345, 988].
14. 'Elegy II', *TCM* 1 (Nov. 1769) 607 [400, 1009].
15. 'The Hirlas I', *TCM* 1 (Nov. 1769) 547 [401, 1009].
16. 'The Complaint', *Universal Magazine* 47 (Nov. 1769) 265 [408, 1013].
17. 'Antiquity of Christmas Games', *TCM* 1 (Dec. 1769) 623 [409, 1014].
18. 'The Copernican System', *TCM* 1 (Dec. 1769) 666 [419, 1020].
19. 'Elegy to the Memory of Mr. Thomas Phillips, of Fairford', *TCM* 1 (Suppl. 1769) 711 [383, 1003].
20. 'The Advice', *TCM* 1 (Suppl. 1769) 713 [427, 1024].
21. 'The Hirlas II', *TCM* 1 (Suppl. 1769) 683 [428, 1024].
22. 'Astrea Brokage Letter', *TCM* 2 (Jan. 1770) 31 [431, 1025].
23. 'The Consuliad', *Freeholder's Magazine* 2 (Jan. 1770) 273 [436, 1029].
24. 'Anecdote of Chaucer', *TCM* 2 (Jan. 1770) 16 [442, 1034].
25. 'The Unfortunate Fathers', *TCM* 2 (Jan. 1770) 32 [443, 1035].
26. 'Heccar and Gaira. An African Eclogue', *Court and City Magazine* 1 (Feb. 1770) 86 [432, 1026].
27. 'February. An Elegy', *TCM* 2 (Feb. 1770) 103 [447, 1037].

28. 'Decimus. To the Duke of G—n', *Middlesex Journal* 24 Feb. 1770 [450, 1038].
29. 'Resignation. A Poem', *Freeholder's Magazine* 2 (Apr., May 1770) 105, 162 [468, 1046].
30. 'Decimus. To the Princess of Gotham', *Middlesex Journal* 17 Apr. 1770 [505, 1062].
31. 'The Hag', *Middlesex Journal* 26 Apr. 1770 [498, 1058].
32. 'The Candidates', *Middlesex Journal* 1 May 1770 [511, 1065].
33. 'Narva and Mored. An African Eclogue', *London Magazine* 39 (May 1770) 268 [543, 1078].
34. 'Decimus. To the Earl of H—h', *Middlesex Journal* 10 May 1770 [564, 1085].
35. 'Decimus. To the P— D— of W—', *Middlesex Journal* 15 May 1770 [566, 1086].
36. 'To the Society at Spring Garden', *Middlesex Journal* 19 May 1770 [563, 1085].
37. 'Decimus. To the Prime Minister', *Middlesex Journal* 22 May 1770 [573, 1089].
38. 'Libertas. A Card. To Old Slyboots', *Middlesex Journal* 22 May 1770 [575, 1090].
39. 'Probus to the Lord Mayor', *Middlesex Journal* 25 May 1770 and *Political Register* 6 (June 1770) 328 [579, 1093].
40. 'Decimus. An Exhibition of Sign Paintings', *Middlesex Journal* 26 May 1770 [576, 1091].
41. 'Elegy III', *TCM* 2 (May 1770) 270 [583, 1094].
42. 'Decimus. To the Freeholders of the City of Bristol', *Middlesex Journal* 31 May 1770 [585, 1095].
43. 'A Song. Addressed to Miss C—am of Bristol', *Court and City Magazine* 1 (June 1770) 280 [559, 1082].
44. 'The Death of Nicou, an African Eclogue', *London Magazine* 39 (June 1770) 320 [590, 1097].
45. 'Letter VI from A Hunter of Oddities', *TCM* 2 (June 1770) 312 [593, 1099].
46. 'Maria Friendless Letter', *TCM* 2 (June 1770) 287 [594, 1100].
47. 'Exhibition of Sign Paintings, at the West End of the Town', *Boddeley's Bath Journal* 18 June 1770 [597, 1102].
48. 'Speech of Sir John de Beauchamp', *TCM* 2 (June 1770) 312 [600, 1104].
49. 'The False Step, a Real History', *TCM* 2 (June 1770) 317 (misnumbered 315) and *Oxford Magazine* 5 (July 1770) 12 [600, 1104].
50. 'To Miss B—sh, of Bristol', *TCM* 2 (June 1770) 327 [605, 1105].

51. 'Memoirs of a Sad Dog', *TCM* 2 (July, Aug. 1770) 374, 431 [651, 1118].
52. 'An African Song', *Court and City Magazine* 1 (July 1770) 326 [662, 1122].
53. 'Menenius. To William Lord M—d', *Middlesex Journal* 16 Aug. 1770 [663, 1123].²

Notes

1. This list is compiled from the tabular notes to the 400+ titles in Donald S. Taylor's *Complete Works of Thomas Chatterton*. While Taylor presents Chatterton's writings in chronological order by date of composition, I have elected to generate a chronology by date of publication. Works appearing in any given month without a day of publication are organized in chronological order by date of composition. Numbers in brackets [ ] at the end of each entry refer to pages for text and notes, respectively, in Taylor's edition.
2. Chatterton died on 25 August 1770. In September, his Ossianic poem 'Gortmund' appeared in the *Town and Country Magazine* 2 (Sept. 1770), 486.

Appendix II: An Analysis of Chatterton's Publications

Total Titles: 53.
Total Publications: 55, including 2 reprinted titles (see Appendix I, nos. 39 and 49).
Total Journals: 11
Publications by Journal: *Town and Country Magazine*: 29,[1] *Middlesex Journal*: 13, *Court and City Magazine*: 3, *Freeholder's Magazine*: 2, *London Magazine*: 2, *Felix Farley's Bristol Journal*: 1, *Bristol Journal*: 1, *Universal Magazine*: 1, *Boddeley's Bath Journal*: 1, *Political Register*: 1, and *Oxford Magazine*: 1.

Pre-London Publications: 31 titles.[2]
Pre-London Journals: 7.
Pre-London Publications by Journal: *Town and Country Magazine*: 22, *Middlesex Journal*: 3, *Freeholder's Magazine*: 2, *Felix Farley's Bristol Journal*: 1, *Bristol Journal*: 1, *Court and City Magazine*: 1, and *Universal Magazine*: 1.

London Titles: 22.
London Publications: 24.
London Journals: 7.
London Publications by Journal: *Middlesex Journal*: 10, *Town and Country Magazine*: 7, *Court and City Magazine*: 2, *London Magazine*: 2, *Boddeley's Bath Journal*: 1, *Political Register*: 1, and *Oxford Magazine*: 1.

Pre-London Journals with No Publications in London Period: *Felix Farley's Bristol Journal*: 1, *Bristol Journal*: 1, *Freeholder's Magazine*: 2, and *Universal Magazine*: 1.

Pre-London Journals Publishing Titles from London Period: *Middlesex Journal*: 10, *Town and Country Magazine*: 7, and *Court and City Magazine*: 2. Thus, 19 of 24, or 79%, of Chatterton's publications while in London came from contacts he had established while in Bristol.

New Journals from London Period: *London Magazine*: 2, *Boddeley's Bath Journal*: 1, *Political Register*: 1, and *Oxford Magazine*: 1.

Journals Reprinting Previously Published Titles: *Political Register*: 1, and *Oxford Magazine*: 1.

Notes

1. When Taylor (*Works*, xlv) mentions in passing that Chatterton had published 32 works in the *Town and Country*, he must be counting three titles printed after Chatterton's death: 'Gortmund' (see preceding note), 'Genuine Copy of a Letter from the Earl of C—d to the Hon. Mr. C—' *TCM* 3 (Suppl. 1771) 696 [642, 1113], and 'The Happy Pair. A Tale' *TCM* 3 (Suppl. 1771) 689 [672, 1127].
2. The term 'pre-London' refers to the period before Chatterton came to London *c.* 25 April 1770. I have included 'The Hag' in this category even though it appeared in the *Middlesex Journal* on 26 April 1770, since the poem was sent from Bristol and, thus, is not indicative of Chatterton's efforts while in London.

II

The Rowley Controversy and After

Chapter 8

Chatterton and the Club

Pat Rogers

When Thomas Chatterton flashed across the sky like a new comet, the Club was ready for him. His appearance presaged the arrival of a Romantic culture which was to subvert many eighteenth-century norms. Yet the members of the Literary Club ('Johnson's Club' or 'the Turk's Head Club') were in various ways prepared and intellectually equipped to enter the fray, as the affair spread from antiquarian and historical concerns to broader literary and cultural issues. At least ten individuals who had been elected to the Club by the time of Johnson's death in 1784 might plausibly have made some contribution to the debate. Their qualifications ranged from localized skills in editing and interpreting older English poetry, along with philological skills grounded in a thorough classical training, down to forensic talents which had been applied to a number of cognate enquiries.

In the event, only a few of the Club's qualified members chose to express their views on Chatterton – or at least, only a few have left any surviving testimony to their interest. These include Johnson, Goldsmith, Lord Charlemont, George Steevens, Thomas Warton, and Malone. Conspicuously absent, as far as public pronouncements go, is the name of Thomas Percy, who pointedly refrained from active involvement in the war of words over Rowley. It should be added that some other literary figures who did take an active role were close allies or associates of Club members. These included Michael Lort, once proposed for the society, but blackballed[1], and John Nichols, who was immediately elected to the Essex Head Club, an organization founded by Johnson and containing a measure of overlap in membership with the more famous Club.

Here, I shall try to give some sense of the impact of the Chatterton affair on the Club, and reciprocally of the group's impact on the debate. The earlier part of the discussion will be devoted to the involvement of particular Clubmen in the affair. This will mean rehearsing some material familiar to all students of Chatterton, but it will be placed in a slightly different light from that thrown by the usual approaches. Samuel Johnson himself will be treated as briefly as the case permits. Elsewhere in this volume, Paul Baines describes the background to Johnson's short interventions in the controversy – most notably, his history as an exposer of previous forgeries. Equally, it is not necessary to discuss at length the involvement, such as it was, of Thomas Percy, since Nick Groom devotes an essay to this topic in the present book. I shall consider the two instances of Johnson and Percy insofar as this is needed for an understanding of the broader Club attitude towards the Chatterton phenomenon.

In the final part of the discussion, an attempt is made to address a somewhat broader and more speculative range of issues. I shall try to narrow down the ideological space contested during the debate, as it helps to define the intellectual position of the Club within British culture of the age. It is clear that the Club had no unified programme or agenda. Moreover, as already suggested, its members were led by diverse paths to their confrontation with Chatterton. Some were professional scholars, others editors and collectors, others literary historians, others journalists and compilers, others merely (if the adverb is allowable) learned students of books and humane culture. No comparable body of trained readers existed in England in the 1770s and 1780s, and even Edinburgh would have struggled to provide a close-knit society with such a dense agglomeration of relevant talent. Since the Club never operated fully in concert, we would be unwise to look for a coherent response. What we may be able to detect are a distinctive flavour and a particular kind of mentality at work. The members who participated were all, by the end, anti-authenticity, but that does not mark them off from many other contemporary figures who were equally sceptical of Chatterton's claims.

I

At the time the affair first came to a head around 1770, the Literary Club had been in existence for six years. The nine founder-members, gathered together at the instigation chiefly of Joshua Reynolds, were all still living, though John Hawkins had seceded. They had been joined by Samuel Dyer, still a figure of some mystery, and then in 1768 by Percy, Chambers, and George Colman. No further elections were made until 1773. After that, a gradual expansion took place, not to the liking of all members. The only Clubmen to die in this period were Dyer (1772), Goldsmith (1774), Garrick (1779), and Topham Beauclerk (1780). As the controversy sputtered on into the 1780s, there came the deaths of John Dunning in 1783 and then Johnson in 1784. By 1774 there were 15 in the group, by 1780 it was 28, and by 1784 the total had reached 36. The average age, it may be added, was steadily increasing in spite of efforts to recruit 'new blood'. Among the new recruits were Lord Charlemont, Garrick, William Jones, and Boswell in 1773; George Steevens, Charles James Fox, and Gibbon in 1774; Adam Smith in 1775; Joseph Warton and Sheridan in 1777; Malone and Thomas Warton in 1782; and Charles Burney in 1784.

Not all these individuals had a direct interest in the Rowleyan dispute, and some such as Sheridan soon lost all contact with the Club. But collectively they help to mould an organization which retained some sense of identity, despite its lack of an instrumental purpose and the increasing heterogeneity of its membership (something Johnson had commented on in 1777).[2] There were other, variously active, members such as the churchman Barnard, the physician Fordyce, the scientist Banks, the lawyer William Scott, the parliamentarian Dunning, the grandee Lord Spencer and the cosmopolite Lord Palmerston. Their gatherings remained social, unofficial and (until Boswell spilt some of the beans) private, though their existence was widely known about in the outside world. Nevertheless, a great deal of mutual aid and networking went on, with some of those who did take up the Chatterton question among the regular collaborators: Percy, Malone, and Steevens for example. The key organizing presence in the group had always been Reynolds, a bachelor who lived near the Club's meeting-place. He was the most assiduous in attendance, but also the one who quietly directed its erratic and sometimes fractious course.

The nominal qualification for the entry into the group was a strong classical background. It was for the lack of this sole attribute that John Hawkesworth, allegedly, was turned down.[3] In practice social acceptability came into the question, and as time went on political considerations sometimes affected choices – though this was more marked after the French Revolution. But even if a degree of snobbery can sometimes be detected, the official line was maintained that 'literacy', i.e. a notional familiarity with classical languages and literature, was the test. It was increasingly implausible to apply this test, in the way we might attempt today with computer literacy, as an essential passport to serious intellectual life. Hence the separation of the Club from much of the culture of the age: though scientists, medical men and businessmen were elected, it would have been fruitless to look for men like Joseph Priestley, Josiah Wedgwood or James Watt in the group. (Thomas Jefferson might have made it, in different circumstances: Benjamin Franklin much more dubiously.) Most of the best-known members were, in fact, provincials who had come up to London looking for success. In this respect, they were not unlike Chatterton himself – and it is worth adding that Reynolds's family background, as the son of a West Country schoolmaster, has a familiar ring.

The Club luminaries were of course older than the young poet, usually by half a generation or more: the average age in 1770 was nearly 44, and it would edge up towards 50 as the years went by. As well as being older, they were naturally more established in every sense: more settled, more financially secure, more celebrated, more integrated into society. Several had creative talents, including the poets Johnson, Goldsmith, and the Wartons – but every one of these had achieved his biggest success in poetry by the time Chatterton fetched up in London. It had never been enough for the Club simply to be a *writer* pure and simple – and novelists were totally unrepresented in the membership right into the nineteenth century, if we exclude *Rasselas* – as the group would probably have done. Finally, the Club was a dining society with definite, though sometimes elastic, notions of manners and propriety. The rejection of Rowley's authenticity in the end was a scholarly and not a social decision, as it had also been in the case of Horace Walpole's shift of position; but it is relevant to the wider enquiry here to point out that Chatterton would have occupied a very different social space from the members even if his poetry had been authenticated and accepted in 1770.

II

In the light of all this, let us turn to individual contributions. For the reason already given, Johnson may be dealt with in a selective fashion. The first record we have of his attitude to the affair comes in the letter which Horace Walpole wrote to William Bewley in 1778, included in the published *Letter to the Editor of the Miscellanies of Thomas Chatterton* (1779). Walpole describes what took place at the first Royal Academy Dinner, held on 23 April 1771. This was apparently the only occasion on which Johnson and Walpole were together in the same company. Joshua Reynolds, who presided, had offered to introduce the two men, but this was declined by Walpole. He did agree to be presented to Goldsmith, and this is what ensued:

> Dr Goldsmith drew the attention of the company with an account of a marvellous treatise of ancient poems lately discovered at Bristol, and expressed enthusiastic belief in them, for which he was laughed at by Dr Johnson, who was present. I soon found this was the trouvaille of my friend Chatterton; and I told Dr Goldsmith that this novelty was none to me.... You may imagine, sir, we did not at all agree in the measures of our faith; but though his credulity diverted me, my mirth was soon dashed, for on asking about Chatterton, he told me he had been in London, and had destroyed himself.[4]

Of course, Walpole was seeking retrospectively to distance himself from the young poet. It is significant, however, in terms of our general theme, that Walpole – a leading actor in the Chatterton narrative, as it is usually constructed – should have found out the truth about this story in these circumstances. It was a gathering hosted by the main promoter of the Club, with founder members like Goldsmith and Johnson among the attendance. In some ways the reluctance of Walpole formally to meet Johnson expresses his embarrassment at straying into Club territory. Any new literary dispute was naturally the business of the Literary Club.

In fact, Johnson intervened directly in the affair on only one occasion. This came with his visit to Bristol on 29 April 1776, which happened to be a momentous year in Club doings as it was in larger respects. Boswell had come down to Bath, where Johnson was staying with the Thrales, and naturally accompanied his friend on the trip:

> ... He and I made an excursion to Bristol, where I was entertained with seeing him enquire upon the spot, into the authenticity of 'Rowley's Poetry', as I had seen him enquire upon the spot into the authenticity of 'Ossian's Poetry.'

Boswell describes a meeting with George Catcott, 'who was as zealous for Rowley, as Dr. Hugh Blair was for Ossian', and who undertook to make Johnson 'a convert'. Catcott had Johnson read aloud 'some of Chatterton's fabricated verses', and sat opposite the great man 'wondering he was not yet convinced.' The visitors then called on William Barrett, with similar results:

We ... saw some of the *originals* as they were called, which were executed very artificially; but from a careful inspection of them, and a consideration of the circumstances with which they were attended, we were quite satisfied of the imposture, which, indeed, has been clearly demonstrated from internal evidence, by several able criticks [Boswell's footnote: Mr. Tyrwhitt, Mr. Warton, Mr. Malone].

'Honest Catcot', undeterred, then asked the visitors to go to St Mary Redcliffe, as Boswell reports, in order to '*view with our own eyes* the ancient chest in which the manuscripts were found'. Johnson duly puffed his way up to the muniment room, as Catcott pointed out the wondrous chest 'with a bouncing confident credulity'. That was the end of it, except for Boswell's recollection of an unconvincing supporter of Ossian they had met in the Highlands, and Johnson's famous remark about the 'whelp'.[5]

Four brief glosses to this passage. First, we note Boswell's buoyant tone in 1791, with an easy (and premature) confidence that the episode is comfortably settled for all time. Second, there is the repeated attempt to align the Chatterton affair with Ossian. In fact, the parallel was far from exact, and Johnson's Caledonian 'enquiry' had been much more exhaustive. Third, there is today some anachronous comedy in the unveiling of the mystic chest, since it brings to our mind the discovery of Boswell's own ebony cabinet and the whole revelation of a new Boswell in the twentieth century. But in eighteenth-century terms such a scene has its own symbolic meaning, inscribed in so many novels which start from a discovery of lost papers – the past viewed as a cache of secret documents, to be dragged out of darkness into the light of understanding. Fourth, there is the distinction between Johnson's resolute determination to be unimpressed by the *evidence* – that is, Rowley, the whole paraphernalia of artefacts brandished by Catcott and Barrett – and his vivid, spontaneous response to the *work*, that is Chatterton's poetry. (What is impressive is perhaps the skill of the forgery, the 'artificial' qualities inherent in the fabrication, rather than the verse considered from a literary point of view, but nevertheless the distinction holds.)

Shortly afterwards, on 16 May, Johnson wrote to Hester Thrale about one aftermath of his visit to Bristol: 'Steevens seems to be connected with Tyrwhitt in publishing Chatterton's poems; he came very anxiously to know the result of our enquiries, and though he says, he always thought them forged, is not quite pleased to find us so fully convinced'. Steevens had been elected to the Club two years previously, and it had been Johnson's task to write to him and offer to make a formal introduction to the society. The relations of the two men had apparently been good while Steevens had helped in the revision of the Shakespeare edition (published in 1773). However, as Johnson moved closer to Malone, their friendship, which had never been especially warm, became much cooler. Three weeks after the letter about Steevens, Johnson told Hester Thrale that 'Catcot had been convinced by Barret, and has written his recantation to Tyrwhitt, who still persists in his edition of the poems, and perhaps is not much pleased to find himself mistaken'.[6]

When Steevens read these letters in Mrs Thrale's edition of Johnson's correspondence (1788), he was visibly wounded: 'Dr Johnson himself was piqued at finding Messrs. Tyrwhitt and Steevens resolved to make their own eyes and understanding their judges in the Chattertonian controversy, instead of expressing complete acquiescence in his decrees'. According to Steevens's account in the *Gentleman's Magazine*, Johnson had tried to deter him from visiting Bristol to inspect manuscripts 'of which the Doctor himself could be no competent examiner, for want of eye-sight keen enough to trace the faint vestiges of almost evanescent ink'. Steevens also claims that Johnson had no knowledge of 'ancient handwriting'. Here we see a kind of professional rivalry behind the personal slight. Finally, Steevens offers to defend Tyrwhitt, who had died in 1786, and claims that Johnson was put out by the fact that the medievalist (and non-Clubman) had reached the right conclusions independently. However, the industrious editor, John Nichols, points out that Tyrwhitt was still a hesitant believer at this stage, and had to correct the proofs of his edition (1777) to eliminate the signs of his earlier faith.[7]

About the only direct reference to the episode after this comes six years later, during which time much water had flowed under Bristol Bridge. Again Ossian is invoked, when Johnson writes to Malone after receiving a copy of the latter's *Cursory Observations*: 'I think this wild adherence to Chatterton more unaccountable than the obstinate defence of Ossian. For Ossian there is a national pride, which may be forgiven, though it cannot be applauded; for Chatterton there is nothing but the resolution to say again what has once been said'.[8] Malone made the same linkage in his exposure of Ireland (1795), when he spoke of Johnson, 'who in opposing the fictions of Ossian and Chatterton was as strenuous as any of their most determined assailants'.[9] Again it needs to be pointed out that Johnson had never gone public as he had done in the former scandal about forgery.

Why not? It is just possible that he was less certain in his own mind about the exact mechanisms of deception in the case of Chatterton. According to Boswell's journal, the topic came up in conversation on 17 May 1781: but this was a phase when Boswell claimed to have 'neglected to keep any regular record', so there is no trace in the *Life*. What we are told is that Johnson 'maintained against Dr Percy the Bristol poetry neither Rowley's nor Chatterton's, but by some middle man'.[10] This is too brief for a convincing interpretation to be possible, but it seems to mean that Chatterton could not have been the ultimate agent of the forgery, not that the poems were in any sense other than forgeries. Bertram Davis has suggested that the remark was made 'probably out of the spirit of contradiction',[11] and it is certainly true that Percy continued to arouse a certain repressed antagonism in Johnson, despite his respect for the Bishop's cloth. But it is possible that (at least until the time when Malone produced his *Observations*) Johnson was satisfied about the exposure narrative only to the extent that the manuscripts were forged and the poems bogus concoctions of a later date. He may have felt, in other words, that Chatterton had not been established as the lone or original perpetrator.[12]

It is probable that Johnson knew little or nothing of the non-Rowleyan side of Chatterton before 1778, the year in which the *Miscellanies* appeared. However, that August he was certainly given a taste of the satirist who had taken up the cudgels of Charles Churchill in works like 'Kew Gardens'. Our informant is Fanny Burney and the location is Streatham:

> Mr. Lort produced several curious M.S.S. of the famous Bristol Chatterton; among others, his *Will*, & divers Verses written against Dr. Johnson, as a *place man* & *Pensioner*; all which he Read aloud, with a steady voice & unmoved Countenance! – *I* was astonished at him; Mrs. Thrale not much pleased; Mr. Thrale silent & attentive; & Mr [William] Seward was slyly Laughing. Dr Johnson himself listened profoundly.... Indeed, I believe he wishes his abusers no other Thing than a *good Dinner* (like Pope).[13]

We cannot know whether the old man was as unmoved by these stinging blows of the impudent young writer as his stoical bearing conveyed. Perhaps the knowledge that his assailant was long gone from the world might have made it easier to dismiss them as pinpricks. The diarist herself writes in the awareness that Johnson could be hospitable to a young talent, especially if she happened to be the daughter of a paid-up Johnsonian and soon-to-be Clubman. Indeed, the next paragraph of the diary alludes to the succeeding topic of conversation – 'a Novel that runs about a good deal, called Evelina'. Lort was not in on the secret of the authorship, or of Johnson's sponsorship of Miss Burney.

One further anecdotal reference is sometimes adduced – Meyerstein, for one, treats it as serious evidence.[14] It occurs in a letter written by Anna Seward in 1800, in which she describes how Johnson brusquely dismissed her enthusiasm for Chatterton (see Paul Baines, below). Seward was not always a reliable witness where Johnson is concerned (by this time she had decided that he was, with other faults, 'a furious Jacobite while one hope for the Stuart line remained'),[15] but this has the hallmark of truth about it. The key phrase is the one about 'enlarging their stock of ideas': a characteristic Johnsonian insistence on the intellectual prerequisites of worthwhile poetry. And the hidden pun in 'coining' guineas is the kind of subliminal reinforcement of an argument at which he was always so adept.

Many years on, the episode had still not been laid to rest. Just before his death in 1811, the elderly Percy wrote to Jane West about the letters of Anna Seward, which had been published by Walter Scott not long before, and defended Johnson against Seward's charges. He noted that Seward 'abuses Johnson for omitting Chatterton in his "Lives of the Poets" although at that time many maintained, and some still believe, that he was not the Author, but only Editor of the poems ascribed to Rowley, which she so much admires'.[16] There was only just time for West to reply, defending Seward but not mentioning Johnson, before Percy himself died on 30 September 1811. So the Clubmen of the 1770s were still preoccupied by the topic until time finally laid their concerns to rest.

III

Since we have reached Percy, the discussion may now turn to his public silence on the theme. According to William Bowles, writing to Boswell in 1787, the question had been put to Johnson as to 'whether Dr Percy meant to write in the controversy about Rowley and Chatterton. "Write Sir about Rowley and Chatterton, no to be sure, why he ought to have his lawn sleeves burned about his ears if he did."'[17] No date is supplied for this exchange: it might well have occurred when Bowles and Johnson were in most direct contact, in 1783; but we might have expected a slightly earlier intervention on Percy's part.

Percy's involvement with Chatterton is explored elsewhere in this volume (see Nick Groom, below). Here I simply draw attention to the evidence of his private concern with the affair. 'Though the Bishop never wrote a line on the subject of the Rowleian controversy', he wrote to T. J. Mathias in 1783, 'nor has ever given his opinion publicly, nor probably ever may, on this difficult question, yet he had the honour to be abused as much respecting it, as if he had stood foremost in the controversy'.[18] Most seriously, he had been accused of suppressing key documents – the full story, exonerating Percy, did not come out until the twentieth century. Yet he remained silent, even though leading actors in the drama like Tyrwhitt and Malone wrote to him regularly about the progress of the dispute, and others such as Lord Hardwicke tried to winkle out his opinions.[19]

As the famous collector and editor of old ballads, who had had access to *the* literary manuscript of recent years, Percy was naturally expected to take a leading share in such a fraught question of authenticity. (We may recall that as late as 1779 Horace Walpole would send a first draft of his own defence to Percy, asking for the clergyman to vet his account.[20]) On 16 April 1773 David Garrick, a newly elected member, brought letters of Chatterton to a Club meeting. Next day Percy went with Goldsmith and William Jones to the site of Chatterton's death three years earlier in Brooke Street: one of the few instances of what could almost be called an organized Club outing. Goldsmith had become an adherent of the Rowley cause, and he and Percy had both been present at the Club on 26 March when Lord Charlemont read from the poems. According to one source, Percy and Goldsmith actually quarrelled over the issue.[21]

We now know that two of the holograph manuscripts, sent by Lord Dacre to Percy for examination in April 1773, should have been returned by Robert Chambers, who had just accompanied Johnson to Newcastle on the first stage of his journey to the Hebrides. Chambers, a fellow Clubman, mislaid the papers, and they had not been returned when he left to become a judge in India the next year. Indeed they did not surface until after Chambers's death in 1803 (see below for a fuller account).

Percy's verdict that the manuscripts were spurious was delivered to Dacre on 6 September. His grounds were those of physical evidence, rather than literary impressions. He had taken the advice of Thomas Butler, and concurred with Butler's view that the handwriting was manifestly spurious, an inept effort on the forger's part to simulate older forms of writing, but done with a modern pen. What emerged was 'a fanciful uncouth alphabet of the writer's own invention'. Further, the parchment examined had been stained with ochre to counterfeit age, but 'the fraud is so unskilfully performed, that you may see stains & besmearings on the other side'. The judgment is unambiguous: this document embodies 'in every respect the most glaring & undoubted fraud'.[22] After his consultations with Butler, Percy was much more secure in his opinions. A little over eighteen months earlier, he had written more hesitantly to the antiquarian Andrew Ducarel, who had sent him some Chatterton materials, 'Dr Percy has seen many former specimens of the same verses, and heard a great deal of the history of the discovery.... At present he can only say, that their *genuineness* is rather *doubted* till the original MS. can be produced'.[23]

If Percy was sure of himself at this relatively early stage in the controversy (6 September 1773), then either uncertainty was not the reason for his silence, or else he lost confidence subsequently. It is more likely that he kept to his views, in view of the growing support mustered for the anti-authenticity party, the more so since his fellow members of the Club took such a leading role here. In particular, Edmond Malone remained Percy's informant on relevant matters, right up to the time of Percy's death. The bishop never tired of asking his friend for information regarding the Club's doings,[24] and this was natural because Malone had become the principal support of the organisation after Reynolds's death. It was Percy who, along with Charles Burney, was most anxious to see the Club records preserved and its activities memorialized. There is clearly a measure of reflected glory looked for here – it seems odd to us that anyone should be anxious to be known to posterity more for hobnobbing with Johnson and Burke than for producing the *Reliques of Ancient English Poetry* or *The History of Music*, but that is because we do not fully comprehend the sense of intellectual solidarity which the Club engendered in men of the highest calibre who achieved distinction in very different fields of enquiry.

Not that personal relations were always on a good footing. Years before, Johnson had taken an active share in the preparation of the *Reliques*, especially in writing the dedication and negotiating with the publisher. It was indeed for Johnson that Percy first had the famous folio manuscript bound, when Percy lent it to him: and Johnson had once promised to help his friend in selecting items for the collection and revising the texts.[25] But those days were past, and when Percy showed his mock-ancient ballad *The Hermit of Warkworth* to the Club on 19 March 1771 (each member received a copy of his own in due course), Johnson's attitude was noticeably cool.[26] The famous quarrel between the two men, described by Boswell, did not occur until 1778,[27] and even then relations were patched up: Percy enquired kindly after Johnson in the last year of the sage's life. Nevertheless, when Chatterton first came to prominence the friendship was under some strain.

Again, as we have seen, Percy and Goldsmith are said to have been at odds when the latter's newly discovered enthusiasm for the young poet ran over too warmly. Goldsmith had been down to Bristol in 1771, very early in the controversy, and allegedly took away scraps of old parchments lying around the muniment room at St Mary Redcliffe. In the same year Goldsmith told Horace Walpole that Chatterton had a reputation as 'the young villain' in Bristol,[28] and (as we have seen) it was he who first gave Walpole news of the young man's death – although this had occurred fully eight months before. If there really was a quarrel, it was of brief duration, for relations were sufficiently restored in the brief remaining span of Goldsmith's life for several contacts to take place. These included the visit to the site of Chatterton's death, in April 1773; as well as attendance at early performances of *She Stoops to Conquer*, just a month earlier. Before Goldsmith died, he had given Percy a large tranche of letters and personal papers, apparently to be used in compiling his biography. In 1776 Percy handed these on to Johnson, who was now expected to take over the job. In the event, these materials would revert to Percy and eventually it was he who would be responsible for the life of Goldsmith which, with assistance from Thomas Campbell and Henry Boyd, made its belated appearance in 1802.[29]

It is unlikely that the shifting dynamics of the Club had any decisive influence on Percy's reluctance to speak out on Chatterton, although they conceivably operated on his mind at some level. One suggestion is that he felt guilty about the doctoring to which his own ballad collection had been subject, and so was inhibited from criticizing what Chatterton had performed.[30] This is implausible. Percy had freely acknowledged the exact nature of his source, had stated that his manuscript had needed interpolation and restoration, and had given no false account of date, provenance or transmission of the texts. His errors were based on the false assumptions of his time, and the limitations of extant scholarship. Nor is it plausible to impute a bad conscience to Johnson, as Ian Haywood does, over the fact that 'he had his own skeletons to hide'.[31] The mock-authentic accounts of the

Senates of Lilliput in the *Gentleman's Magazine* proclaimed their fictionality at every turn; while Johnson may have regretted that some readers supposed they accurately represented the speeches made by individuals in Parliament, no competent person could have supposed that there were actually politicians called Walelop or Jacobites called the Redneterp in a real place called Lilliput. Equally, Horace Walpole's sophisticated artifice in *The Castle of Otranto* incorporates no serious attempt at creating a 'real' historical author or at constructing a phys- ical 'source'. Chatterton's attempt to put Walpole's literary 'fraud' on the same level as his own rests on an erasure of many large points of difference.[32] In the case of Johnson and Walpole, the games were played in accordance with well-established rules and conventions of literary mystification. Chatterton had gone on to an altogether differ- ent plane of deception, moving beyond plagiarism and literary reconstruction into the realm of the fake, once he started to supply corroborative detail, contextual padding, and all the props of bogus authentication.[33]

The most likely explanation is that Percy wished to distance himself from his earlier role of littérateur and gentleman-author.[34] As the bibliographer T. F. Dibdin commented, 'In his latter years Bishop Percy almost wished to *forget* that he had published the Reliques of Ancient Poetry'.[35] This was not an automatic response for a church- man who had advanced to the head of his profession, but it makes sense in terms of Percy's career and character. It may also be that Percy observed the possible links people would make between the *Reliques*, sensation of the 1760s, and Chatterton, sensation of the 1770s.[36] Certainly the book must have impressed the young Chatterton forcibly, as it affected many people of much less sensibility, less rele- vant knowledge and less literary ambition. The thought may have struck Percy that he was in some buried sense one of the progenitors of Chatterton's poetic mode. However, that is very different from imput- ing any feelings of guilt or responsibility for Chatterton's *actions*, or the use to which he attempted to put his forgeries. Otherwise we could blame Arthur Collins for providing in his *Baronetage* a handy basis for Chatterton's genealogical fantasies. In each case Chatterton has adopted a convenient body of material and an appropriate literary practice, for his own wildly discrepant purposes.

Among the minor participants the most interesting is Charlemont. By the time that James Caulfield, Earl of Charlemont was elected to the Club in 1773 as one of the first batch of new men, he had already acquired a reputation as a virtuoso and Irish antiquarian, but his political career with the Irish Volunteers still lay in the future. Charlemont had gone down to Bristol in 1772 and was quickly convinced by Catcott's patter. He asked for a special deluxe transcript to be made of *Ælla* and other items. Catcott complied, for a fee of 15 guineas.[37] It is possible that, as on other occasions, Chatterton's accessory doctored the text, introducing a further thread to follow through the labyrinth of making and remaking. One of the Earl's first acts on joining the Club was to read some or all of these poems to the other members: no doubt some of the audience, including Percy, heard the recital with marked scepticism. Catcott and Barrett, who desperately wanted the suffrage of the literati, had to make do with Charlemont, having failed with bigger names such as Percy and Johnson. Few of the circle proved susceptible to conversion, and Charlemont found himself increasingly isolated. However, during prolonged residence in Ireland he maintained a keen interest in the affair, and sought news from his countryman Malone. When Malone as a 'professed anti-Rowleian' launched his attack in 1782, Charlemont seems to have remained undecided. He told Malone that Jacob Bryant 'might still have some chance with posterity, though the laugh be now against him'. Bryant and others needed to be answered, even if their arguments were weak.[38] It looks as if Charlemont wanted to hold on to some hope of authenticity even at this date, when most of the Club in London had rallied to the Anti-Rowley party.

IV

There were others who took some share in the episode, such as Steevens, who wrote extensively on the affair in the *St. James's Chronicle*.[39] But we are left with two more leading figures in the pamphlet war who were members of the Club. First there is Thomas Warton, who could be seen as an anomalous figure in the Club and also in the controversy. The initial circumstance relates to his affinities and alliances outside, which made him something of a cuckoo in the Club nest at times. The second relates to his position not just as a literary historian and editor, but as an active poet (and brother of a poet). In fact, the future laureate was the only main participant whose own creative needs and capabilities were thrown into question by what Chatterton had done.

Within the Club, Thomas Warton (elected in 1782, five years after his brother) represented an almost deviant streak. He was able to attend meetings only in the Oxford vacations, and indeed gatherings

were held specially around Christmas – that is, outside the parliamentary calendar which normally governed these things – so that he could
be present. He had been chosen partly to strengthen the Oxford presence in the group – Robert Chambers had left for India and William
Jones would follow him in 1783. But the baggage he brought with him
included what should have been a natural alliance with the party of
Horace Walpole and William Mason, which clung to the memory of
Gray, supported Lyttelton against the sneers of the *Lives of the Poets*,
and attracted the following of Elizabeth Montagu. In his *Enquiry*,
published in the same year as his election to the Club, Warton goes
out of his way to defend Walpole's conduct in a lengthy footnote, but
it is not particularly convincing.[40] Though Warton corresponded with
Walpole and Mason, they established no intimacy. Both sides wanted
to establish a New Poetry by supplanting the primacy which Pope had
held in their youth. Walpole's candidate was of course Gray, and in
part this was because he could portray Gray as a better scholar, a more
thoroughly classical writer and a truer gentleman than Pope. The
writing of earlier centuries could be effectively left out of the argument, since Walpole's view was that Warton in his *History of English
Poetry* had dredged through 'the muddy poetry of three or four
centuries that had never a poet'.

For the Wartons, as David Fairer has shown in a number of valuable
studies, poetry was to be taken on a new path – by the example of
their own verse, centrally, as well as that of William Collins. This
involved a new poetic which overlapped in many respects that of the
Romantics a decade or two later; less obviously, it involved a particular version of literary history, reclaiming and even recolonizing the
work of Spenser.[41] Much of this critical enterprise, especially the
dislodging of Dryden and Pope, was unattractive to Johnson and the
more conservative wing of the Club, although Johnson had fond
personal memories of Collins. (There are ways in which Warton's
History and Johnson's *Lives* offer intellectually incompatible views of
literature: their critical touchstones and approach to the verbal texture
of poetry are radically alien.) Nor did the poetic works of the Warton
brothers commend themselves to this group. Yet both brothers, and
particularly Thomas, maintained good relations with the Club,
including the people who might be expected to have an opinion on
Chatterton – that is, Johnson, Percy, Steevens, and Malone. In addition, Thomas kept up a friendly contact with Langton, Boswell,
William Scott, and Colman, amongst others.[42]

Warton's position as an established scholar in literary history conditioned his response to Chatterton in more than one way. When the story first broke, he was already deeply engaged in the researches which came to fruition in the *History of English Poetry*, although the first volume was not published until 1774. The natural development of the history meant that Warton was able to postpone the awkward question of Rowley until the second volume (1778), but then face it he surely must. No other scholar or antiquarian encountered quite such a direct challenge by the new 'discoveries'. Ritson or Bryant, Malone or Steevens, Walpole or Johnson – they could all carry out their existing work without any absolute obligation to confront this awkward case.[43] The scheme to which Warton was committed would allow no evasion. If Thomas Rowley was genuine, he more than deserved his place in the often exiguous records of English poetry in the middle of the fifteenth century.

Understandably, Warton was undecided for some time. The copies of Chatterton items he was shown by Lord Lichfield in 1772 were insufficient to make a judgment: the fragments his brother Joseph obtained from George Catcott, and items received from William Barrett, equally failed to clarify the point. In July 1774 Thomas wrote an anxious letter to Percy, asking his friend what he 'knew' about Rowley, but implicitly posing the supplementary question, what did Percy *think* about the issue of authenticity? No more is heard until January 1776, when Warton told Percy he now inclined to lean to the side of forgery – but he would still be willing to listen to one capital argument in favour of authenticity. 'As for Chatterton', he writes uncertainly, 'I have considered that subject Pro and Con, not professing to enter *minutely* into the Controversy, but just as much as the *general* nature of my work properly required'.[44] The text of the *History* bears out this comment: Warton does finally come down against Rowley, but with seeming reluctance. The antiquarian in him would have liked the poems to be genuine, if only as curious objects – and in fact, he sees, they are more than that. The threat they would then pose to his elaborately constructed scheme of literary history is another matter. There was no room in Warton's plan for a Rowley at this point, precisely because a Rowley could not have appeared at this juncture in the form Chatterton devised for him. It was not just internal evidence, regarding language and allusions, which convicted the forger. The fakes were too good, in a sense, for the function they were meant to fulfil. As Warton was later to say, 'To secure our credulity, he [Chatterton] should have pleased us less. He has shewn too much genius, and too little skill'.[45]

The Pro-Rowley party were able to show up the insecurities in this aspect of the *History*. After Milles and Bryant had stated their side of the controversy, Warton returned in 1782 with a more forthright statement in his *Enquiry*. There is something unconvincing and awkwardly facetious about his opening pages, when he defends his earlier dealings with Chatterton. But the main portion of the text consists of a detailed analysis of primarily textual issues, which serves to document the nature of the forgery – the literary forgery, if not the physical faking of evidence. The headings under which the analysis is conducted include style, composition, and sentiment; metre; ancient language, i.e. lexis; historical allusions; a comparison with Chatterton's miscellaneous non-Rowley verse; and finally a review of the character and circumstances of Chatterton. Warton is naturally able to deploy enough knowledge of medieval English language, poetic modes and history to expose the fraudulence of nearly all the items in Tyrwhitt's edition. His final summary gives priority to literary taste and knowledge of literary history (his own specialisms) over forensic examination:

> It is not from the complexion of ink or of parchment, from the information of cotemporaries, the tales of relations, the recollections of apprentices, and the prejudices of friends, nor even from doomsday-book, pedigrees in the herald's office, armorial bearings, parliamentary rolls, inquisitions, indentures, episcopal registeres, epitaphs, tomb-stones, and brass-plates, that this controversy is to be finally and effectively adjusted. Our arguments should be drawn from principles of taste, from analogical experiment, from a familiarity with antient poetry, and from the gradations of composition.[46]

This piece of literary *jusqu'auboutisme*, rejecting almost every tangible hold on questions of physical identity or provenance, was written by a man who became Camden Professor of Ancient History at Oxford three years later. The Club, however, would have understood. They were antiquarians *malgré eux*, some of them: yet they believed that the key to understanding the mind of the past was to be found not in legal exhibits but in an understanding of texts. Philology, allied to taste, would accomplish what was needed.[47]

It was very different in the case of Edmond Malone. He, if anyone, was a master of what could be dredged up from the herald's office and the parliamentary rolls. His contribution has always been seen as decisive in the argument, perhaps in part because he has gained such a high reputation for his scholarship.[48] Along with Tyrwhitt's *Vindication of the Appendix*, it has been customary to regard Malone's *Cursory Observations* (1782) as a crucial summation of the negative evidence, written as it is with a lighter touch and more literary flair than most of the other contributions. The pamphlet ends, indeed, with a modest proposal to form a committee of Rowleyans to measure the sacred chests and calculate the million-plus documents which they might have contained. Like others on his side of the question, Malone adopts a generous attitude towards Chatterton's literary potential ('I have as high an opinion of his abilities as perhaps any person whatsoever, and do indeed believe him to have been the greatest genius that England has produced since the days of Shakspeare').[49] But the demolition job is remorseless, drawing heavily on Malone's unequalled knowledge of palaeography as applied to earlier English literature, and pronouncing on matters such as Chatterton's handwriting with an authority deriving not from his reputation but from his extensive work at the scholarly coalface. In addition, his critical comparison of Rowley and non-Rowley items, accounting for the superiority of the former, shows some skill in identifying, if not quite analysing, poetic effects. The *Cursory Observations* are just that, and they rely on the physical and textual enquiries which were already in hand when Percy investigated Dacre's manuscripts, all of nine years before. What Malone did was reassemble some of the evidence with a polished wit, set out the implausibility of the opposition case, and reassert what philology, in its broader application, showed about the case. It was by no means one of Malone's most learned or intellectually impressive performances, but it served a purpose.

Malone's reputation has rested chiefly on his Shakespearean researches. These had reached only a preliminary stage in 1782; and anyway his advances in editing related in part to issues concerning the transmission of printed texts, an area irrelevant to Chatterton. It is worth remembering that Malone was a lawyer rather than a classical scholar by training, with a slightly different mind-set from most of the other anti-Rowleyans. However, his attempt to ground authority on authenticity, and his desire to dispel traditional tales, can be seen in the short Chatterton pamphlet, as well as in his more searching contribution to Shakespearean studies. A later exposure of faking, the lengthy *Inquiry into the Authenticity of Certain Miscellaneous Papers* (1796), subjected William Henry Ireland to a merciless battery of documentary evidence. It was Malone's aim to clear away the coral reef of conjecture and plain guesswork which had accreted on the text of Shakespeare. To this end, he assembled an unrivalled range of scholarly aids. He had an excellent private library; access to the collections of others (and he did not always remember promptly to return items he had borrowed); great knowledge of archives; an extensive acquaintance with early English drama; a systematically evolved understanding of Elizabethan linguistic usage; a deep familiarity with historical practices and procedures – and much else. He possessed, for example, the respect for dates which Horace Walpole so singularly lacked. His overall aim was to recover and reinhabit the past, sufficiently to make empirical judgements about what could plausibly be found in an older text and what could not. He was therefore equipped, even at an early stage of his career, to pronounce on Rowley with genuine 'authority' as few of the participants in the long-running squabble could claim to be – not even a man like Joseph Ritson, who certainly had a good deal of relevant experience.

Or so we might have said until recently. Now we must take account of a rather different Malone, who produced the Variorum editions of Shakespeare in 1790 and 1821 (the latter a posthumous work completed by James Boswell junior – the younger son of Malone's Club colleague). In her highly interesting study of these editions, *Shakespeare Verbatim* (1991), Margreta de Grazia depicts a scholar bent on performing the Enlightenment trick of passing off an arbitrary, historically conditioned narrative as a timeless truth, drawing on 'an epistemology that assumes an essential reality outside discourse'.[50] According to this account, Malone creates a concept of 'authenticity' which disguises an editorial construct as an objective standard. He reifies 'Shakespeare', partly by endowing the author with a personal and proprietorial ownership of the text which did not exist in Elizabethan times. And he imposes a particular meaning on the text of Shakespeare's works by enclosing them in a specialized apparatus, which corresponds with the mentality of the editor's period (the late eighteenth century) and violates the assumptions of the dramatist's period, the beginning of the seventeenth century.

This version of Malone as Shakespearean editor, whatever its validity, plainly cannot be extrapolated directly into the Chatterton dispute. However, it would be cowardly to dismiss the rendering of Malone to be found in de Grazia's book as altogether irrelevant to Rowley and his commentators. Insofar as the *Cursory Observations* body forth a theory of historical and textual enquiry, then they do adumbrate the same kind of notional authority as the one located in the Shakespeare editions, although this notion is much more developed and more actively applied in the larger frame of the Variorum. What de Grazia calls the aim of 'situating Shakespeare in an historical period'[51] is close to Malone's intellectual desiderata for settling the Chatterton business – and if the process was an artificial and misleading one with the dramatist (as de Grazia suggests), then it is all the more likely that Malone's reconstruction of a fifteenth-century Bristol and a fifteenth-century poetic climate will be even more bogus. (For one thing, the sources were still less copious for the 1440s than they were for the 1590s.)

It is certain that Malone, like his colleagues among the Anti-Rowleyans, had a naive confidence in the objectivity of his procedures, by modern standards that is. This does not mean that their efforts were invalidated as forensic or heuristic undertakings. Hardly anybody in the Club had much interest in fifteenth-century Bristol anyway. The object of the exercise was to determine the narrow question of authorship (though that single issue naturally got submerged at times in the heat and dust of debate). Different considerations arise when we are trying to assess the validity of establishing a text, or preferring one reading to another. As regards the question of who wrote a text, and when, the tests which Malone brought to bear on the Rowley poems do not seem to be vitiated by any Enlightenment metaphysic.

V

There was one way in which the Club's nominal attachment to classical studies conditioned their response to the imbroglio surrounding Chatterton. We must recall that these men had experienced an education which concentrated almost exclusively on the ancient world and its legacy, and that the instrument of training had been the ancient languages – in practice, overwhelmingly Latin. Their approach to texts was initially philological, rather than literary-critical or even historical. This fact becomes crucial especially for those who had developed this skill in professional directions – for example, Johnson, Langton (who was to edit Johnson's Latin verse in 1787) or Gibbon, who wrote critical observations on the *Aeneid* apart from everything else. Such men were privy to centuries of scholarship, conjecture and emendation which had gone around the canonical texts.

One circumstance of which they were inevitably aware was the role forgery and pseudo-writings had played in the evolution of the literary canon. Almost every ancient author had his or her own apocrypha: many of the most celebrated texts were suspect in one way or another. The fourth-century forgery known as the *Historia Augusta* came with its personal collection of faked documentation and endorsement, very much in Chatterton's style. And it was through the analysis and detection of such frauds that many standard scholarly procedures developed. As Johnson and his colleagues well knew, the question of authenticity was not a recent one which had suddenly arrived with Lauder or Macpherson to trouble the modern investigator. Most of the leading figures in the revival of learning had spent part of their careers looking into cases of forgery, or its cousin plagiarism. The most spectacular instance is provided by Isaac Casaubon, whose peculiar rigour meant that scarcely ever did he stray far from issues of authenticity and authentication. We should need no reminder that it was the work of men like Casaubon which underlay Johnson's entire intellectual enterprise.

But perhaps we do need some sort of reminder. The recent surge of interest in what might briefly be termed the climate of forgery in the late eighteenth century has largely ignored this long saga of investigation. In the words of Anthony Grafton, 'For 2,500 years and more, forgery has amused its uninvolved observers, enraged its humiliated victims, flourished as a literary genre and, most oddly of all, stimulated vital innovations in the technical methods of scholars.' All these responses, from detached amusement to baffled anger, can be observed in the course of the Chatterton affair. As Grafton points out, 'Forgery is as old as textual authority', and as the Club investigators recognized textual authority itself was an issue with a long history – again, it was not something which the historical conditions suddenly produced, even though new factors such as the ownership of copyright might refract the conceptual debate.[52]

We must, then, disengage the Chatterton story from a narrative imposed by modern scholarship, if we are to understand the Club response. In the process we need to regain a sense of many earlier manifestations of literary fraud and plagiarism, such as Johnson, Malone, and their friends possessed. Grafton's book *Forgers and Critics: Creativity and Duplicity in Western Scholarship* (1990) supplies the essential context in a short space, and provides constant pointers in the right direction. It is useful to be reminded that 'Erasmus was not the only grave and learned gentleman to hoax the entire world of learning with an uncharacteristic piece of fakery'.[53] Recent commentary on the spate of eighteenth-century forgeries, from Lauder through Ossian and Chatterton to W. H. Ireland, has seldom fixed its gaze any further back than the work of Richard Bentley. It *is* right to make that particular move, for the battle of the books in England was not just part of the European *querelle* about the status of ancient and modern culture – it was also a contest for ideological ownership of the past, and a struggle between competing modes of apprehending the past. As Joseph M. Levine has shown in a series of excellent studies, it was often the antiquarians who pioneered the new forms of investigation[54] – and this applies to matters of textual transmission, as well as those of archaeology and epigraphy. (There were, by the way, many faked inscriptions, a consideration relevant to some of the physical artefacts Chatterton created.)

One of the central points made by Grafton is that 'if one sets Chatterton's and Ireland's techniques into their long-term context, the tradition of western forgery, it soon becomes clear that there was little radically new in what they did'.[55] The techniques of faking it, and the techniques of discovering the fakes, had changed little over the millennia. This was primarily because physical diplomatics had advanced only in a very gradual fashion. The technology available for dating manuscripts or determining the provenance of a printed book was little better in 1770 than it had been in 1570. Ossian and Chatterton may have attained a particular prominence because people were feeling especially touchy about the whole issue of forgery (one reason often suggested is that a commercial society, placing great dependence on the machinery of credit, needs to be able to rely on written instruments). But it is wrong to suppose that there must be a narrow historical occasion for the existence of such faked literary documents, or a new motivation for the forgers.

The final consideration for our purposes is one raised by Grafton near the end of his book. He remarks, 'Forgery and philology fell and rose together, in the Renaissance as in Hellenistic Alexandria. Sometimes the forgers were the first to create or restate elegant critical methods; sometimes the philologists beat them to it.'[56] In the sense that Macpherson and Chatterton were both attempting to create a new literary mode, they were ahead of the game. But they were fairly soon caught out, as they were deficient (with all their genuine literary qualities) in what might broadly be called philological areas. Of course, the exposers of Ossian in almost every case knew little or no Gaelic, and the exposers of Chatterton were astoundingly inept in Middle English by later standards. But these men were critics and philologists, in Grafton's terms: they applied known procedures, they concentrated on the letter rather than the spirit, and they built on the work of their predecessors in fraud detection. This is even more clear in the case of Ireland, although that hapless young man was trying to reproduce antiques rather than to establish a new brand of writing.

Today it is easy to see the response of the Club to Chatterton as a defensive operation, mounted to preserve the territorial rights of an older generation of classically trained literary gents who feared the coming of the new. The attitude of a Malone, or even a Johnson, can be viewed as positivist:[57] if all history is, as we are sometimes told, equally fictitious, then 'Rowley' has neither more nor less claim on our attention and respect than 'Chaucer'. On this reading, forgery is just scholarship conducted by other means. This is not a conclusion which Grafton's account would support, for he shows that the forger had to move on as soon as the critic caught up with his pretences. Moreover, the claim that Club members were automatically resistant to literary innovation is palpably untrue in the case of Warton, and does not actually hold good in the case of any of them. What gave them a fairly loose connection was not their assessment of current literature, but their view of themselves as inheritors of the traditional role described by Grafton. In their own estimation, they were distinguished alike from mere antiquarians or virtuosi, as with Walpole's haziness about dates, and from pedantic textual scholiasts in the university, who laboured over some unidea'd tract or explained the intelligible. Thomas Warton, who had laboured for quite a few years on his edition of Theocritus, had a foot in this latter camp; but he had another side, and besides was increasingly turning towards subjects such as Milton's shorter poems.

An allied line of reasoning would be that all these issues were ultimately political. In the simplest sense, this would take the form of arguing that Johnson, for example, was motivated by 'political bias' – as Meyerstein actually suggested two generations ago.[58] The proposition is that Johnson 'abstained from admitting [Chatterton] among his poets' because he was vulgar and uneducated, i.e. inadmissible on social grounds. This overlooks the facts, first that several poets of humble origins (Prior, to look no further) were included in the *Lives*; and second, that Johnson never attempted to conceal his own modest origins – as maybe Percy, and certainly Charles Burney, did.[59] It is true that Johnson looked for a 'stock of ideas' in the poet, which would most naturally be acquired through education and wide reading: this if the work was to be 'worth the attention of learning and taste'. Johnson had many defects, but he was as far from being a snob as it is possible to be.

A more sophisticated version of the argument would suggest that hidden ideological blinkers kept the illuminati from understanding the challenge which Chatterton's inventions posed to their too easily naturalized value-system. They thought they were defending objective truth and disinterested scholarship, but really they were stuck in a state of unconscious denial. They would have to admit that an unlettered and still adolescent author could reinvent literature so that traditional assumptions about the poet were invalidated – and that would involve loss of their own status, loss of their prime articles of faith, loss of a *raison d'être* for the whole Club enterprise.[60]

This is a difficult case to sustain, if one has any degree of respect for scholarly enquiry or for its procedures. The new students of forgery are quick to point out that anxiety over literary fakes went with panic about criminal forgeries such as that of William Dodd. But there is hardly any conceivable defence to be constructed which would not have to acknowledge that Chatterton did engage in elaborate, systematic and wilful deception, involving at times direct or indirect attempts to extract money. Even if we wish to argue that such deception could still promote valuable literary innovation, which few today would dispute, it is still necessary for us to *know* the extent of the deception if we are to assess the scale and importance of that innovation.

Malone and his friends were centrally engaged in making that judgment possible, a benefit all of us subsequently take for granted. If the illuminati of the Club were protecting their patch, then that patch was the territory not of aggressive insistence on 'ownership' of literary property, or on the criminalization of plagiarism. It was the territory of traditional scholarship and criticism – above all, getting the facts about a text straight, so we can read it in an unclouded knowledge of its relation to a historical and literary context. Every new claim about Chatterton's originality we may wish to make today rests on our certainty about the (possibly trivial) ways in which he simulated, copied, borrowed and cheated. For that, we have to thank a long series of investigators, beginning with the members of the Literary Club.

Notes

1. Johnson reports Lort's proposal and rejection for the Club in his diary on 10 December and 17 December 1782: see his *Diaries, Prayers, and Annals,* ed. E. L. McAdam, Jr, D. Hyde and M. Hyde (New Haven, 1958), *The Yale Edition of the Works of Samuel Johnson,* vi. 355–6. Lort, the most active antiquarian scholar engaged in the Chatterton episode, was a close and long-standing friend of Hester Thrale.

2. *The Letters of Samuel Johnson*, ed. B. Redford (Princeton, 1992–4), iii. 12.
3. *Thraliana*, ed. K. C. Balderston (Oxford, 1951), ii. 697.
4. Walpole, Horace, *A Letter to the Editor of the Miscellanies of Thomas Chatterton* (Strawberry Hill, 1779), 37–8. For the letter to Bewley, see also *The Yale Edition of Horace Walpole's Correspondence*, ed. W. S. Lewis *et al.* (New Haven, 1937–83), xvi. 121–34.
5. *Life of Johnson*, ii. 30–1.
6. *Letters of Johnson*, ii. 126–7, 129, 336, 339.
7. *Anecdotes*, ix. 529–30. For Tyrwhitt's refusal to commit himself on the issue of authenticity, and his decision to 'leave it to the determination of the unprejudiced and intelligent Reader', see *Poems*, xii.
8. *Letters of Johnson*, iv. 14.
9. Malone's *Inquiry into the Authenticity of Certain Miscellaneous Papers and Legal Instruments* (1796), 354–5, quoted in *The Piozzi Letters*, ed. E. A. Bloom and L. D. Bloom (Newark, NJ, 1989–), ii. 386–7. Someone in a position to know, Hannah More, had a clear idea of Club attitudes. On 13 May 1780 she wrote to Frances Boscawen, 'I suppose you have read Mr Warton's second volume [of the *History*]; I have not seen it, but hear that he totally rejects the authenticity of Rowley's Poems; so does Johnson, so does Percy, so do most of the antiquaries; but neither their authority nor their reasonings have entirely convinced your obstinate friend'. See *Memoirs of the Life and Correspondence of Mrs Hannah More*, ed. William Roberts (London, 1834), i. 181. It is intriguing to see an eighteenth-century writer link 'authenticity' and 'authority' in this way.
10. Boswell, James, *Boswell Laird of Auchinleck 1778–1782*, ed. J. W. Reed and F. A. Pottle (New York, 1977), *Yale Edition of the Private Papers of James Boswell*, 359. Again there is the small but significant fact that this conversation took place at the home of Frances Reynolds, Sir Joshua's sister.
11. Davis, Bertram H., *Thomas Percy: A Scholar-Cleric in the Age of Johnson* (Philadelphia, 1989), 253.
12. It may have been Malone's *Cursory Observations* which settled his mind. After this response to the Rowleyans had come out, Johnson encountered Jacob Bryant. According to a letter from George Steevens to Thomas Warton, in May 1781, Johnson 'heard the other day, with no very grave face, the complaints of Bryant'. See *The Correspondence of Thomas Warton*, ed. D. Fairer (Athens, Ga., 1995), 455. Warton, Steevens, and Catcott were in correspondence about the affair throughout much of 1782, as Fairer's edition reveals.
13. Burney, Fanny, *The Early Journals and Letters of Fanny Burney*, ed. L. E. Troide and S. J. Cooke (Montreal, 1994), iii.1, 112. For Chatterton's satiric treatment of Johnson, see *Works*, 119, 460–4, 520–2, 535–7. The grounds of the attack derive from Churchill and others who had previously assailed Johnson (the pension; the Shakespeare edition, etc.), with a new thrust at *The False Alarm* (in 'The Whore of Babylon', l. 342, reworked in 'Kew Gardens', l. 842). Chatterton, in fact, deals in the currency of newspaper politics and the material of writers such as Shebbeare and Kenrick. He shows no depth of interest in what might be termed 'hard' politics; it is noteworthy that he takes no notice of Burke, who was not to represent Bristol until 1774 but was already a prominent MP.

14. *Life*, 466.
15. Whalley, Thomas Sedgewick, *Journals and Correspondence of Thomas Sedgewick Whalley, D.D.*, ed. H. Wickham (London, 1863), i. 417.
16. *Illustrations*, viii. 430–2.
17. Boswell, James, *The Correspondence of James Boswell relating to the Making of the Life of Johnson*, ed. M. Waingrow, *Yale Edition of the Private Papers of James Boswell* (New York, 1969), 254.
18. *Illustrations*, viii. 213.
19. Ibid. viii. 198. As Paul Baines remarks, 'Oliver Goldsmith even took the advice of Lord Hardwicke (not a sympathetic judge of forgers) before making his enquiries', with citation of a letter from Hardwicke to Goldsmith dated 24 April 1771. See Baines, '"All of the House of Forgery": Walpole, Chatterton, and Antiquarian Commerce', *Poetica* 39/40 (1993), 47. As late as 1781, Hardwicke was reporting to Percy that he had been 'staggered' into belief in Chatterton by the books of Bryant and Milles: see *Illustrations*, viii. 198. By this date Hardwicke had joined the Walpole party in deploring Johnson's *Lives of the Poets*, especially the treatment of their pet Lyttelton.
20. *Walpole Correspondence*, xli. 395–7.
21. For Percy's relations with Goldsmith, and related matters, see Davis, 198–205. William Jones, who may have sympathized with Chatterton's radical views, still retained sufficient piety to visit Brooke Street again in 1779 (*Life*, 391).
22. For Percy's part in the investigation and the loss of the manuscripts, see Davis, 202–4; A. Watkin-Jones, 'Bishop Percy, Thomas Warton, and Chatterton's Rowley Poems (1773–1790)', *PMLA* 50 (1935), 769–84; and Nick Groom, 'Thomas Percy's *Reliques of Ancient English Poetry*: Its Context, Presentation, and Reception', D.Phil. (Oxford University, 1994), 260–72. On 5 November 1773 George Catcott wrote to Lord Charlemont, still regarded as a dependable supporter, concerning Percy's 'sentence': *The Manuscripts and Correspondence of James First Earl of Charlemont*, Historical Manuscripts Commission (London, 1891–4), i. 316.
23. *Illustrations*, viii. 163.
24. See *The Percy Letters: The Correspondence of Thomas Percy and Edmond Malone*, ed. A. Tillotson (Baton Rouge, La., 1944).
25. *Illustrations*, vi. 556; *The Percy Letters: The Correspondence of Thomas Percy and William Shenstone*, ed. C. Brooks (New Haven, 1977), 9–10. Thomas Warton offered assistance with the *Reliques*, although in the event Percy's aid to the *History of English Poetry* was of more consequence (Davis, 83).
26. See *Letters of Johnson*, i. 356; and, less well known, the testimony of Baptist Noel Turner in *Illustrations*, vi. 160–2.
27. *Life of Johnson*, iii. 271–81.
28. See Walpole to William Cole, 13 March 1780, in *Walpole Correspondence*, ii. 205.
29. For the complex story of the biography of Goldsmith, see Balderston, K. C., *The History and Sources of Percy's Memoir of Goldsmith* (Cambridge, 1926); *Thomas Percy's Life of Dr Oliver Goldsmith*, ed. R. L. Harp (Salzburg, 1976); *Dr Campbell's Diary of a Visit to England in 1775*, ed. J. L. Clifford (Cambridge, 1947), 25–30.

30. The most serious accusations of impropriety came from Joseph Ritson, who criticized Percy's treatment of his texts in the *Select Collection of English Songs* (1784) and *Ancient Songs* (1792). Ritson elsewhere kept up his barrage against Warton, Malone, Johnson, Tyrwhitt, and others. His formidable presence must have been forbidding to the sensitive Percy, who actually believed that Warton had been deterred from carrying his *History of English Poetry* to a conclusion after the treatment he had received from Ritson. The fullest coverage of these matters remains that of B. H. Bronson, *Joseph Ritson: Scholar-at-Arms*, 2 vols (Berkeley, 1938), which provides much information relevant to the general topic. Although Ritson was an Anti-Rowleyan, he intimidated the other opponents of Chatterton with his onslaughts on their competence in medieval matters. He actually referred to 'the Literary Club junto' (ii. 379), meaning the dynasty of Shakespearean editors. For Ritson's dealings with individuals, see Bronson as follows: Warton, i. 322–4; Johnson, ii. 430–54; Malone, ii. 495–514; Percy, ii. 543–610. George Steevens's estrangement from the Club after his quarrel with Malone is dramatically revealed by his rapprochement with Ritson, who had formerly launched a fierce attack on the Johnson/Steevens edition of Shakespeare.

31. Haywood, Ian, *Faking It: Art and the Politics of Forgery* (New York, 1987), 63. Haywood's case is not helped by several errors in facts and dating, most obviously his belief that David Garrick (d.1779) took part in the first performance of Ireland's *Vortigern* in 1795 (65). See also Haywood's earlier study *The Making of History* (London, 1986) for a more detailed presentation of a similar case regarding the blurring of the concept of forgery.

32. See *Life*, 271: *Works*, 341. For Lort's defence of Walpole against his accusers, see *Illustrations*, vii. 556–63.

33. See however the opposing view of Haywood (1987), 58–61, where he suggests that the analogies of literary forgery with coining are desperate strategies by Walpole to conceal his embarrassment at having been found out as a kind of fraudster himself.

34. It should also be remembered that after Percy moved to Ireland in May 1782 he was simply more remote from what was going on in the English literary scene. So, for example, Michael Lort had to explain to him who Ritson was (letter of 15 January 1783, in *Illustrations*, vii. 443).

35. See *Illustrations*, vi. 554.

36. Haywood (1986), 47–8, speaks of the way in which Ritson 'undermined the authenticity of the *Reliques*', and compares what Ritson said about Percy with what Johnson had said about Ossian. Again, this seems to be a strained comparison which does not reflect the contemporary sense of Percy's divagations from good practice.

37. *Works*, ii. 923. See Groom (1994), 265–71, for a new account of the episode from unpublished papers.

38. Charlemont, *Manuscripts and Correspondence*, i. 420. For Malone's self-description, see i. 393.

39. It should also be noted that Steevens, even after he broke with Malone and some other members of the Club, still corresponded with Percy, about the Ireland forgeries among other matters: see *Illustrations*, vii. 1–36.

40. Warton, Thomas, *An Enquiry into the Authenticity of the Poems attributed to Thomas Rowley* (London, 1782), 109.

41. There is a large literature on this topic, but the most immediately relevant items include Fairer, David, 'Thomas Warton, Thomas Gray, and the Recovery of the Past', in W. B. Hutchings and W. Ruddick (eds), *Thomas Gray: Contemporary Essays* (Liverpool, 1993), 146–70; and idem, '"Sweet Native Stream!": Wordsworth and the School of Warton', in Alvaro Ribeiro, SJ, and James G. Basker (eds), *Tradition in Transition* (Oxford, 1996), 314–38.

42. Many of these relations are now made more visible by David Fairer's edition of the *Correspondence of Warton* (see n.12 above).

43. I exclude Barrett's private needs for his history of Bristol. The literati were still anxious about this enterprise when publication of the history loomed in 1789: Warton told Lort that Barrett had resolved not to use the Chatterton manuscripts in his work (though we might suppose that this had been the real object of his original interest in the Rowley materials). See *Illustrations*, vii. 554. For the extensive use made of Rowley items in the published history, see *Works*, xxxiii.

44. See *The Percy Letters: The Correspondence of Thomas Percy and Thomas Warton*, ed. M. G. Robinson and L. Dennis (Baton Rouge, La., 1951), 142–4; also printed in *Correspondence of Warton*, 342, 368.

45. Warton, *Enquiry*, 20.

46. Ibid., 124.

47. Malone, for one, recognized himself as an antiquarian, but it was a label most of the group would have been hesitant to adopt: most would have sympathized with Johnson's joking opinion that 'a mere antiquarian is a rugged being' (*Life of Johnson*, iii. 278). Lord Hailes thought that antiquarians had naturally been amongst those most easily duped by Chatterton: 'It is not strange that Antiquaries, who generally deal in bad prose, should have no ear for Poetry, & be incapable of discerning between the rhymes of one age & another' (Hailes to Warton, 27 September 1788, in *Correspondence of Warton*, 606).

48. The most comprehensive modern treatment of Malone's career is that of Peter Martin, *Edmond Malone: Shakespearean Scholar* (Cambridge, 1995). For the Chatterton affair, see 74–80.

49. Malone, Edmond, *Cursory Observations on the Poems Attributed to Thomas Rowley* (London, 1782), 41.

50. de Grazia, Margreta, *Shakespeare Verbatim: The Reproduction of Authenticity and the 1790 Apparatus* (Oxford, 1991), 226.

51. The title of chapter 3 in de Grazia, 93–131. According to de Grazia (223–4), Malone's edition operated so that 'a relation of ownership was inscribed that assigned the texts to Shakespeare both stylistically and hermenutically'. We might see the Rowley exposures as an attempt to *dispossess* Chatterton of his borrowed language, that is to *deprive* the text not only of historicity and authenticity, but of rightful ownership. However, this has nothing to do with copyright or literary property as legally construed: it is a matter of the probity of authorial claims as they affect reading and response.

52. Grafton, Anthony, *Forgers and Critics: Creativity and Duplicity in Western*

Scholarship (Princeton, 1990), 5, 8. In addition, relevant information on Isaac Casaubon and others will be found in Grafton's study *Defenders of the Text: The Traditions of Scholarship in an Age of Science, 1450–1800* (Cambridge, Mass., 1991), 145–61 and *passim.*

53. Grafton (1990), 45.
54. See for example Levine, J. M., *Dr Woodward's Shield* (Berkeley, 1977); and *The Battle of the Books: History and Literature in the Augustan Age* (Ithaca, 1991).
55. Grafton (1990), 122.
56. Ibid. (1990), 123.
57. For example, de Grazia argues that Malone's Shakespearean apparatus was 'constructed on the basis of a positivistic standard that his work ... could never satisfy' (129).
58. *Life*, xvii. One of the problems with this suggestion is that Johnson may not have known anything about Chatterton's political attitudes (his support for Wilkes and Alderman Beckford, say, and his criticism of Lord Bute and the Duke of Grafton). These were of course in line with conventional 'opposition' ideology, and Johnson might well have guessed where Chatterton stood. But there is no evidence that he read any of Chatterton's political writings, or even knew of their existence (beyond what Lort may have read aloud). None of Johnson's comments on the young poet suggest that he has anyone other than Rowley in mind.
59. We might speculate that Johnson was psychologically ill-prepared to admit the claims of a man who might conceivably replace Richard Savage, as the fatherless Bristol poet who scourged a corrupt and insensate ruling class. Chatterton himself saw the link with Savage (*Life*, 390; *Works*, 453). It is likely, too, that Johnson found it distasteful that Chatterton should have constructed the language of Rowley principally from *dictionaries* such as those of Kersey and Bailey. This was a breach of faith with the lexicographical profession. After all, Johnson himself had based his great work in considerable measure on his predecessors, above all Bailey. Chatterton's appropriation of lexicography for his own self-interested purposes becomes a kind of treachery.
60. It was members of the Club who had done most to refigure the map of English culture, through their pioneering efforts to codify the artistic inheritance of the nation. See Lipking, Lawrence, *The Ordering of the Arts in Eighteenth-Century England* (Princeton, 1970). With the lone exception of Horace Walpole, all the key figures treated by Lipking – Hawkins and Burney, Johnson and Warton, Reynolds – were Clubmen. To this list we might add the contributions of Gibbon in reconstructing ancient history; Adam Smith in realigning the study of political economy; Boswell in reformulating the genre of biography; William Jones in developing comparative philology; Joseph Banks in institutionalizing the study of botany; Burke in political rhetoric and Garrick in dramatic expression. Moreover, Robert Chambers (with the help of Johnson) was the first to amplify significantly the great codification of law carried out by Blackstone (himself a friend and associate of several members). It would be understandable if such a group had no desire to see poetic conventions remodelled by a rank outsider. Chatterton is supposed to have told his

sister, 'I wish I knew the classicals, I then could do anything' (*Life*, 62): whatever his individual merits as a creative writer, this lack would have sunk him in the Club's estimation as an arbiter of literary destiny.

1. 'The Last Sleep of Arthur in Avalon' (detail), 1881–98, by Sir Edward Burne-Jones (1833–98), Museo de Arte, Ponce, Puerto Rico.

2. 'Truth Sacrifising to the Muses', Grignion after Ryley, published by Bellamy (1793).

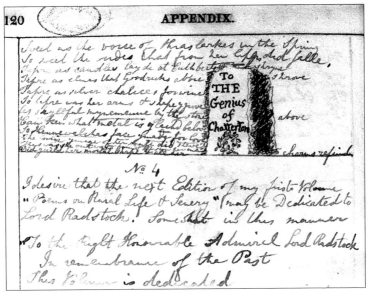

3. John Clare's sketch for a tombstone.

4. The 'goggle-ey'd portrait'; unknown engraver after unknown artist, published by Baldwyn (1797).

5. Frontispiece to John Dix's *Life of Chatterton* (1837): Alais after Branwhite, stipple engraving.

CHATTERTON.

"THE MARVELLOUS BOY WHO PERISHED IN HIS PRIDE." SOUTHEY.

From a picture in the possession of
George Weare Braikenridge, Esq.
Broomwell House, Brislington.

6. Undated pseudo-portrait; unknown engraver after unknown artist, stipple engraving.

"THE DEATH OF CHATTERTON"

AFTER RESTORATION

7. Larry after Wallis, from *Punch* (June 1987), 25.

Chapter 9

'Truth Sacrifising to the Muses': The Rowley Controversy and the Genesis of the Romantic Chatterton

Maria Grazia Lolla

> Hee will goe you forty miles to see a Saint's well, or a ruin'd Abbey: and if there be but a Crosse or stone footstoole in the way, hee'l be considering it so long, till he forgets his journey.
>
> (John Earle, 'The Antiquary')

> The question is the desire of thought ... the answer is the question's misfortune, its adversity.
>
> (Maurice Blanchot)

Before becoming the archetypal Romantic poet, the 'marvellous Boy', and the inspiration for innumerable poems, plays, operas, novels, paintings, and lengthy, uninformative biographies, Thomas Chatterton had been a footnote to Rowley and Canynge, a local attraction in Bristol, and, above all, a function of what became known as the Rowley Controversy.[1]

In the years immediately following his death, Chatterton was remarkably invisible. He was not given life in print until seven years later, in 1777, when Thomas Tyrwhitt felt obliged to provide the reader with a footnote concerning 'the principal circumstances of his short life', since they were 'intimately connected with that of the poems now published'. A fuller biographical account appeared as a digression in Herbert Croft's epistolary novel, *Love and Madness* (1780) three years later – though Croft's contribution was explicitly not 'a formal life of Chatterton'.[2] A full-length biography was published, eventually, in 1789, in the fourth volume of Andrew Kippis's *Biographia Britannica*, 20 years after Chatterton's death, but, tellingly, it was printed in the 'Appendix to the letter C.' (where his life was a little more than a footnote to the entry).

Chatterton's 'scrap of existence', hardly worthy of the appellation of life, as Croft put it, could easily be squeezed into the margin of these narratives – a footnote, a digression, an appendix, or even a cartouche – for the real sensation at the time was the controversy over the authenticity of the Rowley poems. Compared to the magnitude of the issues debated and the stature of the scholars involved in the argument, Chatterton was just 'too trifling to admit any further discussion'.[3] His life counted at most as external evidence, and like paper and ink it was discarded at an early stage as secondary evidence. If it was worth telling at all, it was because it was in some way connected to the controversy – and yet the controversy was known as the *Rowley* Controversy and the paladins of Chatterton went by the name of 'Anti-Rowleyans'.[4]

Where Chatterton was irrelevant to a controversy that effaced his memory even in name (and quite frankly thrived on him being dead and unable to provide a key to the mystery of his forgeries), he hardly existed outside it. The controversy was so integral a part of Chatterton's life that Croft could not even mention Chatterton's date and place of birth without peeking forward: 'Thomas Chatterton, destin'd to puzzle at least, if not impose upon, the ablest critics and antiquarians which the most polished age of England has produced, was born at Bristol, November the 20th 1752'. Similarly, the editor of the *Biographia Britannica* delayed the publication of Chatterton's biography because he 'was in hope that the controversy excited by him would have been so far ended', that he could 'give the history of it in the present volume'.[5] Accordingly, George Gregory, the author of the entry, produced a biography that resembled a monument to all those who had contributed to 'the literary phenomenon of Thomas Chatterton', a cartoon of the funeral procession, rather than a life of Chatterton, as the title deceptively promised.

Although Chatterton was unceremoniously dispensed with for the sake of a controversy that prided itself on being 'the most curious and extraordinary controversy, which, since the days of Bentley has divided the literary world', and on having been 'honoured with the attention of gentlemen of the first erudition in the republic of letters', 'curious and extraordinary' are not the only epithets that have been used to describe the controversy, nor is 'gentlemen of the first erudition' the way those who partook in it are normally referred to.[6] On the contrary, later critics have invariably read the discussion as an embarrassment to scholarship. The judgment of scholars has only become harsher with time. If in 1810 Alexander Chalmers declined to discuss the controversy and contented himself with intimating that its 'object' was 'disproportionate to the warmth it excited, and the length of time it consumed', in 1842 Robert Browning was considerably less restrained when he proclaimed that the fact that 'there should have been a controversy for ten minutes about the genuineness of any ten verses of "Rowley"' was 'a real disgrace to the scholarship of the age in which such a thing took place'. And Walter Skeat in 1871 deplored the controversy as an emblem of the 'existing destitution of philological knowledge' of its participants; Charles Edward Russell belittled their knowledge by comparing it to that of 'the average high school boy of Kansas or Oklahoma'.[7]

This essay argues that the outrage of those who assessed the significance of the Rowley controversy as a monument to the ignorance of the age draws on the double fallacy that the controversy was about the authenticity of Rowley in the first place and that it went on for so long because of the Rowleyans' obstinacy. In fact the controversy was not primarily, or at all, about Rowley; it was neither started nor exacerbated by the Rowleyans but went on for so long largely because those who participated in it had a stake in its continuation which went well beyond a desire for resolution. Rather than proving the ignorance and *naïveté* of early scholars, the controversy fostered research, provided an outlet for the massive amount of information accumulated by antiquaries over the decades and polarized scholars into two groups who, while ostensibly arguing for or against Rowley, promoted conflicting views of the past. In addition, rather than being an unfortunate parenthesis in Chatterton's poetic afterlife, the controversy was crucial to the genesis of the appreciation of Chatterton's poetic persona.

That assessing the authenticity of Rowley was not a priority was obvious from the controversy's (specious) beginning. It is worth recalling that the controversy became public only after (and, to a large extent, because of) the publication of selections from Rowley by editors who were already convinced that the material that Chatterton had fabricated between 1768 and 1770 and attributed to the monk Rowley were modern forgeries. Tyrwhitt's ambiguously entitled edition 'Poems, supposed to have been written at Bristol, by Thomas Rowley and others, in the fifteenth century' appeared in early February of 1777. Since the ostensible purpose of the edition was providing the public with unmediated access to those sources which had 'for some time excited much curiosity', Tyrwhitt studiously avoided revealing his opinion and left it 'to the determination of the unprejudiced and intelligent Reader'.[8] Although Tyrwhitt had undertaken the edition when he believed that the poems might have been authentic, by the time the edition came out, he had made up his mind that they were not. This notwithstanding, he neither stopped the publication nor modified his preface. Indeed, ostensibly to prevent the devaluation of the book, Tyrwhitt kept his preface unchanged through two subsequent editions, one of which bore an appendix 'tending to prove that they were written, not by any ancient author, but entirely by Thomas Chatterton'.[9]

Warton's inclusion of Rowley in the second volume of his *History of English Poetry* (1778) was even more specious. Unlike Tyrwhitt, Warton was not too shy to state his opinion. The section including the poems was entitled 'Poems under the name of Thomas Rowlie supposed to be spurious'. Half-way through the section he announced that 'none of these pieces are genuine', 'an ingenious critic and intelligent antiquary' of his acquaintance having assured him that 'the writing was a gross and palpable forgery ... not even skilfully counterfeited'. Yet there being 'some degree of plausibility in the history of their discovery', their 'merit', the fact that 'many respectable critics' believed them to be authentic, but especially, that 'the world might be furnished with an opportunity of examining their authenticity', were good enough reasons to include them in a history of English poetry.[10]

Both Tyrwhitt and Warton later apologized (obliquely), claiming that they had independently decided to publish their finds to fulfil their felt obligation towards the public, and had merely provided the material that might put an end to a discussion that had been smouldering for a few years.[11] But whether they really hoped to close a discussion by opening it, and they genuinely expected that a few remarks, or a mere edition of Rowley, would be sufficient to quiet controversy, or hoped, instead, to rekindle discussion, their editions were not taken as self-evident proofs of the forgery. Rather than widening the consensus that the Rowley pieces were modern, they brought about a controversy which was destined to last on and off for an entire century. Their editions instantly provoked a flurry of responses in the literary periodicals. Letters were followed by pamphlets the largest of which was Jacob Bryant's *Observations upon the Rowley Poems* (1781) which reached the staggering dimension of a 600-page, two-volume treatise. The controversy came to its peak in 1782, when most of the pamplets were issued, but continued well into the nineteenth century. As late as 1871, Walter W. Skeat claimed that he had 'to begin the whole work of verification *de novo*' to prove that Chatterton's manuscripts were a forgery.[12] Judged with the wisdom of hindsight, the carelessness with which the first editors addressed the issue of the authenticity of the manuscripts appears as either irresponsible or calculated.

Establishing whether the Rowley poems were authentic or not was the goal neither of those editors who published Rowley when they did not need further proof of the forgery, nor of those who, immediately after the appearance of those editions, engaged in the controversy in the periodicals, where discussion moved instantly away from Rowley. Wanting to prove or disprove the authenticity of Rowley generated a number of sub-controversies which were only nominally related to the initial argument. Topics of discussion ranged from the way in which arrows were shot among ancient Britons, the form of their javelins and the usage of armours, to Homer in the Middle Ages, the introduction of worsted stockings and woollen manufactures in Britain, and a myriad of other points.[13] Indeed, much of the controversy did not qualify as a confrontation, for those who participated in the discussion alternatively showed off their knowledge and frankly confessed their ignorance, but also plunged into research and encouraged others to do the same. Take for instance the discussion on the date in which worsted stockings were introduced in England, a topic that saw Rowleyans and Anti-Rowleyans relinquish partisanship and join forces in the common venture to throw light on an obscure portion of their national history. Two months after having argued that the mention of worsted stockings in the Rowley poems were yet more evidence of anachronism, 'A.B.' freely announced that he 'had learnt' since his last 'a bit of history respecting *Hosiers* and *Tailors*' which made him change his mind. Rather than using his research on stockings as evidence of the authenticity of Rowley, 'W' concluded that earlier historians should be used with discretion – 'it is evident how cautiously we ought to admit for truth every thing we find transmitted down to us by our historians' – and that 'the reigns of Henry VIth and Edward IVth want light to be thrown upon them'. The controversy, he argued, provided a precious opportunity to pursue research and he declared himself 'happy in the thought that the Chattertonian controversy may be a means of doing that, and of illustrating a period of our history, from the commotions of the times full of interesting events'. Along the same lines 'A Candid Enquirer', after displaying the result of his research on stockings in a several-page letter, proposed it 'as an Exercise for some of your Antiquarian Readers, to ascertain whether this Art was known in England at the Time this Poem is said to have been written'.[14] Rowleyans and

Anti-Rowleyans alike embraced Rowley as an incentive to pursue research on the national past.

The digressive nature of the controversy is even more glaringly apparent in the lengthy pamphlets that began appearing in 1781. Indeed, the fact that the controversy was not about Rowley was obvious to the participants. Reviewers of Bryant's *Observations*, for instance, though respectful of the 'knowledge of antiquity', the 'learning' and 'acuteness' displayed in the pamphlet, could not fail to notice that 'he sometimes forgets his author to pursue his own views', so that it was 'perhaps, not unreasonable or unjust severity, to observe that *one half* of his work has very little, if any, relation to the dispute'. Another reviewer compared Bryant to Paracelsus, who, though he failed 'in discovering the philosopher's stone, yet, in his wild ranges through nature, made discoveries of much greater consequence, and opened a field of entertainment and information which amply recompensed his assiduity, however distant it might leave him from the original object of his pursuit'. Indeed, Bryant himself was aware and somewhat 'concerned' about the length and range of his digressions.[15]

Far from being a prerogative of the Rowleyans – and far from being stigmatized – digressions were welcomed as the most cherished outcome of the controversy by all parties. George Hardinge proudly announced that 'without any reference to the immediate controversy … many curious points in history and antiquity may be investigated with success, or at least plausibility, which otherwise probably would have remained unnoticed'. Similarly, Thomas James Mathias argued that digressions saved the controversy from the charge of frivolity: 'Why then should these enquiries into the Poems attributed to Rowley be regarded as frivolous, when we consider the various topics they may necessarily introduce, or the pleasing speculations into which they may lead an inquisitive mind?' Trusting that digressions were the best part of the controversy, as late as 1809 John Sherwen entered the discussion knowing from the outset that 'whatever may be the ultimate fate of the main question, its discussion will comprehend so many curious philological inquiries, and will throw light upon so many doubtful and obscure, and even hitherto unintelligible passages in the works of some of our old poets and dramatic writers, as to excite an interest totally independent of the principal subject'. Down to the last pamphlet published in 1857, it was clear that 'perhaps nobody might be particularly anxious to discover whether certain illegible manuscripts were the work of Ischam or Tyb Gorges'.[16]

Just as the authenticity of the Rowley manuscripts has been placed by subsequent observers at the centre of the controversy, when, instead, it was only one of several issues being agitated, the extraordinary length of the controversy has been blamed on the obstinacy, the ignorance, and the gullibility of the Rowleyans. In fact neither Rowleyans nor Anti-Rowleyans wanted controversy to come to an end. Of the two, it was the Anti-Rowleyans – who had opened the discussion in the first place – who were more active in keeping it alive.

From the time that Tyrwhitt and Warton issued their candid appeal to their readers to decide on the authenticity of the manuscripts, the prime obligation of those who took part in the discussion was to keep it from stalling. The already mentioned 'Candid Enquirer', for instance, launched a suspiciously ambiguous appeal to keep the discussion going. He was anxious that 'some will conclude' that what appeared as anachronisms would be taken as 'plain Proof of the Forgery of these Poems', where he 'would by no means draw the same Inference', but 'would rather be induced to search with greater Attention, to try to discover, by other means, if this Art was then known in England'. The leading miscellanies remained committed to the discussion even after disclosure of compelling evidence that the Rowley poems showed spelling mistakes that could be traced back to contemporary dictionaries. As late as 1789 Gregory kept up the pretence that the question was undecided. Robert Anderson declared in 1792 that although he could not 'entertain a doubt but that they were written by Chatterton', he meant not 'to dictate to others'.[17] It was not just that the evidence was not cogent enough. Those who took part in the controversy seemed more interested in arguing and pursuing research than in winning the argument or answering questions.

The ignorance of scholars who could not detect an obvious forgery has been emphasized at the expense of the amount of information that was uncovered along the way and the curiosity, and the eagerness to explore and learn of those who partook in it. More importantly it has not been acknowledged that as well as spurring new research, the controversy provided an occasion for a rare display of knowledge and grew out of the new research on the past. Seen against the background of the ever-expanding research on the national past, the controversy appears neither surprising nor a landmark of the ignorance of the time. On the contrary, in the light of the keenness to open the discussion and keep it going at all costs, it could be argued that it was precisely the exploration of the past tuned to such a fine pitch and turned into a popular, unregulated, enterprise, which moved the controversy in the first instance and kept it going for so long. Not only were a growing number of amateurs, scholars, antiquaries and men of taste engaged in the study of the past, but their finds and research methods had brought them to hold conflicting views of the same past.

Although Rowleyans and Anti-Rowleyans ended up on the same side, having both furthered the cause of scholarship with their questions and participated in the entertainment of the discussion, the controversy was also undoubtedly a fierce confrontation. Contrary to the expectations of the first editors who trusted that a few remarks would settle the question and strengthen their authority, by opening the discussion, they made themselves vulnerable to the attacks of scholars who appeared to be less keen to establish once and for all the authenticity of Rowley than to discredit their opponents' competence, authority and, more generally, 'system' of literature. The so-called Rowleyans, in fact, hardly argued in favour of Rowley. Sometimes they even confessed their suspicion that the poems could be forged. Instead they turned Rowley into the vehicle of a larger offensive on scholars of established reputation.

Of the Anti-Rowleyans, Warton was the one who attracted the most criticism. Beginning with Lionel Chalmers, who, in May 1778, launched an attack on one of Warton's footnotes to expose Warton's misinformation and flawed arguments (rather than to state his allegiance to Rowley), a string of Rowleyans entered the controversy sometimes with the sole purpose of challenging Warton's authority on matters unrelated to Rowley. 'Z.Y.X.', for instance, did not set out to speak either in favour or against the authenticity of the manuscripts, but used the occasion of Rowley and the example of Chalmers to launch an attack on Warton's competence in Spanish and Italian literature. Similarly, the anonymous author of the *Remarks upon the Eighth Section of the Second Volume of Mr Warton's History* aimed at Warton's 'reputed abilities' and '*authority*'. His goal was to alert Warton's readers to the fact that 'his narrative is by no means exact, nor his quotations faithful ... in a word, that the Professor's system throughout, is not supported by a single argument that holds good, or a single fact that may not be questioned'. As to Rowley, he did not pronounce himself an unequivocal supporter, but stated, instead, that 'perhaps it may be a forgery; there are more reasons for thinking so of this than of any other'. Even a committed Rowleyan such as George Catcott claimed to have pointed out Warton's inaccuracies primarily to undermine Warton's authority: 'Had the assertions I intend to examine fallen from a less respectable pen than that of Mr. Warton, they might have passed unnoticed by me; but *his* name will render them *important*, and his *opinion* in this matter, must (as indeed in general it ought) greatly influence the judgment of the *Public'*. (The inaccuracies included having mentioned that Chatterton was 15, instead of 17, when he first offered Rowleyan manuscripts to Catcott; that the manuscripts were found in an iron chest, instead of a wooden one; and that one of the Rowley letters was addressed to Lydgate, instead of Canynge.[18])

Rowley was so much a function of the larger offensive carried out by antiquaries against established scholars that Rowleyans established a connection between Rowley and Joseph Ritson, who was not himself a Rowleyan but was known for his fierce attack on Warton. A correspondent of the *St. James's Chronicle* signed himself 'Rowleiophilus', without mentioning Rowley in his piece. Instead he launched a ferocious attack on Warton:

> You have long lived the Usurper of the Throne of ancient English Literature. Your Words were Law, your Nods Decisions in the Empire of Learning – and Woe to the Wretch who durst dispute your Tribunal. But your Reign is now expired.... The *Observations on the Three first Volumes of your History* ... display such a Fund of Learning, in pointing out and correcting your Errours, as will infallibly demolish that long-established Tory System of Passive Obedience and Non Resistance to your Decrees.[19]

Allegiance to Rowley was the metonym for rebellion against established scholarship.

That their competence and authority had been put in question was clear to the Anti-Rowleyans. Accused of incompetence and mandarin inattention to detail, they replied by invoking taste. Seeing their authority challenged and asked to make room for alternative approaches to the national literary past, they responded by making their authoritarianism even more obvious: they proclaimed their right to be the sole arbiters and custodians of the national literature, dictated the terms of the discussion and, ultimately, sought to oust their opponents from the arena altogether.

After having laughed off the efforts of the Rowleyans as 'too risible for any common power of face', and before engaging in a discussion, Edmond Malone asserted as a 'fixed principle', that 'the authenticity or spuriousness of the poems attributed to Rowley cannot be decided by any person who has not a *taste* for English poetry, and a moderate, at least, if not a critical, knowledge of the compositions of most of our poets from the time of Chaucer to that of Pope'. 'Without this critical knowledge and taste', Malone insisted in a more obviously polemical fashion, 'all the Saxon literature that can be employed on this subject ... will only puzzle and perplex, instead of illustrating, the point in dispute'.[20]

Insistence on taste and 'internal evidence' bespoke even more clearly Warton's aristocratic disdain for the lower classes and their acquired knowledge. Warton's formulation of the same 'fixed principle' was that

> It is not from the complexion of ink or of parchment, from the information of cotemporaries, the tales of relations, the recollections of apprentices, and the prejudices of friends, nor even from doomsday-book, pedigrees in the herald's office, armorial bearings, parliamentary rolls, inquisitions, indentures, episcopal registers, epitaphs, tomb-stones, and brass-plates, that this controversy is to be finally and effectually adjusted. Our arguments should be drawn from principles of taste, from analogical experiment, from a familiarity with antient poetry, and from the gradations of composition.

Earlier in the same pamphlet, Warton had dismissed knowledge 'communicated and even familiarised to all ranks and all ages, by Reviews, Magazines, Abridgements, Encyclopedes, and other works of a similar kind, which form the *school of the people*' – a statement that broke even the ranks of the Anti-Rowleyans.[21]

Animated by unprecedented confidence the Rowleyans challenged not only the Anti-Rowleyans' dubious scholarship but also their 'system', or, in contemporary terms, their history and theory of literature. From the very beginning Rowley was perceived and used as a threat to literary order. Whereas Warton feared that 'If it should at last be decided, that these poems were really written so early as the reign of king Edward the fourth, the entire system that has hitherto been framed concerning the progression of poetical composition, and every theory that has been established on the gradual improvements of taste, style, and language, will be shaken and disarranged', the Rowleyans aimed precisely at what alarmed Warton so much: shaking and disarranging 'the entire system that has hitherto been framed'.[22] In fact it can be argued that Rowley was promoted (if not fabricated) to undermine current views of the past.

Before the controversy exploded, Chatterton's patron William Barrett wrote to Ducarel: 'It has been supposed, I hear, by the critics, that no poetry can be produced, worthy the name of poetry, betwixt the time of Chaucer and Spenser, as if the Muse slept at that interval, &c. ... yet, I will assure you, I have some, though few, originals of Rowley, which totally disprove their assertions'. 'We have been taught to believe', Barrett insisted, 'that a genius for poetical composition, an enquiry into works of literature, researches after antiquities and arts, improvements of sciences, and the like, are no where to be found amongst the English till of very late date.' (Incidentally, Dr Ducarel, Barrett's addressee, did not need to see the documents to agree with Barrett. He believed in Rowley without having read the poems or indeed much literature at all.) Catcott, who was responsible even more than Barrett for promoting Rowley, also reiterated on several occasions the need to rewrite the history of English poetry. 'The following old song', he wrote in a footnote reminiscent of Chatterton's own, 'may vie with any of our Poetry, few of our Modern Compositions, being equal to it wch shows that Literature and even this sublime & engaging part of it was not at so low an ebb formerly as we have been told'.[23]

Chatterton himself had declared that his main 'motive' in producing Rowley was to prove that loss of evidence was responsible for the value-laden views of the literary past. Chatterton had argued that the Normans had 'destroy'd the Mss, paintings &c of the Saxons', and that 'the Poetry of those Days' was 'greatly superior to what we have been taught to believe'. When he contacted Dodsley, he wrote: 'the Motive that actuates me to do this, is, to convince the World that the Monks (of whom some have so despicable an Opinion) were not such Blockheads, as generally thought and that good Poetry might be wrote, in the dark days of Superstition as well as in these more inlightened Ages'.[24]

If authentic, Rowley would have proved the Anti-Rowleyans' history of literature wrong both in its joining of modernity and value and in promoting the notion of the Dark Ages. Rowleyans insisted that poetic value was not a function of time and that what was assumed to be dark, empty and unpopulated, was, most likely, not. The void, for the Rowleyans, was a function of ignorance and distorted, though powerful, vision. But Rowley was both the long-awaited *and* the long-feared evidence that would force historians into rewriting the course of English poetry. For the Anti-Rowleyans it was just as urgent to deny the authenticity of Rowley as it was to preserve their view of the past unchanged. A system of literature that contemplated the gradual improvement of taste, style and language, from 'a rude origin ... to its perfection in a polished age', and a system where the belief in the progress of literature came with disparaging remarks on early English literature, had no room for poetry that showed that literature might not have undergone a linear progress and that early English literature could have some appeal.[25]

It is not surprising that Warton's progressive view of literature became instantly his most cogent 'evidence' of the spuriousness of Rowley. For Warton, Rowley's poetry could not be authentic because it was too refined for its time – so much so that once translated into modern idiom it would have sounded utterly modern!

> Those who have been conversant in the works even of the best of our old English poets, well know, that one of their leading characteristics is inequality ... for many pages together, they are tedious, prosaic, and uninteresting. On the contrary, the poems before us ... are throughout, poetical and animated. They have no imbecillities of style or sentiment ... Rowlie's poetry sustains one uniform tone of harmony; and, if we brush away the asperities of the antiquated spelling, conveys its cultivated imagery in a polished and agreeable strain of versification.[26]

In his 1782 pamphlet – a pamphlet larded with expressions such as 'Of old English poetry ... the bad predominates' and 'In this sort of reading, we are but rarely relieved from disgust, or rouzed from indifference' – Warton argued that the fact that poetry progressed from the beginning to its present perfection, made poetry and its criticism comparable to science, which allowed him to formulate predictions. Warton, then, let himself go on an excited evocation of what should have happened: 'Even allowing that the supposed Rowley was cultivated in literature beyond his times,' Warton wrote,

> he would have cited or named, at least some of the Latin poets ... would have interspersed his poetry with texts of scripture ... We miss the marks ... of old romances ... Had such a poet as Rowley existed in the fifteenth century, he would have been idolized by his age,... and his works would have been multiplied by numerous manuscripts ... He would have been printed by Caxton ... His life would have been written by Bale ...

On the basis of his analysis Warton was confident that 'the few flat and insipid passages that remain in their original state' will 'easily be consigned to Rowley'.[27] To validate the system, only the bad Rowley was accepted as authentic.

Similar arguments were produced by Malone. With Warton, Malone shared a distaste for early English literature, a passion for experiments – he translated Chatterton's *African Eclogues* into medieval English – and the unbound confidence in his hypothesis of what should have happened instead. 'If such a man as Rowley had existed', he argued, 'he would have had half the parchment in the kingdom at his command; statues would have been erected to him as the greatest prodigy that the world had ever seen; and in a few years afterwards, when printing came to be practised, the presses of Caxton and Wynkyn de Worde would have groaned with his productions'.[28]

The controversy over Rowley was largely a contest over the history of English poetry. As such it was by some considered worth fighting. And as such Rowley belonged in a history of English poetry (although Warton's later editors viewed the section as an embarrassment and eventually excised it from the *History*).[29] But arguments in favour of Rowley branched well beyond the rehabilitation of an unsuitably desiccated view of the Middle Ages into the Anti-Rowleyans' very theory of literature and approaches to the study of the past.

Not involved in either the fabrication or the promotion of Rowley, and, it can be added, not primarily interested in Rowley, Bryant launched the most comprehensive attack on the Anti-Rowleyans' belief in a 'system' of literature. Ostensibly arguing for Rowley, Bryant relentlessly aimed at eroding the Anti-Rowleyans' confidence, undermining untenably ordered views of the past and disrupting narratives of continuity. Bryant started by objecting to the notion of a unified English language (to which he opposed a fractured linguistic tradition made up of a variety of dialects) and went on to challenge the presumed homogeneity of literary periods as promoted by the Anti-Rowleyans and finally the hypothesis that literature progresses. According to Bryant there was just not enough evidence. He argued that nothing 'certain' can be determined from 'the texture of a poem, and the mode of compositions' and that we must not 'suppose, because a writer may be in some degree smooth and easy, that he must necessarily be of modern date'. To believe that 'arts take up time to come to maturity; and that poetry must proceed by degrees towards excellence', were 'mere matter of opinion, and by no means well founded'.[30]

As forcefully as he objected to the Anti-Rowleyans' belief in the progress of literature, Bryant questioned their confidence in making

predictions about the past on the basis of their current (scant) knowledge. To those who had objected that it was unlikely that a treasure
of poetry could lie hidden for so long, Bryant responded by recalling
all the manuscripts 'in the Bodleian, and other libraries', which 'lie in
like state of oblivion, and are at this day utterly disregarded'. To those
who had taken mistakes and the apparent smoothness of versification
as evidence of forgery, Bryant responded by invoking the complexity
of the process of transmission: numerous were the cases in which the
intervention of a transcriber was detected without the authenticity of
the original documents being imputed. His all-encompassing scepticism touched even the external evidence. For Bryant there was no
'criterion' by which 'we can certainly determine about the common
hand-writing of people at any time, in the same country'. Definitely,
it was not with experiments that the age of Rowley could be established. To those who had proved Rowley a forgery by arguing that 'if
we only change the spelling, his verses will appear in great measure
modern', he objected that 'The same will be found in many other
writers'. Any modernized author would sound modern.[31]

To the Anti-Rowleyans' hypotheses, assertions, and experiments,
Bryant responded with documents, empirical observations, and above
all with questions. To their unproblematized distaste of early English
literature he did not oppose a vague *laudatio temporis acti*, but doubts.
His was the perspective of a student who was groping in the dark and
had been proven wrong before. His narrative is interspersed with statements such as 'After all I must confess that the whole of this inquiry
is attended with great uncertainty' and 'In these dark researches, it is
not in our power to speak with a thorough degree of certainty'.

The controversy was definitely not about as trifling a subject as
either Rowley or Chatterton. Nor was it susceptible of settlement by
anything we might identify as evidence. The controversy in fact
hinged minimally on evidence and what there was could be used to
draw opposite conclusions. Mistakes in Chatterton's glossary, for
instance, were taken as proof of forgery by the Anti-Rowleyans and as
evidence of authenticity by the Rowleyans. The fact that Rowley made
use of a language not attested in any other author was not reputed
conclusive either. As Samuel Seyer wrote in an unpublished assessment of the arguments of the controversy: 'Homer's works have never
been suspected; & yet we can prove that these writings are totally
different from the language and orthography of Homer's time'. Not
even the discovery of spelling mistakes which coincided with those in
the dictionaries that Chatterton consulted were cogent evidence:

'Cherisaunei makes for neither side. This mistake is in Skinner. Chatt: seeing the word in Rowley's MSS not very legibly written, might consult Skinner, & write it as Skinner has …'.[32] Hence the perpetual motion of the controversy. Blake's oracular statement – 'I believe both Macpherson & Chatterton, that what they say is Ancient Is so' – is a remarkably accurate assessment.[33] No evidence could be definitive, when at play were expectations, biases, assumptions, predilections, and incompatible approaches to research.

What the controversy had allowed to emerge was not only the fact that knowledge of the past was rapidly expanding and that research on national antiquities was being furthered by a wide number of amateurs, who were not necessarily known to each other and who operated on the past with a variety of tools, but also that conflicting (perhaps irreconcilable) views of the past, taste, and scholarship were in existence. Whereas the Anti-Rowleyans viewed the past as the checkpoint of their own refinement, the Rowleyans deferred to the same past with awe and reverence and promoted a version of it which contemplated a large body of attractive literature and the promise of finding more. And whereas the Anti-Rowleyans looked at Rowley from the vantage point of an infallible system – which was naturally validated by what they already knew – and were unwilling to accommodate exceptions, the Rowleyans examined Rowley in the full awareness of their own ignorance and in the keen expectation of new finds.

Not only could the Rowleyans not testify to a system that turned antiquity and antiquarianism into a point of negative reference, but they were also especially uneasy with an approach that organized the past into an all-explicatory system which permitted predictions and experiments. For the Rowleyans, too little was known to formulate judgments on antiquity. They were in fact hammering on just this point: the ways of the past are mysterious; history is not predictable; it is opaque and unfathomable; it is a place where human reason is not supposed to feel at ease. The Rowleyans' was the perspective of scholars for whom what was not known or could be known counted as much as positive evidence; scholars who were working on unfinished, infinite, projects and who had been trained in the exceptional, the curious, the monstrous and the miraculous, rather than the normal and predictable; researchers who, having embraced the unpredictability of the past, were eager to be surprised and startled by discoveries. More importantly, the Rowleyans' was the perspective of students who had come to literature by way of research on the whole of the national past and did not view literary productions as a separate field open only to a privileged and tasteful minority. For the Rowleyans literary texts were a valuable source in the study of the past that could be approached with tools and skills available to all.

Although the Rowleyans were ultimately disqualified by the fact that Rowley was not, in fact, authentic, their arguments had meaning outside the immediate contest over Rowley. Horace Walpole, for one, severed the arguments brought into the discussion by the Rowleyan Jacob Bryant from his verdict on Rowley.[34] Besides, as well as contributing to raising the standards of scholarship, their vociferous criticism made it apparent that, though young, scholarship on the national past was contested or, at least, more contested than the over-confident statements of the Anti-Rowleyans might lead one to believe. Not only did the Rowleyans succeed in engaging their opponents in a dialogue – their criticism, however ridiculous, called for an answer and obtained one – they also posed a perceptible threat.[35] The Anti-Rowleyans' vulnerability was more than a topos of the Rowleyans' propaganda that depicted their opponents as 'astonished' at 'the late unexpected victory', and aware of having 'raised a ticklish fabric'.[36] Both the Anti-Rowleyans' attempt to exclude the Rowleyans from the discussion and their preoccupation that 'the entire system that has hitherto been framed ... will be shaked and disarranged' can be read as a testimony of mounting anxiety, rather than evidence of unshaken confidence.

It was Chatterton's ambiguous performance as a poet and an anti-quary that posed the condition for a dialogue to take place between groups that were not likely interlocutors. As Mathias put it, had Chatterton's papers 'consisted of plain prose narrations ... had they treated of anecdotes, armorial bearings, ancient records or similar points of antiquity, I much doubt whether any question would have been raised of their authenticity'.[37] Outrageous as it may sound to modern ears, it was because documents *and* poetry were in question that both men of taste and antiquaries, critics and philologists, repre-sentatives of the centre of society and academia and those from the school of the people were drawn into the discussion.

The controversy, however, resolved the ambiguity of Chatterton's identity as antiquary and poet with the canonization of Chatterton 'the' poet – the Chatterton known and idolized by the Romantics. With the victory of the Anti-Rowleyan party, in fact, came the codicil of the poetic excellence of the Rowley poetry, which, in their effort to disprove the authenticity of Rowley, the Anti-Rowleyans had extolled with surprising ardour. Walpole confessed that 'nobody [could] admire the poems in question more than [he] did'. Malone believed him to have been 'the greatest genius that England has produced since the days of Shakspeare'. Warton praised the poems as 'throughout poetical and animated' devoid of 'imbecillities either of thought or diction', the works of a poet who 'never offends the ear', 'smooth and mellifluous'. He pronounced Chatterton 'a prodigy of genius', someone who 'would have proved the first of English poets, had he reached a maturer age'. Like Shakespeare, he was a genius whose 'powers of unconquerable mind outgo plans of education and conditions of life'. Mathias outdid them all with the lyricism of his praise: 'we behold a poetical fabric, perfect in all its parts, rising from an abyss of darkness and obscurity, whose foundation is solid, and whose superstructure is elegant. It seems as if the Spirit of Poetry had chosen it for his secret residence'.[38] (Indeed, both the recognition and the construction of Chatterton's poetic persona can be traced back to the controversy, for the 'recognition' of Chatterton 'the poet' was made possible by the labour of Chatterton's early editors, who ignored both Chatterton's gigantic apparatus and his large production of prose, documents, maps, drawings, pedigrees, and music scores and insisted on publishing Chatterton's poetry only, arranging it and translating it as became a true classic.)

But the initial question concerning the authenticity of the manuscripts remained unresolved. The controversy, that is, did not end with a satisfactory answer to the question regarding the authenticity of the manuscripts, but with the denial of the validity of the question. Wanting to know whether the Rowley poetry was authentic or not, or reading literary texts as documents, in the hope to both find and test information about the past, came to be seen as either irrelevant or antiquarian. Readers, instead, demanded that the 'intrinsic merit' of the poems 'independent of any consideration of the period in which or the person by whom, they were written' be discussed. Henry Maty, for instance, mocked those who condemned Chatterton for having written 'excellent' poetry: 'Gentlemen of the jury, the prisoner at the bar, Thomas Chatterton, is indicted for the uttering of certain poems composed by himself, purporting them to be poems of one Thomas Rowley, a priest of the XVth century ... The fact is stated to have been committed by the prisoner between the age of fifteen and seventeen; and the poems are admitted to be excellent'. According to Hardinge, Chatterton deserved gratitude for providing 'momentary amusement' at a time when 'the affairs of our nation are in so deplorable a situation'. In his view, Chatterton was a universal and immortal poet, unfettered by spatio-temporal constraints. 'Whatever be the opinion of their authenticity', Chatterton's poetry was 'worthy of any age or of any country'.[39] That the authenticity of Rowley was irrelevant seemed to have been also the position of the scholar who was most responsible for opening the discussion, Thomas Tyrwhitt. When Tyrwhitt launched Rowley knowing that the poems were forgeries, he undermined the whole question by saying that 'Whether the Poems be really antient, or modern; the compositions of Rowley, or the forgeries of Chatterton; they must always be considered as a most singular literary curiosity'.[40] Truth, to paraphrase the caption of a plate stuck into one copy of Tyrwhitt's edition of Rowley, had been sacrificed to the muses (Fig. 2).[41]

With truth in a suitably subordinate position, the word 'forgery' could be removed from the register and poetry be declared the product of the unruly imagination, free from the constraints of history, scholarship or authenticity. Chatterton could be honoured as a poet, a poet of the first magnitude, if not the archetypal poet. Chatterton was ready, as E. H. W. Meyerstein announced with a sigh of relief, to pass 'from the antiquaries to the poets'.[42]

Notes

1. See Goodridge, below.
2. *Poems*, vii; Croft, Herbert, *Love and Madness, A Story Too True* (London, 1780), 127. See Groom, Nick, 'Thomas Rowley Preeste', in Thomas Woodman, ed., *The Early Romantics* (London, 1998), 242–55.
3. Croft, 127; Warton, Thomas, *Enquiry into the Authenticity of the Poems Attributed to Thomas Rowley* (London, 1782), 7.
4. On the discussion over Chatterton's biography see *Critical Review* 53 (1782), 401; *GM* 53 (1783), 144, 190; *SJC*, 25 March 1783, 26 March 1782; *London Review and Literary Journal*, November 1789, 326.
5. Croft, 127; *Biographia Britannica*, ed. Andrew Kippis, 2nd edn (London, 1778–93), iii (1784). vii–viii.
6. Gregory, George, *The Life of Thomas Chatterton* (London, 1789), 143; *A Complete Edition of the Poets of Great Britain*, ed. Robert Anderson (London, 1792–5), xi (1795). 313–14.
7. *The Works of the English Poets from Chaucer to Cowper*, ed. Alexander Chalmers (London, 1810), xv. 378; Browning, Robert, 'Conjectures and Researches Concerning the Love, Madness, and Imprisonment of Torquato Tasso', *Foreign Quarterly Review* 29 (1842), 465–83 (470); *The Poetical Works of Thomas Chatterton*, ed. Walter W. Skeat (London, 1871–2), ii. ix; Russell, Charles Edward, *Thomas Chatterton the Marvelous Boy: The Story of a Strange Life 1752–1770* (London, 1909), 237. See also Sands, Alexander Hamilton,

Recreations of a Southern Barrister (Philadelphia, 1859), 25.

8. *Poems*, v, xii [i.e. xiii].
9. See *The Canterbury Tales of Chaucer: to which are Added, an Essay upon his Language and Versification; an Introductory Discourse; and Notes*, ed. Thomas Tyrwhitt (London, 1775-8), iii. 318; *GM* 58 (1788), 188; Powell, L. F., 'Thomas Tyrwhitt and the Rowley Poems', *RES* 7 (1931), 314–26.
10. Warton, Thomas, *The History of English Poetry, From the Close of the Eleventh to the Commencement of the Eighteenth Century* (London, 1774–81), ii (1778). 139, 153.
11. See *Poems*, 3rd edn (London, 1778), 311; Warton, *History of English Poetry*, ii. 'Emendations and Additions in the First and Second Volume' (1778), sig. [i2]^r.
12. Skeat, ii. xxxiv.
13. See *GM* 47 (1777), 206, 278, 317, 481; 51 (1781), 557; 52 (1782), 14, 76, 108, 112.
14. *GM*, 52 (1782), 168, 229–30; *SJC*, 8–10 September 1778. See also *GM* 52 (1782), 76. On forgery as an incentive to research see Wellek, René and Austin Warren, *Theory of Literature*, 3rd edn (New York, 1962), 67; Haywood, Ian, *Faking It: Art and the Politics of Forgery* (Brighton, 1987), 67; Grafton, Anthony, *Forgers and Critics: Creativity and Duplicity in Western Scholarship* (Princeton, 1990), 6.
15. *Critical Review* 54 (1782), 86, 98; *Monthly Review* 66 (1782), 433; Bryant, Jacob, *Observations upon the Poems of Thomas Rowley* (London, 1781), i. iii.
16. Hardinge, George, *Rowley and Chatterton in the Shades* … (London, 1782), 19; Mathias, Thomas James, *An Essay on the Evidence, External and Internal, Relating to the Poems Attributed to Thomas Rowley* (London, 1783), 55–6; Sherwen, John, *Introduction to an Examination of Some Part of the Internal Evidence Respecting the Antiquity and Authenticity of Certain Publications* … (Bath, 1809), vi; Maitland, S. R., *Chatterton: An Essay* (London, 1857), 54.
17. *SJC*, 8–10 September 1778; Anderson, xi. 318–19. See also *Monthly Review* 66 (1782), 206–7; *GM* 52 (1782), 195.
18. *GM* 48 (1778), 201–2; *SJC*, 29 December 1778; anon. [H. Dampier or F. Woodward], *Remarks Upon the Eighth Section of the Second Volume of Mr. Warton's History of English Poetry* (London, [1782]), 3, 24, 47–8, 16; *GM* 48 (1778), 347–8.
19. *SJC*, 9–12 November 1782.
20. Malone, Edmond, *Cursory Observations on the Poems Attributed to Thomas Rowley* (London, 1782), Advertisement, iii, 2–3.
21. Warton, *Enquiry*, 124, 111. For responses to Warton see *Monthly Review* 67 (1782), 170; Mathias, 107–8.
22. Warton, *Enquiry*, 7–8.
23. Barrett to Ducarel, 7 March 1772; Ducarel to Barrett, 18 March 1772, *GM* 56 (1786), 460, 463; Bristol Public Library, MS B6489, 36. See also *Monthly Review* 56 (1777), 321; *Poems, Supposed to Have Been Written at Bristol*, ed. Jeremiah Milles (London, 1782), Preliminary Dissertation, 24.
24. Thomas Chatterton to Horace Walpole, 14 April 1769, second draft; 'Bristowe Tragedy'; Chatterton to James Dodsley, 15 February 1769: in *Works*, 273, 6, 172.
25. Warton, *History*, i. ii.

26. Ibid. *History*, ii. 'Emendations and Additions', sig. [i2]^v.
27. Warton, *Enquiry*, 19, 97–100, 32–3.
28. Malone, 30–1.
29. See for instance W. Carew Hazlitt: 'The opinion of modern critics upon these alleged relics of the fifteenth century is so unanimous … that I do not think I have performed an unacceptable service in expunging altogether Warton's remarks and selections.' (*A History of English Poetry*, ed. W. Carew Hazlitt (London, 1871), i. 'Preface to the Present Edition', xiii).
30. Bryant, ii. 426, 429, 443–4. See also i. 1, 8; ii. 425–63.
31. Ibid. ii. 459, 409, 553–4, 204. Similar arguments can be found throughout the Rowleyan literature. See Edward Greene, *Strictures upon a Pamphlet Intitled, Cursory Observations on the Poems Attributed to Rowley* (London, 1782), 51–2, 55; Milles, 24–5; *European Magazine* 1 (1782), 262–3.
32. Bristol Public Library, MS B 4533, f. 117.
33. William Blake, *Complete Writings*, ed. Geoffrey Keynes (Oxford, 1992): annotations to *Poems* by William Wordsworth (1826), 783.
34. Walpole to Cole, 30 December 1781, *The Yale Edition of the Correspondence of Horace Walpole*, ed. W. S. Lewis *et al.* (New Haven, 1937–83), ii. 288.
35. The dialogical nature of the controversy was obvious from the titles of the pamphlets. Malone's was: 'Cursory observations on the poems attributed to Thomas Rowley, a priest of the Fifteenth Century: with some remarks on the commentaries on those poems, by the Rev. Dr. Jeremiah Milles, Dean of Exeter, and Jacob Bryant, Esq; and a salutary proposal addressed to the friends of those gentlemen'. Greene's was 'Strictures upon a pamphlet intitled, cursory observations on the poems attributed to Rowley, a priest of the fifteenth century … with a postscript on Mr. Warton's enquiry into the same subject'. Tyrwhitt's was almost a parody: 'A vindication of the appendix to the poems, called Rowley's, in reply to the answers of the Dean of Exeter, Jacob Bryant, Esquire, and a third anonymous writer; with some further observations upon these poems, and an examination of the evidence which has been produced in support of their authenticity'. Tyrwhitt found it 'absolutely necessary' to reply to Bryant and Milles. Similarly, Warton thought that it was his 'duty' to reply to the Rowleyans' arguments – even to Catcott's objections that Warton had misquoted the material of the chest that contained the Rowley documents (Tyrwhitt, Thomas, *A Vindication of the Appendix to the Poems* (London, 1782), 1; Warton, *Enquiry*, 7).
36. Anon., *The Genuine Copy of a Letter Found Nov. 5, 1782, near Strawberry Hill* (London, 1783), 5–6; 29–30.
37. Mathias, 50.
38. Walpole, Horace, *A Letter to the Editor of the Miscellanies of Thomas Chatterton* (Strawberry Hill, 1772), 39; Malone, 41; Warton, *Enquiry*, 20, 38, 42, 103; Warton, *History*, ii. 157; Mathias, 50.
39. *GM* 51 (Supplement, 1781), 622; Maty, Henry, *A New Review with Literary Curiosities and Literary Intelligence*, April 1782, 218; Hardinge, iv, iii.
40. *Poems*, xii [i.e. xiii]. This statement was reprinted in Tyrwhitt's two subsequent editions published in 1777 and in 1778, and then in the editions by Jeremiah Milles (1782) and Lancelot Sharpe (1794).
41. The drawing 'Truth Sacrifising to the Muses' by C. R. Ryley, was engraved

by Grignion, and published by T. Bellamy in 1793. It was inserted by either Isaac Reeds or Joseph Haslewood in the copy of Tyrwhitt's *Poems* now BL, C 39 f 1. I have been unable to locate this engraving in any other collection.
42. Life, xvii.

Chapter 10

Chatterton and Johnson: Authority and Filiation in the 1770s

Paul Baines

I

A typical literary career: he arrived in London as a young man, determined to make his fortune as a writer. He had left another, respectable but unsatisfying profession in the provinces, having already written a tragedy which represented some of his dearest imaginative achievements, but which was to prove unstageable in the first instance. He had written to the leading bookseller of the day to offer his services, without any very encouraging response. London proved difficult, but he subsisted for a time on periodical journalism and other literary expedients....

For Thomas Chatterton, whom I have been describing, this is almost the end of the story: arrival in London in April 1770 is followed by death from an overdose in August 1770, at the age of 17. Only posthumously did the author of a clutch of political poems and letters and a huge archive of pseudo-medieval documents achieve fame. For Samuel Johnson, whom I have also been describing, it was just the beginning: by 1770, when Chatterton arrived, Johnson was a literary institution, author of a massive English dictionary, editor of the national poet, novelist, essayist, keystone of the whole Augustan edifice; he even had a state pension.

This opposition is easily seen as the crystallization of a literary-historical moment. Who is the last neoclassic if not Johnson? Chatterton, on the other hand, has a strong claim to be the essential pre-Romantic poet, since he was adopted as the very type and totem of the Romantics' own genius, burning out and dying young in an unsympathetic and venal age. Coleridge, Wordsworth, Shelley, and Keats all hymned this perfect dead 'Boy' in a spectral admiration that was already burgeoning before Johnson himself was dead. Johnson was antithetical, admired perhaps but certainly no nurturing father for any sort of Romanticism, with his metropolitan classicism and his privileging of literature and civilization over spontaneity and imagination.[1] But Wordsworth can identify a canon of the pre-Romantic imagination within Augustanism in these terms: 'Thomson, Collins and Dyer had more poetic imagination than any of their contemporaries, unless we reckon Chatterton as of that age.'[2] This odd and uneasy pre-dating (it is actually quite difficult to reckon Chatterton as of that age) seeks to shift the precocious Romantic to a still earlier incipience; and it is this sense of Chatterton as a youthful harbinger, always in a condition of priority, which I wish to explore first.

II

In literary-historical terms, Chatterton (once freed from the damaging aura of 'forgery') might occupy a pre-Romantic niche as an exponent of medievalism, that recuperative opening up of a Gothic past as imaginative resource; Coleridge and Keats have clearly, in the obvious way of influence, learnt something from Chatterton's mode. Medievalism itself can be seen as a response to the complex of nostalgias and fears studied by Walter Jackson Bate in *The Burden of the Past and the English Poet* (1971): the feeling that, by the mid-eighteenth century, everything had been said and done by mightier poets, leaving nothing to do except polish and tidy up. While Johnson turned such a position into a conscious theory, with its own noble stoicism, Chatterton circumvented the problem by reinventing himself as a fifteenth-century poet, eluding the imaginative closedown forced by the Reformation and Enlightenment. To be medieval was to be able to act and write truly, in a kind of soft primitivism which Chatterton, in his editorial guise, explicitly defended. Diction was purer as action was nobler; medieval life was healthier, more manly, than modern; the monks already had essays on the Sublime and Beautiful.[3] Chatterton produced a point of origin for structures now decadent; the archive, in its plural and self-complementing richness of poetry, drawings, documents and letters, gave unmediated and vivid access to a whole society at a notional point of departure.

But this reversal of time's hierarchy and overturning of the tyranny of one's forbears allows for other kinds of priority to be achieved, if we consider how Bate's study was itself subjected to an apocalyptic Freudian reconstruction by Harold Bloom in *The Anxiety of Influence:*

A Theory of Poetry (1973). Here, the struggle with the past in general becomes an explicitly Oedipal 'family romance' in which 'strong' poets battle it out with each other for imaginative space; misreading, absorbing, extending and even begetting the father poet, the strong poet insists upon priority, struggles against mortality, engulfment and castration. Though Bloom sees this agon as archetypal, across history, he nonetheless accords the post-Miltonic eighteenth century a pivotal place, with Johnson as the great theorist of the poetics of belatedness and Blake its first great antagonist.

Chatterton is not mentioned by Bate, or, initially, by Bloom, though the latter does later refer to him (in semi-quotation of Browning) as the 'tragic, suicidal, too-early Romantic poet'.[4] There are good reasons why Chatterton might be considered in this context, however. His career has been subjected to a full-blooded psychoanalytic approach in which his own unconscious 'family romance' is projected into the fictional pseudo-family of Rowley and Canynge. In Louise Kaplan's reading, Chatterton, the posthumous son, predeceased by another male child, makes up for the lack of the father (a writing-master) by mastering the arts of writing himself, and constructing a whole series of benign, nourishing fathers; he goes on to become an impostor as a psychic defence mechanism against castration anxiety.[5] But Kaplan's interpretation of Freud's 'family romance' is Edenic, where Bloom's is Oedipal; and there seems to be room to marry Bloom's archetypal agon with Chatterton's individual father-begetting. Who else situates himself so clearly 'in the anxious position of begetting his own inheritance' (as another critic puts it)?[6] Who else so literally, even consciously, overturns the tyranny of time and invents his own precursors? Chatterton surely sought Bloom's 'ecstasy of priority, of self-begetting, of an assured autonomy' and as surely suffered from 'the primitivizing dream of so many gloriously estranged sensibilities'.

> All quest-romances of the post-Enlightenment, meaning all Romanticisms whatsoever, are quests to re-beget one's own self, to become one's own Great Original. We journey to abstract ourselves by fabrication.[7]

Chatterton seeks this end more consciously than most.

One can understand what Blake means when he says 'I believe both Macpherson & Chatterton, that what they say is Ancient Is so', for there is something strikingly 'primordial, regressive and archaic' about Chatterton's poetic mythology (if not Macpherson's).[8] History, as presented by Chatterton in Welsh and African, as well as Bristolian versions, is a struggle not merely between liberty and tyranny or autonomy and slavery, but between actual titanic figures who fight to the death and are immediately replaced by other pairs of matched warriors in struggles which rarely seem capable of conclusion: both versions of 'The Battle of Hastings' end in mid-battle. Unlike Ossian, where female presence is often used to stimulate 'Gothic politeness', these masculine struggles are rarely offset by palliating or mediating figures: soft primitivism has in Chatterton a core of very hard primitivism. In one sense there is actually a remarkable lack of 'family romance' in Chatterton's imagined past. Rowley after all is a priest, and Canynge (though he has sons) becomes one to avoid the Royal command to remarry after his wife dies in childbirth, so the question of lineage and offspring is partially closed off. Even the fantasy pedigrees, expressed in predominantly male terms and concentrating on noble arms-bearers and the defensive surface of the decorated shield, suggest not so much family, or even the begetting of the son by the father, but the continual defensive displacement of one armed figure by another.

Something of this agonistic mode is retained in Chatterton's political satires, for like Blake, Chatterton can also cast battles in mock-heroic form, as if in recognition of the irony of thinking agonistically in this degenerate age. The 'Consuliad' and 'Constabiliad' constitute debased versions of the Hirlas Ossianics, while 'The Revenge' casts the theogonic desires of Gods and Titans as a sordid little comic opera of infidelity. But satire, the least conciliatory of forms, is itself a personalized revenge, 'my revengeful Quill' as Chatterton puts it: satire's 'sharp avenging steel' replaces the knight's sword in Chatterton's 'poetical vengeance'.[9] Chatterton conceived of his quarrel with Walpole as a sort of conflation of literary and knightly combat; his Anecdote of Chaucer tells how Chaucer physically attacks a friar who has satirized him.[10]

Seeking to throw off the burden of George Catcott's patronage, Chatterton writes,

> Thy Friendship never could be dear to me
> Since all I am is opposite to thee.

It is a nice pre-echo of Blake's epigrams against his patron Hayley, and as with Blake, a kind of all-encompassing resistance.[11] Several times Chatterton rejoices in having burst free from the constraints of his

Bristol apprenticeship (the copying of legal forms being an apt metaphor for regulated penmanship) and this Blakean eruption from system is often fused with a sense of explicitly youthful power. Long before Wordsworth cast him as the 'marvellous Boy', Chatterton had capitalized, as it were, his own youthfulness; the exceptional 'Boy of learning, and Bard of Tropes', as Chatterton styles himself in his 'Will', is locked in opposition to narrow constraints of prudence, the virtue of age and incapacity. He imagines a complacent citizen counselling him to beware the revenge of powerful adults:

> Your infant Muse should sport with other Toys
> Men will not bear the ridicule of Boys.[12]

Naturally he defies this advice in favour of untrammelled conquering prophecy. Yet there is something odd about the way in which Chatterton contemplates his own prematurity or incipience; the Boyness seems already fetishized, an infantilizing gesture, something to be spoken about in a detached, third-person way, as if Chatterton had already become his own elegist for want of a sense of maturity. Indeed, most of the Romantic elegies on Chatterton can only echo his own words; the sense of having come too late despite defiant youthfulness is found not only in the baroque fantasia on death which Chatterton constructed in his 'Will' but also in the way in which he negotiated the problem of inadequacy through elegy.

Bloom is surely right to see the elegy as always the locus of the concern for primacy, for 'in a poet's lament for his precursor, or more frequently for another poet of his own generation, the poet's own deepest anxieties tend to be uncovered'.[13] Many of Chatterton's elegies have no specific occasion or addressee and are thus transparently about his own situation and his attempts to surmount mortality; but one in particular illustrates Bloom's point. The 'Elegy to the Memory of Mr. Thomas Phillips, of Fairford', commemorating the senior boy and usher at Chatterton's school who had been a supportive fellow writer, manages at once to announce the death of poetry and its provisional survival in the elegist. Phillips is the dead master, whose powers in life overawed the elegist and whose death robs him of ability. 'All my little powers' are contrasted with Phillips's universal genius. Nonetheless, the poem also acts as a ritual of separation, specifying emotional differences between the two poets and staking a claim to the mantle of poet. Though the elegist's wish to conjure the spirit of the dead poet through 'negromantic spells' so that they can

'Hymn the Creator and exert the Muse' is denied, the elegist remains, on Phillips's favourite hill, at Phillips's favourite time for writing. This is more than a simple replication and occupation of the precursor's afflatus, however. Though the possibility of following the master into death stands as one of Chatterton's many prospects of suicide ('Phillips is dead, tis Pleasure then to die'), the poem ends with a gesture that could also be read as an overpowering of death through poetic immortality:

> And can the Muse be silent! Phillips gone,
> And am I still alive? My Soul arise,
> The Robe of Immortality put on
> And meet thy Phillips in his native Skys – .[14]

The native skies gesture towards birth, not death, and the Muse is invited to comment on, not acquiesce in death. 'Am I still alive?' is the poet's most important question, a wonder at survival and remaining power rather than a chiding towards suicide. The first version of this elegy concludes with an address to the reader, enjoining us to regard this and all the poet's verses as utterly spontaneous, 'Neat as exported from the Parent brain'; it is the outward consciousness of publication and authorial filiation overcoming the ostensible purpose of the elegy. It may not be beside the point that Chatterton began this elegy while Phillips was still alive.

III

Chatterton fears death, but writes himself to a precarious survival through conventional elegy. But there is another form of elegy available to Chatterton: the mock elegy, a version of covert assassination with more obvious elements of celebration and survival in it. In August 1769, for example, Chatterton wrote the 'Elegy on the Demise of a Great Genius', a vigorous send-off for an unidentified bard-figure, rejoicing in its own burlesque hackneyisms. This lament for lost power concludes with bathetic noise: 'Alas! I cannot sing! I howl! I cry!', a very different sort of statement from the risky conclusion of the elegy on Phillips. But in February 1770, six stanzas of this poem were rewritten as part of a greater satiric elegy, with the colossal figure of Samuel Johnson reanimating the figure of the great genius now dead.

> The pension'd muse of Johnson is no more!
> Drown'd in a butt of wine his genius lies ... [15]

After Johnson's publication of the anti-Wilkes *The False Alarm* the previous month, Chatterton identifies Johnson as the chief enemy writer, pensioned by Bute (in 1763) and effectively dead or blind thereafter. The first elegy on Johnson works to deplore the condition of a prostituted literature, evacuated and engulfed by the power of the state, just as the ministers themselves were held to be hireling servants of a hidden power. But Johnson was also quite consciously killed off by this rhetorical strategy, neutralized and negated as a precursor by the prophet whose living poetry denounces his ventriloqual emptiness.

In 'The Whore of Babylon' (and its revision, 'Kew Gardens'), Chatterton returned to this ghostly Johnson in greater detail. Johnson is antagonized as the rigorous enforcer of critical laws and the enemy of creativity, curbing the flights of inspiration. While not perhaps exactly Bloom's 'covering Cherub', the primordial force of poetic repression and anxiety, Johnson is here a kind of conscious version of the castrating father, and in the kind of travesty of Johnson's thought easily available to the Romantics. But Chatterton contends that Johnson was, as a state author, blind, dead, drunk, or empty, in any of the several available varieties of castration. Chatterton envisions Johnson as a liminal, corrupted figure, a night-walker; but as well as assassinating him in pseudo-elegy, Chatterton perversely resurrects him in a debased version of the necromantic gesture offered towards Phillips, giving us a maggoty, undead writer not so much composing as decomposing on the page ('Whilst from his fancy figures budded out, / As hair from humid carcasses will sprout'). And this 'restless shallow spirit', with his 'venal quill', is opposed to Chatterton, the independent Patriot, in a gesture which further disperses Johnson's identity while retaining Chatterton's authorial integrity: 'every pension'd Johnson' plurally declaims North's wisdom, while the singular 'I' was 'never paid to lie'.[16]

In August 1778, at a gathering at the Thrales's house, Michael Lort, one of the scholars involved in researching Chatterton's life, produced several manuscript verses 'written against Dr. Johnson, as a place man and a pensioner', and read them out, much to Fanny Burney's astonishment and displeasure. But 'Dr. Johnson himself listened profoundly, & Laughed openly. Indeed, I believe he wishes his abusers no other Thing than a *good Dinner*'.[17] Politics was only one of the things one might expect Johnson to have against Chatterton. There was the religious heterodoxy, the most obvious sign of which was the apparent suicide, the 'horrid crime of destroying one's self' as Johnson put it in the *Dictionary*. Johnson castigated Gray's 'The Bard', that over-researched version of primitivizing mythology, for its concluding suicide: 'suicide is always to be had, without expense of thought' – it was, exactly, a failure of imagination, though Chatterton defended it on a number of occasions as a 'noble insanity of the soul'.[18] Medievalism had little appeal to Johnson as a solution for the problems of belatedness; he effortlessly parodied the puerile regression of Percy's and Warton's imitation ballads. One might have expected the editor of Shakespeare to take an interest in the matter of the Rowley poems, especially given the involvement of his co-editor, George Steevens, in their publication. As a lexicographer, and a *recherché* stylist himself, he might have exercised ingenuity on Rowley's language, or criticized Chatterton for 'writing no language' as Ben Jonson said of Spenser's antique diction. As the biographical master of the great canon of English literature (the *Lives of the Poets* sit exactly across the years of the Rowley controversy, 1777 to 1781) he might have taken a strong line on the problems of literary filiation, authenticity, and history, which Chatterton and Rowley represented. In 1775, in *A Journey to the Western Islands of Scotland*, Johnson had published a massively confrontational demolition of the Ossian fabrications, and Rowley was linked with Ossian in the minds of many.

But not, apparently, in Johnson's mind, for the note struck in Fanny Burney's diary is the one maintained throughout Johnson's interest in the case: that of laughter. Johnson laughed at Goldsmith in 1771 for believing in the Rowley poems, and he laughed at George Steevens and Thomas Tyrwhitt for their slow gravitation towards his own instinctive position on the Rowley question.[19] Boswell records Johnson's visit to examine the Rowley material at Bristol in 1776, and while he opens and closes his anecdote with references to Ossian, and compares the examination with the investigative tour he and Johnson undertook in Ossian country in 1773, the scene is one of his best comic set-pieces, almost pure caricature and entertainment. Floating at the end of that record, almost as if Boswell cannot quite place it in his narrative, is Johnson's most appreciative comment on Chatterton:

This is the most extraordinary young man that has encountered my knowledge. It is wonderful how the whelp has written such things.[20]

That 'wonderful' and 'whelp', taken together, give us an interesting pre-echo of Wordsworth's 'marvellous Boy' tag, one which seems closer, more affectionate, less portentous, and perhaps rather more firmly based on a knowledge of what Chatterton actually wrote. It is also interesting that Johnson refers to Chatterton as if he were still alive, a kind of son, rather than a deathly 'sleepless Soul'.

Johnson did not hold to this opinion unwaveringly; as in all literary appreciations, not to mention family romances, there was competition and antagonism as well. Johnson kept an ear on the developing controversy, poking fun at the earnestness of the scholars while nonetheless prodding Tyrwhitt into going to Bristol to examine the Rowley material he was about to publish. Steevens was piqued at Johnson's amused references to his Chatterton studies in letters to Mrs Thrale and declared Johnson's attitude was borne of authoritarian jealousy that he and Tyrwhitt would not simply express 'complete acquiescence in his decrees' about Rowley; and though Steevens's own narrative is prone to error, there is some evidence of a high-handed attitude towards Chatterton in later years. Johnson may have laughed at Chatterton's satires, but when they were published in the *Miscellanies of Thomas Chatterton* in 1778, and Anna Seward expressed her admiration of the collection, Johnson is said to have retorted:

> Pho, child! don't talk to me of the powers of a vulgar uneducated stripling.... It may be extraordinary to do such things as he did, with means so slender; – but ... what could Chatterton do, which abstracted from the recollection of his situation, can be worth the attention of learning and taste? ... No man can coin guineas, but as he has gold.[21]

Johnson said much the same thing about the poetry of the St Kildans, in a literary version of his 'don't cant in defence of savages' – though even here he may have the *Miscellanies* in mind rather than the Rowley poems, and the 'extraordinary' nature of the talent is not quite eclipsed. Nonetheless Johnson occasionally expressed the view that the Rowley poems, though not ancient, were not by Chatterton either, so the problem of authorship did trouble him on occasion. His most balanced view was a succinct summary of the 'probability' arguments on both sides, which he called (appropriately enough given the material under discussion) 'a sword that cuts both ways'.

It is as wonderful to suppose that a boy of sixteen years old had stored his mind with such a train of images and ideas as he had acquired, as to suppose the poems, with their ease of versification and elegance of language, to have been written by Rowlie in the time of Edward the Fourth.[22]

Inconclusive as this is, it returns us to Johnson's initial admiration; no lover of the marvellous, Johnson must consider the 'wonderful' possibility that Chatterton had acquired what (his own syntax seems to assert) he had indeed acquired.

The final note is again one of laughter, cutting across the mawkish language in which everyone else spoke of Chatterton. At Beilby Porteous's house, in April 1782 (Hannah More records) Johnson 'continued his jokes and lamented that I had not married Chatterton, that posterity might have seen a propagation of poets'.[23] Chatterton was not at this stage canonical; the 'whelp' did not qualify for the *Lives of the Poets* series, though that is hardly surprising given the state of the authorship question at that time. Johnson never really settled his own views on Chatterton, which remained at variance with each other to a far greater degree than his views on Ossian, authoritarian, neoclassical, and offensive as those are. At times, it seems impossible for normal modes of literary filiation to be maintained in the face of Chatterton's supposed precocity; at other times, it is almost as if Johnson, the last of the childless Augustans, glimpsed in Chatterton a miraculous youth who might have eluded the trap of belatedness and fathered a new poetic line.

IV

There is another possible reason why the expected antagonism between the youthful Chatterton and the aged Johnson does not explode. My opening paragraph, superimposing the two careers, was suggested by a passage in a poem by Samuel Rogers. Imagining a viewpoint at the city gate, Rogers sees Chatterton and Johnson arriving at London to await their different fates, and at the liminal moment of crossing the gate, their immediate prospects appear not dissimilar: death and poverty. Though Chatterton is awarded poetic primacy, as one might expect, it is nonetheless striking to see common ground between the two writers being found by anyone writing in 1822.[24]

But if we think of Johnson specifically as a youth, the strangeness is considerably lessened. Chatterton and Johnson shared provincial origins and impoverished families; both fathers dealt professionally in books, both sons were given to voracious random reading, both were influenced by black letter printing, both were fond of courtly romances. If Chatterton cast himself as notoriously proud, Johnson displayed fierce disregard of 'all power and authority'. Johnson's own religious sense was hardly orthodox until he went to Oxford. Chatterton was a 'mad genius'; Johnson was 'mad and violent'. Both rejected charitable offerings (food, shoes) as humiliating insults to manly self-sufficiency.[25] There is even a little literary forgery right at the inception of Johnson's career, in the epitaph on a duckling which Johnson was supposed to have extemporized at the age of three and which Anna Seward saw as an early sign of Johnson's poetic genius: Boswell set things right by reporting, on Johnson's authority, that the verses were by Johnson's father, who wished the story of his son's precocity to circulate.[26] The Child may well be father of the Man, but one also has to beware of the father's incursions on the child.

There are further parallels between Chatterton and the young Johnson: abandoning the dull, normative jobs for risky creativity, lobbying booksellers, trying to push a precious tragedy (*Ælla, Irene*); the struggles with poverty, the survival through journalism. Though Chatterton and Johnson were on opposite sides in the political wars of the 1770s, when Johnson started out his relation to politics was more skewed than that opposition suggests. He wrote the semi-fictional debates of the 'senate of Lilliput' for the *Gentleman's Magazine*, and was alternately proud and troubled to hear his own work quoted as the speech of this or that politician.[27] His direct political writing was precisely in opposition, attacking the corruption of Walpole as Chatterton attacked the corruption of Bute and North. In *Marmor Norfolciense* (1739) he even used an antiquarian device, a discovered inscription with a spoof commentary, which both imagines and satirizes an antiquarian world-view (the prime minister's son, Horace Walpole, was later the butt of Chatterton's own antiquarian satires, and we may need to be reminded of Chatterton's sometimes ambivalent relation to the medieval). And despite Johnson's later contempt for soft primitivism, he wrote two whole issues of *The Rambler* devoted to the heroic poetry of two lovers in Greenland. Without quite losing a gently satiric control, the heroic story is invested with considerable imaginative power, and the final disappearance of the lovers into a world of speculation and romance refuses to close the primitive story with an enlightened convention.[28] At least when Johnson declared that anyone could write like Ossian (as for example Chatterton did), he spoke from experience.[29]

Indeed, Ossian is in many ways the exception rather than the rule as far as Johnson's supposed authority and mastery goes, for it is the one literary forgery which really provoked Johnson to a combative answer. Ossian challenged a whole complex of standards (literary, historical, authorial) and for once was demonized into rejection. But Johnson's relation to all the other forgers is much more inward. Psalmanazar, the self-proclaimed 'Formosan', and all-round reformed character, he revered: 'I should as soon think of contradicting a BISHOP'. For William Lauder, who manufactured evidence to suit his charge that Milton had plagiarized earlier Latin poets, he wrote a brilliantly dignified confession, as he did on a vast scale for Dr William Dodd, convicted and hanged in the Rowleyan year of 1777 for a criminal forgery. Though his sense of literary orthodoxy may not be compromised by these acts, his voyage into the transgressions they represent is interesting, perhaps a kind of necessary sacrifice.[30] Johnson never condemned Chatterton as a forger (as plenty of his other admirers casually did) and there were times when Chatterton's precocity and situation might have recalled his own.

The only sign of such recognition in the other direction that one might cite is the late 'Maria Friendless Letter' which Chatterton substantially condensed from Johnson's story of Misella in *The Rambler*. Johnson's powerful version of the Harlot's Progress narrative, in which an ordinary respectable woman is gradually degraded, abandoned, and sold into prostitution through the deceitful power of a great man (a quasi-father), seems so invested with sympathetic identification that one begins to wonder if Johnson is not covertly comparing the situation of a struggling freelance writer with the feminized economics of dependence endured by Misella. And when Chatterton, who had demonized Johnson exactly as a prostitute writer, chooses this of all stories to plagiarize, one wonders further if there isn't some kind of doubly-displaced confession from the young writer who found that there was so little money in writing for the opposition that he would have to consider writing for the side of interest and power – to submit in other words to the prostitution of talent. Maria Friendless testifies to the economics of copy-supply, at least, and it may also embody a rueful homage to Johnson and a further recognition of the changed nature of the Muse, whose incestuously begotten offspring dies at birth in both stories.[31]

V

That borrowing, or plagiarism, was noted very early, in Jacob Bryant's *Observations upon the Poems of Thomas Rowley* (1781), a book on which Johnson commented.[32] Bryant's note was one of a whole series of such linkages put in motion by the Rowley controversy and which gradually undid the entire fabric. Though Chatterton attempted to circumvent the tyranny of time by inventing his own precursors, critics assiduously tracked down borrowings from Shakespeare, Pope, and others, in order to detach the Rowley archive from its putative fifteenth-century author and deposit it in the juvenile reading of a 16-year-old boy. When it was further noticed that Chatterton's London writings were mostly in borrowed styles (Junius, Ossian, Churchill, and Johnson), the process of turning Chatterton into an author virtually overloaded itself in its exfoliation of any individual integrity to the *œuvre*. Herbert Croft mentioned as possible influences on Chatterton the ballad 'Auld Robin Gray', the narrative of Alexander Selkirk, Junius, Ossian, Psalmanazar, Walpole's *Historic Doubts on the life and reign of King Richard the Third* and *Castle of Otranto*, Mickle's *The Concubine, Hardyknute*, Parnell's hoax with a Latin source for *The Rape of the Lock*, and Fontenelle's story about a Russian pretender.[33] Such a shopping-list of multiple filiations almost renders the concept of individual authorship untenable even while seeming to validate it. What then did Chatterton really write?

This kind of source-hunting is one of the many property-based concepts of authorship which Barthes attacks as 'the process of filiation' in his attempt to replace 'work' with 'text'.[34] Filiation for Barthes peddles a version of literary history in which a genealogy of canonical and possessive poets transmit ideas, phrases, and images to each other in gestures of poetic inheritance. This again is emphatically not the kind of inheritance Bloom has in mind in writing of 'influence', though his version of intertextuality still inhabits a kind of generative model and genetic language. But 'the filiation of a literary performance' was very much an issue in the property-conscious eighteenth century, Boswell in particular using a genetic language to locate and police the author's patriarchal presence in the text and to fend off the threat of dispossession, infiltration, and castration.[35] Johnson, who defined filiation as 'the relation of the son to the father; correlative to paternity', spoke of Macpherson as 'the father of Ossian', and Walpole, the powerful father-patron to whom the Boy Chatterton self-consciously appealed, commented on the publication in 1772 of Chatterton's *Bristowe Tragedie*:

it grows a hard case on our ancestors, who have every day bastards
laid to them, five hundred or a thousand years after they are dead.
Indeed Mr. Macpherson, etc., are so fair as to beget the fathers as
well as the children.[36]

(One might call this a weak pre-misreading of Bloom.) But as Boy, or
as whelp, what is Chatterton's standing amongst the 'propagation of
poets', the genealogy of literary history?

Wordsworth claimed that Macpherson's *Ossian*, admired as it was,
had been 'wholly uninfluential upon the literature of the country....
No Author in the least distinguished, has ventured formally to imitate
them – except the Boy, Chatterton'.[37] This manages to dispose of any
literary affiliation between the forgers and the Romantics at a stroke:
the forgers influence each other, but not authors of distinction (or
Bloom's strong poets). Bloom writes how Shelley's *Adonais*, while
ostensibly elegizing the immortal talent of Keats, covertly seeks to
subvert the other poet's immortality as if to prolong his own (even in
this 'sublimely suicidal' poem).[38] But Chatterton, another sublime
suicide, is also there in the poem, one of too many 'inheritors of
unfulfilled renown'. Chatterton belongs to those legions 'whose
names on earth are dark, / But whose transmitted effluence cannot
die / So long as fire outlives the parent spark'. Individually within this
plurality of Promethean begetters, Chatterton 'Rose pale – his solemn
agony had not yet faded from him'; which suggests that, syntactically,
it must have since faded, perhaps to a greater glory 'beyond mortal
thought', but perhaps altogether, into the very oblivion that Shelley
seeks to negate. Chatterton remains only as a figure of transition;
'solemn agony' may be all he has. Perhaps the Romantics could not,
as Johnson put it, abstract Chatterton from his situation; perhaps
Chatterton could only exist for them as the 'Boy' who showed marvellous promise (to be safely fulfilled by other, surviving poets) but who
did not himself grow up to produce a work strong enough to wrestle
with – or even to read. Again, the Child may well be father of the Man,
but the Romantics may have found it more comfortable to keep safe
in conscious elegy a poet who was too young to beget anything at all.
At the historical point where literary genealogy, in Bloom's argument,
is supplanted by a history of influence as the dominant model of literary inheritance, Johnson's estimations, looking at once forward and
back, may include the more paternal recognition; at any rate, they
indicate that there is more to the 'family romance' that writers inhabit
than the titanic struggle of Romantic ideology.

Notes

1. See Levine, William, 'The Genealogy of Romantic Literary History: Refigurations of Johnson's *Lives of the English Poets* in the Criticism of Coleridge and Wordsworth', *Criticism* 34.3 (Summer 1992), 349–78.
2. Wordsworth, Christopher, *Memoirs of William Wordsworth* (London, 1851), i. 215.
3. See, for example, *Works*, 6n, 17n, 145–6n, 172, 409–12.
4. Bloom, Harold, *A Map of Misreading* (Oxford, 1975), 115. Bloom referred to Chatterton in similar terms in *The Ringers in the Tower: Studies in Romantic Tradition* (Chicago, 1971), 15.
5. Kaplan, Louise, *The Family-Romance of the Impostor-Poet Thomas Chatterton* (Berkeley, 1987).
6. Stewart, Susan, *Crimes of Writing: Problems in the Containment of Representation* (Oxford, 1991), 149, and see 146–53.
7. Bloom, Harold, *The Anxiety of Influence: A Theory of Poetry* (Oxford, 1973), 19, 26, 56, 64, 116.
8. William Blake, *Complete Writings*, ed. Geoffrey Keynes (Oxford, 1957, repr. 1969), 783; Bloom (1973), 59, 71.
9. *Works*, 377, 419, 504, 551.
10. To Stephens, 20 July 1769, *Works*, 338, 442–3.
11. *Works*, 501; *Blake: Complete Writings*, 544–5.
12. *Works*, 465, 502.
13. Bloom (1973), 150.
14. *Works*, 383–92.
15. 'February: An Elegy', in *Works*, 447–9.
16. Ibid. 535–58.
17. *The Early Letters and Journals of Fanny Burney*, iii: *The Streatham Years, Part 1. 1778–1779*, ed. Lars E. Troide and Stewart J. Cooke (Oxford, 1994), 112 (23–30 August 1778).
18. *Works*, 443–5, 501–5; Johnson, Samuel, *Lives of the English Poets*, iii. 441. See further the entry on suicide in Rogers, Pat, *The Samuel Johnson Encyclopedia* (Westport, Conn., & London, 1996).
19. Walpole to Bewley, *The Yale Edition of the Correspondence of Horace Walpole*, ed. W. S. Lewis *et al.* (New Haven, 1937–83), xvi. 129–30; Powell, L. F., 'Thomas Tyrwhitt and the Rowley Poems', *RES* 7 (1931), 314–26.
20. *Life of Johnson*, iii. 50–1.
21. Seward to Thomas Park, 30 Jan., 1800, *Letters of Anna Seward*, ed. Archibald Constable (London, 1811), v. 270.
22. *Johnsonian Miscellanies*, ed. G. B. Hill (London, 1897), ii. 15 (Sir John Hawkins).
23. More, Hannah, *Memoirs of the Life and Correspondence of Mrs. Hannah More*, ed. William Roberts (London, 1835), i. 25.
24. 'Italy, A Poem', ll. 24–37, in *The Poetical Works of Samuel Rogers* (London, 1848), 176.
25. For Chatterton, see *Life* as follows: father, 7–11; reading habits, 21–2, 37–62; pride, 69, 73, 98 (and see *Works*, 341, 494); refusal of food, 433. For Johnson, see *Life of Johnson* as follows: father, i. 34–7; reading habits, i. 43, 49 & iv. 17; 'power and authority', i. 74 (for more early pride see i. 39);

'mad and violent', i. 73; refusal of shoes, i. 77; religion, i. 68–9. Percy's comment (i. 49) offers both first and second thoughts on chivalric romance: 'When a boy he was immoderately fond of reading romances of chivalry, and he retained his fondness for them through life.... Yet I have heard him attribute to their extravagant fictions that unsettled turn of mind which prevented his ever fixing in any profession'. See further Henson, Eithne, *'The Fictions of Romantick Chivalry: Samuel Johnson and Romance* (Rutherford, NJ, & London, 1992).

26. *Life of Johnson*, i. 40–1.
27. Rizzo, Betty, '"Innocent Frauds": By Samuel Johnson', *The Library*, 6th ser. 8.3 (September 1986), 249–64.
28. *The Rambler* 186 and 187, 28 and 31 December 1751.
29. See *Life of Johnson*, i. 396 and iv. 183.
30. Bogel, Fredric, 'Johnson and the Role of Authority', in *The New Eighteenth Century: Theory, Politics, English Literature*, ed. Felicity Nussbaum and Laura Brown (New York & London, 1987), 189–209.
31. *The Rambler* 171 and 172 (2 and 5 November 1751); *Works*, 594–5.
32. *Works*, 1101–2.
33. Croft, Herbert, *Love and Madness: A Story Too True* (1780), 209–11.
34. Barthes, Roland, 'From Work to Text', in *Image–Music–Text*, tr. Stephen Heath (London, 1977), 155–64, at p. 160.
35. *Life of Johnson*, ii. 259 and i. 254.
36. To Mason, 25 May 1772, *Correspondence of Walpole*, xxviii. 36.
37. For Wordsworth's comment and Blake's response, see *Blake: Complete Writings*, 783.
38. Bloom (1973), 151.

Chapter 11

Fragments, Reliques, & MSS: Chatterton and Percy

Nick Groom

> He who venerates a contemptible relique is actuated with a
> degree of the pilgrim's superstition, less pernicious indeed in
> its effects, but scarcely less absurd in its principle.
>
> Vicesimus Knox, 'Objections to the Study of Antiquities
> when Improperly Pursued'.[1]

Vicesimus Knox, an eloquent commentator on, among other things, eighteenth-century letters and the Rowley Controversy, found considerable entertainment in the antiquarian scramble for scraps of old literature and the ensuing uncritical eulogies sung over ancient poetry in the later eighteenth century. He laid blame for this revolution in literary taste clearly, if discreetly, at the door of Thomas Percy and his *Reliques of Ancient English Poetry*, an anthology of ballads and songs first published in 1765.[2] When Knox published his essays in 1782, Percy, a persistent social climber, had just been promoted from Dean of Carlisle to Bishop of Dromore and over the next 30 years of life in his corner of Ireland, would assiduously distance himself from his early antiquarian interests. But the influence of Percy's *Reliques* remained palpable – not simply in the encouragement it offered to subsequent collectors of antique literature (including Walter Scott), but to the succeeding generation of Romantic poets (notably in Wordsworth and Coleridge's *Lyrical Ballads*). And yet perhaps the most significant impact of the *Reliques* was on Thomas Chatterton.

Although Percy's presence in the Rowley Controversy was spectral, the following essay demonstrates that he haunted the composition, publication, and reception of the Rowley works: Percy unwittingly inspired Chatterton and determined the presentation of Rowley, he thwarted publication of the forgery for four years, and he laid the ground for reading and debating the forgery.[3] Just as Percy's *Five Pieces of Runic Poetry* (1763) and the *Reliques* were written in direct response to James Macpherson's *Ossian* and so became exemplars of antiquarian authenticity, the *Reliques* and Percy's *Hermit of Warkworth* (1771) established the context for the posthumous publication of Chatterton's Rowley. Rowley's fate was sealed in literary salons long before the controversialists went to the press, but these private discussions structured the public debate, and their touchstone was Percy's *Reliques*.[4]

I

Percy was, of course, oblivious of Chatterton until the boy was dead and Rowley was being toasted across the Town. But Chatterton was not ignorant of Percy. Meyerstein, Taylor, and Holmes all agree that Percy's *Reliques* was one of the principal influences on Rowley, and Meyerstein goes so far as to declare that the *Reliques* was 'the efficient poetical cause of Rowley ... a model to anyone who wished to produce antique verse, and appeal to his century at one and the same time'.[5] Percy's anthology characterized literary antiquarianism: exotic and idiosyncratic language, swarming footnotes and references, authoritative historical underpinning, an interfering Enlightenment editorial sensibility, and an enticingly loose intertextuality. Chatterton plundered the *Reliques*: he took vocabulary from Percy's glossary, imitated specific pieces such as 'Lucy and Colin', and used a primitive ballad metre and diction (for example in the ballad of the 'Bristowe Tragedy'). The direct influence of Percy's *Reliques* on Chatterton has been clearly established. But Chatterton's work was also a startling reconfiguration of Percy's political theory of ancient English minstrelsy.

Percy's ancient English minstrels in the *Reliques* were a response to Macpherson's Celtic bard Ossian, who after 1500 years erupted onto the literary scene in *Fragments of Ancient Poetry* in 1760. Percy's minstrels were instruments of the state: guardians of history and genealogy, the wards of culture and nation. This status was exemplified not so much in their epic ballad singing as in their symbolic association with writing – and therefore with both historical documentation and literature, with legal and aesthetic truth. Percy attacked Macpherson's *Fragments*, and his epics *Fingal* (1762) and *Temora* (1763), for relying on oral sources for Ossian. He replaced this faith in the oral tradition by demonstrating the value of physical sources (runes, writing). In doing so, Percy argued that the literate source was a peculiarly English characteristic of cultural history and national identity that derived from the ancient Goths, and he positioned the medieval minstrels in the context of Gothic literacy and poetry. The English minstrels were the inheritors of national poetry.[6]

The *Reliques*, of course, supposedly derived from a compendious 'folio MS' of ballads and metrical romances that Percy had rescued from a basket of kindling, freely edited and adapted, and then kept under lock and key. His theory of minstrelsy was, therefore, methodologically expedient. But although Percy was utterly convincing in demonstrating the empirical dogma of literate documents, Chatterton was still able to challenge him. Chatterton's revolutionary innovation was to reimagine the culture of the manuscript. He disputed Percy's imperious yet covert use of a single, authoritative written source, proposed a new version of manuscript culture, and consequently devised a new national myth. Chatterton's England was not determined by mystical Goths pragmatically reinvented for the good old cause of Tory patronage; rather, Chatterton imagined medieval manuscripts as circulating commodities that confirmed the Whigs' devotion to the marketplace.

The historical positioning of Thomas Rowley was therefore crucial. Macpherson's Ossian was supposedly so ancient as to be virtually preliterate, whereas Percy was focused on the absorption of manuscript culture into print, which allowed him to rewrite the works of anonymous transcribers and printers as if they were a motley rabble of hacks. In contrast, Thomas Rowley wrote at the culmination of manuscript culture. He embodied the calligraphic word on the very eve of print: the 'Bristowe Tragedie or the Dethe of Syr Charles Bawdin', possibly the first Rowley piece fabricated, was dated 1462 by Chatterton, just a few years before Caxton set up his press in Westminster in 1476.[7]

For Chatterton, the principal characteristic of the manuscript in the fifteenth century was as a potent form of cultural currency. Manuscripts were, in effect, paper money. Inspired by the 1760s market in literary antiquarianism, Chatterton commodified the past as a trade in manuscripts driven by the connoisseurship of men like Rowley's patron, William Canynge. In other words, Whig capitalism was rooted in a market economy of Gothic poetry. It was an immediately attractive proposition to Bristolians, citizens of one of the economic centres of the empire. Chatterton theorized the economic status of the manuscript as an artefact, as a commodity, and delineated the fifteenth-century literati as Whiggish: they traded, and what they traded in was, appropriately enough, the Gothic myth – architectural plans, antiquarian documents, and poetic manuscripts.

Chatterton took a contemporary vision of England as a free, entrepreneurial, economy and imposed it on the past. His Gothicism was resolutely English, and resiliently provincial: indeed, it was antagonistic to the Anglo-Normanism of London, and Chatterton specifically defined the Saxon spirit as resistance to the Normans in 1066. In an unsent letter to Walpole, the Goths have a clear Saxon identity:

> However Barbarous the Saxons may be calld. by our Modern Virtuosos; it is certain, we are indebted to Alfred and other Saxon Kings for the wisest of our Laws and in part for the British Constitution – The Normans indeed destroy'd the Mss, paintings &c of the Saxons that fell in their way; but some might be and certainly were recoverd. out of the Monasteries &c, in which they were preservd.[8]

The Battle of Hastings provided an elemental distinction. In 'Goddwyn. A Tragedie', the Kynge remarks, 'Thou arte a Normanne, Hughe, a straunger to the Launde'.[9]

Moreover, the very provenance of the manuscript of the Saxon epic 'Hastings' actually exemplified the pecuniary advantages of the Saxon myth: the profits to be made from the Gothic spirit. Rowley's initial investment was to purchase the poetic papers of the Saxon monk Turgot from a Durham monastery, in order to translate them. This paid off when Canynge and another Bristol merchant and aristocrat (named John Pelham) each 'bargayne[d]' for copies 'to be manuscripted'.[10] The language ('manuscripted') emphasizes the medium, and consequently the value. Rowley profited from the past, evidently heeding his employer's advice: 'Excellent ande pythey was the saying of Mr. Cannges [*sic*] "Trade is the Soule of the Worlde but Moneie the Soule of Trade"'.[11]

In his imaginative use of manuscript culture and free-market version of the Gothic myth, Chatterton was profoundly at odds with Percy, for whom manuscripts were little more than the raw material of the printing-press. This difference necessitated a revision of Percy's figure of the minstrel. Although Chatterton's 'mynstrelles' were part of the fabric of medieval artistic life, they were really no more than performing musicians, and had none of Percy's court status. For example, Rowley's 'Epistle to Mastre Canynge on Ælla' began, '"Tys songe bie mynstrelles, thatte yn auntyent tym', and in the following play there were a number of 'Mynstrelles Songes', some improvised, sung by men and women. The play ended, 'Inne heaven thou synge of Godde, on erthe we'lle synge of thee'.[12] They acted as a Saxon chorus in 'The Tournament' and followed 'The Freres of Seincte Augustine':

> Behynde theyre backes syx mynstrelles came,
> Who tun'd the strunge bataunt.[13]

In a later article written for the *Town and Country Magazine*, 'Antiquity of Christmas Games', Chatterton wrote that the primary entertainments of Old England were ecclesiastical dramatics, after which

> Minstrels, jesters, and mummers, was the next class of performers: every knight had two or three minstrels and jesters, who were maintained in his house, to entertain his family in their hours of dissipation;

and he quoted from 'Sir Thopas'.[14] Minstrels were songsmiths, not bards.

Thomas Rowley was not a minstrel: he was primarily a writer who left his physical signature lacing through elaborate manuscripts. Significantly, then, Chatterton's interest lay in the production of plausible documents. The poet was a calligraphic craftsman, a producer of things – scrolls, rolls, and parchments – who sold the fruits of his labour. For Chatterton, in fact, the poet was ultimately a maker: a forger.

II

On 29 February 1776, Percy wrote to Samuel Henley, later the translator of William Beckford's *Vathek*. Henley had requested further particulars of the entertainments at Eltham and Killingworth and proposed an edition, and Percy gave a step-by-step guide to publishing literary-antiquarian works.[15] Throughout the 1770s, Percy himself was engaged in similar projects: *Northern Antiquities* (his translation of Paul-Henri Mallet) and *The Northumberland Houshold Book* (an edition of the regulations and establishment of the household of Henry Algernon Percy, 1512–25) were issued in 1770; *The Hermit of Warkworth* (his Northumberland ballad) was published in 1771 and went through three editions in its first 12 months; he revised the

Reliques for a third edition in 1775, and so on.[16] In addition to this, Percy gave advice to a number of researchers and aspiring writers: Horace Walpole, Thomas Warton, '*Don*' Bowle, and John Pinkerton, as well as Henley.

Percy seemed to be conducting an entire ensemble of antiquarian literature, and at some point he also began collecting Rowleyana: a transcript of the 'Bridge Narrative' made by Catcott, Chatterton's own copy of 'Elinour and Juga', and he was later sent Walpole's manuscript of the *Letter*.[17] Among Michael Lort's papers in Bristol Reference Library is a four-page 'List of Chatterton's Letters MS' in Percy's hand: a bibliographical list of Chatterton's letters and periodical publications.[18] Whatever inspired Percy to take this intimate interest in Chatterton, it perhaps encouraged Chatterton's literary executors to imitate the editor of the *Reliques*, irrespective of any differences in poetical theory. The first publication of Rowley after Chatterton's death followed closely the standards and formats espoused by Percy, and notably employed in *The Hermit of Warkworth*.

The Hermit has received most of its critical attention from Bertram Davis, Percy's most diligent biographer, who while openly admitting it 'simply lacks the fire and color of the ballads in the *Reliques*', remarks that, at 200 stanzas, it was considerably longer than anything in the *Reliques* and demonstrated that the sustained ballad narrative might be a suitable vehicle for poetic expression.[19] Today, this poem is unfortunately chiefly remembered as the occasion for Johnson's extemporized ballad parodies, and as another example of Percy's valorization of the Northumberlands.[20] It takes its inspiration from the Hermitage at Warkworth on the Alnwick estate, a vaulted chapel carved into the rock, sheltering two stone figures. From this architectural enigma, Percy spun a romantic tale of love and tragedy, securely grounded in the English ballad tradition revived by the *Reliques*. The poem was written in outright homage to his patrons, the Northumberlands: describing their lands and their ancestors in the style of the old Northumbria ballads and using 'Chevy-Chase' as its model. In other words, Percy was aspiring to be a minstrel.

The poem began life as a souvenir epistle in a letter to the Bishop of Carlisle in 1767, but it eventually emerged as a lavishly printed ballad four years later.[21] *The Hermit of Warkworth. A Northumberland Ballad. In Three Fits or Cantos* was printed by Edmund Allen for Thomas Davies and Samuel Leacroft on 21 May 1771, and followed most of the recommendations Percy later made to Henley. It was a quarto, set in generous type, and the title-page featured an impressive engraving by Samuel

Wale, the *Gentleman's Magazine* and *Reliques* illustrator. There was no hint that it was written by Percy – his name was absent from both the title-page and dedication – although his authorship was an open secret, and naturally the name 'PERCY' reverberated through the text. *The Hermit* was dedicated to the Duchess of Northumberland, and Percy prefaced the ballad with a Spenserian sonnet asserting the inextricable ties between poetry and patronage. There followed a two-page Advertisement describing the situation and layout of the Hermitage, and a note on the word 'FIT' which referred the reader to the *Reliques*.[22] The ballad itself was very much a Percy ballad – full of references to the family, their history, and estates, and freighted with elucidatory footnotes. Hotspur was described in an endnote and there were supporting historical documents appended to the text in a postscript.

The Hermit was an immediate – and evidently an unexpected – success. Percy had taken Johnson's advice for a moderate first run of only 500 copies, but the demand of the public was not met by a second, or even a third, edition.[23] Johnson had entirely underestimated the taste for pseudo-historical ballads, and it was perhaps this miscalculation that provoked his teasing of ballad 'simplicity', although it is interesting that Percy was still deferring to Johnson at this time. *The Hermit* remained popular: it went through another eight editions before the end of the century and the hermitage was celebrated as a picturesque tourist spot.[24] Percy seemed to have succeeded in establishing for himself the position of courtly minstrel, and yet published no more in this vein. Enter Rowley, in borrowed garments.

It is likely that Percy's decision not to follow the success of *The Hermit* was caused by the first Rowley publication. On 10 April 1772, George Catcott had unwisely agreed to the publication of the 'Bristowe Tragedy', the most derivative and least convincing of the Rowleyan works.[25] It appeared early in May 1772, in a style which aped *The Hermit of Warkworth*. Although *The Execution of Sir Charles Bawdin* was a cheap and anonymous pamphlet, devoid of the grandeur of Percy's effort, it was prominently (and unjustifiably) dedicated on the title-page to:

THE DUTCHESS OF NORTHUMBERLAND, IN HER OWN RIGHT BARONESS PERCY, LUCY, POYNINGS FITZ-PAYNE, BRYAN, AND LATIMER, BEHIND WHOSE ILLUSTRIOUS NAME THE *RELIQUES* OF ANCIENT ENGLISH POETRY WERE WITH PROPRIETY INTRODUCED INTO THE WORLD, THIS PIECE IS WITH ALL HUMILITY DEDICATED BY THE EDITOR.[26]

Rowley was, from his first public incarnation, a fraud. Worse, he besmirched the patron whom Percy had cultivated with such scrupulous regard since 1764. Indeed, Walpole wrote to William Mason on 25 of the month:

> Somebody, I fancy Dr. Percy, has produced a dismal dull ballad called *The Execution of Sir Charles Bawdin*, and given it for one of the Bristol poems called Rowley's – but it is a still worse counterfeit than those which were first sent to me.[27]

Hence Thomas Percy, and his Northumberland patrons, were unwittingly enlisted by the Bristol literati (George Catcott and William Barrett) in the burgeoning Rowley Controversy. Not only did Percy risk being contaminated by this doubly fraudulent association; as became increasingly clear, the servile role of minstrels in the Rowley corpus was quite at odds with Percy's pretensions that they were noble civic bards.

We now need to focus more minutely on the precise ebb and flow of opinion. In London, Oliver Goldsmith informed Walpole of Chatterton's death, and Walpole, who had only involved Gray and Mason in detecting the forgeries he had been sent in 1769, fell silent on the subject (except to make the comment noted above). Goldsmith, however, sought an introduction to Catcott and opened the subject to discussion at the Club.[28] On 1 February, Barrett wrote that, 'Mr. S. Johnson I hear has denied ye Authenticity of "the Song to Ella"'.[29] Percy was also interested in the manuscripts, but told Ducarel as early as 13 January 1772:

> Dr. Percy has seen many former specimens of the same verses, and heard a great deal of the history of the discovery; which, when he has the pleasure to see Dr. Ducarel, he will relate at large: at present he can only say, that their *genuineness* is rather *doubted* till the original MS. can be produced.[30]

Percy, then, actively collected and discussed Chattertoniana. But to appreciate the part he played in the early publication of Rowley it is necessary to return to George Catcott's unpublished papers and the plans of the Bristol literati.[31] The following account fundamentally rewrites the history of the publication of the Rowley forgery, and demonstrates Percy's crucial role in assessing the pre-publication texts.

In September 1772, Dr Francis Woodward, a crony of Catcott's, interested Lord Charlemont, a patient of his at Bath, in the Rowley poems.[32] Woodward sent Charlemont to read the poems at Catcott's house, 'and after a very minute Examination said he was perfectly satisfied of their Authenticity'.[33] Charlemont then sent precise instructions for a quarto book of foliated transcripts of 'The Tournament', *Ælla*, and the Prologue and Chorus to 'The Tragedy of Godwynn', for which he paid Catcott 15 guineas. Catcott stipulated that Charlemont should not copy or print the pieces, or even learn them by heart.[34]

In November 1772, Catcott dined with Lords Dacre and Camden, also patients of Woodward, and the three of them read *Ælla*, 'The Tournament', and 'Charles Bawdin'. Dacre and Camden only doubted the authenticity of the latter, which they believed modernized by Chatterton (it had of course already been published by this time). Nevertheless, Catcott won their patronage:

> Lord Camden assured me, that if I would print them in his Name, with my Introduction ... Lord Dacre and himself, would each subscribe 20 Guineas towards defraying the Expence; and Lord Camden further promised, that when he return'd to London, he would propagate his own Opinion of their Authenticity, wherever he went.[35]

Plans for publication seemed to be progressing nicely: during the season at Bath, three influential Lords had been persuaded of the poems' authenticity and dispatched to London to spread the word. But it was also in November that, in spite of Catcott's extreme care in only allowing transcripts to circulate, Barrett lent Lord Dacre the actual parchments of 'Songe to Ælla' and the 'Yellow Roll', hoping to have them authenticated in London.[36]

After the November meeting, Camden wrote to Catcott on 27 December, requesting some further Rowley pieces.[37] Catcott sent copies of the 'Songe to Ælla', and various extracts from *Ælla* on 1 January 1773, and directed that Camden should defend the pieces in London:

> I have been credibly inform'd several Gentlemen well-known in the literary World, particularly M^r. Horace Walpole, D^r. Johnson &c have not only expressed their Doubts concerning the Antiquity of Rowley's writings, but have even gone so far, as to treat the whole

as a forgery; but if the request should not be thought too presuming, I would humbly beg Leave to refer them to your Lordship, as I am well assur'd, you can give them the most convincing proofs of their Authenticity.[38]

Camden replied on 11 January:

> I am more pleased with them upon a further perusal, and shall make it my Business to propagate my own Opinion of their Authenticity, & more particularly to Mr Horace Walpole the first time I see him. As to Dr Johnson, I am not acquainted with him, and so can do no more than communicate my Sentiments to Mr Garrick, who is intimately acquainted wth. him.[39]

Catcott had no further word from his missionaries for six months.

In the meantime, Percy had been dining with Dacre, Camden, and Charlemont, and discussing Rowley.[40] On 26 March 1773, he intriguingly recorded in his diary, 'I was at the Club: Dr. Goldsmith came to us with a bloody Face. L^d. Charlemont read the Bristoll Poetry' – presumably reading from the deluxe book prepared for him by Catcott.[41] By 3 April, Johnson's ridicule of 'modern imitations of ancient ballads' such as *The Hermit* and *Charles Bawdin* shows that the verses were topical in literary salons.[42] On 16 April, Garrick arrived with some of Chatterton's letters, and caused a great row between Percy and Goldsmith on the subject, but the following day Percy went with Goldsmith to visit Chatterton's garret.[43] Percy, it seems, was the man to convince: by dealing with the Bristol representatives Dacre, Camden, and Charlemont he had made himself pivotal to the acceptance or rejection of the poems. On 22 April, Percy spent 'a good part of the Morning' with Camden: 'he gave me some of Chatterton's Publications', and six days later, Dacre sent him a transcript of the parchments obtained from Barrett.[44] But still Percy could not decide whether they were authentic or not.

Percy left for Alnwick in July, where he remained until October. By then, contemporary tradition had it that Percy was the editor of *Charles Bawdin*, and possibly he was chastised by the Duchess for allowing her name to be used so freely.[45] While at Alnwick, and having just returned from a week in Scotland, Percy secured the original parchments from Dacre on 15 August and examined them with Thomas Butler, the Duke's agent and an expert in antique hands and documents.[46] Dacre, Camden, and Charlemont had had their suspicions raised by Percy and were awaiting his verdict. Sensing all was not well, Catcott wrote to Camden again on 19 August 1773:

> I am very anxious to know what your Lordship's Friends, particularly M^r. Garrick, D^r. Johnson, & M^r. Walpole, think of the Authenticity of the Poems in your Lordship's Possession … I am inform'd, they are universally admir'd for the elegance of the Compositions; but that their Authenticity with some few, still remains a doubt, and that this incredulity, is chiefly founded on the unfortunate Publication of *Sir Charles Bawdin*, which the learned President of Saint John's Oxford i.e Dr Fry and my present worthy Friend Dr Woodward, say, has serv'd more to stab their reputation, than anything else could possibly have done.[47]

The London Rowleyans awaited Percy's final judgement; Catcott was right to have feared 'the unfortunate Publication of *Sir Charles Bawdin*' Camden replied to Catcott on 27 August 1773:

> I am sorry to say, that I remain in great doubt; The Literati in Town are much divided, & those who are most conversant in the old English writings, make <so> many Objections to the Stile, the Grammar, and the use of words; Lord Dacre has been favoured by Mr Barrett, with the Original of Ella's Ode, which he has sent to D^r. Piercy for his inspection. Much will depend upon the judgment which those who are skilful in old hands, shall make of this parchment …
>
> I shall know the Opinion of Dr Piercy before I come to Bath in the Autumn, at which time, if I have the pleasure of seeing you, I will acquaint you, with every thing I have been able to collect in London touching this most extraordinary youth; Give me leave, before I conclude, to return you my Thanks for those Extracts you were so good to send me. I keep them as choice Relicks.[48]

The debate among the literati here alluded to deserves a much more detailed treatment – from the unpublished letters I have seen opinions changed on an almost daily basis. Catcott waited until he 'knew Dr Piercy's final Opinion concerning the Authority of the Original Mss' before he replied a month later.[49] Percy wrote Dacre a long and learned report from Alnwick on 6 September, declaring 'these are undoubtedly spurious and modern', and Butler had described them as the 'most bungling attempts to imitate old Writing that he ever saw'.

In all points of calligraphy, punctuation, and orthography they were inconsistent and anachronistic, as was the local historical detail. Percy also applied forensic tests and discovered the parchments had been aged with ochre and an infusion of gall, and written in thin ink: 'in every respect the most glaring & undoubted Fraud'.[50] In a long post-script he assured Dacre that the originals would be returned to him in London via Justice Robert Chambers, and gave Dacre permission to copy the letter for Barrett – which he evidently quickly did. On 14 September Dacre wrote to Barrett with a copy of Percy's letter, and explained: 'As to myself, whatever I might have thought on a cursory view of these Parchments, D^r. Piercy's and M^r. Butler's Opinion have great weight with me'.[51]

When Catcott replied to Camden on 23 September, he was understandably disappointed. He felt his trust misplaced, and wrote forcefully:

> I am extremely sorry to find your Lordship's Opinion, (who I fondly imagined would by your Perswasions have made many Proselytes to the Cause) so very much changed ... I thought the Sight of the Originals sent by Mr Barrett, would have settled that matter, beyond the possibility of a doubt.[52]

Catcott went on to say that Jeremiah Milles, President of the Antiquarian Society, had come to rather different conclusions. He then quoted from Percy's letter to Dacre.

> Tho' D^r. Piercy does 'em the justice to say they are highly deserving [of] Publication on Account of their great Poetical Merit, and that for his own part, he would subscribe to such a publication with great pleasure, and lend all the Assistance in his power, to promote the Sale and formation of such a work ... But if the Mss lately perused by D^r. Piercy and his Friend, (which I think impossible to be forg'd) cannot attest their own Authenticity, I shall despair of doing it by any other evidence ... And I beg further to observe to your Lordship, that if I find, after so many incontestable Proofs of their Authenticity, they should be condemn'd as spurious, and the writings are to stand or fall by the Opinions of the two Gentlemn above mentioned, *when I fondly imagin'd they were just on the Eve of Publication* [my emphasis].[53]

Amazingly, Catcott went on to press another manuscript into

Camden's hands. The question of authenticity had overtaken Rowley's 'great Poetical Merit', and it is significant that Percy obviously could not judge the poetry of the pieces with any certainty. There was no critical language for assessing the value or validity of ancient poetry, and so it was the physical status of the manuscript by which opinions were being carried.

Only Charlemont kept the faith with his book of transcripts, writing to Woodward two and a half years later on 28 February 1775:

> As to our Friend Rowley my endeavours have succeeded so far as to render him a general subject of Conversation, but I cannot flatter myself, that I have made many Converts to my own Opinion concerning his work. Horace Walpole is still an Infidel, and in general I find a great deal of Incredulity with regard to his claims of Antiquity, tho' all concur in admiring his Poetry.[54]

On 5 November 1773, Catcott had written to Charlemont again, to inform him that Percy had declared the Rowley manuscripts to have been forged, and again quoted from Percy's letter to Dacre.[55] Nevertheless, Catcott's hopes had been dashed, 'when I fondly imagin'd they were just on the Eve of Publication'.

Percy had managed to acquit himself with propriety, but it is tempting to imagine that he was also exacting a revenge on the Bristol Rowleyans who with *Charles Bawdin* had embarrassed him before the House of Northumberland and more significantly tarnished the standing of the minstrel. Needless to say, Percy did not offer any help in the eventual publication; he gave his advice instead to Thomas Warton. On 29 July 1774, Warton wrote to Percy asking him to 'conveniently communicate to me what you know about Rowlie's poems of Bristol'. Warton needed help with the second volume of his *History of English Poetry*. He had been sent a parchment by Barrett, and felt duty-bound to include a discussion of Rowley in the *History*, 'whether spurious or not'.[56] Percy's reply has not come to light, but Watkin-Jones notes that in the second volume of the *History*, Warton included an account of the parchments lent to Percy by Dacre: 'We may safely assume from the close resemblance of this account to Percy's Report either that Warton read the Report written for Dacre, or more probably, that Percy recapitulated his arguments in a letter to Warton, sometime between 1774 and 1776'.[57] Warton joined Percy as an Anti-Rowleyan.

But Percy's involvement with Rowley was not yet over. Percy entrusted the Dacre manuscripts to Justice Robert Chambers who was returning to London, imagining that this would be a safer conveyance than the mail.[58] Percy also gave Chambers instructions to show the parchments to Thomas Tyrwhitt, the Rowley heir apparent, before they were returned, and wrote to him twice to remind him to do so.[59] Tyrwhitt, whose edition of Chaucer was published in 1775, had not yet been approached by the Bristol Rowleyans. Chambers, however, in a hurry to leave for judicial office in Bengal, mislaid the parchments among his papers, failed to return them, and inadvertently carried them half-way across the world to India, where they remained until his widow discovered them after his death in 1803.[60] It was an unfortunate, a preposterous, *dénouement*.

Eventually hearing of the loss of these priceless papers, Catcott wrote to Charlemont on 20 March 1775:

> I am sorry to acquaint you, that Dr Piercy and his Friend Mr Butler, have lost or mislaid Mr Barretts curious originals of the Ode to Ælla & the yellow Roll ... which were sent them for their inspection, the latter of these Mss mentioned (as your Lordship well knows) the whole Contents of M[r]. Canynge's Folio Ledger, certain it is, they never yet have, nor probably never will be returnd, which in my humble Opinion, is a very convincing Proof those Gentlemen them selves, are well convinced (had they Candor enough to own it,) they are too authentick to be doubted.[61]

This claim was repeated in the ensuing controversy: Percy, finding the parchments authentic, had spread word that they were forged and destroyed them. Percy's fears were justified: 'a large party of pseudo antiquaries, and critics' made 'a great clamour about the disappearance of these two parchments' he told Chambers in 1778.[62] Catcott and the Rowleyans took revenge on Percy for demolishing their plans to publish in 1772. It was not until 1797 that Joseph Cooper Walker quoted the Chambers letters to Catcott and reported Percy's surprise that Catcott was ignorant of the story. Catcott replied on 10 May 1797 that he at last accepted Percy's version of events, but by then it was too late.[63]

III

Percy's entire reputation – his career – was at stake in the Rowley Controversy. Attacks on his integrity ranged from snide insinuation to outright libel. Herbert Croft was in no doubt that Rowley was faked.

In his rank and opportunistic sentimental novel, *Love and Madness* (1780), he wrote, 'Is any one fool enough to believe C. was only the blind, subterraneous channel, through which these things were to emerge to day, and float for ever down the stream of fame?'[64] But he blamed others for creating an ambiguous context for the literary source: notably Percy's *Reliques* and the almost forgotten Chinese pot-boiler *Hau Kiou Choaan* (1761):

> and [Chatterton] must have seen through the *pretended* extract of a letter from *Canton* to James Garland, Esq; at the end of the third volume [of the *Reliques*], which vouches for the *truth* of Percy's *Hau Kiou Choaau* [*sic*], there advertised as *translated from the Chinese*.[65]

In the face of such a clamour, Percy had very little to say. He collected most of the Rowley pamphlets, but, as Meyerstein notes, 'it is notice-able that Percy does not figure as one of the disputants in the Rowley Controversy, where some of the foremost antiquaries in England took sides'.[66] By delaying publication for four years, losing a brace of parch-ments, and contributing to Warton's immediate riposte, Percy had probably done enough damage already, and he had also been prevailed upon by James Dodsley to publish a third edition of the *Reliques* in 1775, presumably to capitalize on the burgeoning Rowley fashion. But Percy's involvement was not common knowledge, and on 21 July 1777, a W. Harington (friend of John Miller) wrote to him from Bath, adding the following postscript to his letter:

> I find *Rowlies Poems* are publishing by Mr Tyrwhi[tt.] I presume the Learned are divided in Opinion respecting their Authenticity and wish Dr Percy cou[l]d visit this part of the World to collect the Testimonies on each Side [of] the Question – what appears hitherto, I confess prejudices many in favour of their being Originals muti-lated by an Ignorant Boy.[67]

If Percy replied, his letter has not survived. He made only brief comments in letters to Astle and Ducarel although he later wrote in detail to Edmond Malone, on receipt of the latter's pamphlet (1782).[68] Percy had no doubts that Rowley was forged, but did not want to remind the public that he still jealously guarded the *Reliques'* folio MS.[69] It is telling, however, that the Rowley Controversy should have fixated upon manuscripts, the most vulnerable aspect of Percy's Gothic theory. For Percy, manuscripts were merely traces of minstrelsy that the antiquarian editor could realise on the printed page; for Chatterton, however, manuscripts were the very matter of literature, the stuff of history itself.[70]

In other words, Rowley manuscripts circulated in a literary-antiquarian environment in which manuscripts had previously played only a symbolic role. Although Percy's folio MS was proclaimed as the fundamental source of the *Reliques*, the document itself was carefully hidden away because publication superseded the manuscript and therefore literally revised the status of the original. The folio MS was merely a signifier of origins. By restoring physical qualities to these abstract manuscripts, Rowley therefore threatened to destabilize literary antiquarianism and topple its most prominent support: Percy's *Reliques*. If the *Reliques* had inspired Chatterton, not least to move away from Percy's assumptions about minstrels and manuscripts, it now characterized the world that would receive Rowley, and critics and satirists were quick to recognize the problem Rowley posed. William Mickle's satire *The Prophecy of Queen Emma* (1782), for example, was supposedly derived from 'a fair MS. in good preservation' which had turned up in the false lid of a chest in Durham Cathedral.[71] Mickle parodied the recovery and publication of Ossian and Rowley and other antique poetry:

a person who makes a discovery of a long-lost poetical MS. ought never to suppress it on account of its inferiority: and every nation has its poets of different degrees, the lowest of which no true Antiquarian, or *Collector of Reliques*, would wish to be destroyed.[72]

The poetic superiority of Percy's minstrels was denied and the folio MS was threatened with being classed as a forgery.

But Percy, who had set the context for literary-antiquarian poetry, refused to enter the controversy himself – with the effect that each side pressed the *Reliques* into service. The very status of the work was ambiguous. Edward Greene, for example, argued that the *Reliques* appeared to endorse the free translation of ancient poetry:

And here stop we a moment to pay a tribute justly due to the accurate arrangement of venerable 'balades' by the ingenious Percy; from these, ancient versification, no less than ancient phraseology, if stripped of their weeds, and decorated with the finery of modern 'apparamentes,' would be experienced to flow 'smooth as the smoothest stream,' smooth as the melody of Pope.[73]

Here, Percy's editorial emendations and conjectures were a character-istic proof of literary antiquarianism.

Some attacks were simply good-natured mockery. John Baynes's *An Archaeological Epistle to the Reverend and Worshipful Jeremiah Milles* (1782) included an 'Epistelle to Doctoure Mylles': a piece of Rowleyese verse describing the controversy and its participants, including Percy:

> Deane Percy, albeytte thou bee a Deane,
>   O whatte art thou whanne pheered[a] with dygne Deane Mylle?
> Nete botte a groffyle[b] Acolythe[c] I weene;
>   Inne auntyante barganette[d] lyes alle thie skylle.
> Deane Percy, Sabalus[e] will hanne thy soughle,
> Giff mo thou doest amate[f] grete Rowley's yellowe rolle.

> [a]Matched, or compared. [b]Grovelling, or mean. [c]Candidate for Deacon's Orders. [d]Ballads. [e]The Devil. [f]Derogate from, or lessen.
>   [Baynes's notes][74]

Others were less circumspect. The Rowleyans answered the mockery of Mickle and Baynes in a venomous satire, *The Genuine Copy of a Letter Found Nov. 5, 1782, near Strawberry Hill, Twickenham* (1783), supposedly addressed to Walpole. This suggested that Walpole, Steevens, Croft, Warton, and Percy had planned 'the Ochre affair', a conspiracy to destroy every Rowley manuscript they could lay their hands on.[75] And in a sense, when one considers Percy's use of the folio MS, they were right. At the very least, such attacks recognized that the canons of liter-ary antiquarianism derived from Percy's *Reliques* could not adequately deal with manuscripts. Scholars needed to reassess their use of sources.

There is a coda to Percy's entanglement in the Rowley Controversy: at the time, he was embroiled in a public row with Adam Ferguson about Ossian. *The Genuine Copy* made specific reference to this sorry affair, 'that plaguy [*sic*] scrape which his L-rdsh-p [Percy] contrived to get into about Ossian, and which was so near akin to this, made me fearful lest men should no longer shut their eyes'.[76] The coincidence of the two disputes, here noted by contemporaries, can hardly be acci-dental. William Shaw reminded the public that, while visiting Adam Ferguson in Edinburgh in 1766, Percy had heard a Highlander (appar-ently John Macpherson) reciting *Fingal* in Erse, and that in consequence he had briefly been an advocate for Macpherson's Ossian. Shaw, suggesting that Percy had been deliberately imposed upon, succeeded in provoking Ferguson to write to the papers and deny the meeting had ever taken place. Percy remembered otherwise, and an ill-natured public squabble erupted. His first newspaper advertisement attacking Ferguson in December 1781 appeared just as the Rowley Controversy was about to rise to its greatest ferocity.[77] The reading public was forcibly reminded that Ossian's claims to be authentic oral verse had been successfully challenged by Percy's insistence on written sources for ancient poetry, exemplified in his *Runic Poetry* and *Reliques* – which was precisely the point under current debate regarding the folio MS and Rowley. Although Rowley was soon dispatched as a forgery, attention shifted to deifying Chatterton as an extraordinarily precocious genius, and although Percy had opportunely fled to Dromore, he was still scarred by the controversy. When the fourth edition of the *Reliques* appeared in 1795 (dated 1794) not only was it attributed to his eponymous nephew (Dr Thomas Percy of St John's), but it was entirely re-edited from the folio MS, and published with an unlikely story claiming that this mysterious source had been recently exhibited in London.

In the dozen years between the Rowley Controversy and the 1794 *Reliques*, ancient manuscripts blossomed as literary tropes. Freed from the carefully contrived historical context of Percy's Goths, they filled journals and newspapers. Manuscripts exercised a profound fascination on writers. There was, for example, a revival of 'Hardyknute', a pseudo-antique Scottish ballad included in the *Reliques*. Although Percy proved 'Hardyknute' to be forged, he could not resist repeating the tale of its discovery: 'written on shreds of paper, employed for what is called the bottoms of clues' – that is, scrap paper in tailoring. Consequently, the case was seized upon as another Percian precedent for Rowley, and raised another storm in a teacup when John Pinkerton 'discovered' and published a second part in 1786.[78]

But perhaps the most striking influence was on a poet and painter who was inspired by the revolutionary quality of Chatterton's Rowley manuscripts to go far beyond language into art, beyond the alphabet into signs, and beyond printed verse into illuminated books. In about 1787, William Blake began to experiment with relief etching for the exquisite works *All Religions are One*, *There is No Natural Religion*, and *Songs of Innocence*.[79] The fabrication of the manuscript became a spiritual exercise to retrieve a lost world, perhaps the same world lamented by Percy and Warton. Warton had ended the second volume of his *History of English Poetry* (1778) with what was almost an epitaph for Chatterton:

... we have lost a set of manners, and a system of machinery, more suitable to the purposes of poetry, than those which have been adopted in their place. We have parted with extravagancies that are above propriety, with incredibilities that are more acceptable than truth, and with fictions that are more valuable than reality.[80]

The next generation would turn his lament into a celebration.

Notes

1. Knox, Vicesimus, *Essays Moral and Literary* (London, 1782), ii. 322.
2. For another arch comment on Percy, see 'On the Prevailing Taste for the Old Poets', ibid. 214.
3. The relationship of Percy to Chatterton and the Rowley Controversy is appreciated only by A. Watkin-Jones ('Bishop Percy, Thomas Warton, and Chatterton's Rowley poems (1773–1790) (Unpublished Letters)', *PMLA* 50 (1935), 769–84) and Pat Rogers (in the present collection).
4. See also my essay 'Richard Farmer and the Rowley Controversy', *NQ* 239 (1994), 314–18.
5. *Life*, 56–7; *Works*, 1178–9; Taylor, 81, 86–7; Holmes, Richard, 'Thomas Chatterton: The Case Re-Opened', *Cornhill Magazine* 178 (1970), 218. Bertrand Bronson, however, argues that Elizabeth Cooper's *The Muses Library* was more significant ('Thomas Chatterton', in *Facets of the Enlightenment: Studies in English Literature and its Contexts* (California, 1968), 187–209).
6. For my argument on Macpherson and Percy, see 'Celts, Goths, and the Nature of the Literary Source', in Alvaro Ribeiro, SJ, and James G. Basker (eds), *Tradition in Transition: Women Writers, Marginal Texts, and the Eighteenth-Century Canon* (Oxford, 1996), 274–96; and *The Making of Percy's Reliques* (Oxford, 1999), ch. 3.
7. *Works*, 6–20. Chatterton was irrepressible: Rowley even anticipated the invention of moveable type (*Works*, 60).
8. Ibid. 273.
9. Ibid. 304.
10. Ibid. 52, 54.
11. Ibid. 63.
12. Ibid. 228.
13. Ibid. 284–6, 290, 16 [bataunt: an unidentified musical instrument].
14. Ibid. 411.
15. Boston Public Library, Ch H 3 46.
16. There were also some failed projects: a fourth volume of the *Reliques*, *Ancient Songs chiefly on Moorish Subjects* (ready for issue in 1775), editions of the *Tatler* and *Spectator*, and of Buckingham and Surrey.
17. These were kept in a folder titled 'Chatterton & Rowley MS. Adversaria &c. carefully to be preserved T[homas]. D[romore]'. They probably arrived in April 1773 (see below) (Clarke, Ernest, 'New Lights on Chatterton', *Transactions of the Bibliographical Society* 13 (1916), 230–6).

18. Bristol Reference Library [hereafter BRL], B11457, fos. 214–16; see also Bodl., MS Eng poet b6, fo. 46ᵛ. Lort was one of the first researchers into Chatterton and Rowley, and, by 1774, a friend of Percy's (Davis, Bertram H., *Thomas Percy: A Scholar-Cleric in the Age of Johnson*, (Philadelphia, 1989), 207, 214). Percy's bibliography is also important in its own right: it notes a lost Chatterton letter to Thomas Carey, 25 June 1770 (*Works*, 776).
19. Davis, 180–3.
20. Cradock, Joseph, *Literary and Miscellaneous Memoirs* (London, 1828), i. 207; Johnson, Samuel, *The Complete English Poems*, ed. J. D. Fleeman (Yale, 1982), 128, 220n.
21. Similarly, the Northumbrian *Ride to Hulne Abbey* (privately printed, 1765) began as a letter to Edward Lye.
22. See *Reliques of Ancient English Poetry*, ed. Nick Groom (London & Bristol, 1996), ii. 161–4, 383–4. Evidently Lewis Carroll was sufficiently tickled by the word to subtitle 'The Hunting of the Snark' as 'An Agony in Eight Fits'.
23. *Illustrations*, vi. 160–2. Baptist Noel Turner gave this as the unlikely reason for Percy abandoning his poetic career.
24. For example, there are two engravings of Warkworth Hermitage in Grose, Francis, *The Antiquities of England and Wales* (London, 1773 [1772]–87), iii (1776) (unpaged): one is a floor-plan, the other a picturesque projection with an account of the scene.
25. *Life*, 451.
26. Chatterton, Thomas, *The Execution of Sir Charles Bawdin*, ed. Thomas Eagles (London, 1772), A1ʳ.
27. *The Yale Edition of the Correspondence of Horace Walpole*, ed. W. S. Lewis *et al.* (New Haven, 1937–83), xxviii. 36.
28. *Life*, 273.
29. BRL, B11457, fo. 72ᵛ.
30. *Illustrations*, iv. 573.
31. Catcott's accuracy has been confirmed by L. F. Powell, 'Thomas Tyrwhitt and the Rowley Poems', *RES* 7 (1931), 315n.
32. *Life*, 453.
33. BRL, B5342, 172.
34. Ibid. 174–8.
35. Ibid. 154. There are also transcriptions in Catcott's hand of his correspondence with Camden at BRL, B5304, 153–73.
36. *Life*, 454–5.
37. BRL, B5342, 155.
38. Ibid. 157.
39. Ibid. 159.
40. Percy dined at the Club at least seven times in a dozen weeks in 1772 (BL, Add MS 32336, fos. 157–71). Percy ruthlessly edited his memoranda books before he died and excised hundreds of pages, undoubtedly taking with them records of other visits during this period.
41. BL, Add MS 32336, 175ᵛ.
42. *Life of Johnson*, ii. 212.
43. 'Went with Dr. Goldsmith & Mr. Jones [Sir William Jones]: to inquire after the House where Chatterton died. Harry with me' (BL, Add MS 32336, fo. 177ᵛ). Cradock, i. 206; Davis, 198–9.

44. BL, Add MS 32336, fo. 178^v; Davis, 202. Presumably the 'Bridge Narrative' and 'Elinour and Juga' were also sent at this time.
45. Clarke, 235–6.
46. Watkin-Jones, 770; Davis, 202.
47. BRL, B5342, 161.
48. Ibid. 162–3.
49. Ibid. 163.
50. Clarke, 227–9; Watkin-Jones, 773–6.
51. BRL, B5304, 195.
52. BRL, B5342, 163–4.
53. Ibid. 164–5.
54. Ibid. 183.
55. Ibid. 179–81.
56. Fairer, David (ed.), *The Correspondence of Thomas Warton (1728–90)* (Athens, Ga., & London, 1995), 342.
57. Watkin-Jones, 783.
58. Clarke, 224; Watkin-Jones, 770; Davis, 202–4.
59. 15 October and 28 [?October: the manuscript is damaged] 1773 (Houghton Library, Harvard, fMS 1279 (3–4). These letters are currently unpublished, and Watkin-Jones even claims that 15 October is not extant (771), although Davis notes them (203).
60. *Life*, 457.
61. BRL, B5342, 182–3.
62. Watkin-Jones, 771.
63. *Illustrations*, vii. 740–1; BRL, B5304, 178–88. In 1783, Percy described the incident to Thomas James Mathias (*Illustrations*, viii. 213–14). See also Bodl., MS Eng poet b6, fos. 56–7, and BL, Add MS 32329, fo. 126.
64. Croft, Herbert, *Love and Madness: A Story Too True* (London, 1780), 126.
65. Ibid. 211. This obviously caught the public imagination: the passage was copied into 'MS Life of Thomas CHATTERTON, written in a small notebook by Orton SMITH', ed. Georges Lamoine, *Caliban* 8 (1971), 26. The authenticity of Percy's *Hau Kiou Choaan* (1761) has not been adequately established (see V. H. Ogburn, 'The Wilkinson MSS. and Percy's Chinese Books', *RES* 9 (1933), 30–6).
66. *Life*, 456. Percy's copies of *Poems* and *Miscellanies* are almost entirely unannotated, and there is no evidence that Percy compiled scrapbooks of magazine articles as many of his fellows did.
67. Bodl., MS Percy c 1, fo. 45^r.
68. 'Miscellaneous Correspondence of Thomas Percy', ed. A. H. Ashe, B. Litt. thesis (Oxford, 1964), i. Appendix, 32; *The Correspondence of Thomas Percy and Edmond Malone*, ed. Arthur Tillotson (Baton Rouge, La., 2nd edn 1960), i. 303–7.
69. In his dotage, Percy was tempted to change his mind after he received Southey and Cottle's edition (see *The Correspondence of Thomas Percy and Robert Anderson*, ed. W. E. K. Anderson (New Haven, 1988), ix. 146).
70. For some ruminations on this theme, see 'Thomas Chatterton was a Forger', *Yearbook of English Studies* 28 (1998), 276–91.
71. Mickle, William Julius, *The Prophecy of Queen Emma; An Ancient Ballad lately discovered Written by Johannes Turgotus, Prior of Durham, in the Reign*

of William Rufus (London, 1782), 21.

72. Ibid. 16.

73. Greene, Edward, *Strictures upon a Pamphlet intitled, Cursory Observations on the Poems attributed to Rowley, a Priest of the Fifteenth Century* (London, 1782), 56.

74. Baynes, John, *An Archeological Epistle to the Reverend and Worshipful Jeremiah Milles, D. D. Dean of Exeter, President of the Society of Antiquaries, and Editor of a Superb Edition of the Poems of Thomas Rowley, Priest* (London, 1782), 13.

75. anon., *The Genuine Copy of a Letter Found Nov. 5, 1782, near Strawberry Hill, Twickenham. Addressed to the Hon. Mr. H–ce W–LE* (London, 1783), 19–20.

76. Ibid. 9.

77. *GM* 51 (1781), 568. Richard Sher ignores the Rowley dimension in his article on Percy and Ferguson, 'Percy, Shaw, and the Ferguson "Cheat": National Prejudice in the Ossian Wars', in Howard Gaskill (ed.), *Ossian Revisited* (Edinburgh, 1991), 207–45. See also Davis, 256–9.

78. *Reliques*, ii. 88 [italics reversed] (noted in *Life*, 115). For example: Croft, 211; Malone, 58–62; anon., *An Examination of the Poems attributed to Thomas Rowley and William Canynge. With a Defence of the Opinion of Mr. Warton* (Sherborne, n.d. [1782]), 36n. In 1782, Nichols capitalized on this resurgence by advertising *Hardyknute, An Heroic Ballad*. 1782 also saw the fifth and sixth editions of Percy's *The Hermit of Warkworth*.

79. Viscomi, Joseph, *Blake and the Idea of the Book* (Princeton, 1993), 187–97.

80. Warton, Thomas, *The History of English Poetry, from the Close of the Eleventh to the Commencement of the Eighteenth Century*, ed. David Fairer (London & Bristol, 1997), ii. 463. The passage is strikingly reminiscent of Percy's conclusion to *Northern Antiquities* (London, 1770), i. 394, and Richard Hurd's *Letters on Chivalry and Romance* (London, 1762), 119.

Chapter 12

Nostalgic Chatterton: Fictions of Poetic Identity and the Forging of a Self-Taught Tradition

Bridget Keegan

In September 1824, John Clare was at work on his autobiography. He notes in his journal of Sunday, 12 September: 'as I did not keep a journal earlier I have inserted the names of those from whom I have recievd letters and to whom I have written in cronological order as near as I can reccolect'.[1] In writing about his life as a poet, Clare acknowledges that he must rely on imaginative reconstruction based upon other texts and texts from others. As the journal reveals, those texts include both letters and literary works. In this entry and the next, Clare mentions what he is currently reading: the first chapter of Genesis, Shakespeare's sonnets, and Chatterton's poems. Such eclectic reading was not uncommon for Clare. Despite the fact that his earliest patrons and critics presented him as 'unlettered' and 'artless' – a 'natural' (and hence completely uneducated) genius, Clare was a voracious and intelligent reader, whose self-imposed programme of study was as rigorous as it was unsystematic.

The conjunction of Clare's autobiographical activity with these particular texts may be purely fortuitous. However, it suggestively indicates some of the contours of Thomas Chatterton's significance for self-taught poets such as Clare, 'Poetical Shoemaker' James Woodhouse, 'The Bristol Milkwoman' Ann Yearsley, and Isabella Lickbarrow. While many recent critics of plebeian poetry, including Donna Landry, Moira Ferguson, Morag Shiach, Martha Vicinus, Richard Greene, and H. Gustav Klaus have been careful to demonstrate the combined influences of a number of 'popular' and 'polite' authors on the work of labouring poets, none has investigated the role that Chatterton, and the myth of his life, had in shaping plebeian poetry.[2] While Greene does note that the vogue of primitivism in the eighteenth century can be seen as a common root of the growth of interest in both antiquarianism (and antiquarian hoaxes) and in self-taught poets, to date only John Goodridge has elaborated upon the way in which Chatterton can be identified as a crucial part of the broader cultural nexus linking questions of literary and national origins and originality.

As such, besides revealing the interpretative possibilities of a deeper connection between Chatterton and other autodidact writers, Clare's reading also underscores his constant concern with origins and originality, as he juxtaposes the Judeo-Christian myth of origins with works by two authors whose originality was, at various times and for different reasons, subject to popular suspicion. It may be no accident that, in meditating on his poetic development, Clare was simultaneously studying two authors for whom the question of authorial identity and its relationship to textual authority was vexed. Clare knew that both Shakespeare's and Chatterton's less-than-perfect pedigrees invited some readers to question the authenticity of their literary production – much as Clare's detractors distrusted the achievements of a 'peasant poet'.[3]

Clare's journal as a whole (and a good portion of his poetry) touch upon aesthetic questions important to the eighteenth and early nineteenth centuries: whether artistic genius was natural or acquired; how to define poetic identity and whether it was due to an inherent originality or a training in literary tradition; what literary effects resulted from the poet's relationships to patrons, publishers, and the public; and, finally, how to account for the period's fascination with literary biography. While these topics are relevant to a discussion of any poet of the period, they assume a revealing new dimension when read through the relationships that the self-taught poets constructed between themselves and Chatterton. These intertextual relations have only recently begun to receive the attention they merit, yet an exploration of their extent yields important insights into the work of Chatterton and of all the poets, rustic or refined, whom he influenced.

Chatterton's significance to the generation of poets now categorized as 'Romantic' is a critical commonplace. In their desire to articulate an authentic poetic identity, many major poets of the age enshrined Chatterton as the model of an original creative subject, one whose tragic devotion to his art was untainted by material ambitions. Wordsworth famously invokes the 'sleepless Soul' in his vocational crisis lyric, 'Resolution and Independence'. Chatterton's fate provided the subject for an early monody by Coleridge. Keats dedicated *Endymion* to Chatterton, curiously calling the Rowley dialect 'the purest English', preferable even to Milton's. And Shelley considered Chatterton significant enough to include among the parade of illustrious mourners in *Adonais*.

It is this nostalgized 'Chatterton', a poet whose existence was conjured in the very act of mourning his loss, who became a privileged prototype for concepts of Romantic genius.[4] The neglected 'outsider poet' – and not the ambitious forger of the Rowley poems – was transformed into the paradigm for a poetic subject whose talents were presumably unaffected by social or educational contingencies. Chatterton's poverty merited mention as a factor in his untimely demise. But such poverty could be ascribed to the abuses of patrons and publishers and the lack of public taste – an effect, and not a cause, of the poet's creative ability. In order to produce their nostalgic fiction, later poets had to ignore salient facts of Chatterton's life (such as his relentless desire to turn a profit) and much of his poetry. Indeed, the Romantic 'forgery' of the life of the great forger almost entirely neglects his literary production. An overview of the mainstream Romantic texts invoking Chatterton reveals that he was commemorated as a great poet with only scant indication of what it was about his poetry that made him so very great.

For the self-taught poets of the Romantic era, however, there is no comparable neglect of the poetry. Yearsley's and Clare's relationships to Chatterton, in particular resemble and differ from those of their contemporaries.[5] While all sympathize with certain (sometimes specious) details from Chatterton's life, the self-taught poets do not always suppress the fact that Chatterton's 'originality', such as it was, came in promulgating an elaborate imposture, passing off what was his own (certainly highly original) work as the work of another. Yearsley's and Clare's writings about Chatterton explicitly invoke, cite, and celebrate Chatterton's *work* as much as his *life*. Perhaps more importantly, their assimilation of Chatterton's poetry into their own poetry and their reinscription of the Chatterton myth into their own poetic self-fashionings reveal the historical possibilities of a nascent but self-conscious parallel plebeian poetic tradition.

In *The Daring Muse*, Margaret Doody characterizes Chatterton as 'two tongued'; he 'illustrates the Augustan poetic ideal, that every utterance should speak twice at the same time'.[6] This double-voicedness is particularly pertinent to the self-taught poets, precisely because plebeian poetry had always, necessarily, to speak in two languages. Because most self-taught poets of the eighteenth and the early nineteenth centuries rarely composed explicitly for readers of their own social class, their poetry spoke to a refined audience from a social space alien to that audience. Labouring-class poets, from Stephen Duck onwards, were expected to employ a refined poetic idiom, revealing at least partial knowledge of a learned tradition, while at the same time, speaking from (and often about) another discursive position. They had to speak like 'real' rural inhabitants – but not too realistically – giving some evidence of their knowledge of poetic conventions – but not too much, lest they lose that level of 'authenticity' or 'artlessness' that made them interesting to polite audiences in the first place. Yearsley's and Clare's increased unwillingness, over the course of their respective careers, to speak in 'two tongues' and to continue what they may have felt to be an imposture, created practical difficulties in their careers and affected their poetry. Both would have been aware of what became of Duck and his poetry when he attempted to impersonate too closely the discourse of the aristocratic world into which he was adopted. It is possible that Chatterton may have provided an alternative to Duck's concessions, particularly if we analyse how Yearsley and Clare turned to Chatterton's life and his work to explore how issues of rank and education were both formative and limiting for their own vocational identities.

The self-taught poets' connections with Chatterton, then, complement and contest those of his other Romantic admirers. The plebeian authors are more alert to the construction of poetic identity within Chatterton's work, thus troubling the more prevalent Romantic construction enabled by a nostalgized reading of Chatterton's life. Yearsley's and Clare's literary responses to Chatterton indicate that they were attuned to how Chatterton's Rowley poems, in particular, expose the 'double voicedness' and imposture sometimes needed to express a marginalized poetic identity. Chatterton's imposture, and the representations of imposture and ventriloquism within the Rowley poems, were especially significant to the plebeian poets, as the role of poet was not one to which lawyer's clerks, milkwomen, or agricultural day-labourers might aspire without accusations of fraud or duplicity. In fabricating, impersonating, and simultaneously critiquing patrons and precursors to authorize himself, Chatterton provided a blueprint for the later labouring-class poets to follow.

To appreciate Yearsley's and Clare's responses to Chatterton, it is useful to sketch how identity and originality are already troubled concepts in Chatterton's work. Chatterton forged a vocational identity for himself through the sublimation of its origin in Rowley. Furthermore, Chatterton represented Rowley as establishing an authorial identity in its displacement and erasure through his relation to his patron, Canynge, and his own fictional predecessor, Turgot. Chatterton thus creates a nostalgic infinite regress that will be imitated by Yearsley and Clare. That Yearsley and Clare would have responded to this component of Chatterton's project may be connected with their perception that Chatterton's strategy for inventing a fictional poetic alter ego was motivated by his understanding of the relationship of social class to poetic production. Chatterton doubtless discerned that a public who welcomed *Ossian* and *Otranto* would more readily accept literary experimentation if it came from a 'larned' fifteenth-century priest than from a 16-year-old Bristol charity-school boy. Chatterton's ingenious exploitation of the manufactured antiquarianism practised by Walpole and Macpherson allowed him to hide behind a more authoritative voice than his own to gain access to a literary world from which he would have otherwise been excluded.

Yet Chatterton's simultaneous critique of his own nostalgic narratives demonstrates a resistance to the need to fix a better-credentialed source for the expression of his self-taught poetic voice. This is evident in one of the earliest documents of the Rowley period, the 'Extracts from Craishes Herauldry'. By concocting genealogies for his family and friends, Chatterton grants himself and his peers a false sense of importance derived from a fabricated aristocratic past, using fiction to elevate himself and his friends to a nobler rank. By contriving several specious patrilineages, this text presents the paradoxes – the 'double-cross' – of Chatterton's larger antiquarian hoax. As Donald Taylor points out, that double-cross becomes apparent in the penultimate entry on the name 'Cross' – the only name that did not belong to anyone in Chatterton's circle.[7] In this passage, the men described are not all members of the same family. Instead, each has merely taken on the name 'Cross' out of greed or ambition. Several of those who share this assumed name die 'issueless'. The final entries explicitly mock those who claim a false heritage:

> 1140   Rys ap Tewdewr da toke up the bearing of the Cross declarynge he was descended from Arthur ap Uther Pendragon he was therefore called Tudore the great of the Crosse but his Sonne Griffydh ap Tewdewr despising such Follie layd down that Armes and toke the Arms of Rys an Eagle between two Cotizes –
> 1460   John of Welles was so foolish that he gave out he was descended in a strait male Lyne from Ina Kyng of the West

Saxonnes in the yeere 690 and accordinglie bare a Cross Patee gayning thereby the name of Cross John but leevynge only a Dawter the name sunke....[8]

The moral is clear: there are risks attendant to pretending to be of a higher station. Those who do so may be remembered as foolish and may not produce a lasting legacy. This is certainly a fate that Chatterton (indeed, most poets) would wish to avoid. Hence Chatterton creates Rowley. Yet, as Taylor notes: 'The method of "Extracts" is that used throughout the imagining of the Rowley world: the names are quite authentic, drawn from histories and heraldic works; the connections to Chatterton, his friends, and his city are ... strictly of his own invention.'[9]

With Rowley, Chatterton's antiquarian deception grows more sophisticated while his reflexive critique of the trap of such nostalgic self-deception becomes more subtle. Rowley 'is' Chatterton, but Chatterton is not Rowley. Through Rowley, Chatterton indulges in a nostalgic fantasy and invents poetic identities in the past. Because of how Rowley is drawn, however, Chatterton maintains a delicately ironized distance through a double-voicedness that might, albeit temporarily, protect him from accusations of impudently speaking beyond his social position. Such a strategy is tenuous, as each Rowley text reveals that Rowley's poetic identity is always dependent upon other, more authoritative voices. In particular, the gradual collapse of Rowley's identity into that of his wealthy merchant-patron, Canynge, is critical. Seemingly from the moment of his creation, Rowley's singularity as a creative agent is displaced by attention to his work, his patron and his poetic precursors. Even in the earliest texts, the emphasis quickly moves away from the persona of Rowley to his work as translator and biographer of others. Rowley's identity disappears (just as Chatterton's would), but it is not replaced by a fiction of his life (since that life was already a fiction). After his 'birth' as a poet, Rowley comes into being obliquely, through a nostalgic network of other texts.[10]

It is not insignificant that one of Rowley's central activities is as the biographer of his patron. Among the first Rowley documents which Chatterton produced is 'A Brief Account of William Cannings from the Life of Thomas Rowlie Preeste'. Here, the patron's life is presumably contained in a specious autobiography, yet the only portion which is provided brings Rowley into view solely in terms of his relationship with Canynge. This relationship is grounded on their common antiquarian interests and has an undisguisedly financial foundation. Further evidence of how Rowley's authorial persona disappears is provided by the two epic fragments on the 'Battle of Hastings', where Rowley is depicted not as original author but as translator. The 'original' author is identified as Turgot, another historical but biographically embellished monk, this time from the tenth century. Turgot, like Rowley, is both a poet and a collector of antiquities, which will go on to form the foundation of the history of Bristol that Chatterton has Rowley write in 'A Discorse on Brystowe by Thos. Rowleie wrotten and gotten at the Desire of Wm: Canynge, Esqur'.

Not secure in inventing an authoritative other voice for himself in the past, Chatterton ultimately depicts his fictional forebear as also practising two-tongued strategies, looking towards a patron or an older source to warrant his work. While the relationships of Chatterton to Rowley, Rowley to Canynge, and Rowley to Turgot are not completely analogous, in each case, we see Chatterton experimenting with different representations of the double-voicedness which characterizes his condition as a poet. The various impostures he adopts illustrate the dilemmas confronted by the self-taught artist: to authorize his activity he must locate (and sometimes create) suitable patrons and precursors. What is particularly ingenious about Chatterton's scheme is that he takes the operation a step further, depicting those patrons and precursors as pursuing precisely his own path. Chatterton supplies prototypes both for himself and for possible patrons, and he cleverly gives this gesture a 'history' by having those prototypes engaging in the self-same activity. In distinction from their more privileged contemporaries, the plebeian poets appear to be more attuned and responsive to this facet of Chatterton's method.

The poem, 'Elegy on Mr. Chatterton' from Yearsley's second collection explicitly addresses her fellow Bristolian but implicitly addresses Yearsley's well-documented disagreement with her first patron, Hannah More, the friend and correspondent of Chatterton's infamous would-be patron: Horace Walpole.[11] The elegy is one of many poems in the second book, one whose production was superintended by Yearsley, in which the poet is preoccupied with asserting her freedom to express her identity. She knew that in so doing she must answer charges that she was aspiring to transcend her rank by speaking in a voice that should not have been 'her own'. Since Yearsley had learned from her falling-out with More that she could not entirely rely upon patrons' support, in the second collection, she turns to poetic tradition to protect and sanction her endeavours.

The question of whom she might claim as precursor is explored first by the poem 'Written on a Visit'[12] which directly precedes 'Elegy on Mr. Chatterton'. The poem depicts Yearsley's vocational pilgrimage to Twickenham. As Donna Landry has noted, Pope was a privileged figure for working-class women poets, 'the quintessence of the high literary mode to which their writing must achieve some relation in order to be considered "literary" at all'.[13] Yearsley had gone to Pope's pastoral utopia to claim a forefather. Despite her description of the raptures of her sojourn there, by the poem's conclusion, however, she is made only to feel her isolation and exclusion more acutely. This leads her to turn to Chatterton. Yearsley would have already felt a natural affinity, as both had been victimized by patrons or potential patrons. In Yearsley's elegy, More's friend Walpole is unquestionably guilty of causing Chatterton's death. Both More and Walpole attempted, in Yearsley's view, to ruin the careers of their potential protégés, and problems with patronage and self-filiation are at the centre of 'Elegy on Mr. Chatterton'.[14] While Yearsley does myth-ologize Chatterton's life in what are now recognizable as conventional ways, in her work (as in Clare's), Chatterton's poetry is granted a significance typically absent from other Romantic tributes. As with the poem offered to Pope, the piece is overtly self-effacing. Yearsley's poetic persona disappears as she hides it behind an image of Chatterton. The poet finds herself unworthy of approach, and the poem opens with the self-deprecating lines: 'Forgive, neglected shade! my pensive lay' (1). As if to underscore the modesty of the tribute, the poet brings to the forgotten grave a fragile violet as tribute, beginning an extended and conventional simile. Like the violet 'this joyless Youth was quickly hurl'd, / From Hope's fair height, to Death's unlov'd embrace' (15–16). However, in the fifth stanza, the poem takes a curious turn. The voice switches to that of Chatterton's 'sad Ghost' and, for nearly half the poem, Yearsley hauntingly imperson-ates her precursor.

The lament of Chatterton's ghost is addressed to the 'patrons of the tuneful Nine' (17), who are responsible for failing to rescue the poet as he was snatched from 'Apollo's shrine' by the 'haggard fiend' of 'Mis'ry'. Yearsley thus repeats a point she had made in another poem in the volume, 'On being presented with a silver pen': that is, while the untutored genius may be able to thrive without formal education, she cannot survive without a generous and sympathetic patron. Yearsley's desire to identify with Chatterton and to claim a privileged relationship with him appears to be great enough to produce a fantasy along the lines of that of Canynge's patronage of Rowley. The Ghost's last request contradicts all we know of Chatterton's ambitions for himself:

> I ask no laurel, claim no late-born sigh;
>   Yet should some rustic Muse, in Nature drest,
> Strike her soft bosom with a tearful eye,
>   While keen Emotion's in her strain confest,
> Resting on yon white cloud, I will be near.
>
> (37–41)

In constructing this self-serving version of her precursor, Yearsley adopts and usurps the voice of Chatterton, much as Chatterton adopted the voice of Rowley or Turgot to create a fiction for his own origins and originality.

Yet Yearsley's forged genealogy is built not only from a fiction of Chatterton's life but is constructed to include his work. Yearsley assumes the poet's voice and incorporates two Rowleyan heroes, 'Bawdin' (of the 'Bristowe Tragedy') and 'Ella' of the drama of the same name. What is more compelling, and what distinguishes Yearsley's identification, is not merely that she actually mentions Chatterton's poems, but that she is herself indicated in the elegy's final stanza. As unfortunate and marginalized herself, the speaker sees herself as unsuited to the commemorative task. But who better can understand the fate of a fellow 'hapless Genius'? Yearsley alerts the reader to her double-voiced strategy in memorializing her precursor:

> Now rest, too hapless Chatterton, whose strain
>   My bosom warms while singing Bawdin's fate;
> Yet shalt thou live! nor shall my song be vain
>   That dares not thine, but dares to imitate.
>
> (57–60)

Yearsley labels herself as imitator, through the imposture of the poem's earlier voice-over. Her 'imitation', however, is entirely original. Just as Chatterton, in 'imitating' a medieval monk, produced original poetry, Yearsley too is able to have it both ways. She appears to maintain a subordinate position, derivative of Chatterton, and like Chatterton she pretends to erase her own voice in assuming that of one with greater authority. But that 'authoritative' voice remains one of her own creation. Chatterton created Rowley and his poetry and antiquarian writing to authorize his own marginalized plebeian voice. Yearsley does the same with the figure of Chatterton. Yet unlike the mainstream Romantics, she does so in a way that does not entirely erase Chatterton's poetic production. That the poem includes Chatterton's work has other implications. As marginal poets, both Yearsley and Clare attracted many readers intrigued by the un-commonness of their lives and not necessarily by their poetic achievement. By awarding lasting fame to Chatterton's song and by making him live through the repetition of his work (and not solely through sentimentalized, nostalgic tales of his life) Yearsley could also be wishing that attention to *her* life would not occlude the memory of her *poetry*.

The nature of a plebeian poet's possible fame and whether it would be based on the work or the life, is the subject of extensive meditation for Clare: in many of his prose discussions of his condition as 'peasant poet' Clare ponders Chatterton's fate. It was a persistent problem for Clare that readers were drawn initially to his work because he was a curiosity, and Clare quickly became dissatisfied that what he wrote was of subordinate interest to the fact that he wrote at all:

> the first publication of my poems brought many visitors to my house out of a mere curosity to expect to know wether I realy was the son of a thresher and a laboring rustic as had been stated and when the[y] found it realy was so they lookd at each other as a matter of satisfied supprise askd some gossiping questions

It is not astounding that despite his desire for recognition, Clare remarks 'I was often annoyd by such visits and got out of the way when ever I coud'.[15]

The public's sometimes prurient fascination with his life helped confirm Clare in his identification with Chatterton, who, in fact, inspired Clare's earliest steps toward a poetic vocation. As Clare reminisces in his autobiographical writing: 'My mother brought me a picturd pocket hankerchief from Deeping may fair as a fairing on which was a picture of Chatterton and his Verses on Resignation'. Such items bespeak Chatterton's popularity, and it is this celebrity that caused Clare to consider the difficulties which ensue when a poet's reception is dominated by his biography, 'for Chattertons name was clouded in mellancholly memorys which his extrodinary Genius was scarcly know[n]'.[16] Clare would struggle throughout his career to turn his audience's gaze from the person of the poet to the poetry itself. In 1832, Clare wrote to Eliza Emmerson, 'all I wish now is to stand on my own bottom as a poet without any apology as to want of education or anything else'.[17] What is further significant about Clare's anecdote is that the keepsake encouraged one of his earliest poetic productions. He notes, 'I was fond of imatating every thing I met with and therefore it was impossible to resist the oppertunity which this beautiful poem gave me'.[18]

Clare's poem is 'The Resignation', and is 'Supposed to be Written by the Unfortunate Chatterton Just Before he Took the Deadly Draught that Put a Period to his Existance.'[19] As Yearsley did, Clare ventriloquizes 'Chatterton'. It is uncertain when Chatterton's 'Resignation' was composed, so it is difficult to guess if it had any relation to his possible suicide. If anything, Chatterton's poem would argue against swallowing deadly draughts: it is a pious piece which praises a just God. Though the speaker suffers from 'languid Vitals' that 'The Sickness of my Soul declare', any tension is ultimately resolved, hymn-like, in the final stanza:

> The gloomy Mantle of the Night,
> Which on my sinking Spirit steals,
> Will vanish at the Morning Light
> Which God, my East, my Sun reveals.

(29–32)[20]

Clare's imitation reveals more differences than similarities. While Clare's includes a divine address, it is enclosed in a more complex thematic discussion of hope and despair, and ends less optimistically. Clare's version opens not with an assertion of divine magnificence, but with a painful admission of human failure and frailty:

> Since disappointment & dispair
> The vainess of all hopes declare
> Since toss'd upon this Restless main
> I strive 'gainst wind and Waves in vain
> The more I struggle for the shore
> Misfortunes overwhelm the more
> Then since I struggle to maintain
> And strive alass – to live in vain

(1–8)

Hope does not dawn in the end but 'only burns to dye away' (12), leaving the speaker already 'resolv'd to take the plunge' (20) by the conclusion of the first stanza.

It is the poem's final stanza that reveals Clare's most interesting innovations, and, because of its strangely prophetic quality for Clare's own life, its effect is even more powerful for the modern reader. Moving from the possible comfort of a caring Creator, the speaker turns his address to the 'Grizly Ghosts that seem to rise / And swim before these frantic eyes / My blood runs chill – your hollow screams / But serve to terrify my dreams' (51–4). Chatterton haunts his literary progeny, and even at this early stage in his career, the poem discloses Clare's sensitivity to the emotional turmoil that could induce a person to take his own life. Turning his thoughts to others who have chosen the same route, the speaker again asserts: 'that last resource is mine / Stern Fate resolve – & I resign' (65–6).

Like Yearsley, and like other Romantics, Clare does emphasize Chatterton's death. The poem, then, might seem of a piece with more mainstream nostalgic appropriations of Chatterton's biography. Yet a closer reading reveals that Clare's ventriloquizing, and his attempt to understand the feelings that might have driven Chatterton to his purported suicide, show a more profound, and certainly more sustained, effort at identification. Though Clare could not know it at the time, no one of his generation would suffer more than he from the consequences of the Romantic nostalgic myth of the outsider poet that the figure of Chatterton had been used to epitomize.[21]

The fate of Clare's tribute is also telling. In his autobiographical fragments, Clare tells us that this poem was among the very first he showed to anyone outside of his family, in the hopes of initiating a literary career. Bookseller J. B. Henson liked the poem so much that, as Clare tells us, 'he wanted to print [it] in a penny book to sell to hawkers but I was doubtful of its merits and not covetous of such fame so I declind it'.[22] One wonders to which kind of fame Clare is referring. That of a popular-ballad writer, not of a 'refined' literate poet? Certainly Clare had aspirations beyond that of a rural hack. Nonetheless, he was interested in having an audience. Perhaps it was the anonymity of such 'penny books' that Clare resisted. Whatever the case may be, the poem remains an instructive document for understanding the unique nature of Clare's relationship to Chatterton.

But the poem is not the only time Clare 'impersonates' Chatterton. John Goodridge has written of the several times when Clare, long prior to his institutionalization, tried his hand at more overtly

Chattertonian impostures. Goodridge reveals, 'Clare made several attempts in 1825, some of which were successful, to pass off his own poetry as the work of well-known seventeenth-century poets'. Mischievously claiming to be 'Steven Timms', 'Percey Green', or 'James Gilderoy', Clare, like Chatterton, demonstrated that there was more than one facet to his double-voicedness. As Goodridge comments: 'The important Chattertonian features of these early impostures lie not so much in their content ..., but more in the way they reveal the temper of their author. By dressing up in his new disguises, Clare expresses his discomfort in the literary clothes he has been made to wear'.[23]

Though Goodridge sees Clare's discussion of Chatterton in his correspondence as a sign of Clare's greater concern for Chatterton's biography rather than his poetry, I would argue that time and again, Clare underscores his investment in his forebear's work, particularly as he sketches a broader poetic genealogy for himself. In one of his very earliest letters, to J. B. Henson, mentioning his plans for publishing, Clare invokes Chatterton:

> Good God, how great are my Expectations! what hopes do I cherish! As great as the unfortunate Chattertons were, on his first entrance into London, which is now pictured in my Mind – & undoubtedly like him I may be building 'Castles in the Air' but Time will prove it.[24]

Clare has a good notion of the poetic tradition and of a model of the poet that he sees himself assuming. As in the imitation, Clare is attempting to understand more fully what Chatterton may have been feeling at a parallel stage in his career. Clare acknowledges that his hopes may be as 'Castles in the Air'. But considering that Chatterton achieved eventual fame, Clare's claims for himself are not so self-deprecating as they might first appear. While Wordsworth made invocations of Chatterton something of a cliché for young poets at crucial vocational junctures, in a letter to Captain Sherwill in 1820 Clare shows himself to be familiar with popular accounts of the story of Chatterton's life, but desirous of better knowing his poetry, as Clare asks Sherwill to forward him a copy of Chatterton's works.[25] Mark Storey notes that Sherwill sent Clare *Chatterton's Life and Works* (as well as Currie's *Life of Burns*!) with money donated by Sir Walter Scott. Thus from very early in his career, we have evidence that Clare was reading Chatterton's poems.

It is useful, also, to pause once more over Clare's several journal entries discussing Chatterton. In September 1824, again as Clare is writing his autobiography, he also 'lookd in to the Poems of Chatterton to see what he says about flowers and have found that he speaks of the Lady smock'.[26] Clare then inscribes several lines taken from the Rowley poems. Eric Robinson and David Powell, editors of Clare's journals, identify the verses as from 'The Battle of Hastings I' and from the 'Songe toe Ælla'.[27] During the remainder of the month, Clare continues to pore through Chatterton, 'in search for extracts to insert in my natural history'.[28]

At first, it might seem odd for Clare to study Chatterton for lines relating to nature, as Chatterton is better known for his emphasis on the legendary and heroic. However, Clare reveals a fine appreciation for this neglected dimension of Chatterton's achievement and demonstrates himself to be a shrewd critic. Goodridge justly remarks that 'Clare's extracts show that he is reading "against the grain", looking for things which it is not Chatterton's first aim to deliver. One nevertheless finds oneself, having worked through his extracts ..., looking anew at Chatterton's characteristic words and forms of writing. Clare ... *reads Chatterton to us* in a way that is interesting and refreshing.'[29]

Despite this, Clare does simultaneously participate in some unoriginal sensationalizing of Chatterton's death:

what a wonderful boy was this unfortunate Chatterton   I hate the name of Walpole for his behaviour to this Genius and his sneering and cold blooded mention of him afterwards when his gossiping fribble had discoverd them to be forgeries   why did he not discover the genius of the author – no because they surpassd his Leadenhall forgery of 'Otranto'[30]

Clare sentimentalizes the poet and blames Walpole for the suicide. However, in his reading of the relationship between Chatterton and the author to whom he turned as a possible patron, Clare shows good insight into motives. He expresses genuine anger that Walpole, a member of the literary establishment, failed to recognize Chatterton's genius and went so far as to defame him through the 'sneering and cold blooded mention' in 'gossiping fribble'. By the time Clare was making these entries, he had felt something of the same chilly reception.

But Clare also announces himself as more than a sentimentalist. In a subsequent entry, he further imparts his admiration for the Rowley poems, identifying particular favourites:

> Finishd the reading of Chatterton admire his tradegy of Elia and Battle of Hastengs noticd a good description of a Thunder storm in the Ballad of Charity.   v.29 etc and a beautiful one of a ladye inserted it in Appendix No 3   Chatterton seemd fond of taking his similes from nature   his favourite flower seems to be the 'kingge coppe' and his favourite bird the 'pied Chelandrie' (Red cap)   the only trees he speaks of are the oak and elm[31]

Clare appropriates these verses, however, not for imitation, as with the earlier efforts, but in the service of a project that is uniquely his own, namely, his natural-history writing. His incorporation of Chatterton's lines shows his identification with his precursor, his 'misreading', and his subsequent incorporation of that 'misreading' into work that is no longer imitation but which reveals his own achievement as an independent writer.

While there is another notice of Chatterton later in the journal (an expression of his admiration for Coleridge's 'Monody'), the final significant mention dates from late September 1824 in a letter to Henry Francis Cary.[32] Here Clare reveals something that was not mentioned in the journals: that he had been reading Cary's *Life of Chatterton*, which is what had inspired him to reread the poems. In this letter, Clare asks Cary if he would consider reading Clare's auto-biography. After doing so, he invokes Cary's *Life*, mentioning that it 'turnd me to read his poems over seriously   I was often struck with remarkable passages & happy expressions   did the reading strike you as such'. Clare presses Chatterton's biographer about his subject's poetry, in the same moment as he enlists his help with his own autobiography. What confirms Clare's purposes in establishing Chatterton as a key figure in a plebeian genealogy of poetic origins, however, is his next comment to Cary: 'I hope in your lives of the Poets you will think of Bloomfield he is a great favourite of mine'. Clare's request is, I believe, entirely purposeful. Clare felt a deep rever-ence for Robert Bloomfield, another 'peasant poet' whose *Farmer's Boy* (1800) had been a best-seller, but who had died nearly penniless. Clare's admiration for both Bloomfield and Chatterton, and his mention of them within the discussion of his autobiography suggests that Clare saw himself as heir to a (doomed) plebeian tradition in which they were the esteemed forefathers. This identification is further supported by a sketch Clare (who was at one point in his career an apprentice stonecutter) made among his manuscripts of several tombstones, one 'To the Memory of Thomas Chatterton' and two others bearing the names of Chatterton, Bloomfield, and, interestingly enough, Keats as well (Fig. 3).

In forging his genealogy, Clare, like Yearsley, emphasized his precursor's literary achievements as well as his remarkable life. Yearsley and Clare commemorate Chatterton as one imagines they would want to be remembered themselves, as poets first – but poets whose significant origins contributed to their originality in ways that were productive as well as limiting. It was in part according to Chatterton's model that they created themselves as independent and original, if always necessarily double-voiced, poetic subjects.

Notes

1. *John Clare by Himself*, ed. Eric Robinson and David Powell (Ashington and Manchester, 1996), 173.
2. Greene, Richard, *Mary Leapor: A Study in Eighteenth-Century Women's Poetry* (Oxford, 1993); Klaus, H. Gustav, *The Literature of Labour: Two Hundred Years of Working-Class Writing* (New York, 1985); Shiach, Morag, *Discourse on Popular Culture: Class, Gender, and History in Cultural Analysis, 1730 to the Present* (Cambridge, 1989); Vicinus, Martha, *The Industrial Muse: A Study of Nineteenth-Century British Working-Class Literature* (London, 1974); and see below.
3. In 'Identity, Authenticity, Class: John Clare and the Mask of Chatterton' (*Angelaki* 1.2 (1993/4), 131–48), John Goodridge remarks on another passage from the journals in which Clare conjoins Chatterton and Shakespeare. He writes: 'Clare seems interestingly to engage here with (and perhaps means to make ironic comment on) the common eighteenth-century habit of comparing Chatterton favourably with Shakespeare. (One also wonders what he knew about the Rowley Controversy, and the accusations that Chatterton had plagiarized Shakespeare)' (135). The present essay is indebted to Goodridge's article, the most complete discussion of Clare's complex relationship with Chatterton.
4. My definition of nostalgia is drawn from Susan Stewart, *On Longing: Narratives of the Miniature, the Gigantic, the Souvenir, the Collection* (Durham, NC, 1993). In *On Longing,* Stewart describes the processes of nostalgia as 'a sadness without an object, a sadness which creates a longing that of necessity is inauthentic because it does not take part in lived experience. Rather, it remains behind and before that experience. Nostalgia, like any form of narrative, is always ideological: the past it seeks has never existed except as narrative, and hence, always absent, that past continually threatens to reproduce itself as a felt lack' (23).
5. James Woodhouse includes a brief invocation to Chatterton in the opening lines of his lengthy autobiography. Lickbarrow's poem is entitled

'Stanzas Supposed to be written at the grave of Chatterton' and appeared in her first collection of 1814. (See Goodridge's 'Rowley's Ghost', in the present volume, below.) While an analysis of both works would certainly prove an interesting complement to the current discussion, the present study will limit itself to Yearsley's and Clare's tributes only.

6. Doody, Margaret, *The Daring Muse: Augustan Poetry Reconsidered* (Cambridge, 1985), 231.
7. Taylor, 53.
8. *Works*, 49.
9. Taylor, 53.
10. As this essay was being finalized for press, I was made aware of Nick Groom's piece, 'Thomas Rowlie Preeste', in the collection edited by Thomas Woodman, *Early Romantics: Perspectives in British Poetry from Pope to Wordsworth* (London, 1998). In his essay, Groom ingeniously reconstructs Rowley's biography through a network of texts devoted to Canynge, and convincingly argues, contrary to my position, that 'Rowley's life of Canynge is really a secret life of Rowley'.
11. Yearsley's troubled relationship with More has been the subject of several excellent and contrasting recent interpretations in the works of Donna Landry (*The Muses of Resistance: Laboring-Class Women's Poetry in Britain, 1739–1796* (Cambridge, 1990)), Moira Ferguson (*Eighteenth-Century Women Poets: Nation, Class and Gender* (Albany, 1995)), and Mary Waldron (*Lactilla, Milkwoman of Clifton: The Life and Writings of Ann Yearsley, 1753–1806* (Athens, Ga., 1996)).
12. Yearsley, Ann, *Poems on Various Subjects* (Oxford, 1994), 139.
13. Landry, 47.
14. Yearsley, 145.
15. Clare, *By Himself*, 121.
16. Ibid. 99.
17. Storey, Mark (ed.), *Clare: The Critical Heritage* (London, 1973), 218.
18. Clare, *By Himself*, 99.
19. Clare, John, *The Early Poems of John Clare*, ed. Eric Robinson, David Powell, and Margaret Grainger (Oxford, 1989), i. 325.
20. *Works*, 684.
21. Although it is unrelated to Clare's technique in this imitation, it is an interesting and tragic fact that a symptom of the mental illness that would afflict Clare during the last thirty years of his life would be delusions that he was someone else. During those years, he did not however envision himself as Chatterton, but as Byron. One might say that this imitation of an archetypal poet figure is unconsciously prescient in more ways than one (though Byron's great popular success and lifestyle was certainly as much of a contrast with Clare's and Chatterton's as one could imagine).
22. Clare, *By Himself*, 104.
23. Goodridge, 141, 143.
24. Clare, John, *The Letters of John Clare*, ed. Mark Storey (Oxford, 1985), 1.
25. Ibid. 45.
26. Clare, *By Himself*, 173.
27. Ibid. 315.
28. Ibid. 174.

29. Goodridge, 139.
30. Clare, *By Himself*, 174.
31. Ibid. 174.
32. Clare, *Letters*, 304.

Chapter 13

Chatterton's Poetic Afterlife, 1770–1794: A Context for Coleridge's *Monody*

David Fairer

Perhaps no other poet offers such a contrast between a brief and obscure life and a vast and powerful posthumous existence as the figure of Thomas Chatterton. When he died in his Holborn garret in 1770 at the age of 17, all he could claim were a scattering of anonymous poems and letters in the newspapers, squibs, imitations, satires and love verses, and a bundle of documents rather amateurishly forged or 'transcribed', many purporting to be the writings of a fifteenth-century priest and poet, Thomas Rowley. In the years after Chatterton's death, curiosity became intense about this odd conjunction of youth and age, the charity boy who had recovered the voice of a fifteenth-century priest – a language whose words were ancient yet seemed new-minted for an age tiring of politeness and wit. Chatterton fast became an object of wonder to those who, like Dr Johnson, made their way to the muniment room of St Mary Redcliffe. The young man's writings began to take their ambiguous place in the literary canon. By 1777 Rowley's poems had been given a scholarly edition by Thomas Tyrwhitt, and in the following year the fifteenth-century writer was awarded a chapter in Thomas Warton's *History of English Poetry*.[1] This was not merely Rowley's triumph, but that of his youthful creator: Warton declared that he considered the poems spurious but their teenage originator an undoubted genius. The historian of poetry, however, could not bear to leave them out of his account, knowing that single-handedly they would, if genuine, redeem the fifteenth century from tedium. Rowley was the vital missing link that continued the Chaucerian tradition to Tudor times. Somehow, as with the *History of Bristol* which William Barrett printed in 1789 with many of Chatterton's concocted documents, the youth had the knack of supplying just what ought to have been there, but was not. He supplied connections, completed fragmented stories, provided origins (the first English pastoral, the first native classical epic, the earliest verse tragedy), and brought alive scenes and voices from oblivion. In a strange way the figures of Thomas Rowley and Thomas Chatterton appeared to be real and distinct (they met and conversed in George Hardinge's *Rowley and Chatterton in the Shades*, 1782). Whether Rowley had been rediscovered or simply invented was equally a matter for wonder, and Chatterton's twin selves entered a debate about fact and fiction, life and art, and how one could be subsumed into the other. Indeed in 1780 Chatterton himself began his slippage into the realm of fiction with Herbert Croft's sensational docu-novel, *Love and Madness*, which combined the contemporary scandal of a vicar and an actress (the Reverend James Hackman's murder of his mistress Martha Reay) with a series of genuine letters written by Chatterton and unscrupulously purloined from the boy's mother. In this book the tragic young poet found a context of emotional frustration, senti-mental gesture, and flawed genius that would never be disentangled from him.

In the Rowley Controversy of 1782 the battle lines were drawn up between the scholarly establishment, represented by Edmond Malone, Thomas Warton, Thomas Tyrwhitt, and George Steevens, and the antiquarian believers, Milles, Barrett, Catcott, and Jacob Bryant. At the centre of the debate was Chatterton himself, with the Anti-Rowleyans tending to assert his wonderful genius, and the Pro-Rowleyans char-acterizing him as an ill-educated apprentice quite unequipped to write such poetry.[2] Thus Chatterton was caught between being a fraudulent genius or an honest ignoramus. It began to seem that this lad could be anything you wanted him to be. Fact and fiction, life and art, creator and created, had become so intertwined.

Inevitably, Chatterton was himself becoming a subject for others' poetry. Ode-writers who wished to address a personified Fancy, Pity or Despair, found they could address Chatterton and thereby evoke all three. One after another versifiers wrote elegies and laments for a figure who awkwardly combined Orpheus and the Grub-Street hack – the pure-voiced songster expiring in a filthy garret – and his example could enliven a poetic discussion of unjust neglect, blighted hopes, or the nature of poetry itself. Henry Headley, 'Perdita' Robinson, Ann Yearsley, Thomas Russell, William Hayley, John Scott, Henry James Pye, Hannah Cowley, and Helen Maria Williams were only the most notable of many poets who addressed or invoked the figure of Chatterton in this period, and in 1790 the 17-year-old Samuel Taylor

Coleridge copied out his own 'Monody on the Death of Chatterton' into the headmaster's Golden Book of his pupils' literary productions.[3]

Coleridge, in his final year at Christ's Hospital, found much in the figure of Chatterton with which he could identify: youthful poetic aspirations, high hopes for changing the world, a feeling of estrangement from family and home – and Chatterton's garret was only a short walk from the school. Most strikingly, both were blue-coat charity boys (Colston's School in Bristol, where Chatterton was educated, was founded as a charitable institution by Edward Colston, a Christ's Hospital boy himself). The connections would if anything grow closer during the 1790s with Coleridge's move to Bristol, his intimacy with Southey, Cottle and the Frickers, and his own marriage on 4 October 1795 in the church of St Mary Redcliffe ('poor Chatterton's Church … The thought gave me a tinge of melancholy to the solemn Joy, which I felt').[4] By the late 1790s Coleridge, now known as 'the author of the Monody on Chatterton', found he could use the image of the suicidal young poet to his advantage.[5] Conversely, his friends employed the identification to warn or admonish him.[6] Wordsworth's 'Resolution and Independence' (composed 1802, published 1807) is only the most famous example of how the figure of Chatterton could be used for this purpose. In a poem that moves from joyous energy to static endurance, from the hare 'running races in her mirth' to the old man beside the pond, it is that figure of 'dire constraint' who carries the message, and Coleridge who should be listening to it:

> I thought of Chatterton, the marvellous Boy,
> The sleepless Soul that perish'd in its pride;
> Of Him who walk'd in glory and in joy
> Behind his plough, upon the mountain-side:
> By our own spirits are we deified;
> We Poets in our youth begin in gladness;
> But thereof comes in the end despondency and madness.

$$(43\text{--}9)[7]$$

In *Coleridge and the Literature of Sensibility* (1978) George Dekker sees the identification with Chatterton as 'Coleridge's problem'. Indeed it is tempting to turn the Chattertonian Coleridge into a psychological case history, and the poet's use of Chatterton can be overplayed in terms of a personal fixation. There is a danger of letting notions of psychological development shape Coleridge's career too neatly:

At Nether Stowey, I think, Coleridge simply outgrew the identification with Chatterton: the *Monody* became a literary
embarrassment, and as a husband and father in his middle twenties
he could no longer picture himself as a 'wond'rous boy'.[8]

Dekker has dealt interestingly with the way the tragic figures of
Chatterton, Burns, and Werther recur in Coleridge, and in his
biographical reading of the early career the 'Dejection Ode' takes its
place as the pivotal text. His view of Sensibility as a morbid and self-
indulgent mode means that Chatterton comes to be associated with
suicidal tendencies and depressive illness – the 'despondency and
madness' of Wordsworth's warning. He is made to represent an
unstable adolescence that Coleridge fruitfully outgrew.

But I want in this essay to steer the discussion away from the
pathology and back to the poetry, thinking less about Coleridge's
emotional and psychological progress than about the artistic influences and choices that characterized his poetic use of Chatterton in
the 'Monody'. I have already stressed how unstable the figure of
Chatterton was during the two decades after his death, and this
instability is reflected in the poem itself. The teenage Coleridge was
faced with a wide range of possibilities. What he made of these in
1790, and what he then proceeded to do when he rewrote the poem
for its first publication in 1794,[9] can perhaps tell us something about
Coleridge's early development, and also about the development of
Chatterton's posthumous image. What we now call the Romantic
myth of Chatterton involved a narrowing down and weakening of a
figure who had earlier offered writers so much.

For this purpose the essay will concern itself with the earliest two
versions of the poem completed in 1790 and 1794. The 'Monody on
the Death of Chatterton' is remarkable in that it spans Coleridge's full
poetic career from about 1785 (if we accept that some lines of the first
version were written as a school exercise in his 13th year)[10] up to the
final text published in 1834, the year of his death – a range of almost
50 years. He continually rewrote and revised it. The 90 lines of 1790
became 107 lines in 1794, 143 lines for his 1796 *Poems*, 135 in 1797,
119 in 1803, 143 again in 1828, 154 in 1829, and swelled to 165 lines
in 1834. It is unhelpful, however, to see this as a single poem in course
of development as I. A. Gordon does ('the *Monody* took him no less
than forty-four years to beat into its final form').[11] We begin with
irregular Pindarics and end with a poem in pentameter couplets, and
the texts of 1790 and 1794 are so distinct as to amount to separate

poems. In terms of the two earliest versions, of the 90 lines of the 1790 text, only 17 reappear in 1794. I shall therefore be treating them as two separate texts embodying different constraints and opportunities. They are emphatically not part of an organic process by which Coleridge is trying to work a single poem into shape.

But before looking at these two monodies it is necessary to establish a fuller context for assessing what Coleridge does with the figure of Chatterton. As the beginning of this essay suggested, in the 20 years following his death Chatterton was a figure who could be manipulated and packaged in different ways. Wordsworth's 'marvellous Boy, / The sleepless Soul that perish'd in its pride' is disembodied (unlike his companion Burns who is holding a plough), and the Chatterton celebrated by the young Keats in 1815 is a figure whose voice 'melted in dying murmurs' and who perished like 'a half-blown floweret which cold blasts amate'.[12] But the delicate spirit of poetic myth was only one of several Chattertons available in the 1770s and 1780s. It is important to realise that during the quarter century after his death there were various competing Chattertons who could be used to make a range of points about poetry and society.

It is necessary first to confront the image of the boy, which has become inextricably attached to Chatterton. As the material listed in 'Rowley's Ghost' makes clear, the 'marvellous Boy' has regularly attached itself to works about or inspired by Chatterton. The popular nineteenth-century representation of the poet pictured at the age of 9 with long hair and chubby cheeks (the portrait which gained currency in Dix's *Life* of 1837 and a copy of which was owned by Wordsworth: see Fig. 5) though spurious, is still being used today.[13] The picture's popularity must come from the fact that we need to have an image of Chatterton in which he looks like a boy. And the need has been a long-standing one: the engraved programme for a Chatterton commemorative concert on 3 December 1784 showed 'Genius conducting Chatterton in the habit of a Blue-coat boy, to her altar'.[14]

In the early years of his posthumous existence, however, Chatterton was also regularly represented as a manly youth who had grown up quickly and was mature beyond his years. This is, after all, closer to the truth. He had ceased to be a charity boy and had been released from his apprenticeship by the Bristol attorney, Lambert. By the summer of 1770 he had set himself up in London and had climbed the first rung of a journalistic career, arranging an interview with the Lord Mayor and negotiating on his own behalf with publishers. The earliest of the elegies on Chatterton, written by his friend Thomas

Cary and published in the *Town and Country Magazine* in October 1770 two months after his death, stresses his 'manly soul' which even in infancy had evinced 'that heroic mental fire, / Which reign'd supreme within the mighty whole'. There is nothing diminutive or boyish about Cary's portrait: though he had not been allowed to grow to maturity, Chatterton was a heroic figure who, rather than nurturing a delicate, private voice, had already made his mark on the public stage:

> The public good was ever in his view,
> His pen his lofty sentiments bespoke,
>   Nor fear'd he virtuous freedom to pursue.
> Yes, Liberty! thy fair, thy upright cause,
> He dar'd defend, spite of despotic force,
> To crush his much-lov'd country's wholesome laws,
>   Its noble constitution's only source.[15]

This image of Chatterton as the public defender of liberty became widely known when the elegy formed the epilogue to the *Miscellanies*.[16] The 'manly soul' of Cary's poem is the Chatterton of the 'Decimus' letters, whose attacks on the political establishment rivalled Junius in their controlled invective on behalf of 'the liberty of the subject'.[17] These subversive papers, along with the most uncompromising of Chatterton's political satires, 'Kew Gardens', 'Resignation', and 'The Whore of Babylon', may have remained out of the public eye during the 1790s,[18] but Horace Walpole had already revealed Chatterton as 'Decimus' and the author of 'Kew Gardens'. Furthermore, his *Letter to the Editor of the Miscellanies* (1779) reiterates Cary's description of the satiric and political Chatterton as mature and far from boyish.[19] Walpole's Chatterton is dangerous and aggressive, 'a bold young man', one who 'had formed disciples – yes, at eighteen' – 'he demanded his poems roughly and added, that I should not have *dared* to use him so ill'.[20]

Admittedly, Walpole had a personal investment in offering his readers a strong, even threatening Chatterton; but some of his statements found support the following year when the satiric and mature Chatterton was again emphasized by Sir Herbert Croft in *Love and Madness* (1780). This book gave for the first time a full picture of Chatterton's London activities, his projected alliance with John Wilkes, and his ambitions as a political journalist. It also printed the precociously satiric 'Apostate Will' (his earliest known poem) and the satire 'Happiness'. Croft (in the persona of Hackman) concluded that 'Satire was his sort, if any thing can be called his sort' (p. 148). Once again the emphasis was reinforced by a picture of Chatterton as manly: 'with regard to Chatterton's face and person, all agree that he was a manly, good-looking boy' (p. 241). In support of this statement Croft presents evidence from the poet's Shoreditch landlord, Mr Walmsley, that 'there was something manly and pleasing about him, and that he did not dislike the wenches' (p. 190), and Walmsley's niece told him that 'but for his face and her knowledge of his age, she should never have thought him a boy, he was so manly' (p. 191). In *Love and Madness* readers also encountered for the first time Chatterton's letters from London, in which he tells his mother about Wilkes's interest in him: 'Mr. Wilkes knew me by my writings since I first corresponded with the booksellers here. I shall visit him next week ... He affirmed that what Mr. Fell had of mine could not be the writings of a youth: and expressed a desire to know the author.'[21]

The image of a manly young satirist was again to the fore in the 'Chatterton' article in *Biographia Britannica* (1789). This substantial and well-researched account by George Gregory was also published as an independent *Life of Chatterton* in the same year.[22] In his *Life* Gregory repeatedly praises the satiric verse and prose and underplays the Rowley material. He emphasizes the satiric side of the poet's work by printing for the first time an extract from 'Kew Gardens' and the whole of 'The Prophecy' as Chatterton's. It should by now give us no surprise to find that Gregory's politically engaged poet is also grown-up: 'The person of Chatterton, like his genius, was premature: He had a manliness and dignity beyond his years'.[23]

Cary's poem, Walpole's pamphlet, Croft's *Love and Madness*, Gregory's *Life*, present a satirically inclined and politically aware poet, and each links this to his maturity and manliness. It is important to remember that such an image of the poet was widely available by 1790, and that to keep Chatterton a boy was partly to shut off his politico-satirical side and exploit the lyricism and sentiment instead. For a poet like Coleridge writing in 1790 and 1794 the manly, Wilkesite Chatterton could be a powerful, even dangerous model. In this decade the cry of 'Liberty' was an increasingly incendiary one, and it was possible to look back to Wilkes as having inaugurated English political radicalism. Therefore, what Coleridge did between 1790 and 1794 with the identity of Chatterton – specifically the degree to which he presented the manly satirical figure – is of some significance for assessing the two earliest texts of the 'Monody'. A glance at what other poets made of Chatterton during the 1770–94 period will suggest that there was a range of alternative possibilities.[24]

Some poets were ready to exploit the political implications of Chatterton-as-victim. Excluded by the establishment, the young poet was killed by a haughty lord and neglected by a society that left social provision in the uncertain hands of Charity. This approach tends to exploit Chatterton's vulnerability for satiric purposes in order to accuse society of failing to value its finer spirits. A notable example is William Hayley, in book four of his *Essay on Epic Poetry* (1782), who uses Chatterton to convey a message to the wealthy:

> Search the dark scenes where drooping Genius lies,
> And keep from sorriest sights a nation's eyes,
> That, from expiring Want's reproaches free,
> Our generous country may ne'er weep to see
> A future *Chatterton* by poison dead,
> An *Otway* fainting for a little bread.

> (iv. 337–42)

Hayley's point about the social conscience of the rich ('Too oft the wealthy, to proud follies born, / Have turn'd from letter'd Poverty with scorn', iv. 333–4) was picked up by Henry James Pye, the future Poet Laureate, in *The Progress of Refinement* (1783), which uses the 'cold despair' of Chatterton to bring into question poetry's relationship to the political establishment. Pye points out that Poverty could become Tyranny's weapon in that it forced the starving poet to pen slavish flattery to those in power: 'Too oft has Poesy with servile aim / By tyrants favor'd, sung a tyrant's fame' (ii. 591–2). In each case, thoughts of Chatterton introduce a political dimension into the poem, which in neither case is followed through. Hayley and Pye were far from radical figures, but it is significant that at the point of Chatterton's appearance their respective poems become momentarily tinged with radical possibilities.

In the 1780s Chatterton often raised issues of this kind. Ann Yearsley, the Bristol milkmaid, in her 'Elegy, on Mr. Chatterton',[25] speaks in the voice of the dead Chatterton's ghost to reiterate Pye's point about poverty encouraging servility:

> Scorning to fawn at laughing Insult's knee,
>   My woes were doubled, deeper rais'd my groan;
> More sharp, more exquisite, came Agony ...

(29–31)

Part of the tragic scenario of Chatterton's suffering could be his refusal to surrender to the establishment. In a poem sent to *The Gentleman's Magazine* in 1788, the author, 'R.F.' supported his picture of Chatterton as the victim of 'Lords selfish views' with a footnote reference to the 'Balade of Charitie' and its statement that 'Lordis and Barons live for pleasure and themselves'.[26] Chatterton's 'Balade', one of his most admired poems, was seen as satirically reworking the Good Samaritan parable into a poem about how a wealthy society should deal with its poor.

In this regard the unfortunate Horace Walpole is regularly attacked, and a poetic lament for Chatterton will sometimes pivot round to take a swipe at him. Another example is Sonnet XI 'Written on the Blank Leaf of Chatterton's Poems' in John Rannie's *Poems* (2nd edn 1791), where the sestet opens:

> [Walpole] was wealthy – wealth engender'd pride;
> Pride steels the heart when meanness rules the mind;
> With pride the poor petition was denied,
> And thence the woes of Chatterton combin'd.[27]

Rannie was circumspect, and for the word 'Walpole' we have merely a dash.

In the poems which pre-date Coleridge's 1790 *Monody* there is a noticeable divide in treatment. Those mentioned so far exploit an element of indignation to make points about social hierarchy, poverty and charity, with one eye on Chatterton the satirist. If this 'satiric' mode takes its cue from texts like the 'Balade' and the chorus from 'Goddwyn' (which became known as the 'Ode to Freedom'),[28] the lyric-descriptive Chatterton of sweet showers, soft dews, and drooping flowers was easily combined with images of the poet's own 'budding genius' to form what we might term the 'lyric' mode of Chatterton celebration. Here the traditional flower-passage of classical elegy is combined with the boy's frail body and blighted hopes. The flower-image indeed can sometimes be obsessive. In Ann Yearsley's poem the unfortunate youth is a delicate harebell, a 'languid flow'r' whose 'beauties drop ungather'd as I sing, / And o'er the precipice by winds are cast' (it is quite a terrifying picture of the boy's vulnerability):

> Emblem of Merit in a frozen world,
>   Thine azure tints shall yet our garland grace;
> Like thee this joyless Youth was quickly hurl'd,
>   From Hope's fair height, to Death's unlov'd embrace.[29]

The gentle harebell is a pathetic picture of compliance ('In vain it humbly bends to ev'ry blast', 10), and this is in a poem which speaks a few lines later of Chatterton's refusal to fawn to power – a useful example, if one were needed, of how the same poem can offer contradictory pictures of the poet, depending on the mode being employed at the time.

Where Ann Yearsley gives us a harebell, Mary Robinson, in her 'Monody to the Memory of Chatterton', comes up with the more conventional primrose:

> So the pale primrose, sweetest bud of May,
> Scarce wakes to beauty, ere it feels decay.
>
> (29–30)[30]

Robinson's Chatterton is the author of the Rowley poems, whose 'timid talents own'd a borrow'd name', and who was deluded by the fragile allure of the imagination ('Frail are the charms delusive *Fancy* shows, / And short the bliss her fickle smile bestows', p. 77). Evidently Robinson saw neither boldness nor substance in Chatterton's imagined Rowleyan world.

This lyric mode of Chatterton celebration often extends the evanescent and delicate into an utterly disembodied strain in which the poetic voice is vulnerable and transitory. Robinson's airy phantom 'glides along the minster's walls' to the sound of a 'mournful echo', and Yearsley's 'sad Ghost sings on the buoyant air', and once the voice has reached us it merges into the breathings of nature ('Hush'd dies the sound, shrill as the midnight wind').[31] The elusiveness becomes a celebratory transcendence when the disembodied spirit is the poet's soul embraced by higher powers ('thy soul, immers'd in purest air / Smiles at the triumphs of supreme Despair').[32] This intangible strain is characteristic of the lyric mode of Chatterton celebration.

The most beautiful and effective of the disembodied Chattertons is offered by Henry Headley in his 'Ode to the Memory of Chatterton' from his *Fugitive Pieces* (1785). In this poem William Collins meets Keats as Chatterton's spirit is released into the cycle of the seasons. Headley's ode hovers between Collins's 'Ode to Evening', his 'Ode to the Memory of Mr Thomson', and Keats's 'To Autumn':

> When jocund Summer with her honied breath
> (Sweetening the golden grain and blithsome gale)
>   Displays her sun-burnt face
>   Beneath the hat of straw,
> The lily's hanging head, the pansy pale,
> (Poor Fancy's lowly followers) in meek
>   Attire, shall deck thy turf,
>   And withering lie with thee ...
> Remembrance oft in Pity's pensive ear,
> At silent eve shall sorrowing toll thy knell,
>   And tell to after days
>   Thy tale, thy luckless tale.[33]

The poem fades away in assonance and echoes, haunted by Chatterton's unseen presence.

There could be no greater contrast to the 'disembodied spirit' strain than my final category of the 'dramatic'. Contemplation of the tragic youth can turn, as in Headley, to the lyrical invocation of a spirit; but, in quite an opposite move, the contemplation (like the mystical procedure of Pope's Eloisa) can bring a disturbing and disturbed body before us. If Collins often lies behind the lyric response, the dramatic frequently reproduces the febrile immediacy of Pope's 'Eloisa to Abelard' or his 'Unfortunate Lady'. In this next example they both meet at Elsinore:

> See! see! he comes! shield me ye gracious pow'rs!
>   How pale and wan his lifeless cheeks appear;
> Those cheeks once blooming as the new-blown flowers,
>   Now only boast a deadly sallow there.
>
> By yonder aged beech e'en now he stands,
>   He spreads his arms and beckons me, I fly!
> Stay, friendly shade, alas! it 'scapes my hands,
>   It sinks! it's gone! I come! I rave! I die!

This is James Thistlethwaite, a friend of Chatterton, writing as early as November 1770 in *The Gentleman's Museum*.[34] Other examples of the dramatic mode focus on the visual set-piece of the death scene to draw the reader into active emotional involvement, like Edward Rushton's *Neglected Genius* (1787):

> See, where thy wretched Victim lies,
>   What frantic Wildness in his Eyes:
> Hark! how he groans! see! see! he foams! he gasps!
> And his convulsive Hand the pois'nous Phial grasps.[35]

The keynote is immediacy and emotional response. Sometimes to achieve this the writer becomes the stage director and designer, as here with William Hayley in 1782:

> In a chill room, within whose wretched wall
> No cheering voice replies to Misery's call;
> Near a vile bed, too crazy to sustain
> Misfortune's wasted limbs, convuls'd with pain,
> On the bare floor, with heaven-directed eyes,
> The hapless Youth in speechless horror lies!
> The pois'nous vial, by distraction drain'd,
> Rolls from his hand, in wild contortion strain'd[36]

In the dramatic mode, instead of stillness and spirit we have the grotesque body, its contorted hands gesturing to us. It was this mode that would so powerfully affect Thomas De Quincey in a dream:

> I see Chatterton in the exceeding pain of death! in the exhausted slumber of agony I see his arm weak as a child's – languid and faint in the extreme – stretched out and raised at midnight – calling and pulling (faintly indeed, but yet convulsively) some human breast to console him.[37]

A visual representation of the dramatic mode is John Flaxman's drawing, 'Chatterton receiving Poison from the Spirit of Despair',[38] in which the youth reaches out for the dish of poison offered to him by a frightful dark figure, while behind him Apollo's airborne chariot waits to carry him away. In Hannah Cowley's well-known 'Monody' (1778) Flaxman's three characters enact a little stage drama. Here the speaker is a frustrated participant in the scene:

> And now Despair her sable form extends,
> Creeps to his couch, and o'er his pillow bends.
> Ah see! a deadly bowl the fiend conceal'd,
> Which to his eye with caution is reveal'd –
> Seize it, Apollo! – seize the liquid snare!
> Dash it to earth, or dissipate in air!
> Stay, hapless Youth! refrain – abhor the draught ...
> In vain! – he drinks – and now the searching fires
> Rush through his veins, and writhing he expires![39]

My division of the early poetic responses to Chatterton into the three modes of satiric, lyric, and dramatic, is not meant to suggest they are mutually exclusive: several poems move from one mode to another and the strands interweave differently from poem to poem. An awareness of these dynamics should help us to gauge the individual character of Coleridge's 1790 and 1794 monodies and appreciate the implications of his extensive revisions. Confronted by the multifariousness of Chatterton's image during the 1770s and 1780s, a poet was faced with a range of choices.

What is immediately noticeable about Coleridge's earliest version of his 'Monody', transcribed into the Christ's Hospital *Liber Aureus* in 1790, is its affinity with the dramatic and satiric modes of Chatterton elegies. The irregular Pindaric form assists Coleridge in charting the shifts of emotion and response that play between the poet and his subject. A conventional opening in the first four lines is pushed aside with the image of Chatterton's corpse 'on the bare ground' (8).[40] The presence of the picture of death generates the ebb and flow of the contemplation that follows. The poet himself becomes the highly sensitized reader of Chatterton's image, the site for the poem's alternation between pity and anger:

> Thy corpse of many a livid hue
> On the bare ground I view,
> Whilst various passions all my mind engage;
> Now is my breast distended with a sigh,
> And now a flash of Rage
> Darts *through* the tear, that glistens in my eye.

> (7–12; my italics)

In other Chatterton poems before this date the pity and anger were often present, but never so intertwined, and so absorbed into the poet-voice. Rather than the reader being invited to 'look!' or 'hear!' the voice of the monodist is enacting the response for us. The identification is partly conveyed through a syntactic ambiguity that hints at the writer's own suicide: in the phrase 'Athirst for Death I see thee drench the bowl!' (l. 6) the dangling non-finite clause attaches itself to the subject of the sentence, the 'I' of the poem, a formula that is later repeated to exaggerated effect:

> Fated to heave sad Disappointment's sigh,
> To feel the Hope now rais'd, and now deprest,
> To feel the burnings of an injur'd breast,
>   From all thy Fate's deep sorrows keen
>   In vain, O youth, I turn th'affrighted eye

> (40–4)

By a kind of syntactical sympathy the poem's 'I' gathers up Chatterton's miseries and makes them his own.

By favouring the immediacy of a dramatic rather than lyric contemplation, Coleridge dispenses with the organic imagery of growth being nipped in the bud and the traditional cycle of nature which is the staple of classical elegy. Instead he draws on some of those elements of what I have called the 'satiric' mode of response to Chatterton, and exploits the radical possibilities that enter with them. On the waves of emotion generated by his dramatic contemplation, Coleridge's indignation and anger give voice to rhetorical questions. With the tear glistening in his eye, he turns to accuse his country: 'Is this the land of liberal Hearts!' (l. 13). Where the poem's first exclamation ('I see thee drench the bowl!') had ushered in the dramatic mode, this second one introduces the satiric. Alongside the tragic figure of Otway (conventionally linked with Chatterton as another victim of poverty) there enters at line 16 the more surprising figure of 'Hudibras' Butler, representative of the native English satiric tradition, who specialized in exposing religious hypocrisy.[41] This overt reference to a dramatist and a satirist helps establish the terms on which Coleridge's poem is written:

> … Yet Butler, 'gainst the bigot foe
> Well-skill'd to aim keen Humour's dart,
> Yet Butler felt Want's poignant sting;
>   And Otway, Master of the Tragic art,

> Whom Pity's self had bade to sing,
> Sunk beneath a load of Woe.
> This ever can the generous Briton hear,
> And starts not in his eye th'indignant tear?

> (16–23)

In the summary of Chatterton's writing career that follows, Coleridge continues to emphasize the national context, and the poet's 'many a vision fair' (30) are not merely those of an immaterial fancy, but instead issue in active benevolence, a concept to which Chatterton himself had given a political meaning:

> He listens to many a Widow's prayers,
> And many an Orphan's thanks he hears;
> He sooths to peace the care worn breast,
> He bids the Debtor's eyes know rest,
> And Liberty and Bliss behold

> (33–7)

And the monody moves on to make direct allusion to Chatterton's political writings:

> And now he punishes the heart of steel,
> And her own iron rod he makes Oppression feel.

> (38–9)

At line 55 the pity and indignation, which had earlier combined within the speaker, and were then satirically externalized as the nation's response, now become the terms of a dramatic psychomachia enacted in Chatterton himself. Pity's vision paints for him a sentimental picture of his 'native cot' with his lamenting sister and mother; but set against this is a pressing reminder from Despair and Indignation, who retell his woes and recall the miseries of 'dread dependance', 'Neglect and grinning Scorn, and Want combin'd'. Chatterton, with the bowl poised at his lips, is torn between the two pictures as Pity and Indignation now compete for him.

Coleridge therefore stages as the dramatic climax of his poem a confrontation between sentiment and satire, pity and indignation. And in this monody it is the latter that wins as Chatterton embraces death.

The final paragraph evokes Chatterton's liberated spirit, but avoids etherializing him. Instead Coleridge models his ending on that most famous of monodies, *Lycidas*. The climax is a vindication of Chatterton's 'fire divine' as a poet. But where Milton's Lycidas is a passive auditor who 'hears the unexpressive nuptial song, / In the blest kingdoms meek of joy and love', in Coleridge's poem Chatterton soars through 'the vast domain' and is himself the singer who keeps the angelic host entertained. He does not evanesce, but ends the poem as a lesson in the necessity of fortitude:

> Grant me with firmer breast t'oppose their hate,
> And soar beyond the Storm with upright eye elate.

> (89–90)

Coleridge's 1790 monody is conscious of the literary tradition to which it contributes, and of the range of Chattertons celebrated in the poetry of his day. What is striking is the teenage Coleridge's integration of pathos and anger, and the poet's staging as drama the contending responses within himself. Particularly noticeable, too, is his avoidance of the lyric mode with its tendency to evanesce, fade, and wither. On the contrary, the 'hateful picture' of the poet's death scene is forced on his sight. Also missing is any sign of the delicate boy. The picture of Chatterton that he sees is not childlike, but actually prematurely aged:

> In vain I seek the charms of youthful grace,
> Thy sunken eye, thy haggard cheeks it shews,
> The quick emotions struggling in thy Face,
>   Faint index of thy mental throes.

> (49–52)

This is a man of passion, whose face is lined by his experiences of life.

It is also the prematurely aged poet figured on the Chatterton handkerchief. That exemplary sentimental text now in the British Library was designed to absorb the very tears it caused to flow. Its visual representation of the tragic youth, engraved from a painting that was 'the work of a friend',[42] holds the central position on the fabric and is read emblematically in the prose and verse descriptions on either side. This triptych of Sensibility offers just such a haggard figure as Coleridge is transfixed by. The prose text on the handkerchief explains

Chatterton's far from youthful appearance: 'Anxieties and cares had advanced his life, and given him an older look than was suited to his age.'

It is possible to go further and to see Coleridge's 1790 monody as in part a response to the emotive verses that occupy the right-hand column of the handkerchief. These 38 lines urge the reader to contemplate the picture in an itemized meditation on its details (the handkerchief is in several ways a sentimental development of the old emblem books):

> Pale and dejected, mark, how genius strives
> With poverty, and mark, how well it thrives.
> The shabby cov'ring of the gentle bard,
> Regard it well, tis worthy thy regard;
> The friendly cobweb, serving for a screen,
> The chair, a part of what it once had been.
> The bed, whereon th'unhappy victim slept,
> And oft unseen, in silent anguish, wept ...
>
> (7–14)

The reader-spectator is not merely prompted, but prodded and cajoled into an emotional reaction. What is more, the handkerchief-poem closes with a remarkable curse on anyone who coldly turns away from the picture:

> Whoe'er thou art, that shall this face survey,
> And turn, with cold disgust, thy eyes away,
> Then bless thyself, that sloth and ign'rance bred
> Thee up in safety, and with plenty fed,
> Peace to thy mem'ry! may the sable plume
> Of dulness, round thy forehead ever bloom!
> Mayst thou, nor can I wish a greater curse,
> Live full despis'd, and die without a nurse.
> Or, if some wither'd hag, for sake of hire,
> Should wash thy sheets, and cleanse thee from the mire,
> Let her, when hunger peevishly demands
> The dainty morsel from her barb'rous hands,
> Insult, with hellish mirth, thy craving maw,
> And snatch it to herself, and call it law.
> 'Till pinching famine waste thee to the bone,
> And break, at last, that solid heart of stone.
>
> (23–38)

These verses set the 'honest warmth' of the sentimental reader against the 'cold disgust' of one who turns his eye away. In its own responsive way Coleridge's monody also begins in coldness ('For cold my Fancy grows .. / .. When Want and cold Neglect had chill'd thy soul', ll. 4–5) and then moves to generate warmth. The enemy in Coleridge's monody, as in the handkerchief, is 'th'unfeeling heart' (l. 74). Coleridge's poem is an exercise in that 'honest warmth' urged by the linen. Both texts are passionate responses to a man of passion ('his passions were too impetuous', says the handkerchief; 'each strong Passion spurn'd controll', l. 53 of the monody); both present a prematurely aged face marked by its cares; both also use the satiric mode to accuse their country (Coleridge's 'Is this the land of liberal Hearts!' finds its equivalent in the handkerchief's remark that Chatterton's fate was 'a satire upon an age and a nation'). It is impossible to say whether Coleridge had seen the handkerchief and recalled it when he wrote the first version of the monody, but what is clear is that the two texts belong closely together in the way they exploit the satiric and dramatic modes of Chatterton celebration. The poet is physically present, mature, marked by his experiences, and he arouses warmth, indignation and a wider sense of national injustice which is radical in its implications. In other words, both texts resist the lyric mode which eventually won the day and came to preoccupy Romantic responses to Chatterton. In that fiction the poet becomes a wondrous spirit rather than a marked body, an evanescent being rather than a standing reproof.

By avoiding the palpable immediacy of Chatterton, the lyric mode lets slip the radical possibilities of Sensibility, and we have seen its prevalence in several of the 1780s treatments of the dead poet (notably those of Headley and Robinson). It is particularly interesting that when Coleridge revised the monody for publication in 1794 it was chiefly to introduce lyrical passages that quite alter the poem's character. In 1794 It became a very different text, and it was this poem which brought Coleridge a degree of public popularity and was influential in establishing the lyric mode's primacy in poetic presentations of Chatterton.

As soon as we encounter the 1794 text we can see that it features those key elements of the organic, evanescent, and transcendent that his 1790 version had excluded:

> When faint and sad o'er Sorrow's desart wild,
> Slow journeys onward, poor Misfortune's child,

> When fades each lovely form by Fancy drest,
> And inly pines the self-consuming breast;
> No scourge of Scorpions in thy right arm dread,
> No helmed Terrors nodding o'er thy head,
> Assume, O DEATH! the Cherub Wings of PEACE,
> And bid the heart-sick Wanderer's Anguish cease!

(1–8)

The new opening creates a figure that is generalized, diminutive, isolated, childlike, and insubstantial – all those things that the 1790 Chatterton was not – rather than specific, embodied, engaged, communicative, manly. The poor child of line 2 is not even Chatterton, but some lorn, fanciful surrogate.

The poet's tearful reaction to the dead poet is no longer an immediate personal response (the drama is diffused by generalizing it as 'Nature's bosom-startling call', 15), and the *now* of this poem is not the dramatic present, but a term of continuity ('Now ...; And now ...'). The political exclamation of 1790 ('Is this the land of liberal Hearts!') has in 1794 become a literary question: 'Is this the Land of song-ennobled Line?' Even more pointedly, the figure of the satiric Butler has been replaced by the predictably elegiac Spenser:

> Ah me! yet Spenser, gentlest Bard divine,
> Beneath chill Disappointment's deadly shade
> His weary Limbs in lonely Anguish lay'd!

(26–8)

Samuel Butler's highly relevant battle against 'Want' and 'the bigot foe' have become a vague and world-weary 'Disappointment'.

Some of the urgency of the 1790 version is retained, as in the line 'And her own iron rod he makes Oppression feel' (48). But in the 1794 text the grasping of the 'patriot steel' (47) becomes incongruous three lines later when the lyric mode fully establishes itself (the whole passage is added in 1794):

> Sweet Tree of Hope! thou loveliest Child of Spring!
> How fair didst thou disclose thine early bloom,
>   Loading the west-winds with its soft perfume!
> And Fancy hovering round on shadowy wing,
>   On every blossom hung her fostering dews,

That changeful wanton'd to the orient Day!
Ah! soon upon thy poor unshelter'd Head
Did Penury her sickly mildew shed:
And soon the scathing Lightning bade thee stand,
In frowning Horror o'er the blighted Land!

(51–60)

Chatterton is invoked as a marvellous boy, an early bloom nipped in the bud, a delicate, evanescent figure accompanied by a sylph-like Fancy and perfumed breezes. In the passages added for the 1794 version, the monody moves away from Chatterton's discomforting presence. He is not even really dead, but becomes an anticipation of the Scholar Gipsy who in the following added passage haunts the landscape as a heart-sick, disengaged wanderer:

Ye Woods! that wave o'er Avon's rocky steep,
To Fancy's ear sweet is your murm'ring deep!
For *here* she loves the Cypress Wreath to weave,
Watching with wistful eye the sad'ning tints of Eve.
Here far from Men amid this pathless grove,
In solemn thought the Minstrel wont to rove,
Like Star-beam on the rude sequester'd Tide,
Lone-glittering, thro' the Forest's murksome pride.

(92–9)

Fancy is again in evidence, but the beautiful images cannot conceal the fact that the dead poet, now suffused by lyric melancholy, has been taken out of society and history. We are furthest of all from fact in the final lines when Chatterton's suicide is Wertherized. The despondent wanderer is closer to the psychic depressive of Thomas Warton's 'Suicide'[43] than to the indignant patriotic bard of Gray:

With wild unequal steps he pass'd along,
Oft pouring on the winds a broken song:
Anon upon some rough Rock's fearful Brow,
Would pause abrupt – and gaze upon the waves below.

(104–7)[44]

It should be pointed out that when Coleridge later turned against the 'Monody on the Death of Chatterton' it was in fact the 1794 dematerializing additions that he singled out for criticism.[45] Clearly he felt dissatisfied with it, and part of the reason is that the 1794 poem is a mixed and compromised work which runs through too many moods and makes too many different gestures. It is a more generalized and less focused text than its predecessor. In fact the distinctly characterized 1790 poem deserves to be appreciated in its own right, and the Chatterton that it presents is a more disturbing and radical figure.

Critical focus on the posthumous Chatterton has tended understandably to concentrate on the delicate boy of Romantic legend. Certainly it was this image that conquered the field (we have seen it do so in Coleridge's 1794 monody). However, during the first decades after his death, 1770–94, the responses were much more varied, and one of the Chattertons competing for the poet's attention was a mature (even prematurely aged), disturbing, satiric, and questioning presence. To encounter the early posthumous Chattertons can encourage a more attentive reading of Chatterton himself as a writer less elusive and more socially engaged than poetic myth eventually made him. At the same time we may begin to discern elements of tension and contradiction in the evoking of Chatterton by a Romantic poet. The evanescent spirit of the tragic boy can play against a sense of toughness and indignation. This happens, I would suggest, in the preface to *Endymion* (1818), inscribed 'to the memory of Thomas Chatterton', where in a single ambitious breath John Keats bids a lyric farewell to his insubstantial poem as if it were the marvellous boy himself, but then immediately hints at poetic sedition to come: 'It is just that this youngster should die away: a sad thought for me, if I had not some hope that while it is dwindling I may be plotting and fitting myself for verses fit to live'. Alongside Keats's dream of the fading poet stood Chatterton's manly presence in the building-blocks of his native language: ''tis genuine English Idiom in English Words'.[46] Blake, too, with the dead charity child in his mind, could juxtapose the notes of lyric evanescence and satiric indignation: 'Is that trembling cry a song? / Can it be a song of joy – / And so many children poor? / It is a land of poverty!'[47]

Chatterton did not enter Romantic culture as a single myth. He found his way in as part of a continuing dialogue within later eighteenth-century Sensibility which articulated the demands of body and spirit and engaged the satirical with the sentimental. As we have seen, the young Coleridge found in Chatterton not merely a figure with whom he could identify, but one that posed problems for his own art and raised questions about the kind of writer he himself would be. To confront or to transcend? To embody or to idealize? By 1794, the year of Coleridge's revised 'Monody' and of Blake's *Songs of Experience*, such questions were developing a more urgent political cast, as they would for Keats during 1818–19. Within Romantic culture Chatterton was no mere myth, but a figure whose varied literary afterlife articulated problems and choices that were crucial to the age.

Notes

1. Warton, Thomas, *The History of English Poetry* (London, 1774–81), ii. 139–64.
2. Jeremiah Milles, Dean of Exeter and President of the Society of Antiquaries, compared Rowley favourably with Homer, describing Chatterton as merely an 'illiterate charity-boy' (*Poems, Supposed to have been written at Bristol in the Fifteenth Century* (London, 1782), 3, 23).
3. Christ's Hospital *Liber Aureus*, BL, MS Ashley 3506, vol. i. fos. 44^r–46^v.
4. Coleridge to Thomas Poole, 7 October 1795 (*Collected Letters of Samuel Taylor Coleridge*, ed. E. L. Griggs (Oxford, 1956-71), i. 160).
5. Writing to Poole, 13 Dec. 1796, Coleridge invoked the ghost of Chatterton to impress on his friend an image of his own frantic state: 'the Ghosts of Otway & Chatterton, & the phantasms of a Wife broken-hearted, & a hunger-bitten Baby! O Thomas Poole! Thomas Poole! if you did but know what a Father & Husband must feel, who toils with his brain for uncertain bread! I dare not think of it – The evil Face of Frenzy looks at me!' (*Letters*, i. 275). After receiving this letter Poole invited Coleridge to live at Nether Stowey.
6. See Charles Lamb's poem 'To Sara and Her Samuel', sent to Coleridge 7 July 1796 (*The Letters of Charles and Mary Anne Lamb*, ed. Edwin W. Marrs, Jr. (Ithaca & London, 1975–8), i. 39), and Poole's comparison of Coleridge and Chatterton as wayward geniuses (Poole to Henrietta Warwick, 6 February 1796: Mrs Henry Sandford, *Thomas Poole and His Friends*, i. 132–4). See also George Dekker, *Coleridge and the Literature of Sensibility* (London, 1978), 64–5.
7. Wordsworth, William, *Poems, in Two Volumes, and Other Poems, 1800–1807*, ed. Jared Curtis (Ithaca, 1983), 125.
8. Dekker, 60, 62–3.
9. Coleridge's rewritten 'Monody' was prefixed to the 1794 Cambridge edition of the Rowley poems, edited by Lancelot Sharpe, xxv–xxviii ('The Editor thinks himself happy in the permission of an ingenious Friend, to insert the following Monody'). An abridgement of the 1790 text (in 72 lines) was going to be printed and was set in type, only to be cancelled at the last minute and replaced by the rewritten poem. See Freeman, Arthur, and Hofmann, Theodore, 'The Ghost of Coleridge's First Effort: "A Monody on the Death of Chatterton"', *The Library* 11 (1989), 328–35.
10. As Coleridge told William Worship on 22 April 1819. See *The Complete Poetical Works of Samuel Taylor Coleridge*, ed. E. H. Coleridge (Oxford, 1975), i. 125–6.

11. Gordon, I. A., 'The Case-History of Coleridge's *Monody on the Death of Chatterton', RES* 18 (1942), 49.
12. Sonnet 'To Chatterton'.
13. See both the recent *Dictionary of Literary Biography* article on Chatterton, and *TLS*, 6 May 1994, 3–4. The picture of the boy Chatterton features in both. See Richard Holmes, below.
14. *Life*, 476. See also Goodridge, items 205 and 234, below. It was Chatterton the bluecoat boy who was set up as a monument in St Mary Redcliffe churchyard. See Russell, Charles Edward, *Thomas Chatterton, The Marvellous Boy* (London, 1909), 262–3.
15. 'Elegy to the Memory of Mr. Thomas Chatterton, Late of Bristol', 26–8, 42–8. In a letter printed by Milles (19), Cary remarks that Chatterton's 'natural inclination' was to satire, and he maintains that his friend was not the author of the Rowley poems.
16. *Miscellanies*, 241–5. The poem is reprinted in *Life*, 540–2.
17. 'To the Duke of G—n', *Middlesex Journal*, 16 February 1770 (*Works*, 451). The 'Decimus' letters, published between February and May 1770 were first printed as Chatterton's by Dix (1837).
18. A short extract from 'Kew Gardens' and an account of 'The Whore of Babylon' were given in Gregory's *Life* and *Biographia Britannica* article (1789), but the three poems were not printed in full until 1803. By 1789, however, the libertarian and satiric Chatterton was well established in the public's mind when his non-Rowleyan writings reached print. The 1778 *Miscellanies* included 'The Consuliad' and 'The Prophecy', the 1784 supplement added 'The Defence' and 'Epistle. To the Revd. Mr. Catcott', and *Love and Madness* (1780) gave 'Apostate Will' and 'Happiness. A Poem'.
19. In Appendix 2 to his *Letter to the Editor of the Miscellanies* (1779) Walpole catalogues the pieces he has seen in manuscript, including the three 'Decimus' letters ('scandalous' and 'very abusive') and 'Kew Gardens' ('a long satirical rhapsody of some hundred lines, in Churchill's manner, against persons in power'). Walpole also reveals Chatterton to be the author of 'Probus to the Lord Mayor' ('a violent abuse of government').
20. Walpole, 15, 39, 37.
21. Chatterton to Sarah Chatterton, 6 May 1770 (*Works*, 560). This letter, along with others of Chatterton, was well known. Besides its inclusion in *Love and Madness* (1770), 170–1, it was reprinted in Gregory's *Life* (1789). Isaac Fell, publisher of Chatterton's 'Resignation' and 'The Consuliad' in the *Freeholder's Magazine*, was in the same week as Chatterton's letter arrested and imprisoned for his anti-ministerial publications. See Suarez, Michael F., SJ, 'What Thomas Knew: Chatterton and the Business of Getting into Print', *Angelaki* 1.2 (1993/4), 85–6, and his essay above.
22. *Biographia Britannica*, 2nd edn (ed. Andrew Kippis), iv (London, 1789), 573–619; Gregory, G., *The Life of Thomas Chatterton, with Criticisms on his Genius and Writings, and a concise view of the Controversy concerning Rowley's Poems* (London, 1789).
23. *Biographia Britannica* (1789), 589; Gregory, 101–2.
24. An incomplete list of poetic references to Chatterton is given by Harvey, A. D., 'The Cult of Chatterton amongst English Poets *c.* 1770–*c.* 1820',

Zeitschrift für Anglistik und Amerikanistik 39 (1991), 124–33. See Goodridge, below.

25. Yearsley, Ann, *Poems on Various Subjects* (London, 1787), 145–9. See Keegan, above.
26. *GM* 58 (Dec. 1788), 1106–7.
27. Rannie, John, *Poems*, 2nd edn (Aberdeen, 1791), 13.
28. In Charles Cowden Clarke's commonplace book (Brotherton Library, Leeds University, Novello–Cowden Clarke Collection MS 6) the chorus is anthologized as 'Ode to Freedom' and takes its place alongside other extracts of a radical tendency. See Roe, Nicholas, *John Keats and the Culture of Dissent* (Oxford, 1997), 95.
29. *Poems on Various Subjects* (1787), 146 (ll. 5–16).
30. *Poems by Mrs. M. Robinson* (London, 1791), 75–9. The obvious debt is to Perdita's own 'pale primeroses, / that die unmarried, ere they can behold / Bright Phoebus in his strength' (*The Winter's Tale*, IV. iv. 122–4). But Robinson may also have in mind Egwina's description of the tragic Birtha, 'Lyche prymrose, droopynge wythe the heavie rayne' (*Ælla*, 1276).
31. Yearsley, *Poems on Various Subjects*, 146, 148 (ll. 18, 38).
32. *Poems by Mrs. M. Robinson*, 75.
33. Headley, Henry, *Fugitive Pieces* (1785), 76.
34. See Meyerstein, E. H. W., 'An Elegy on Chatterton', *TLS*, 8 Feb. 1934, 92.
35. *Neglected Genius: or, Tributary Stanzas to the Memory of the Unfortunate Chatterton* (London, 1787), 11. 'R.F.' gives a similar picture: 'Stretch'd on the floor, aghast, he lies! / Now rises, sinks again!' (*GM* 58 (1788), 1107). See Goodridge, item 145, below.
36. *Essay on Epic Poetry*, iv. 235–42. The full passage was quoted in *Biographia Britannica* as 'uncommonly animated and poetical' (595).
37. *A Diary of Thomas De Quincey. 1803*, ed. Horace A. Eaton (London, 1927), 156–7.
38. Dated *c.* 1775–80 by Raymond Lister, *English Romantic Painting* (Cambridge, 1989); see plate 23.
39. Hannah Cowley's poem appeared in *The Morning Post*, 24 Oct. 1778, and was reprinted in later editions of *Love and Madness*. Gregory gives the whole of the 'beautiful monody' (124–6).
40. All quotations from the 1790 monody are transcribed from the *Liber Aureus* (see note 3 above). This version survives in another manuscript in Coleridge's hand *c.* 1792–3, BL Add MS 47551, fos. 8ᵛ–11ᵛ ('the Ottery Copybook'). The text given by E. H. Coleridge (*Poetical Works*, 1912) described as 'First version, in Christ's Hospital Book – 1790' differs in 62 places from the manuscript. EHC's changes include silent verbal adjustments such as 'taught' for MS 'bade' (l. 20), 'th'eternal Throne' for MS 'the endless throne' (81), and 'blest' for MS 'vast' (84). It is difficult to explain his tinkerings.
41. Samuel Butler (1612–80), author of the satiric poem *Hudibras* (1663–78), died in penury.
42. The engraved plate appeared in *Westminster Magazine*, 10 (July 1782) facing p. 342, along with a slightly different version of the prose commentary. The handkerchief, which must have been printed shortly afterwards, is BL, C 39 h 20. See Goodridge, item 244, below.

43. Warton's poem, first printed in his *Poems. A New Edition, with Additions* (1777), 42–7, does not name Chatterton, but the suicidal youth was taken by many to refer to him. Coleridge thought Warton's ode 'exquisite' (letter to the editor of *The Monthly Magazine*, January 1798, *Letters*, i. 381–2).
44. Cf. Warton's 'Suicide', 28–30: 'Oft was he wont, in hasty fit, / Abrupt the social board to quit, / And gaze with eager glance upon the tumbling flood'.
45. '[O]n a life & death so full of heart-giving *realities*, as poor Chatterton's to find such shadowy nobodies, as cherub-winged DEATH, Trees of HOPE, bare-bosom'd AFFECTION, & simpering PEACE – makes one's blood circulate like ipecacacuanha [*sic*]' (Coleridge to Southey, *c.* 17 July 1797. *Letters*, i. 333). The references are to the 1794 text, lines 7, 51, 71–2, and 77 (all were added in 1794 and remained in 1796).
46. Keats to Reynolds, 21 September 1819.
47. Blake, 'Holy Thursday', 5–8, from *Songs of Innocence and of Experience* (1794).

Chapter 14

Forging the Poet: Some Early Pictures of Thomas Chatterton

Richard Holmes

> Look in his glommed** face, his sprighte there scanne;
> Howe woe-be-gone, howe withered, forwynd, deade!

> **clouded, dejected. A person of some note in the literary world is of opinion, that *glum* and *glom* are modern cant words; and from this circumstance doubts the authenticity of Rowley's Manuscripts.

(from 'An Excelente Balade of Charitie', with Chatterton's footnote)

What did Chatterton look like?

The great scholar E. H. W. Meyerstein closed this subject definitively in his biography of 1930: 'It cannot be repeated too emphatically that there is no authentic portrait of Thomas Chatterton.'[1]

But of course an *inauthentic* portrait of Chatterton might still tell us something very interesting about the poet. It might suggest how his readers imagined him to be, or what they thought he represented in the *mythos* of Romantic genius. It could show how he was transformed into a popular icon of the creative prodigy, the 'marvellous Boy, / The sleepless Soul that perished in his pride'. It might also provide a revealing extension of the theme of forgery which shapes his career: Chatterton first forged himself and was then posthumously forged by others.

There is some anecdotal evidence of Chatterton's physical type, emphasizing his youth, his air of eccentricity and disorder, and his peculiar eyes. The eighteenth-century investigator Michael Lort, after his extensive enquiries in London and Bristol, produced this brief composite picture of the young poet. 'He had a large quick grey eye; rather slovenly in his dress; not vain, but proud; something like his sister, who was of sallow complexion'.[2]

Chatterton's sister, Mary Newton, was reported as describing her brother as 'thin of body, but neatly made', not handsome, but of striking appearance, owing to his eyes – the left eye seemed to 'flash fire'. 'He was always very reserved, and fond of seclusion; we often missed him for half a day together.'[3]

To this can be added various folk-traditions which circulated back in Bristol, after Chatterton's death in London in 1770. One of his eyes was larger and brighter than the other. His 'manly' and provocative manner was much more mature than his physical appearance, though in the last months suffering aged him with terrible swiftness. He had fits of melancholic distraction, and bouts of fury and sleeplessness, which left him continuously drawn and pale. He had extraordinary energy and intensity ('I give and bequeath all my Vigor and Fire of Youth to Mr George Catcott, being sensible he is most in want of it').

Recurrent is the idea that there was something unstable about him, and a strong suggestion of insanity in his features. Chatterton himself wrote famously in his 'Will': 'The most perfect Masters of Human Nature in Bristol, distinguish me by the title of the Mad Genius therefore if I do a mad action it is conformable to every Action of my Life which all savored of Insanity.'[4] His editor Southey (who never met him) added long after: 'Chatterton *was* insane – better proof of this than the coroner's inquest is that there was insanity in the family. (His sister, Mrs Newton, was for some period confined in a madhouse). His biographers were not informed of this important fact ...'[5]

The iconographic tradition exploited these hints, mixing claims to historical accuracy with particular forms of artistic licence and sensationalism. Henry Wallis's languid masterpiece, for which the young George Meredith posed in blue silk pantaloons, 'The Death of Chatterton' (1856, now in the Tate Gallery) is well known. Its mixture of sentimental melodrama and antiquarian detail tells us little about its subject, but a great deal about Chatterton's Victorian reputation as a beautiful, rather androgynous prototype of the doomed Romantic (a style and pose curiously echoed in the supine Memorial of the drowned Shelley, sculpted by E. Onslow Ford in 1894).

However, there are at least three other *inauthentic* portraits, which because they are much earlier in date, have remained obscure. For that very reason they have much greater historical interest.

The first appeared as an engraving in the *Westminster Magazine* for July 1782, just 12 years after Chatterton's death. In the same year it was widely distributed in the form of a memorial handkerchief, some examples of which are in the British Museum printed on red linen and others on blue. This was entitled 'The Distressed Poet, or a True Representation of the Unfortunate Chatterton'. It conforms to a popular eighteenth-century image of the Grub Street poet, though the face is almost schematic, and his 'distress' is shown by traditional emblematic means in the furnishings of his garret. Chatterton sprawls on a broken chair, leaning forward over a sheet of poems spread across a trestle table. One hand holds a quill pen, the other is held pensively against his left cheek. He wears a cloth nightcap against the cold, his ill-fitting coat has holes in the elbow, and his stockings are tangled round his ankles. His shoes are trodden down at the heel. Behind him, a torn truckle bed is upended against the wall, and on the table is a large flask that might hold either wine or laudanum.

Two commentaries, one in prose, one in verse, frame the image.

The painting from which the engraving was taken on the distressed poet, was the work of a friend of the unfortunate Chatterton. The friend drew him in the situation in which he is represented in this plate. Anxieties and cares had advanced his life, and given him an older look than his age. The sorry apartment portrayed in the print, the folded bed, the farthing candle, and the disorderly raiment of the bard are not inventions of fancy. They were realities, and a satire upon an age and a nation of which generosity is doubtless a characteristic. But poor Chatterton was born under a bad star; his passions were too impetuous.... Unknown and miserable while alive, he now calls forth curiosity and attention. Men of wit and learning employ themselves to celebrate his talents, and to express their approbation of his writings. Hard indeed was his fate, born to adorn the times in which he lived, yet compelled to fall a victim to his pride and poverty!

The verse points the same moral:

> Ah! what a contrast in that face portrayed.
> Where care and study cast alternate shade,
> But view it well, and ask thy heart the cause,
> Then chide, with honest warmth, that cold applause,
> Which counteracts the soft'ning breath of praise,
> And shades with cypress the young Poet's bays.
> Pale and dejected, mark, how genius strives
> With poverty, and mark, how well it thrives....

The second portrait is something of a shock. It is both strikingly individualized and hauntingly ugly. It appeared in *The Monthly Visitor* magazine for January 1797. It was also engraved as the frontispiece to a copy of Chatterton's *Works*, by the publisher Thomas Baldwyn of Newgate Street at this time (Fig. 4). In 1816 the Keeper of Prints in the British Museum christened it the 'goggle-ey'd portrait'. It shows Chatterton like a prematurely aged child, dressed in ragged adult clothes, with long shaggy unkempt hair, dark frowning brows, and huge hungry eyes. What is shocking and memorable about the portrait is the grotesque rendering of mental suffering: here is genius on the very edge of madness. The very crudeness of the image gives it force and conviction.

The third picture appeared as the engraved frontispiece to John Dix's immensely popular and notoriously unreliable *Life of Chatterton* of 1837 (Fig. 5). (Characteristically, Wordsworth's famous line is used as a motto, but assigned incorrectly to Southey.) It has some resemblance to a softened version of the 'goggle-ey'd' portrait, turned in right profile. But its subject appears much younger, and considerably prettified. Chatterton has been barbered, washed, combed, and laundered and is presented as a Bristol bluecoat-boy, rather clever and intense, apparently aged about 14.

In fact, this engraving is an ingenious fake, based on an eighteenth-century oil portrait, the original of which still hangs in the Bristol Museum. It is dated 1762, signed Morris, and is actually a portrait of the artist's son. (In the original the boy's coat is red.) The elaborate details of the forgery were finally uncovered in 1891, after extensive investigation by Sir George Scharf, the curator of the National Portrait Gallery.

A copy of the Morris portrait, signed on the back 'HS Parkman, Bristol, 1837', was presented to the ageing Robert Southey at Keswick. It is intriguing that although the picture is now known to be false (at two removes: the copy of a fake) it was instantly 'recognised' by Southey as genuine, because it was so like Chatterton's elder sister Mrs Newton, whom Southey had met several times in Bristol.

Scharf noted that all three images – the original Morris oil, the engraving, and the Parkman copy – showed subtle differences, in response to their intended clientele. 'Taken as a whole, the engraving in Dix's book does not accurately render the character of Mr Braikenridge's [Bristol] picture. It is a darker & shorter face, with a less amiable expression. It is, comparatively speaking, more pugnacious. The Guelph picture [Southey's] is altogether milder.'[6] Yet Southey wrote to Walter Savage Landor in 1839: 'The portrait of Chatterton, which Mr Dix discovered, identifies itself if ever portrait did. It brought his sister, Mrs Newton, strongly to my recollection. No family likeness could be more distinctly marked, considering the disparity of years'.[7]

This 'recognition' of inauthenticity presents us with a significant paradox. Throughout this early series of pseudo-portraits, anonymously invented or commercially imagined or consciously faked, there does seem to be a genuine visual tradition – or folk memory – of what Chatterton actually looked like in the flesh, and one might add, in the spirit. The faked or forged picture of Chatterton was in some sense an acknowledgement of the essence of a shared, agreed idea of the real Chatterton. The artists had somehow inherited an idea of what they should be picturing – an image of extreme youth, extreme poverty, and extreme instability. It was not in the least sentimental. It was a tough, pre-Victorian idea of genius, as something uncanny, solitary, and even savage.

It was to this image that a 17-year-old schoolboy, S. T. Coleridge of Christ's Hospital, London, responded in some naive and moving lines copied into his school's Golden Book in the summer of 1790 from his prize-winning poem entitled 'Monody on the Death of Chatterton':

> In vain I seek the charms of youthful grace,
> Thy sunken eye, thy haggard cheeks it shews,
> The quick emotions struggling in the Face
> Faint index of thy mental Throes,
> When each strong Passion spurn'd control,
> And not a Friend was nigh to calm thy stormy soul.[8]

What that same image eventually became is shown in a final, undated late-Victorian or twentieth-century version of nursery-book charm. It is still distantly related to the 'goggle ey'd' portrait, with its now girlish locks and saucer-eyed wistfulness. The hand has come back under the chin, as in the Grub Street portrait, to indicate melancholy and brooding, but the plump, genteel little finger suggests that high tea, rather than laudanum, will soon be served (Fig. 6).

Portraits of Chatterton continue to surface, the most recent being sold at Sotheby's in July 1990. ('Portrait of a Young Gentleman Thought to be Thomas Chatterton', English School, eighteenth century, from the collection of Doyne C. Bell Esq., FSA, Catalogue

No. 95. Oil on an oval panel: full face, large eyes, fringed hair, blue coat over white waistcoat.) None has been authenticated, but the tradition of his 'likeness' continues to haunt the literary world. It should not be forgotten that when the alcoholic poet Francis Thompson decided to commit suicide one night in Covent Garden, he claimed that he was saved by a vision of Chatterton: 'I recognised him from the pictures of him – besides, I knew that it was he before I saw him.'[9]

Notes

1. *Life*, 521.
2. Bristol Library MSS.
3. Ireland, William Henry, *The Confessions of William-Henry Ireland* (London, 1805), 15–16, 13.
4. *Works*, 503.
5. Appendix to *Chatterton's Poetical Works* (London, 1842), 625.
6. Scharf MS, National Portrait Gallery archives.
7. Southey, Robert, *Life and Correspondence*, vi. 384–5.
8. Coleridge, Samuel Taylor, *Poetical Works*, ed. E. H. Coleridge (Oxford, 1980), 14.
9. Blunt, Wilfred, *My Diaries* (1907).

Afterword

Michael Wood

> Besides, who can boast of being a mere impostor?
>
> Jorge Luis Borges, 'The Babylon Lottery'

'But he is a poor writer', Chatterton says in a letter quoted earlier in this book, 'who cannot write on both sides'. In context he means writing both for and against the government of the day, but it's hard to resist the larger applications of the remark; and hard to miss its casual ambiguity. A writer who is any good will be able to write on both sides; but a writer who can't is likely to stay poor.

In another letter Chatterton announces confidently that 'A character is now unnecessary; an author carries his character in his pen'. 'Character' here is presumably a reference or guarantee as to one's actual, non-textual character, but again the assertion points towards a performance, towards writing as both a production and a dismissal of the self. The self is present in the writing, but only there. Similarly, the ability to write on both sides makes all questions of authorial sincerity irrelevant – or relevant only as investigations of a movable literary effect. Is Chatterton describing a version of what Michel Foucault called the author-function; foreshadowing the New Criticism and/or the death of the author? None of those things, probably; but he is certainly joining a controversy which includes those phrases and that movement among its twentieth-century ripples. 'Do we know what writing is?' Stéphane Mallarmé asked, in a phrase which haunts much modern criticism and theory in many languages. *Sait-on ce que c'est qu'écrire?* Chatterton wrote to his sisters as if he knew: writing is mobility and self-certification, a form of imposture even when the 'character' is true. But then it is precisely such views of writing that make us wonder, again and again, whether we know what it is.

In this light both Chatterton and Rowley become images of an ongoing hesitation not only about fiction and fakery but about every form of absence and presence in writing. The death of the author is too emphatic a metaphor for this, a fine intuition rhetorically over-sold. We don't know the author is dead, any more than we know that the intentional fallacy is always a fallacy. Some authors are dead and some are not, both literally and figuratively; and some authors, it seems, do have precisely the intentions we naively ascribe to them. 'Who can boast,' as Borges asks, 'of being a mere impostor?' How do we know the lies we tell are not true? The critical question concerns the relation of the life of the text to other forms of life. All authors are absent, in a pedestrian sense; in the sense in which we are all away from home when we leave a note on the door. What bothers us and enchants us is the array of ghostly presences which that permanent absence is able to create.

Among the many things we learn from this collection of essays is how much is at stake in this interplay of absence and presence; how thoroughly the presences we get follow from our particular predicates of absence. David Fairer even suggests that Chatterton was a kind of diviner of absence: 'the youth had the knack of supplying just what ought to have been there, but was not'. He converted absence into presence, but the knack was to know which absence to choose – that is, which story of absence was calling out for presence. Chatterton produced not just any old poet but precisely the poet the fifteenth century hadn't got – or rather, precisely the poet the eighteenth century thought the fifteenth century lacked or couldn't have. That was how Warton knew the works were a forgery. 'The fakes were too good', as Pat Rogers says, that is, too good as poems, not quite good enough as fakes. There are splendid collusions and confusions here, and the wonderful central paradox recurs again and again. The supporters of Rowley needed an absent author in the eighteenth century, an ignoramus who just found the stuff; the dead author had to live. Conversely, as Claude Rawson points out, the recognition of Chatterton's own genius 'actually depended on the exposure of the forgery'. Chatterton could be a Romantic icon only if he was a faker. The unbelievers needed an absent author in the Middle Ages, a mere fiction, but were pretty much unanimous about the gifts of the eigh-teenth-century prankster – 'the greatest genius that England has produced since the days of Shakespeare', Malone said. With enemies like these, what forger needs friends? If Johnson was dismissive in one (famous) mood – 'for Chatterton there is nothing but the resolution to say again what has once been said' – he was dazzled in another:

> It is as wonderful to suppose that a boy of sixteen years old had stored his mind with such a train of images and ideas as he had acquired, as to suppose the poems, with their ease of versification and elegance of language, to have been written by Rowlie in the time of Edward the Fourth.

Why was no one saying the schoolboy joke was an elaborate schoolboy joke, or that most of the poems were terrible by any standards and for any age? Because they weren't terrible, because the gifts of the author, whoever he was and whenever he wrote, were incontestable? Because of certain assumptions about schoolboys? Certain assumptions about poems and ease and elegance? Because the combined idea of fraud and ineptitude was more than anyone could manage?

If Chatterton 'first forged himself', as Richard Holmes suggests, 'and was then posthumously forged by others', then the very notion of forgery is entangled with a surviving or reconstituted authenticity. Something has to be genuine here, even if it is only the talent. But what is the force of 'has to'? Does it express a core of truth, an irreducible nugget of perception commanding critical and cultural agreement? Or does it reflect the pressure of a demand or need, the horror of a landscape which would be all waste? Perhaps it is enough, at this time and in this space, to see the extraordinary reach of the riddle. A real forgery is a false text, but then the forger is real. A falsely suspected forgery is a true text, but then the author was shady enough to arouse suspicion. Claude Rawson suggests, rightly, that the time is long between the age of Swift and the age of Thomas Mann's *Felix Krull*, but his own brilliant idea of 'unparodying' closes the gap considerably. Even the unparodied fails to return to straight sense. It's not that there is no difference between parody and impersonation, or between fiction and forgery. On the contrary, there is all the difference in the world. But important differences are not always large or easily visible ones, and the difficulty of detecting or fixing them is just what the riddle is about. Readers and writers are fillers of absences. Some fillings are manifestly more persuasive than others, historically sounder, interpretatively richer. But in writing and reading absence keeps washing back over the best and the worst projections. If there was no Rowley, we may say, we have Chatterton. But who was he? An author carries his character in his pen, and it's a poor reader who cannot read on both sides.

Rowley's Ghost: A Checklist of Creative Works Inspired by Thomas Chatterton's Life and Writings

John Goodridge

> Then Aradobo began, 'In the first place I think, I think in the first place that Chatterton was clever at Fissic, Follogy, Pistinology, Aridology, Arography, Transmography, Phizography, Hogamy, Hatomy, & hall that, but, in the first place, he eat wery little, wickly – that is, he slept very little, which he brought into a consumsion; & what was that he took? Fissic or somethink, – & so died!'
>
> William Blake, 'An Island in the Moon'

Introduction

This is a lightly annotated summary of material, especially poetry, which responds creatively to Thomas Chatterton. While Chatterton is central to the majority of items listed, his fleeting presence in poems, novels, etc., is also recorded, though more selectively. Although it is rather fuller than earlier lists, it cannot be exhaustive, so that for example the magazines for the period 1782–1800 would reward further patient searching. To keep within reasonable limits it concentrates on work which seems *overtly* fictional and imaginative, though one recognizes that Chatterton is a figure who attracts storytellers of all kinds. It might be argued, indeed, that even such notorious *fabrications* as the 'inquest report' on Chatterton, or his 'secret reburial' at St Mary Redcliffe, are a kind of creative response, involving (like the Rowley project itself) ingenious impostures, and the creation of narrative and mythic structures.[1]

The material is arranged alphabetically by author within four general areas: (A) Poetry, (B) Fiction, (C) Dramatic and musical works, and (D) Visual representations, with subsections for unidentified or pseudonymous material at the end of sections A, C, and D, filed by title. It is numbered in a single sequence, with some grouping (e.g. of several poems by one author, etc.). Inevitably some interesting marginal material remains beyond the scope of this system, for example the letter which 'Thomas Chatterton' published in *Macmillan's Magazine* in February 1872, offering the 'true source' for Lewis Carroll's 'Jabberwocky'.[2] Although French, German, Italian, and Polish responses to Chatterton are included, I have not traced what B. Keith-Smith (126) describes as Chatterton's '[l]ess well known [...] influence on the work of the father of Portuguese Romanticism João Baptista da Silva Leitão Almeida-Garrett' (1799–1854). Among Anglophone writers who failed to qualify for inclusion, see Meyerstein (489n.) on Hannah More (1745–1833); David Fairer's essay (above) and *TLS* (8 May 1930), 394, on Thomas De Quincey (1785–1859); *NQ* 4th ser. 7 (1871), 279–80 on Walter Savage Landor (1775–1864); and Rowles (C1473–5 and C1478–81) on John Masefield (1878–1967). Joanna Baillie (1762–1851) is reported in *NQ* 5th ser. 6 (1876), 60, to have been 'affected' by the Morris portrait (item 231), but if she printed any response it has eluded me. The film *Love and Death on Long Island*, dir. Richard Kwietniowski (1997), and the story by Gilbert Adair from which it is was adapted by Adair and Kwietniowski (Gilbert Adair, *Love and Death on Long Island*, London: William Heinemann, 1990) make use of Chatterton material, particularly the Henry Wallis painting (item 241). A television film about Chatterton is also in production.

Principal sources are listed below: they are cited by surname in this Introduction and in the entries. Useful chronological surveys may be found in Harvey and Rowles. I am much indebted to these earlier scholars, and Jean C. Rowles's 'C' numbers are used as a standard reference throughout. I would also like to thank for their help Celia Coates and Mary Dawson (Library and Information Services, The Nottingham Trent University), Peter Cox, David Fairer, Nick Groom, Bob Heyes, Richard Holmes, Robert Jones, Bridget Keegan, Kaye Kossick, Claire Lamont, Maria Grazia Lolla, Alison Ramsden, Simon Turner (Prints and Drawings, British Museum), and Robert Woof.

Principal sources

Anderson, Robert, *Complete Edition of the Poets of Great Britain* (Edinburgh, 1795), xi. 295–405.
Barker, W. R. (ed.), *A Catalogue of the Autograph Manuscripts and Other*

Remains of Thomas Chatterton now in the Bristol Museum of Antiquities (Bristol, 1907).

Chatterton Bibliography (*c.* 1900), typescript, Bristol Central Library, B20988.

Clarence, Reginald (comp.), *'The Stage' Cyclopaedia: a Bibliography of Plays,* (London, 1909).

Dix, John, *The Life of Thomas Chatterton* (London, 1837). See also *NQ* 4th ser. 9 (1872), 294–6, 365–6, 429–30; 4th ser. 10 (1872), 55, 229–30.

English Poetry: The English Poetry Full-Text Database, CD-ROM edn (Cambridge, 1995), via lion.chadwyck.co.uk.

Graves, Algernon, *The Royal Academy of Arts: A Complete Dictionary of Contributors,* 4 vols (London, 1905; reprinted Wakefield & Bath, 1970).

Groom, Nick, 'Thomas Chatterton Was a Forger', *Yearbook of English Studies,* 28 (1998), 276–91.

Harvey, A. D., 'The Cult of Chatterton amongst English Poets *c.* 1770–*c.* 1820', *Zeitschrift für Anglistik und Amerikanistik,* 39 (1991), 124–33.

Hyett, Francis Adams, and William Bazeley, *Chattertoniana* (Gloucester, 1914).

Ingram, John H., *The True Chatterton* (London, 1910).

Jackson, J. R. de J., *Annals of English Verse 1770–1835: A Preliminary Survey of The Volumes Published* (New York & London, 1985).

Johnson, C. R., *Provincial Poetry 1789–1839: British Verse Printed in the Provinces: The Romantic Background* (London, 1992).

Kaplan, Louise J., *The Family Romance of the Impostor-Poet Thomas Chatterton* (New York, 1988).

Keith-Smith, B., 'The Chatterton Theme in Modern German Literature', in *Affinities: Essays in German and English Literature,* ed. R. W. Last (London, 1971), 126–38.

Kelly, Linda, *The Marvellous Boy: The Life and Myth of Thomas Chatterton* (London, 1971).

Martin, Edward and Bill Pickard (eds), *600 Years of Bristol Poetry* (Bristol, 1973).

Mathews, E. R. Norris, 'Thomas Chatterton, a Bibliography', in his *Bristol Bibliography* (Bristol, 1916), 55–82.

Meyerstein, E. H. W., *A Life of Thomas Chatterton* (London, 1930).

Rowles, Jean C., 'Thomas Chatterton 1752–1770: an Annotated Bibliography' (Fellowship of the Library Association thesis, Bristol, 1981). The most important source: two copies are held at Bristol Central Library, ref. nos. 31853 and 31448.

Russell, Charles Edward, *Thomas Chatterton, the Marvellous Boy* (New York, 1908; London, 1909).

Smith, Michael Quinton, *St Mary Redcliffe: An Architectural History* (Bristol, 1995).

Warren, Murray, *A Descriptive and Annotated Bibliography of Thomas Chatterton* (New York & London, 1977).

Wilson, Daniel, *Chatterton: A Biographical Study* (London, 1869).

A. Poetry

David Fairer's essay (above) quotes, discusses and groups together a significant number of the early verse responses. For a poetry competition on the theme of Chatterton see Rowles, C1369, C1532. For Rowley modernizations see items 70, 74 and 83, and unlisted poems in *GM* 47 (1777), 277; 48 (1778), 327–8, 429–30 and 534.

1. Bailey, Philip James (1816–1902), *Festus: A Poem*, 10th edn (London: Longmans, Green and Co., 1877), 261 (Bk. XVIII, ll. 11542–3), 'Here Chatterton's proud spirit / Self-tumbled'.

2. Barham, Francis Foster (1808–71), *The New Bristol Guide, a Comic Poem* (London: Longman and Co., 1847), 36–7, 64, and *passim*.

3. Barham, Richard Harris (1788–1845), (a) 'Relics of Ancient Poetry', I ('When good Kynge Wyllyam ruled this lande') and II ('It was a Butcher wyth hys traye'), first printed in *The Intelligence* (1831), quoted in Martin and Pickard, 37; (b) 'The Bulletin' ('Hark! the doctors come again'), in the style the third minstrels' song from *Ælla*, written May 1845, first pub. in *Bentley's Miscellany* (July 1862); both collected in *Life and Letters* (London: Richard Bentley, 1870), ii.

4. Barker, R. W., 'On Chatterton', *Mirror of Literature, Amusement and Instruction* (23 Jan. 1830), 16; C1259.

5. Baynes, John (1758–87) or William Mason (1724–97), *An Archaeological Epistle to the Reverend and Worshipful Jeremiah Milles* (London: J. Nichols and others, 1782); C72–3. An important parody of the Rowley Poems, which includes 'Paradise Lost, Book I' ('Offe mannes fyrste bykrous volunde wolle I singe'), 'To blynne or not to blynne the denwere is', and the 'Epistelle to Doctoure Mylles'. Extracted in the *Public Advertiser* (19 Mar. 1782), *A New Review* 1 (Mar. 1782), 133, and Anderson, xi. 402–4. The attribution to Baynes, made by John Nichols in his *Anecdotes* (viii. 113) is strongly refuted by a correspondent in *GM* 86

(1816), 489–91, who attributes to Mason. Meyerstein (472–3) re-attributes to Baynes without argument. Recent critics tend to assume it is by Mason, though opinion is divided. See Groom, 280–1, and Groom, above.

6. Beattie, James (1735–1803), *The Minstrel; or, The Progress of Genius* (London: E. and C. Dilly, 1771), Bk. I, stz. xvi ('And yet poor Edwin was no vulgar boy'). See Meyerstein, xii; Kelly, 59.

7. Bell, Henry Thomas Mackenzie (1856–1930), 'The Boy Chatterton to Himself', *Poems* (London: J. Clarke and Co.; Kingsgate Press, 1909), 128–9.

Bell, Neil: see Southwold, Stephen.

8. Blacket, Joseph (1786–1810), 'The Bards of Britain', *Remains*, ed. Samuel Jackson Pratt (London: Sherwood, Neely and Jones, 1811), ii. 47.

9. Blaikie, John Arthur, 'Ode on the Death of Thomas Chatterton, August 24, 1970: the supposed utterance of a contemporary of the poet', *Love's Victory: Lyrical Poems* (London: Percival and Co., 1890), 67–81; C1301. An apparent earlier publication is untraced.

10. Blake, William (1757–1827), several echoes, including lines from 'A Memorable Fancy' in *The Marriage of Heaven and Hell* (*c.* 1790–3). See Meyerstein, 92, 357; Kelly, 81; *Blake Quarterly* 4.2 (1977), 27–9; *NQ* 230 (1985), 328–9; Fairer, above; and item 173, below.

11. Bobrowski, Johannes (1917–65), 'Ode auf Thomas Chatterton', *Sinn und Form: Beitrage zur Literatur*, 7 (1955), 500–1. For a translation and commentary see Brian Keith-Smith, *Johannes Bobrowski* (London: Oswald Wolff, 1970), 32–4, 84–65; see also Keith-Smith, 131–2; C1362–7.

12. Brooke, Arthur (=John Chalk Claris, 1797?–1866), 'The Curse of Chatterton', *Durovernum; with Other Poems* (London: Longman, Hurst and others, 1818), 91–102.

13. Brown, James Pennycook (d. 1863), 'The Death of Chatterton' ('One struggle more, and then I shall be calm'), *Poetical Ephemeras* (Aberdeen: A. Brown, 1831).

Browning, Robert: see *Dramatic and Musical Works*.

14. Brydges, Samuel Egerton (1762–1837), *Human Fate: A Poem* (Great Totham: Charles Clark's Private Press, 1850), 5, and 11. Links Bloomfield and Chatterton.

15. Buchanan, Robert Williams (1841–1901), 'Poet's Prologue: To David in Heaven', *Complete Poetical Works*, 2 vols (London: Chatto and Windus, 1901), 21–3.

16. Byron, George Gordon, Lord (1788–1824), *Monody on the Death of the Rt. Hon. R.B. Sheridan* (London: John Murray, 1816). Opening lines echo Chatterton's 'Narva and Mored'. See Meyerstein, 507; *NQ* 162 (1932), 207; 191 (1946), 281.

17. Carpenter, Maurice (*fl.* 1935–71), 'The Descent of Chatterton', *Peninsula: An Anthology of Verse from the West Country*, ed. Charles Causley (London: Macdonald, 1957), 33–5; C1368.

18. Cary, Thomas (b. 1752), 'Elegy to the Memory of Mr. Thomas Chatterton, Late of Bristol', *Town and Country Magazine*, 2 (Oct. 1770), 551; Anderson, XI, 402; C1193. See Meyerstein, 540–2; Kelly, 43.

19. Clare, John (1763–1864), (a) 'The Resignation (Supposed to be Written by the Unfortunate Chatterton Just Before he Took the Deadly Draught that Put a Period to his Existance)'; (b) 'To the Muse', ll. 53–4. See *Early Poems*, ed. Eric Robinson and David Powell (Oxford: Clarendon, 1989), i. 325–7; ii. 207. See also John Goodridge, 'Identity, Authenticity, Class: John Clare and the Mask of Chatterton', *Angelaki*, 2.1 (1993/4), 131–48; Keegan, above; and item 244.

Claris, John Chalk: see Brooke, Arthur.

20. Coleridge, Samuel Taylor (1772–1834), 'Monody on the Death of Chatterton', versions of 1790, 1794, 1796, 1803, 1828, 1829, and 1834 (see David Fairer's essay, above); C1231–4. 'The Foster Mother's Tale' and 'Kubla Khan' also have Chatterton resonances. See Meyerstein, 356, 502–4; Kelly, 84–90, 93; Kaplan, 17; *TLS* (21 Aug. 1937), 606, (28 Aug. 1937), 624; *Review of English Studies* 18 (1942), 49–71; n.s. 17 (1966), 391–402; n.s. 18 (1967), 174; *The Library* 11 (1989), 328–35.

21. Cooper, Thomas (1805–92), *The Purgatory of Suicides: A Prison Rhyme* (London: Jeremiah How, 1845), 137–8 (Bk. IV).

22. Corso, Gregory (b. 1930), 'I am 25' ('With a love a madness for Shelley / Chatterton Rimbaud'), first pub. in *Gasoline* (San Francisco: City Lights, 1958); collected in *Mindfield* (New York: Thunder's Mouth Press, 1989), 35.

23. Cottle, Joseph (1770–1853), *Malvern Hills*, 4th edn (London: T. Cadell, 1829), (a) title poem, ll. 55–6, see also pp. 382–432, and (b) 'Epitaph for a Proposed Monument to Chatterton, at Bristol' (*c.* 1827), on p. 169, reprinted in Martin and Pickard, 18; C1257; (c) *Early Recollections* (London: Longman, Rees and Co.; Hamilton, Adams and Co., 1837), 256–74, 281–302; C576. Cottle co-edited the 1803 edition of Chatterton.

24. Cowley, Hannah (1743–1809), 'A Monody', unauthorized version first pub. in *Morning Post*, no. 1878 (24 Oct. 1778); heavily revised as 'The Death of Chatterton', *Works* (London: Wilkie and Robinson, 1813), iii. 75–6; Anderson, xi. 401–2; C1196–9.

25. Crabbe, George (1754–1832), 'The Patron', *Tales* (London: Hatchard, 1812), ll. 118–19. See Meyerstein, 506–7.

26. Cunningham, Allan (1784–1842), 'The Legend of Richard Faulder, Mariner', *Sir Marmaduke Maxwell ... and Twenty Scottish Songs* (London: Taylor and Hessey, 1822), 163.

27. Curnick, Thomas, 'Ode on the Death of Chatterton, Written on St. Vincent's Rock's at Clifton, near Bristol', *Jehoshaphat, with Other Poems* (Bristol: M. Bryan, 1815), 104–7; C1253.

28. Dainty, John (*fl.* 1873–1902), 'Thomas Chatterton', *Leicester Lyrics* (Gloucester: privately printed by the author, 1902), 54; C1310.

29. Dallaway, James (1763–1834), *Sonnets to an Aeolian Harp; on the Death of Chatterton* (Rodborough, Stroud: privately printed, 1788); C1227. See also Smith, 137–42. Elsewhere listed as *Stanzas on the Death of Chatterton*, and with the place of publication as Gloucester: see Harvey, 129.

30. Daniel, George (1789–1864), *The Modern Dunciad: Virgil in London and Other Poems* (London: William Pickering, 1835), 48–9.

31. Davies, J., ('Still, Chatterton! Rowley, and Milles, and old Bryant!'), *SJC* (1 June 1782); *GM* 52 (1782), 303; quoted by Kelly, 50.

32. Dermody, Thomas (1775–1802), (a) 'The Pursuit of Patronage', *Poems* (London, 1800), 49; (b) 'A Monody on Chatterton' (*c.* 1801), *The Harp of Erin*, ed. James G. Raymond (London: Richard Phillips, 1807), ii. 129–33; C891.

33. Dibdin, Charles Isaac Mungo (1768–1833), 'Invocation to the Spirit of Chatterton', *Mirth and Metre* (London: Vernor, Hood and Sharpe, 1807), 17–19.

34. Dowden, Edward (1843–1913), 'Prologue to Maurice Gerothwohl's Version of Vigny's "Chatterton"' [item 198], *Poems* (London and Toronto: J.M. Dent and Sons, [1914]), 217–18.

35. Dun, Aidan Andrew, *Vale Royal* (Uppingham, Rutland: Goldmark, 1996). Chatterton is a key figure in this 2000-line poem.

36. Dyer, George (1755–1841), *The Poet's Fate* (London: Robinson and others, 1797), dedicated to the 'Society for the Establishment of a Literary Fund'; collected with 'The Balance', 'Poetic Sympathies', and 'The Redress. To the Young Poet', *Poems* (London: Longman and Rees, 1801), 206–331. The four poems form a sustained

argument on poverty and poetry, with Chatterton as a key figure, notably in 'The Balance' (232, 251).

37. Eagles, John (1783–1855), Lines inscribed on the Chatterton Monument (item 226), beginning 'A poor and friendless Boy was he' (1840); C1396. See Russell, 263; Kaplan, 31; *NQ* 2nd ser. 4 (1857), 325.

38. Eagles, Thomas (1746–1812), 'Rowley's Ghost to the Right Reverend the Lord Bishop of Dromore and the Rev. Thomas Warton', *NQ* 2nd ser. 4 (1857), 264–5; C1286.

39. Eastmead, John Shepherd, 'Chatterton: A Poem', *Poems* (Bristol: W.S. Matthews, 1843), 65; C1282.

40. Elliott, Ebenezer (1781–1849), 'Inscriptions' (I) and 'Love', *Poetical Works*, ed. Edwin Elliott, revised edition (London: Henry King, 1876), i. 13–14, 65–6.

41. Elton, Charles Abraham (1778–1853), 'Sonnet on the Church of St. Mary Redcliffe, Bristol', *Boyhood* (London: Longman and Co., 1835), 85; C1264. Reprinted in Martin and Pickard, 35.

42. Fitzgerald, William Thomas (1759?–1829), 'An Address to the Literary Fund, Recited by the Author, at Freemason's Hall, May 3, 1798', *Miscellaneous Poems* (London: J. Wright, 1801), 105–7. There are three other 'addresses' in the volume: see Harvey, 130. Chatterton was an emblematic figure in the campaign to promote the Literary Fund: compare items 36 and 80.

43. Forman, Henry Buxton (1842–1917), [Chatterton,] *Five Rondeaux* (*c.* 1870), 29; C1290. BL, 1870 c 28.

44. Galt, John (1779–1839), 'Epitaph for a proposed monument to Chatterton', *Greenock Advertiser*, 23 Nov. 1837.

45. Greene, Edward Burnaby (d. 1788), 'To the Lerned Deane Percy: Greteying', in *Strictures upon a Pamphlet* (London: J. Stockdale, 1782), also printed in *GM* 52 (1782), 342. A sonnet in the style of the Rowley Poems.

46. Gregory, John (*fl.* 1877–1911), 'Sonnets on Chatterton's Church, Bristol', *Song Streams* (Bristol: published by the author, 1877), 108–10.

47. Grinfield, Charles Vaughan, (a) 'Epigram on Chatterton', *Pickings from my Portfolio* (Bristol: J. Lavars, 1857), 44; C1285; (b) 'Acrostic on "Chatterton"', *Western Daily Press* (4 Dec. 1895); *Bristol Times and Mirror* (27 Dec. 1895); C1304–5.

48. Grinfield, Thomas (1788–1870), Verses on Chatterton, *Western Daily Press* (4 Dec. 1895); *Bristol Times and Mirror* (27 Dec. 1895); C1304–5.

Hardinge, George: see *Dramatic and Musical Works*.

49. Hayley, William (1745–1820), *An Essay on Epic Poetry in Five Epistles to the Revd. Mr. Mason* (London: J. Dodsley, 1782), 81–2 (Ep. IV, ll. 207–48, 333–42); *GM* 52 (1782), 302, 344–7; Anderson, xi. 320; C1204–8. See also *NQ* 193 (1948), 195.

50. Headley, Henry (1765–88), 'A Dirge to the Memory of Chatterton' and 'Ode to the Memory of Chatterton', *Fugitive Pieces* (London: C. Dilly, 1785), 8, 76; C1215. The 'Ode' is misattributed by Meyerstein, 501, to 'William Headley'. Reprinted, ed. P. M. Spacks (Los Angeles: Augustan Reprint Society, 1966).

51. Hobday, Charles (b. 1917), 'Chatterton', in Martin and Pickard, 80; first published in the *Bristol Evening Post*; C1370.

52. Hobhouse, Thomas, *Kingsweston Hill: a Poem* (London: John Stockdale, 1785), 14–15 (ll. 139–56); C1216–17. Extracted in Martin and Pickard, 13.

53. Holford, Margaret (later Hodson, 1778–1852), 'Experience to the Poet', *Monthly Mirror* 15 (1803), 411–12; C1243.

Home, Anne: see Hunter, Anne.

54. Hood, Thomas (1799–1845), and John Hamilton Reynolds (1794–1852), 'Ode to the Great Unknown', *Odes and Addresses to Great People* (London: Baldwin, Cradock and Joy, 1825), 44 (stz. 5). Witty Scott–Chatterton comparison.

55. Hunter, Anne (*née* Home, 1742–1821), 'To the Memory of Thomas Chatterton', *Poems*, 2nd edn (London: T. Payne, 1807), 27; C1240.

56. Hunter, John (*fl.* 1798–1805), *A Tribute to the Manes of Unfortunate Poets* (London, 1798), 90–2.

57. Ireland, William Henry (1775–1835), the 'second Chatterton', (a) 'Elegaic Lines to the Memory of Thomas Chatterton', *Rhapsodies* (London: Ellerton and Byworth, 1803), 17–21; revised as (b) 'Elegaic Stanzas ...' in *Neglected Genius: A Poem* (London: G. Cowie and Co., 1812), which includes some dozen poems on Chatterton, 57–98, 121–7, 144–51; C882; C1249; (c) *Chalcographimania; or, The Portrait-Collector and Printseller's Chronicle*, by 'Satiricus Sculptor' (London: R. S. Kirby, 1814), 28, 85. Many other allusions, and an unpublished manuscript, 'Chatterton: A Tragedy', mentioned by G. Hilder Libbis (Huntington Library, HM 287175). See Kelly, 71–9; Meyerstein, 494–5. See also item 219.

58. James, Charles (1765?–1821), 'Modern Patronage: An Ode', *Poems* (London: J. Davis for J. Debrett, 1792), 320–2; C1236.

59. James, Joseph, 'Lines on Reading the Recently Published Life of

Chatterton', *Bristol Mirror* (20 Oct. 1837); C1277; 'Lines, Written After Seeing in the Exhibition Room, in Broad-Street, the Model of a Monument to the Memory of Chatterton, by a Lady', 'Lines, on Seeing the Picture of the Dying Chatterton Exposed for Sale in a Broker's Shop, Close Beside his Monument', *Poetry* (Bristol: Mirror Office, 1841), 128 and 131; C1280–1.

60. Keats, John (1795–1821), (a) Sonnet to Chatterton beginning ' O Chatterton! how very sad thy fate', written 1815, pub. in *Life, Letters and Literary Remains* (London: E. Moxon, 1848); C1254; (b) 'To George Felton Mathew', written 1815, pub. in *Poems* (London: Charles and James Ollier, 1817), ll. 55–6; (c) *Endymion* (London: Taylor and Hessey, 1818), dedicated to the memory of Chatterton and influenced by *Ælla*. The 'Ode to a Nightingale' also has Chatterton resonances. See also Meyerstein, 247, 507–12; Kelly, 94–103; *Keats–Shelley Journal* 4 (1955), 47–55; 5 (1956), 103–8; 30 (1981), 100–17; *Keats–Shelley Review* 10 (1996), 35–50.

61. King, Harriet Eleanor Hamilton (1840–1920), 'The Shade of Chatterton: Brooke Street, Holborn', *Ballads of the North and Other Poems* (London: Paul, 1889), 111–20.

62. Kipling, Rudyard (1865–1936), 'Recessional', *The Times* (17 July 1897); collected in *The Five Nations* (London: Methuen, 1903). An imitation of Chatterton's 'The Resignation' ('O God, whose thunder shakes the sky').

63. Lamb, Charles (1775–1834), 'To Sara and Her Samuel', in a letter to Coleridge dated 5 July 1796, *The Letters of Charles and Mary Lamb*, ed. Edwin W. Marrs (Ithaca & London: Cornell University Press, 1975), i. 38–9. Lamb's quip about Chatterton's Rowleyan spelling and the 'mob of gentlemen who write with ease' is recorded in *Henry Crabbe Robinson On Books and Their Writers*, ed. E. J. Morley (London: Dent, 1938), entry for 30 Dec. 1813.

64. Le Grice, Charles Valentine (1773–1858), (a) untitled poem beginning 'Dear Sharpe, this work by Mr Dix', dated 30 May 1838; (b) 'Sonnet. On Visiting the School at Bristol in which the Poet Chatterton was bred', dated Bristol, 22 July 1826; C1256; *NQ* 4th ser. 9 (1872), 429–30. Le Grice's essay on Chatterton appeared in *GM* n.s. 10 (July 1838), 128–33.

65. Levy, Amy (1861–89), 'A Minor Poet', *A Minor Poet and Other Verses* (London: T.F. Unwin, 1884); *The Complete Novels and Selected Writings of Amy Levy*, ed. Melvyn New (Gainesville: University Press of Florida, 1993), 370–7.

66. Lickbarrow, Isabella (*fl.* 1811–18), 'Stanzas supposed to be written

at the Grave of Chatterton', *Westmorland Advertiser* 4, no.142 (12 Mar. 1814); reprinted in *Poetical Effusions* (Kendal: M. and R. Branthwaite; London: J. Richardson, 1814), 58–60. See *The Wordsworth Circle* 27.2 (1996), 113–28.

67. Lott, Henry F., Sonnet ('Tread softly! Here the gifted hand that penned'), *Home Companion Magazine* (Apr. 1854), 248.

68. Lovell, Robert (1770?–96), *Bristol, a Satire* (London: printed for the author, 1794), ll. 133–54; extracted in Martin and Pickard, 21.

69. MacSweeney, Barry (b. 1948), Three Chatterton odes, *Odes 1971–1978* (London: Trigram Press, 1978), 16, 21, 50; C1371. MacSweeney's *Elegy for January : An Essay Commemorating the Bi-Centenary of Chatterton's Death* (London: Menard Press, 1970), is also dedicated to Chatterton.

70. Malone, Edmond (1741–1812), (a) 'Chatterton in Masquerade' and 'Chatterton Unmasked', in *Cursory Observations on the Poems Attributed to Thomas Rowley* (London: J. Nichols and J. Walter, 1782), a 'Rowleyized' version of Chatterton's 'Narva and Mored' and a modernized version of the 'First Eclogue' (see Groom, 280); (b) 'The Remonstrance of Mr Bryant', *SJC* (28 May 1782); *GM* 52 (1782), 303, a satire on the Rowleyans.

71. Mant, Richard (1776–1848), 'Religious Comfort', *Poems* (Oxford: Oxford University Press, 1806), 16.

Mason, William: see Baynes, John.

72. Mathias, Thomas James (1754?–1835), (a) *The Pursuits of Literature. A Satirical Poem*, 7th edn, revised (London: T. Becket, 1798), 74 and 144; (b) 'The Bard of the Severn', *Lyrick Poetry*, new edn (Naples: privately printed, 1832), 23–37. Item 201 is sometimes misattributed to Mathias.

73. Meek, George, 'Monody on the Death of Chatterton', *Evening Hours: A Collection of Original Poems* (London, 1817).

74. Merivale, John Herman (1779–1844), 'From Chatterton's "Aella"', *Poems* (London: William Pickering, 1844), 102–4.

75. Meyerstein, E. H. W. (1889–1952), (a) 'Chatterton at Shoreditch; a Sonnet', *Bristol Times and Mirror* (24 Aug. 1929); C1329; (b) 'Song to Chatterton', *Oxford Magazine* (26 Feb. 1931); C1333–4; (c) 'Chatterton; or, The Apotheosis', *Eclogues* (London: The Richards Press, 1940), 104–7; C1349; (d) 'Thomas Chatterton', *Division: A Poem* (Oxford: B. H. Blackwell, 1946), 15–18; C1353; (e) 'Chatterton in Holborn: A Vision', *English* 7 (1948–9), 19–20; C1355–6. See Kelly, 129–37; *Some Poems of E. H. W. Meyerstein*, selected by Maurice Wollman (London: Neville Spearman, 1960),

30–3. See also item 210.

76. Mickle, William Julius (1735–88), *The Prophecy of Queen Emma, by Turgottus, Bishop of St Andrew* (London: J. Bew, 1782). A parody of the Rowley Poems. See Groom, above.

77. Middleton, Christopher (b. 1926), 'The Glummonging' ('Ah, Thomas Chatterton, I hear / They cut you short'), *PN Review* 111 (Sept.–Oct. 1996), 67.

78. Montgomery, James (1771–1854), 'Chatterton: Stanzas on reading the verses entitled "Resignation" written by Chatterton', *The World Before the Flood* (London: Longman, Hurst and others, 1813), 225–7; C1250-2, extracted in Chatterton, *Poetical Works*, ed. W. W. Skeat (London: Bell and Daldy, 1871), i. 264–5.

79. Montgomery, Robert (1807–55), 'The Age Reviewed' and 'Oxford: or, Alma Mater', in *The Age Reviewed: A Satire*, 2nd edn (London: William Charles Wright, 1828), 250, 262, 395, and 416.

80. Morris, (Captain) Thomas (b. 1737), 'Lines, addressed to the Society for a Literary Fund', in *Claims of Literature: The Origin, Motives, Objects and Transactions of the Society for the Establishment of a Literary Fund*, ed. David Williams (London: W. Miller, 1802), 169.

81. Musser, Benjamin Francis, *Marvelous Boy* (North Montpelier, Vt.: The Driftwind Press, 1937); C1348.

82. Musset, Alfred de (1810–57) and George Sand (=Aurore Lucile Dupin, 1804–1876), 'Aux Critiques du *Chatterton* d'Alfred de Vigny' (item 217), two sonnets, written 1835; C1273. See Alfred de Musset, *Oeuvres Complètes*, ed. Philippe Van Tieghem (Paris: Editions de Seuil, 1963), 236; Kelly, 111.

83. Nares, Robert (1753–1829), modernization of 'Elinoure and Juga', *Town and Country Magazine*, June 1769. See also *TLS* (25 June 1931), 504, item 9. The first documented creative response to Chatterton.

84. Nicholson, John ('The Airedale Poet', 1790–1843), 'Genius and Intemperance', *Poetical Works*, ed. W. G. Hird (London: Simpkin Marshall and Co.; Bradford: Thomas Brear, 1876), 162 (l. 823 ff).

85. Oram, Samuel Marsh (1767–93), 'To the Woodlark', *Poems*, Introduction by Percival Stockdale (London: printed at the Philanthropic Press for T. Cadell, 1794), 20; C1238.

86. Ord, John Walker (1811–53), *England: A Historical Poem* (London: Simpkin and Marshall; Edinburgh: Baldwin and Craddock, 1834), 11, 55, and 128.

87. Pennie, John Fitzgerald (1782–1848), 'On the Death of Chatterton', *The Tale of a Modern Genius, or the Miseries of Parnassus* (London: J. Andrews, 1827), i. 139–45.

88. Poe, Edgar Allan (1809–49), verse motto by 'Lancelot Canning', who is also the 'author' of 'Mad Tryst', in 'The Fall of the House of Usher', first pub. in *Burton's Gentleman's Magazine* (1839). See *NQ* 177 (1939), 77–8, and 160.

89. Polidori, John William (1795–1821), 'Chatterton to his Sister', *Ximenes, The Wreath, and Other Poems* (London: Longman, Hurst and others, 1819), 135–43.

90. Preston, William (1753–1807), 'Epistle to a Young Gentleman, on his having addicted himself to the Study of Poetry', *Poetical Works* (Dublin: printed for the author and sold by J. Arthur, 1793), i. 181; Anderson, xi. 295 and 319.

91. Prince, John Critchley (1808–66), 'The Child of Song', *Poetical Works*, ed. R. A. Douglas Lithgow, 2 vols (Manchester: A. Heywood, 1880), 109 (ll. 21–4).

92. Pye, Henry James (1745–1813), *The Progress of Refinement* (Oxford: Clarendon-press; London: J. Dodsley and others, 1783), Part II, ll. 579–92; Anderson, xi. 319; C1211–12.

93. Rannie, John (*fl.* 1789–91), Sonnet XI, 'Written on a Blank Leaf of Chatterton's Poems', *Poems*, 2nd edn (Aberdeen, 1791), 13.

94. Rawnsley, Hardwick Drummond (1851–1920), 'St. Mary Redcliffe', 'Chatterton', 'The Oak Chamber at Jefferies', and 'Redcliffe Street', *A Book of Bristol Sonnets* (London: Hamilton, Adams and Co.; Bristol: I. E. Chilcott, 1877), 16–21.

Reynolds, John Hamilton: see Hood, Thomas.

95. Rhys, Ernest Percival (1859–1946), 'Chatterton in Holborn', *Century Magazine* 42 (1891), 350; C1302.

96. Roberts, William Isaac (1786–1806), 'Chatterton, or the Mynstrelle. A Fragment', *Poems and Letters* (London: Longman, Hurst and others, 1811), 56–7; C1248. See *Publications of the Bibliographical Society of America* 57 (1963), 184–90.

97. Robinson, Mary ('Perdita', 1758–1800), 'Monody to the Memory of Chatterton', *Poems* (London: J. Bell, 1791–3), i. 75–9; C1237.

98. Rogers, Samuel (1763–1855), 'The Lake of Geneva', *Poetical Works* (London: George Bell, 1875), 189 (ll. 27–9), in the sequence 'Italy'.

99. Rossetti, Dante Gabriel (1828-82), 'Thomas Chatterton: A Poem', and 'Tiber, Nile and Thames', *Works*, ed. William M. Rossetti, rev. and enlarged edn (London: Ellis, 1911), 230, 233, C1298–9. See also Hall Caine, *Recollections of Rossetti*, rev. edn (London: Cassell, 1928), 118–19; Meyerstein, 515–17; Kelly, 119–22; Kaplan, 27.

100. Rushton, Edward (1756–1814), *Neglected Genius: or, Tributary*

Stanzas to the Memory of the Unfortunate Chatterton (London: J. Philips, 1787), abridged in *Poems and Other Writings* (London: Effingham Wilson, 1824), 45–53; C1222–5. See also Meyerstein, 501–2; *The Times* (13 Jan. 1916), 21c, and (20 Jan. 1916), 33b.

101. Russell, Charles Edward (1860–1941), 'In the Church of St Mary Redcliffe', *Such Stuff as Dreams* (Indianapolis: Bowen-Merril Co., 1901), 9–16; C1309.

102. Russell, Thomas (1762–88), 'Sonnet II', *Sonnets and Miscellaneous Poems* (Oxford: D. Prince and J. Cook, 1789), 2; C1230.

Sand, George: see Musset, Alfred de.

103. Sassoon, Siegfried (1886–1967), *On Chatterton, a Sonnet* (Winchester: printed at Mr Blakeney's private press, 1930); C1332. A limited edition of 14 copies.

104. Scott, John, (1730–83), 'Ode XV' and 'Ode XX1', *Poetical Works* (London: J. Buckland, 1782), 206, 224.

105. Scott, Sir Walter (1771–1832), *The Lay of the Last Minstrel* (Edinburgh: A. Constable; London: Longman, Hurst and others, 1805). Influenced by Chatterton's 'The Unknown Knight': see Meyerstein, 507; Kelly, 81–2. For Scott's fullest comment on Chatterton see *Edinburgh Review* 4 (1804), 214–30.

106. Scott, William Bell (1811–90), 'Sonnet X: Chatterton', *A Poet's Harvest Home* (London: Elkin Mathews and John Lane, 1893), 126.

Seward, Anna: see Stevens, William Bagshaw.

107. Shelley, Percy Bysshe (1792–1822), (a) 'Fragment: Omens', written 1807, recast as 'Ghasta or, the Avenging Demon!!!' ('Hark! the owlet flaps her wing'), Jan. 1810, *Complete Poetical Works*, ed. Neville Rogers (Oxford: Clarendon, 1972), i. 4 and 56–62; (b) *Adonais* (Pisa, 1821), stz. 45 (stz. 31 also cited by Dix, 297). Possibly other echoes: see Russell, 249; Meyerstein, 246, 297, 512; Kelly, 94–5.

108. Shepperley, William, *Chatterton* (London: Bowyer Press, 1914); C1314. Seven poems on Chatterton.

109. Sherif, S., 'Sonnets to the Poet Chatterton', *Oddfellows Quarterly Magazine* 9 (Jan. 1846), 39; C1284.

110. Slade, Edward Walker, 'The Skull: XVIII. The Poet', *The Skull and Other Poems* (Bristol: Mirror Office, 1829), 71–2; C1258.

111. Smith, Thomas Enort, of Hammersmith, 'Sonnet to Misfortune: supposed to be written by that unfortunate youthful Bard CHAT-TERTON, a few Moments previous to his unfortunate Exit from this Life,' *European Magazine and London Review* 42 (Dec. 1802), 461; C1242.

112. Southey, Robert (1774–1843), 'The Young Spirits XI', *Poetical Works* (London: Longman, Orme and others, 1838), l. 47 ff. Southey's *Thalaba the Destroyer: A Rhythmical Romance* (London: Longman and Rees; Bristol: Biggs and Cottle, 1801) was influenced by the *African Eclogues*. Southey co-edited the 1803 edition of Chatterton: see Kelly, 82, 85, 91–3. See also C1396; *NQ* 2nd ser. 4 (1857), 325.

113. Southwold, Stephen (='Neil Bell', 1887–1964), 'To Chatterton', *The Common Day* (London: G. Allen and Unwin, 1915), 40; C1315–16. See also item 171.

114. Steevens, George (1736–1800), (a) 'The Deans of Exeter, or Rowley-Powley' and 'Another', *SJC* (30 Mar. 1782), signed 'Oliver', two squibs aimed at the pro-Rowleyan Dean Jeremiah Milles; (b) 'Ode to William Duke of Cumberland', *SJC* (13 Apr. 1782), a modernized parody of the 'Songe toe Ella'. See also item 238.

115. Stevens, William Bagshaw (1756–1800), 'Retirement', *Poems* (London: R. Faulder and G. Kearsley, 1782), 1–29 (20–1). This is praised and quoted by Anna Seward (1742–1809) in her 'Epistle to the Rev. Bagshot [sic] Stevens', *Poetical Works*, ed. Walter Scott (Edinburgh: J. Ballantyne, 1810), ii. 168–9.

116. Stockdale, Percival (1736–1811), 'Siddons: A Poem', *Poetical Works*, 2 vols (London: Longman, Hurst and others, 1810), 107. On Chatterton and Walpole.

117. Stuart-Wortley, Lady Emmeline Charlotte Elizabeth (1806–55), *The Visionary: A Fragment, with other poems*, 2 vols (London: Longman, Rees and Co., 1836–9), i. 171.

118. Tasker, William (1740–1800), (a) 'A Poetical Encomium on Trade, Addressed to the Mercantile City of Bristol', *Poems* (London: Dodsley, Bew and others, 1779), 48–9; (b) 'Impromptu on the honour paid to Chatterton by Thicknesse' (1798), in *Anecdotes*; C562.

119. Thistlethwaite, James (b. 1750), 'An Elegy, to the Memory of a Young Man lately deceased', *Gentleman's Museum and Grand Imperial Magazine* 5 (Nov. 1770); C1194–5. See *TLS* (8 Feb. 1934), 92.

120. Thompson, Francis (1859–1907), lines in the style of the 'Third Mynstrelles Songe' ('Come listen to my roundelaie'), quoted by Kelly, 123.

121. Thornbury, George Walter (1828–76), 'Temple Bar', *Historical and Legendary Ballads and Songs* (London: Chatto and Windus, 1876), 178.

122. Thurlow, Edward, Lord (1781–1829), 'Moonlight: A Poem' and 'A Song to Amoret', *Moonlight: A Poem* (London: White, Cochrane and Co., 1814), 15 and 177.

123. Warton, Thomas (1728-90), 'Suicide', *Poems, a New Edition, with Additions* (London: T. Becket, 1777), 42–7, discussed by Fairer, above.

124. Waugh, Edwin (1817–90), 'A Little Brief Authority', *Poems and Songs, Second Series* (Liverpool: Gilbert G. Walmsley; Oldham: W. E. Clegg, 1889), 63.

125. White, Henry Kirke (1785–1806), 'Genius, an Ode', *Poetical Works* (London: Bell and Daldy, 1830), 154–7 (ll. 57–9); C1247.

126. Whitehead, Charles (1804–62), 'The Death of Chatterton', *The Amaranth*, ed. Thomas Kibble Hervey (London: A. H. Bailey, 1839), 65–8; C1279.

127. Wilde, Oscar (1854–1900), sonnet beginning 'With Shakespeare's manhood at a boy's wild heart', printed in Richard Ellmann, *Oscar Wilde* (London: Hamish Hamilton, 1987), 269.

128. Williams, Helen Maria (1762–1827), 'Sonnet to Expression', *Poems* (London: A. Rivington and J. Marshall, 1786), ii. 201–2; Anderson, xi. 401; C1219–20.

129. Williams, John (='Anthony Pasquin', 1761–1818), 'The Children of Thespis', *Poems: by Anthony Pasquin*, 2nd edn (London and Edinburgh; J. Strahan and others, 1789), 160. On Chatterton and Walpole.

130. Wolcot, John ('Peter Pindar', 1738–1819), 'A Poetical, Supplicating, Modest and Affecting Epistle to Those Literary Collossuses the Reviewers' and 'Ode I', *The Works of Peter Pindar*, 4 vols (London: Walker and Edwards, 1816), i. 6 and 38.

131. Woodhouse, James (1735–1820), 'The Life and Lucubrations of Crispinus Scriblerus', written *c*. 1800, *Life and Poetical Works*, ed. R. I. Woodhouse (London: Leadenhall Press, 1896), 9. The poem's Invocation (ll. 1–10) is to Chatterton.

132. Wordsworth, William (1770–1850), (a) *Salisbury Plain*, written *c*. 1793, first pub. *Poems* (London, 1842); (b) 'Resolution and Independence', written 1802, first pub. *Poems in Two Volumes* (London, 1807), ll. 43–9; C1244–6, C1376. See Meyerstein, 504–6; Stephen Gill, *William Wordsworth* (Oxford: Oxford University Press, 1990), 75; *TLS* (21 Oct. 1926), 722; *NQ* 221 (1976), 103–4; *TLS* (6 May 1994), 3.

133. Worgan, John Dawes (1791–1809), 'Recollections of a Summer's Day', *Select Poems* (London: Longman, Hurst and others, 1810), 152.

Wortley: see Stuart-Wortley.

134. Yearsley, Ann (1756–1806) 'Elegy, On visiting the Hermitage, near Bath', undated clipping from *SJC*, BL, C 39 h 20(1), probably *c.* 1785, revised as 'Elegy, on Mr. Chatterton', *Poems on Various Subjects* (London: printed for the author and sold by G.G.J. and J. Robinson, 1787), 145–9; C1226.

135. Yeoman, William Joseph, 'Chatterton', *Fugitive Fancies* (London: Digby, Long, 1895), 71; C1306.

Poems by unidentified or pseudonymous authors

An Archaeological Epistle: see Baynes, John.

136. 'Bristol Beauties', by 'The Man in the Sun', 1848, included in Martin and Pickard, 40–1. Two verses on Chatterton and his Memorial (item 226).

137. 'Chatterton' ('Averse to ev'ry childish toy'), in *An Asylum for Fugitive Pieces in Prose and Verse*, new edn (London: J. Debrett, 1793), iv. 235–6; C1239; attributed to 'Albert' in an unidentified newspaper cutting (hand-dated Jan. 1792) in BL, C 39 h 20(1); C1235.

138. 'Chatterton', *Bristol Observer* (26 May 1860), 6, by 'Simara', of Clifton; C1289.

139. 'Chatterton: a Poem Inspired by Wallis's Picture' (item 241), *National Magazine* 1 (1857), 125–6, by 'F.R.N.'; C1287.

140. 'Chatterton's Tomb, the Hermitage, near Bath', *General Advertiser* (1 Sept. 1785), by 'A——a H——h'; C1214.

141. 'The Death of Chatterton', *William Tyndale, and Other Pieces* (Bristol: J. Wright, 1825), 29–46; C1255. A dramatic poem in blank verse.

142. 'The Death of Chatterton', *Tait's Edinburgh Magazine* 9 (1839), 585–6, by 'Cecini'; C1278. A monologue in blank verse.

143. 'The Death of Chatterton', *Tait's Edinburgh Magazine*, 25 (1858), 81–2, by 'W.B.B.S.'; C1288.

144. 'The Death of Chatterton: A Fragment', *Bath and Bristol Magazine* 2.4 (1833), 453–6, introduced by 'A.D.'; C1263. Nine stanzas of verse.

145. 'Elegy on T. Chatterton, the Boy of Bristol', *GM* 58 (1788), 1106–7, by 'R.F.'; C1228.

146. 'Epigram' ('The Antiquarian's skill, how bright'), *GM* 52 (1782), 40, by 'W.O.'

147. Epigram on the Rowley Controversy ('Who now believes in Ossian and Rowley?'), *GM* 52 (1782), 437.

148. 'Epigram, On two late Writers in Defense of Rowley's Poetry' ('From Glossaries and Doom's-Day Books'), *SJC* (Jan. 1782).
149. 'Epilogue to the Tragedy of Werter', undated poem headed 'Spoken by Mrs. Bernard', cutting possibly from *SJC*, Bodl., G A Glouc b 4a (50).
'Epistelle to Doctoure Mylles': see Baynes, John.
150. 'Epitaph to the Memory of Thomas Chatterton' (Mar. 1787), publication unidentified, Bristol Central Library, B26062; C1221.
151. 'Genius. A Sonnet', by 'Benedict', headed 'For the Oracle', dated 6 Apr. 1791, printed copy stuck into a 3rd edn of the *Rowley Poems* (London: T. Payne, 1778), formerly owned by Francis Douce (1757–1834), Bodl., Douce C244.
152. 'The Grave of Chatterton: a Poem', *Mirror of Literature, Amusement, and Instruction* 2 (7 Dec. 1844), 379, by 'L.M.S.'; C1283.
153. 'Impromptu, On seeing some late incomprehensible Strictures', *SJC* (25 May 1782); *GM* 52 (1782), 253. On the Rowley Controversy.
154. 'The Lamentation of Birtha. Bie Thomas Rowleie', *SJC* (6 Apr. 1782), with a letter signed by 'W.S.' of Bath.
155. 'Metrical Epistle' ('Does prudery haunt you in ——'s boasted form'), *European Magazine and London Review* 45 (Feb. 1804), 85–6. Offered as Chatterton's by 'W.K.' of Exeter, but exposed as a forgery, taken from his own verses, by 'E.G.' of Aylesham, Norfolk, in the July issue, 18.
156. 'Monody to the Memory of Chatterton', *European Magazine and London Review* (June 1791), 440.
157. 'Ode, Addressed to Edmund Malone, Esq', *GM* 52 (1782), 379. On the Rowley Controversy.
158. 'On First Seeing a Portrait of Chatterton', dated Bristol, 12 Mar. 1836, by 'Ion', publication unidentified; C1276.
159. 'On the learned Dispute respecting the Authenticity of Rowley's Poems', *SJC* (11 Apr. 1782).
160. 'On the Poems Imputed to Rowley', from the *Bury Post*, dated 9 Dec. 1782; *GM* 52 (1782), 590; C1209; Anderson, xi. 401.
161. 'The Ossiad', *SJC* (4 Apr. 1782), signed 'J.N.B.I.' Satirical poem championing Ossian over Rowley.
Paradise Lost, Book I ('Offe mannes fyrste bykrous volunde wolle I singe'): see Baynes, John.
162. Parody of Chatterton's 'Songe toe Ella' ('Oh thou, orr what remaynes of thee, / Rowley, thou preacher of antiquitye'),

European Magazine and London Review 1 (Apr. 1782), 307, by 'B.R.' of Dorsetshire; C1210.

163. 'Poem on Chatterton's Burial-Place', *Mirror of Literature, Amusement, and Instruction* 5 (1825), 170.

164. 'Sonnet on Chatterton' ('O Chatterton! fair Genius' eldest born'), *c.* 1783, *Bonner and Middleton's Bristol Journal* (16 Aug. 1800); C1241.

165. 'Sonnet, supposed to be written by Chatterton', *GM* 56 (1786), 513; C1218.

166. 'Thomas Chatterton' ('Pride, Genius, Energy in endless stream'), *Bristol Times and Mirror* (20 Nov. 1924), by 'M.R.'; C1318. A sonnet.

167. 'Thomas Chatterton, Written on the Banks of the Avon', by 'G.H.T.', unidentified cutting in BL, 1870 c 28.

'To blynne or not to blynne the denwere is': see Baynes, John.

168. 'Verses' ('Long has Blackstone of law the great oracle shone'), *GM* 52 (1782), 591. On the Rowley Controversy.

169. 'Written on reviewing the Portrait of Chatterton', printed on the Chatterton handkerchief (*c.* 1782, item 244); C1378. Reproduced in Meyerstein, 476; Kelly, opp. 29.

B. Fiction

170. Ackroyd, Peter (b. 1949), *Chatterton: A Novel* (London: Hamish Hamilton, 1987).

Adair, Gilbert, *Love and Death on Long Island* (1990): see Introduction.

171. Bell, Neil (=Stephen Southwold, 1887–1964), *Cover His Face: a Novel of the Life and Times of Thomas Chatterton* (London: Collins, 1943); C1350–2. See also item 113.

172. Bester, Alfred (1913–87), *Extro* (London: Eyre Methuen, 1975), 2–4. Chatterton in science fiction: a time-traveller fails to save him from poverty-induced suicide.

173. Blake, William (1757–1827), 'An Island in the Moon', written *c.* 1784, pub. in Edwin John Ellis, *The Real Blake* (London: Chatto and Windus, 1907), ch. 3 and 6. See William Blake, *Complete Writings*, ed. Geoffrey Keynes, corrected edn (Oxford: Oxford University Press, 1970), 49, 783. Satirical fantasy. See also item 10 and epigraph.

174. Collins, [William] Wilkie (1824–89), *The Woman in White*, first pub. in *All the Year Round* (1860), Second Epoch, ch. 3. Chatterton is discussed by Count Fosco, the villain.

175. Croft, Sir Herbert (1751–1816), *Love and Madness, A Story Too True, in a Series of Letters* (London: G. Kearsley, 1780); as *The Love Letters of Mr. H & Miss R., 1775–1779,* ed. Gilbert Burgess (London: W. Heinemann, 1895). An influential Wertherian novel, incorporating primary Chatterton material. See Russell, 230–2; Ingram, 287–9; Meyerstein, 467–8; Kelly, 60–70; Kaplan, 254–7; *NQ* 4 ser. 8 (1871), 319–20.

176. Dane, Clemence (=Winifred Ashton, 1888–1965), 'The Marvellous Boy: A Sketch', *The Listener* (6 Feb. 1941), 201–2. See also item 194.

177. Dix, John (alias John Ross, ?1800–?65), *Pen and Ink Sketches by a Cosmopolitan to which is added Chatterton: A Romance of Literary Life* (Boston, 1845; London: David Bogue, 1846). One could also argue for the inclusion of much of Dix's biography of Chatterton (1837) in the category of fiction.

Imbs, Bravig: see Stein, Gertrude.

178. Kruger, Rayne (b. 1922), *Young Villain with Wings. A Novel* (London and New York: Longmans, Green, 1953); C1357–8.

179. Marshall, Emma (1830–99), *Bristol Bells: A Story of the Eighteenth Century* (London: Seeley; New York: Macmillan; Leipzig: B. Tauchnitz, 1892); C1303. The Leipzig edition is sub-titled 'a story of the days of Chatterton'. A second London printing of 1893 boasts '8th thousand'.

180. Masson, David (1822–1907), *Chatterton: A Story of the Year 1770* (London: Macmillan, 1874), first pub. in *Dublin University Magazine* (1851), then in Masson's *Essays* (Cambridge: Macmillan, 1856). A novelized biography.

181. Maty, [Paul] Henry (1744–87), 'The Trial of Thomas Chatterton', *A New Review* 1 (1782). A parody of the Rowley controversy by the founder and editor of *A New Review.* See Meyerstein, 473; Kelly, 43; Lolla, above.

182. Melville, Hermann (1819–91), *Bartleby, the Scrivener: A Story of Wall-street,* first pub. in *Putnam's Monthly* 2, nos. 11–12 (Nov.–Dec., 1853).

183. Penzoldt, Ernst (1892–1955), *Der arme Chatterton. Geschichte eines Wunderkindes* (Leipzig: Insel Verlag, 1928); C1324–28; trans. John J. Troustine and Eleanor Woolf as *The Marvellous Boy* (New York: Harcourt, Brace and Co., 1931; London: Harrap, 1932); C1340–4. Discussed by Keith-Smith, 126–8.

Poe, Edgar Allan: see *Poetry.*

184. Stein, Gertrude (1874–1946), *The Autobiography of Alice B. Toklas*

(1933; New York: Random House, 1960), ch. 4, p. 84. 'Alice' recounts that Stein supplied Bravig Imbs with source materials for his life of Chatterton, which she admired. (There is a typescript of the first 307 pages of the Imbs biography in Bristol Central Library, ref. 21598; publication untraced.)

185. Susman, H., 'Chatterton. An Echo', *McBride's Magazine* 81 (1908), 251–3; C1311. Short story.

186. Vigny, Alfred de (1797–1863), *Stello* (Brussels: J.P. Meline, 1832), chs 14–19; C1260–2. Chatterton is one of the novel's three heroes: see Kelly, 108–9. See also item 217.

C. Dramatic and Musical Works

See Clarence; *Western Daily Press* (7 Oct. 1925). For bicentenary music (1952), see C1497–8.

187. Arnold, Matthew (1822–88), *Empedocles on Etna* (London: B. Fellowes, 1852). For Chatterton as a possible source of Arnold's dramatic poem see his letter to Henry Arthur Jones, 20 May 1884; *NQ* 160 (1931), 393; 163 (1932), 228.

Ashton, Winifred: see Dane, Clemence.

188. Blau, Heinrich, *Thomas Chatterton. Tragödie in Vier Akten* (London: Hirschfield Brothers, 1887); C1300. Discussed by Keith-Smith, 133–5.

189. Browning, Robert (1812–89), *The Return of the Druses: A Tragedy* (London: Edward Moxon, 1843). See *Browning's Essay on Chatterton*, ed. Donald Smalley (Cambridge, Mass: Harvard University Press, 1948), 5, on the resemblance between the play and the essay. (Chatterton is also mentioned in Browning's poem 'Waring'.)

190. Chevalier, Albert, 'Shattered 'Un', a burlesque sketch on Chatterton, performed at the Vaudeville Theatre, 3 June 1891, in a matinee with W. S. Gilbert's 'Rosencrantz and Guildenstern'. The characters are 'Shattered 'Un', 'Bold 'Un' and 'Mary'. See Clarence, 409; J. P. Wearing, *The London Stage 1890–1899* (Metuchen, NJ: The Scarecrow Press Inc., 1976), i. 130 (91.171).

191. Clark, Richard (1780–1856), a setting of Chatterton's 'Resignation' to the music of Henricus Loritus (d. 1563), undated. See *NQ*, 157 (1929), 190; 171 (1936), 228–9.

192. 'Mademoiselle Coquelicot', 'Thomas Chatterton', play in three episodes, performed at Ladbroke Hall, 25 July 1901. Listed in Clarence, 441.

193. Cuciniello, Michele (*fl.* 1873–1904, *Tomaso Chatterton o genio e sventura. Dramma in quattro atti* (Milan, 1904).

194. Dane, Clemence (=Winifred Ashton, 1888–1965), and Richard Addinsell, *Come of Age: The Text of a Play in Music and Words* (Garden City, New York: Doubleday, Doran and Co., 1934; London: Heinemann, 1938), verse drama, performed at the City Centre Theatre, London, 1938; C1345–6. Excerpted by Ann Mathisen, http://www.the-spa.com/anna/comeofage.htm. See also item 176.

195. Fletcher, J. Kyrle, 'Spirit of Adventure', radio programme including a sketch of Chatterton, broadcast by the Cardiff Broadcasting Station, 22 July 1925; C1320.

196. Forster, Joseph, 'Chatterton', a tragedy, adapted from the French of Alfred de Vigny (item 217), performed at Ladbroke Hall, 23 Jan. 1888. Listed in Clarence, 74.

197. Gainsbourg, Serge (1928–91), 'Chatterton', song recorded in London, June 1967; Melody Nelson Publishing. Re-issued on the Gainsbourg compilation CD *Comic Strip* (Philips, 1996, 528951–2). Also covered by Mick Harvey, on *Intoxicated Man: Songs of Serge Gainsbourg Sung in English by Mick Harvey and Anita Lane* (Mute, 1995, CDSTUMM144), translated by Alan Chamberlain.

198. Gerothwohl, Professor Maurice Alfred, 'Chatterton', play adapted from Alfred de Vigny (item 217), with a prologue by Professor Edward Dowden, produced by the Dramatic Productions Club and the Revival Co., Court Theatre, London, 25 Apr. 1909, with S. Esmé Percy as Chatterton. Clarence, 74; J. P. Wearing, *The London Stage 1900–1909* (Metuchen, NJ and London: The Scarecrow Press Inc., 1981), ii. 744 (09.99). See also item 34.

199. Grattan, Francis William (b. 1854), *Thomas Chatterton, the Marvellous Boy in The Foes and Woes of a Poet: A Four Act Drama* (Astoria, Long Island: J. F. Odewadell, 1918); C1317.

200. Gutch, John Matthew (1776–1861), 'Rowley's Ghost' (1857), untraced play. 'This represents a meeting in the shadow world and has neither literary nor historical value' (*Western Daily Press*, 7 Oct. 1925).

201. Hardinge, George (1743–1816), *Rowley and Chatterton in the Shades: or, Nugæ Antiquæ et Novæ: A New Elysian Interlude, in Prose and Verse* (London: T. Becket, 1782); extracted as *The Genius of Chatterton: An Irregular Ode* (London: T. Becket, 1788); ed. Joan Pittock (Los Angeles: Augustan Reprint Society, 1979); C1200–3, C1229. A parody in the form of a dialogue between the shades

of Chatterton, Rowley, and others, in prose and verse, sometimes mis-attributed to T. J. Mathias. Anderson, xi. 400; Clarence, 391; *Monthly Review* 67 (1782), 235–7; *NQ* 2nd ser. 2 (1856), 30–1.

202. Hocking, A. Trevoso, 'The Marvellous Boy: Thomas Chatterton', performed at the Everyman Theatre, Hampstead, 30 June 1932, and at The Pump Room, Bath, 25 Aug. 1932; C1335–9. Peter Ridgeway produced the play, played Chatterton, and is credited as co-author for the Bath production.

203. Hoffman, Maurice H., 'Chatterton', performed at the Washington Music Hall [Battersea Palace], 15 Apr. 1901. Clarence, 74.

Ireland, William Henry: see items 57 and 219.

204. Jahnn, Hans Henny (1894–1959), *Thomas Chatterton. Eine Tragödie* (Frankfurt/Main: Suhrkamp Verlag, 1955); C1359-61. See also 'Zur Tragödie "Thomas Chattertons"' in *Sinn und Form: Beitrage zur Literatur* 6 (1954), 805–29; Keith-Smith, 128–31. 'Thomas Chatterton', an opera in two parts adapted from Jahnn, with a libretto by Claus H. Henneberg and the composer Matthias Pintscher, was premiered in Dresden in May 1998.

205. Jenkins, Richard (*c.* 1754–1836), *The Ode, Songs, Choruses, &c., for the Concert in Commemoration of Chatterton* (London: J. Bew, 1784); C1213. Two concerts were held, the first on 2 Nov. and the second on 3 Dec. 1784, at the Assembly Room, Princes Street, Bristol. The 'Ode' had been separately published in a journal (unidentified), *c.* 1778. See Harvey, 131; Russell, 259–60; item 234.

206. Jones, H[enry] A[rthur] (1851–1929) and Henry Herman (1832–94), 'Chatterton: A New and Original Play in One Act', performed at the Princess's Theatre, London, 22 May 1884, produced by Wilson Barrett (1846–1904), who played the lead; collected in *One-Act Plays for Stage and Study: Seventh Series*, with a Preface by Zona Gale (New York: Samuel French, 1932), 17–37; C1294–7. See Clarence, 74; Meyerstein, 520; *NQ* 7th ser. 10 (1890), 128; 160 (1931), 224, 393; 163 (1932), 228.

207. Knowles, Josephine Pitcairn, 'Chatterton', three act play performed at the Theatre Royal, Bristol, by the Forbes Robertson Company, 2 Sept. 1925; C1321–3, text untraced. See Meyerstein, 520n; review in *Western Daily Press*, 7 Oct. 1925.

Kwietniowski, Richard (dir.), *Love and Death on Long Island* (film, 1997): see Introduction.

208. Lacy, Ernest (1863–1916), (a) *Chatterton: A Drama in One Act* (Philadelphia: Globe Printing House [privately printed], 1893),

collected in *Plays and Sonnets* (Philadelphia: Sherman and Co., 1900), 1–28, with frontispiece etching of Julia Marlowe as Chatterton (first performed 1894); C1307–8; (b) *The Bard of Mary Redcliffe* (Philadelphia: Sherman and Co., 1910), a five-act play; C1312–13. See also *Chatterton*, with an Introduction and Biographical Sketch by Louis Filler (Ann Arbor: Edwards Brothers, 1952); Charles Edward Russell, *Julia Marlowe – Her Life and Art* (New York and London: D. Appleton and Co., 1926).

209. Leoncavallo, Ruggero or Ruggiero (1858–1919), *Chatterton: Melodramma in 4 Atti* (Bologna: Societa Tip. dei Compositori, 1877); C1291–3. Opera, based on Alfred de Vigny's play (item 217); first performed in Rome, 1896. For a photograph of the tenor Thomas Salignac in the title part for the 1905 production at Nice see Kelly, opp. 108, and 113–15.

210. Meyerstein, E. H. W. (1889–1952), *Redcliff Hill: A Colloquy in One Act* (Bristol: G.H. Holloway, 1948); C1354. See also item 75.

211. Ostrowski, Krystyan Jósef (1811–82), 'Chatterton', *Dziela dramaticzne [Short Plays]* (Crakow, 1861), 1–83.

212. Owlett, F[rederick] C[harles], *Chatterton's Apology* (Hoddesdon, Herts: printed for the author by T. Knight, 1930), collected in *The Spacious Days and Other Essays* (n. p.: Herbert Joseph and the Globe Memorial Association, 1937), 89–110; separately reprinted in 1939, 1969 and 1976; C1330–1. A dialogue between Chatterton, Burgum, and Walpole.

Pintscher, Matthias: see Jahnn, Hans Henny.

213. Reznikoff, Charles (1894–1976), *Chatterton, the Black Death, and Meriwe Ther Lewis* (New York, 1922), collected in *Nine Plays* (New York: published by the author, 1927).

214. Russell, Mrs E. M., 'The Life of Thomas Chatterton', performed at Redcliffe Parish Hall, 20 Nov. 1924, with Miss Elsie Hanks as Chatterton; C1319. See *Bristol Times and Mirror*, *Western Daily Press*, both 21 Nov. 1924. This seems to be unpublished, but there is a mimeographed copy in the New York Public Library, *C p v 1947(k).

215. Sackville-West, Vita (1892–1962), *Chatterton* (Sevenoaks: privately printed, 1909). A play in blank verse, quoted in Kelly, 129, and in Michael Stevens, *V. Sackville-West* (London: Joseph, 1973), 27–8. Her first publication.

216. Tyler, Froom, 'The Sleepless Soul: Scenes from a Radio Play', *Bristol Evening World* (20 Nov. 1935), 10. The play was broadcast on 28 Mar. 1935; C1347.

217. Vigny, Alfred de (1797–1863), *Chatterton: A Play in Three Acts* (Paris: Hippolyte Souverain, 1835); C1265–75. See Meyerstein, 519–20; Kelly, 104–15; *NQ* 7th ser. 10 (1890), 237. See also items 34, 82, 186, 196, 198, and 209.

Dramatic and musical works by unidentified or pseudonymous authors

218. 'The Marvellous Boy', improvised play, devised and performed by Public Parts Theatre Company, Bristol, at the Bush Theatre, Hammersmith, London, Jan. 1992, and toured. See *The Guardian* (7 Jan. 1992), 30; *TLS* (24 Jan. 1992), 17.

219. 'More Reliques of Rowley: Wortigerne, A Playe', undated, BL, C 39 f 11. 'Vortigern' is the title of W. H. Ireland's forged Shakespeare play, which was frequently compared to Chatterton, especially in the controversy that erupted in the magazines in 1795–6. Ireland himself compared his own life and works with Chatterton's, for example in *The Confessions of William-Henry Ireland* (London: Thomas Goddard, 1805), 11–18, and indeed his entire *oeuvre* may be read as a creative response to Chatterton. See John Mair, *The Fourth Forger* (London: Cobden-Sanderson, 1938), and Bernard Grebanier, *The Great Shakespeare Forgery: A New Look at the Career of William Henry Ireland* (London: Heinemann, 1966); item 57.

D. Visual Representations

This section includes, for the cultural interest inherent in rumours of their existence, some notorious 'ghosts'. There is no authenticated portrait of Chatterton taken from the life: see *DNB*; Wilson, 313–15; Ingram, 335–38; Meyerstein, 521. See also Barker, 49–50; *Western Daily Press* (20, 22, 26, 27, and 30 Aug., and 5 Sept. 1910); C1079, C1644–51; and Richard Holmes, 'Forging the Poet', above. There is a fine collection of printed portraits, including many of those listed below and related ephemera, in the British Library, 1870 c 28. On memorials see items 226 and 247. On Chatterton-inspired images of St Mary Redcliffe see the illustrations reproduced in Smith.

Baldwyn, Thomas: see Symonds, H. D.

220. Barker, John Joseph, of Bath (*c.* 1820–1904), 'The Poet Chatterton', Royal Academy (1860), Bath Art Gallery (1930). See Graves, i. 113.

Blake, William: see Flaxman, John.

221. Braddon, Paul, 'Haunts of Chatterton' (*c.* 1900), a series of eight water-colour drawings; C1637.

'Braikenridge' portrait: see Morris, A.

Branwhite, Nathan C: see Morris, A.

Chatterton, Thomas, 'Self-portrait': see Pocock, Nicholas.

222. Cranch, John (1751–1821), 'The Death of Chatterton', engraved by J. T. Smith in 1795. See Meyerstein, 490.

223. Ernst, Max (1891–1976), 'Vivant seule sur son globe-fantôme, belle et parée de ses rêves: Perturbation ma sœur' (1929), in *Max Ernst: Loplop* (London: Thames and Hudson 1983). This is reproduced in the *TLS* (10 June 1983), 590, with this comment: 'In the foreground, it seems, Thomas Chatterton dreams of being *le petit prince*, his perforated planet aground in a disconsolately regimented landscape.'

224. Flaxman, John (1755–1826), (a) 'Sketch for a Monument to Chatterton', Royal Academy, 1780 (untraced: Meyerstein, 525 note, writes of 'a slight sketch in terra cotta'); (b) Thomas Chatterton receiving a bowl of poison from Despair, *c.* 1775–80, pen and ink and wash over graphite, with two associated studies in graphite, chalk and wash, British Museum, British Imp PIV and British Roy PIV, from the collections of E. H. W. Meyerstein and Iolo A. Williams; (c) English Metamorphoses, Thomas Rowley's Poems, Book I, Verse 84, pen and ink with wash over graphite, British Museum, British Imp PIV, formerly attributed to William Blake; C1584–5. See also Kelly, frontispiece; Graves, ii. 123; Raymond Lister, *English Romantic Painting* (Cambridge: Cambridge University Press, 1989), Plate 23; *Angelaki* 2.1 (1993/4), cover illustrations and studies by Frances Burden.

225. Fourau, Hugues (1803–73), 'Chatterton mourant', also listed as 'Dernière moments de Chatterton' (1842), sold in Paris, 1933; C1181. Reproduced in Kelly, opp. 93.

226. Fripp, S. C., The Chatterton Monument, Bristol. First mooted in 1792, erected in 1838–40 on unconsecrated ground to the north of the church of St Mary Redcliffe, removed to the crypt in 1846, resited in 1857, removed altogether in 1967, the pedestal and its inscriptions destroyed. (In 1998, to Bristol's disgrace, the statue still lies in an outhouse at the back of Chatterton's birthplace, badly eroded.) Meyerstein (528) described it as a 'pentagonal monument, thirty-one feet high, in three stages, crowned by a capped and standing figure of a bluecoat boy with a scroll

inscribed "Ella, a tragedie" in his left hand'. On this and other memorials to Chatterton see Wilson, 323–4; Russell, opp. 258 and 260–3; Meyerstein, 489, 525–8, 529; Kaplan, 30–2, 263–4; *NQ* 2nd ser. 4 (1857), 325; 4th ser. 7 (1871), 279–80; 12th ser. 8 (1921), 108; 12th ser. 9 (1921), 148; 146 (1924), 440; 155 (1928), 419–20; *TLS* (21 Oct. 1926), 722; C1374–1530; and items 37 and 136. For artists' impressions of the statue see Barker, 49; Smith, 145; *Bristol Times and Mirror* (13 Nov. 1937); C1596.

227. Gainsborough, Thomas (1727-88), Portrait of Chatterton. But descriptions of the painting are inconsistent, and this is a 'ghost'. See Ingram, 335; *NQ* 2nd ser. 2 (1856), 171–2; 2nd ser. 3 (1857), 53–4, 492; 2nd ser. 4 (1857), 11–12, 38; 6th ser. 5 (1882), 367; 8th ser. 6 (1894), 308, 394; 10th ser. 8 (1907), 309; C1597–1602, C1624, C1634–6, C1642–3, C1652.

228. Hogarth, William (1697–1764), 'Thomas Chatterton', exhibited at the second National Portrait Exhibition, Royal Academy (1867), lent by Salford Royal Museum, donated by Alderman Thomas Agnew (1853). Another 'ghost': not Chatterton but a self-portrait. See Algernon Graves, *A Century of Loan Exhibitions 1813–1912* (London, 1913–15; Bath: Kingsmead Reprints, 1970), i. 525; Ingram, 335. For Hogarth and St Mary Redcliffe see Smith, 120–5.

229. Lewis, Richard Jeffreys (*fl.* 1843–9), 'Chatterton writing Rowley,' mezzotint (Bristol: C. Mitchell, 1846), engraved by R. McInnes; also recorded as being engraved by 'Griffiths of College Green', and entitled 'Chatterton composing the Rowleian MSS'. See C1651.

230. Loxton, Samuel J., 'A Chatterton Souvenir' (Bristol, 1901), a series of six etchings; C1638–41. See Barker, 50 (no. 9).

231. Morris, A. (a Bristol painter), Portrait, claimed to be of Chatterton but probably of Morris's son, painted before 1837, spuriously dated 1762; engraved by Richard Woodman (1784–1859) from a drawing by Nathan C. Branwhite; presented to Bristol Art Gallery by G. W. Braikenridge; widely reproduced, notably as a frontispiece in Dix, Ingram, Kaplan, and most recently in the *TLS* (6 May 1994), 3. There is a variant image in Russell, opp. 94: for more on variants see Holmes, above. See also Russell, 264–7; Ingram, 337; Meyerstein, 522–3; Algernon Graves, *A Century of Loan Exhibitions 1813–1912* (London, 1913–15; Bath: Kingsmead Reprints, 1970), II, 1427; C1590–5, C1625–33, C1642; *NQ* 2nd ser. 2 (1856), 171–2, 231; 2nd ser. 3 (1857), 53–4, 100; 4th ser. 9

(1872), 294–6; 5th ser. 6 (1876), 60; 6th ser. 4 (1881), 108; 6th ser. 6 (1882), 97; *Athenaeum*, (4 Apr. 1891), 447, and (18 Apr. 1891), 512. See Fig. 5.

232. Morris, William Bright (*fl.* 1869–1900), 'Chatterton's holiday afternoon', Royal Academy, 1869; engraved by W. Ridgway (London: Virtue, undated); C1589; Graves, iii. 303.

233. Orme, Edward (1775–1848), 'The Death of Chatterton', engraving (London: D. Orme, 1794) from an unlocated painting by Henry Singleton (1766–1839), with a four-line epigraph from Hannah Cowley (item 24) beginning 'Behold him Muses!'; C1586. See Barker, 49; Meyerstein, 490; Kelly, opp. 44.

234. Pocock, Nicholas (1741?–1821), 'Genius conducting Chatterton in the habit of a Blue-coat boy, to her altar' (1784), engraving for the commemorative concert programme (item 205). There is a dubious tradition that this is based on a lost self-portrait of Chatterton: see Ingram, 336; Meyerstein, 476, 523.

Ridgway, W.: see Morris, William Bright.

235. Rippingille, Edward Villiers (?1790–1859), 'The Funeral Procession of William Canynge to St. Mary Redcliffe, 1474' (1820), now in the Elton collection at Clevedon Court. Among the mourners are Chatterton (with a lute) and 'Rowley'. See Francis Greenacre, *The Bristol School* (Bristol: City of Bristol Museum and Art Gallery, 1973), 130–1.

236. Rowbotham, Thomas [Charles] Leeson (1823–75), 'Chatterton's route to St. Mary Redcliffe from Pike Street' (1826), watercolour, Braikenridge Collection, Bristol City Museum and Art Gallery. Reproduced in Smith, 127.

Singleton, Henry: see Orme, Edward.

237. [Stead, George,] painting of the middle-aged Chatterton (1802). Readers of Peter Ackroyd's novel (item 170) will recognize this as the ghost of a ghost.

238. Steevens, George (1736–1800), woodcuts of the Rowleyan poets Turgot and Cheddar, with a periwig, spectacles and threadpapers, the whole designed to satirize the Rowleyans. 'Turgottus Dunelmensis' appears in *SJC* (23 May 1782); all are in *GM* 52 (1782), 276 and 288, above the signatures 'H.B.' and 'God Save the King!' See item 114, and George Steevens to Thomas Warton, 25 May 1782, *The Correspondence of Thomas Warton*, ed. David Fairer (Athens: Georgia University Press, 1996), 453–4.

239. Symonds, H. D., 'Thomas Chatterton' (London: H. D. Symonds, 1797), also printed in the *Monthly Visitor* (Jan. 1797), steel

engraving; C1587. The National Portrait Gallery records this engraving as having been published at this time by Thomas Baldwyn of Newgate St., London (Fig. 4). This sketch, supposedly from a picture belonging to the poet's sister, is sometimes called the 'goggle-ey'd' portrait. See Ingram, 336, 338; Meyerstein, 521–2; Holmes, above.

240. Tassie, James (1735–99), Miniature of Chatterton, undated, The Wordsworth Trust, Grasmere (1997), on loan from the Scottish National Portrait Gallery, PG 1274.

241. Wallis, Henry (1830–1916), 'Chatterton', Royal Academy (1856), Tate Gallery; C1603–18. The most famous image of Chatterton, widely disseminated, imitated, and parodied.[3] See Graves, iv. 115; Barker, 49; Meyerstein, 518; Kelly, 116–19; Kaplan, 15, 261, and Bryden, above. A small sketch for it was stolen from Birmingham Museum and Art Gallery in 1991 ('Tipsy art thief flees by bus', *The Times* (13 Dec. 1991), 1b).

242. Ward, Mrs. Edward Matthew [Henrietta Maria Ada] (*fl.* 1849–1877), 'Chatterton, 1765', Royal Academy (1873), Bristol City Museum and Art Gallery; C1619–23. See Graves, iv. 138–9; reproduced in Smith, 127.

243. Wheatley, Francis (1747–1801), Portrait of Chatterton. This is alleged to exist by 'Mrs Edkins' in the discredited Dix biography, and is another 'ghost': see Ingram, 335–6.

Woodman, Richard: see Morris, A.

Visual representations by unidentified or pseudonymous artists

244. Chatterton handkerchief, printed in red and blue (from *c.* 1782), headed 'The Distressed Poet. Or a True Representation of the unfortunate Chatterton', depicting a youth writing with a quill amidst shabby furniture, flanked by a description of the painting this is allegedly based on, and a poem (item 169). The description and the picture are printed in the *Westminster Magazine* 10 (July 1782), 342–3. See also Barker, 19; Ingram, 338; Meyerstein, 475–6; Kelly, opp. 29; Fairer, and Holmes, above; C1372, C1378, C1490. John Clare, *By Himself*, ed. Eric Robinson and David Powell (Ashington and Manchester: Mid-Northumberland Arts Group and Carcanet, 1996) 99, describes another souvenir handkerchief, with 'Resignation' on it.

245. Chatterton in the muniment room at Bristol, by 'W.H.K.' (*c.* 1800), steel engraving; C1588.

The Distresst Poet: see Chatterton handkerchief.

246. 'Portrait of a Young Gentleman Thought to be Thomas Chatterton', sold at Sotheby's, July 1990, Catalogue no. 95, English School, 18th century, from the collection of Doyne C. Bell, FSA, oil on an oval panel: full face, large eyes, fringed hair, blue coat over white waistcoat. See Holmes, above.

247. Profile of Chatterton, in relief (1784), commissioned by Philip Thicknesse (1719–92) for his rustic monument, raised between two hills in the grounds of The Hermitage, near Lansdowne Crescent, Bath, and decorated with a broken lyre over a gothic arch, with an inscription quoting Vicesimus Knox (1752–1821). An engraving of it is in the *Lady's Magazine* 15 (Feb. 1784), 62; C1373. See Ingram, opp. 335, 336; Meyerstein, 475; Kelly, opp. 45; *NQ* 2nd ser. 4 (1857) 39; items 134, 140.

Notes

1. On the 'inquest' see Wilson, 308; *Athenaeum* (5 Dec. 1857), 1518–19, and (23 Jan. 1858), 114–15; *NQ* 1st ser. 7 (1853), 138–9; 2nd ser. 11 (1861), 457; 4th ser. 9 (1872), 294–6; 6th ser. 1 (1880), 295, 322, 343. On the 'reburial' see Wilson, 309–11; Russell, 232–6; Kaplan, 28–30, 263; *GM* n.s. 10 (July 1838), 133; *NQ* 2nd ser. 3 (1857), 361–2; 2nd ser. 4 (1857), 23–4, 54–5, 92–4; 12 ser. 8 (1921), 108.

2. *Macmillan's Magazine* 25 (Feb. 1872), 337–8. The real author was the classicist Robert Scott: see Lewis Carroll, *Alice's Adventure's in Wonderland and Through the Looking Glass*, ed. Hugh Haughton (Harmondsworth, 1998), 330n. 'Jabberwocky' parodies Percy's *Reliques*, a favourite Chatterton text.

3. The following adaptations of the Wallis image are noted:
   (a) Martin Rowson, 'Logorrhoea' cartoon, *Independent on Sunday*, 15 Dec. 1991, review section, 1. A masked figure poses as Chatterton, headed with the text 'Or do you prefer the gaunt image of the suffering romantic, true to his *ideal* but *stone cold dead*?'
   (b) 'Biff' cartoon, dated Nov. 1994, reproduced in *Biff Weekend: The Missing Years* (Cambridge: Icon Books, 1996), 66. Chatterton holds a coffee cup, and the torn-up papers include an 'Ode to an Estate Agent'. The cartoon is headed, 'Insight derived from *suffering?*…', and Chatterton is saying 'You think I *enjoy* dying in this garret? I was planning a late flowering!'
   (c) 'Larry' cartoon, 'The Death of Chatterton / after Restoration', from *Punch* (June 1987), 25 (Fig. 7).
   (d) Susan Herbert, 'The Death of Chatterton' from 'The Cats Gallery of Art', series of greetings cards (1990). A corpulent cat in blouse and breeches lies in the pose of Chatterton.
   (e) Tableau vivant, undated, captured in a photograph with no date or identifying text glued into a copy of the Dix *Life* owned by John Goodridge. The tableau is meticulously carried out, with poison-phial, buckled shoe, and copious amounts of rather neatly torn-up

'manuscripts' on the floor (whose bare boards, however, run the wrong way).

(f) A tiling design at Pimlico Tube Station, London (where the Tate Gallery is situated),adapted from the Wallis painting.

(g) Edward Burne-Jones (1833–98), 'The Last Sleep of Arthur in Avalon' (1881–98), Museo de Arte, Ponce, Puerto Rico, West Indies. See Bryden, above (Fig. 1).

(h) Kim Stringfellow, 'The Death of Chatterton', San Francisco Camerawork (1991). A photographic construction designed as a triptych, in which the left and right panels contain shredded paper, and the central photograph is a negative of the Wallis painting. The body is reversed, and portrays the young black artist Jean-Michel Basquiat, who died of a heroin overdose. The construction may be found at http://www.kimstringfellow.com/chat.html.

(i) Sam Taylor-Wood, '5 Revolutionary Seconds: XIII' and 'Soliloquy I', in *Sam Taylor-Wood*, catalogue of an exhibition at Fondazione Prada, Milan, 19 Nov. 1998–6 Jan. 1999, curated by German Celant, 37–9, 154–5, 278–9.

Index

References to endnotes are occasionally given where citations may not be inferred from the text. The Appendices and 'Rowley's Ghost' have been only very lightly indexed. Chatterton's titles have been slightly simplified.